T0384058

# Ethical Leadership and Global Capitalism

This book is a very practical guide to help managers put their own and their employees' professional values to work. Through real life stories and case studies, the author brings to life and light the ethical challenges that present themselves in corporate and institutional settings.

The reader gets to see that ethics lies not only in the big, dramatic defining moments, but in the everyday behaviors of people as they work together in the service of organizational goals. The text is punctuated with summaries, exercises, and opportunities for reflection where the reader has an opportunity to review their own ethical frameworks and to see how these show up in the daily choices they make. Ideas are provided to help managers coach their employees to strategize around ethical issues, how to communicate their views with clarity and conviction, and how to find support in the organization to tackle difficult issues.

**Annabel Beerel**, PhD, has worked with multinationals as well as educational and non-profit organizations. She was the Founder and CEO of an international A.I. company, has been a Corporate Financier and Investment Banker in the City of London, and is the President and CEO of the New England Women's Leadership Institute. She is the author of nine books.

"It is a real honor to be included in Dr. Beerel's *Ethical Leadership and Global Capitalism: A Guide to Good Practice*. As a business leader trained in the Baldrige framework for performance excellence, I cannot overstate the importance of ethics in the workplace. Dr. Beerel has a wonderful way of 'connecting the dots' and delivering high-level theory in an easy to understand format that any manager can follow. You won't regret adding this book to your reading list."

*Tom Raffio, President and CEO, Northeast Delta Dental*

"This book is a tour de force text on ethical leadership, particularly in the context of business, but relevant for any organization. It explains the ethical mess we are in, why we are in it and how to get out of it; how each leader can and must take personal responsibility to be consciously ethical. Annabel not only demonstrates an amazing knowledge of the history and philosophy of ethics but also provides an unparalleled analysis of the dire situation today. Further, she provides the solution that leaders must first develop themselves in order to create ethical cultures. And last but not least, this academic text is such a good read with all its no-holds-barred style and punchy case studies, it's difficult to put down."

*John Knights, Chairman, LeaderShape Global*

# Ethical Leadership and Global Capitalism

A Guide to Good Practice

**Annabel Beerel**

LONDON AND NEW YORK

First published 2020
by Routledge
2 Park Square, Milton Park, Abingdon, Oxon OX14 4RN

and by Routledge
52 Vanderbilt Avenue, New York, NY 10017

*Routledge is an imprint of the Taylor & Francis Group, an informa business*

*British Library Cataloguing-in-Publication Data*
A catalogue record for this book is available from the British Library

*Library of Congress Cataloging-in-Publication Data*
Names: Beerel, Annabel C., 1953– author.
Title: Ethical leadership and global capitalism : a guide to good practice /
    Annabel Beerel.
Description: Abingdon, Oxon ; New York, NY : Routledge, 2020. |
    Includes bibliographical references and index.
Identifiers: LCCN 2019037048 (print) | LCCN 2019037049 (ebook) |
    ISBN 9780367197445 (hardback) | ISBN 9780429243172 (ebook)
Subjects: LCSH: Business ethics. | Leadership. | Capitalism—Moral and
    ethical aspects.
Classification: LCC HF5387 .B4255 2020 (print) | LCC HF5387 (ebook) |
    DDC 174/.4—dc23
LC record available at https://lccn.loc.gov/2019037048
LC ebook record available at https://lccn.loc.gov/2019037049

ISBN: 978-0-367-19744-5 (hbk)
ISBN: 978-0-429-24317-2 (ebk)

Typeset in Bembo
by Apex CoVantage, LLC

# Contents

# Foreword

If you have come to this book, *Ethical Leadership and Global Capitalism: A Guide to Good Practice*, because you are seeking answers to questions pertaining to ethics in the field of business, then you have come to the wrong place. I say this not because the book isn't superbly written (it is), nor because it doesn't demonstrate an authoritative command of the subject matter (it does), nor because in reading it you won't learn a great deal about ethics and ethical leadership in the context of business (I did, and I have been teaching ethics for over 20 years). I say this because you would be missing possibly the most important point of the book. Allow me to explain.

The Delphic Oracle of ancient Greece was revered as the place where one could receive guidance on life's most difficult decisions – straight from the mouth of the high priestess of the god Apollo. Before undertaking a long journey, or going off to war, or making any other life-changing decision, people (especially important people) would tramp off to consult the Oracle. Unfortunately, it was often the case that the answers that they received were subject to a variety of interpretations, leaving them uncertain of how they should proceed. Even more unfortunate was the fact that it was only afterwards (often when the wrong choice was already made), that it became clear what the Oracle had really meant. In one famous case recounted by Herodotus, the ancient King of Lydia consulted the oracle when he was deciding whether or not to wage war on the Persians. The Oracle told him that if he did wage war on the Persians, a great empire would be destroyed. The King of Lydia thought "Perfect! I have just the answer I wanted!" and eagerly attacked the Persians. It was sadly much later – after the attack had failed and the Persians had responded by sacking Lydia – that the Lydian King realized that it was his own great empire that was foretold to be destroyed.

Similar to the Oracle of Delphi, when it comes to life's decisions, this book will provide guidance but will not relieve us of the hard business of thinking. Ethics, as Dr. Beerel tells us, is not about following the prescriptions and rules that others hand us – whether it be our parents, our teachers, our employers, our society, or even our religion. Rule-following is all fine and good, especially when the rules are sound, but it has nothing to do with ethics. That becomes evident when the rules go bad – as they are in any corrupt regime or organization. It was, after all, rule-following that made the holocaust possible, and arguably a kind of rule-following that brought on the recent scandal at Wells Fargo. However – and this is key – one cannot know whether the rules are good or bad unless one gets into the business of thinking, and sound thinking about right and wrong requires more than simply knowing facts and theories; it requires honesty and courage and reflection about our responsibilities and duties and a great many other things. Above all else, ethical thinking requires us to think about ourselves, which leads us back to our Oracle of Delphi.

Inscribed above the opening of the Delphic Oracle was the phrase "know thyself" (Gr. *gnothi seauton*). In this phrase the Delphic Oracle was saying the following to all of those people seeking easy answers from the priestess: "no matter how much advice and guidance you might get from other people, if you wish to make good choices in life, be aware of yourself and your weaknesses." Indeed, if the Lydian King had been a bit more self-aware, a bit more attentive to his own pride, arrogance and complacency and lust for greater power and wealth, he would not have destroyed his kingdom and come within a whisker of being burned alive. In the same way, Dr. Beerel will tell you in this book that without constant attentiveness and vigilance to our dark side (what she calls, following Jung, our "shadow"), we will fall prey again and again to moral error. In life and business alike, we will never be relieved of the painful work of doing ethics. And this book calls us to this work again and again and provides us with the tools to do it.

Anyone who is in any position of leadership in any organization will benefit tremendously by reading this book. Dr. Beerel brings to bear on the topic of ethical leadership a constellation of experiences that are, to my knowledge, unmatched in the field. She has worked in business and finance at the executive level; she has studied and taught ethics at the highest academic levels; she has provided leadership consulting to dozens of executives; she has conducted numerous seminars for corporate leaders on developing an ethical culture; and she has provided mindfulness training to countless individuals. To all of these experiences she brings thoughtfulness, humor, insight, and humility. The result is a book full of wisdom. It is full of wisdom about the pressures placed on decision-makers today, from age-old tensions inherent in capitalism to recent developments in globalization. It presents, with insight, the perils of organizational culture and organizational behavior, often with delightful anecdotes and vexing moral dilemmas that will send our moral compasses spinning. It shares with us all of the great ethical theories with remarkable clarity and provides us with a decision-making matrix that readers will find extremely useful. It teaches us the value of honesty and courage and mindfulness. And perhaps most importantly, like the priestess of the Oracle of Delphi, Dr. Beerel calls us to reflect upon ourselves and how we should act.

Max Latona, PhD
Saint Anselm College

# Preface

## A first career

At five years of age, I was given the formal role of "Returns Checker" in my father's factory in Johannesburg, South Africa. The factory manufactured cold drinks. The drinks were mostly sweet, fizzy drinks, that appealed to the sweet-toothed, particularly those who labored under the sweaty South African sun.

As Returns Checker, my job was to track the empty bottles that people brought to the factory in order to claim their returnable deposits. In those days, the most expensive part of purchasing a case of cold drinks was the deposit on the glass bottles and the wooden box in which they were transported known as the "case." Deposits amounted to more than the cost of the drinks, so relatively speaking, they had significant monetary value.

Promptly at 8 a.m. every Saturday morning, as the factory opened its doors, I would dutifully take up my stance at the entrance of the Returns Bay. After a meticulous counting of all the customer's empties, I would scribble a note stating the number of bottles and wooden cases that had been returned. This note would be given to the customer who would hand it to the cashier where a credit would be given against any further purchases.

Now, counting the empties and connecting them to a specific customer was not always easy. Frequently, impatient and hurried people would try to jump the line, placing their returns next to each other, claiming empty cases that weren't theirs, and causing confusion while often yelling at me to hurry up. Some people got quite nasty and tried to bully me into writing numbers that were not true. Other people were downright rude calling me a "stupid kid!" As you can imagine, the whole checking and counting business could become quite unpleasant.

Well, at five years I learned a lot about human nature. I learned that people, in fact many people, if they get the opportunity, are dishonest and cheat. I also learned that on occasion people would alter my handwritten (rather scrawly but always accurate!) note for the cashier. I learned that people fabricate things, sometimes saying that I was too young to be able to count properly. I learned that people were particularly nasty if they were having a bad day. The more agitated they were, the more they seemed to want to cheat, lie, shout at people and be rude.

I learned a lot at five years. I learned that people, both women and men, are not always nice. I learned that many people are self-interested and self-absorbed.

I learned that some people are just downright bullies, and some are angry and disgruntled no matter how nice you are to them. And I learned that one had to work at not becoming angry and cynical oneself.

I also learned how important it was that the employees of the factory remained dignified, calm and above the frenzy of the Saturday morning fever. I learned a lot about business, people, and myself at five. I learned that to stay calm and not be afraid, intimidated or become angry, I had to stay inside myself. This staying inside myself gave me strength and an inner confidence that I was not a stupid kid. It helped me rise above the fray and just observe the circus; at times with amusement.

That was the beginning. I have been learning, and learning, and learning since then, and I want to share some of what I have learned with you.

My main message in this business ethics book is that we rarely consciously hurt who or what we love. Business ethics is about loving what we do and who we do it with – employee, supplier, customer, the environment, you name it, no matter who they are, or how nasty or grouchy they might be. Business ethics – in fact ethics – is about staying inside yourself. Because when you stay inside yourself you realize that everything is about love. When one looks at it like that, it is quite simple really.

## From counter to accountant

Fast forward several years and I embarked on the next stage of my career. Encouraged by my eager parents, I decided to become an accountant. After all, I had been well trained as a counter and I understood what it meant to be accountable, so why not be an accountant? In truth, I wanted to be an actress and a dancer, but that is another story.

Now in the early 1970s in South Africa, women were supposed to take care of the home and not venture out into the challenging world of professional work. The role of doctor, lawyer and accountant was reserved for white men only. Common thinking held that women would never be able to participate competently in the demanding work environment. To this day, I recall the astounded look on the face of the recruitment partner as I stood before him, all of sixteen years of age, insisting that I was applying to become a trainee accountant. Three months later, the London head office granted permission to hire me. I was duly accepted into the then prestigious firm of Cooper Brothers, Chartered Accountants. And so, on January 5, 1970, my training as an accountant began.

There were many challenging times during those six years of accounting apprenticeship known as "doing one's articles." It was certainly not easy (and often not safe) to be the only female trainee amidst a firm of over one hundred and twenty men. Yet, despite many challenging times, I am enormously grateful for the rigorous professional training I received. To this day, that training stands me in good stead in every aspect of my work. I am also thankful for the professionalism and business acumen of the partners of the firm who taught me invaluable lessons about the dynamics of a business, and who instilled in me a deep pride of what it meant to be a professional accountant. Even though I know that time has dulled and possibly distorted my memory, recollections of those days remind me of a deep commitment to honesty and fair-mindedness. During my seven years with the firm, I was unaware of any dubious collusions, cover-ups or corruption. In those days, accountants were proud of being "squeaky" clean and supposedly only the very small, one-time operator, in the pocket of his client, was led astray.

In the 1970s, training as an accountant was a rigorous affair. Not only did you require at least four years of university study in the disciplines of accounting, tax and law, but you also had to apprentice yourself to an accounting firm for a minimum of four years. For financial reasons, I took the longest option where I was "articled" for six years while simultaneously attending university most nights of the week. It was a grueling experience to say the least.

What made us good accountants in those days is that we received a great deal of hands-on experience. The focus back then was not so much on compliance, which seems to be the current emphasis, but on understanding the basis of a sound business. If you spend six years, day after day working inside different companies, auditing their books, understanding how they make and lose money, and what makes for effective and ineffective management, you learn a great deal.

Working for Coopers and in South Africa exposed me to a wide range of different organizations. Over my seven years with the firm, I audited coal and gold mines, the huge Cahora Bassa dam project on the Zambezi River in western Mozambique, the Fish River tunnel in the Orange Free State, several large insurance companies, investment banks, book publishing, construction and manufacturing companies, the largest bookstore in South Africa, hotel chains, real estate companies, Walls Ice Cream, several stock brokers and a few high tech engineering companies. All in all, I gained extensive training into how to evaluate a business and the critical ingredients that constituted effective management.

## Hidden in plain sight

The first day of every audit was dedicated to reconnaissance. This meant that each person on the audit team was assigned a duty to investigate what was going on inside the company. The focus was on what had changed since last time; what was new or what might require special scrutiny.

This first day was consumed with talking to people; mostly to people one did not normally talk to in the normal course of the audit. There was the janitor; people who worked in the canteen; the CEO's chauffeur; the person responsible for the building and the grounds; maybe a truck driver; the in-house nurse; the security guard and the switchboard operator, to name a few. (We had switchboards in those days!)

The goal of each encounter was "just to chat." We would ask how things were going; what was new; what changes were going on; was so-and-so still working in such-and-such department; why the canteen had been moved to a new building; what happened to the CEO's old Mercedes; when did he get a new one;

why there were now two security guards; and so on. On and on we chatted and questioned with no apparent agenda just getting the feel of the place and how it had changed, if at all, since the last time we were there.

Come four o'clock in the afternoon, the audit team would gather in an office and share the spoils of the day. My, what a lot we had learned, and we had not yet opened a book or looked at one cancelled check! We had learned about hirings and firings, misappropriated money, scandals, new homes purchased by the senior management team, court cases in progress, inventory being stolen, office affairs and the true picture about whether the company was doing well or not. These supposedly "low level" employees were delighted at the attention they received and the opportunity to talk about their work and what they observed. They unwittingly happily spilled the beans. The audit after that was a piece of cake!

The brilliant theory that lay behind the reconnaissance day is that 1) if a fraud is going on everyone knows about it even if or when they feign ignorance, and 2) people low on the hierarchical totem pole, who are immersed in the daily minutiae of the organization, see what is really going on. They appreciate attention and enjoy disarming chat that does not put them on the spot. After our debriefing, all we needed was to find the necessary evidence. The evidence is always there, one just needs to know where to look. The real story of how the firm is performing and its ethical behaviors is hidden in plain sight.

## The evolution of business ethics

In the 1970s we did not talk about business ethics as such. There was no such phrase in common parlance, and we certainly did not have a separate subject called Business Ethics as part of the accounting curriculum. There was a professional ethics code that as accountants we had to study. We also had to be able to define a situation that constituted a conflict of interest as well as knowing the extent to which we could receive gifts or favors from our clients. At the time we did not explicitly "audit" the ethical behavior of management although our tests and questionnaires addressed business conduct from a variety of perspectives.

The early 1970s heralded the emergence of a new business discipline called Business Ethics. This discipline gained increasing momentum and interest with the growing number of corporate scandals throughout the 1970s and 80s, the most infamous being those of Ivan Boesky and Michael Milken, along with the infectious Savings and Loan crisis. Within no time business schools were mandating classes on business ethics and a whole new genre of literature was spawned. Professors and consultants jumped on the bandwagon to claim their turf in this rapidly growing landscape. The now infamous accountants, Arthur Anderson, stood out as symbolic forerunners of the emerging business ethics stampede.

The early textbooks on business ethics emphasized protecting the most immediate and direct stakeholders of the organization. These were the owners or shareholders as well as the business's financiers, notably the banks. Over time, as corporate scandals persisted, the stakeholder circle was expanded to include customers and suppliers. Attention to employees and the need for organizational justice and human rights received acknowledgment much later.

Business ethics, has in the last twenty to thirty years, extended its reach to include now well-known terms such as corporate social responsibility, environmental sustainability and global citizenship. With globalization, the number of stakeholders impacted by business activities and who claim their rights to receive just treatment by businesses has grown exponentially. If we read stockholder reports or follow the media carefully, we notice how public opinion has trended towards businesses now being accountable to just about every stakeholder on the planet, including the planet itself. Many business texts discuss the well-known Millennium Development Goals and the United Nations Global Compact initiatives that, among others, encourage corporations to take up their global citizenship responsibility.

Acting as a corporate citizen is supposedly now a big deal yet the scandals continue. As I am writing, I am looking at the front page of the *Financial Times* dated September 29, 2018, where UK Business Secretary Ken Clark is insisting on an investigation into the behavior of the "Big 4 Accountants." These accountants have signed off on audits of companies that were clearly in dire straits. The question is, why and what is really going on? It is not just the big public corporations that perpetuate malfeasance, but the very "cops" who are supposed to protect the system. This fact alone – not a new one by any means – alerts us to the reality that ethical lapses are a systemic problem, and as such need to be approached systemically.

## From accountant to ethics professor

Fast forward many years and many careers, in April of 2003, I defended my doctoral dissertation in Social Ethics at Boston University. Having by then worked for over thirty years in a variety of business organizations – both public and private – in various countries, on three different continents, I had decided to embrace the academic life – for a while at least.

My dissertation focused on how the influence of power dynamics in organizations, and the prevalence of a culture of fear affects the ethical deliberations and moral behavior of employees. As a result of my exposure to a wide range of industries, I firmly believed that these two factors – there are of course others – hold great sway over people's behavior at work. It has also been my experience that a culture of fear has intensified over the years, especially in public companies.

My dissertation covered topics relevant to the factors that inhibit employees, at all levels, from experiencing the moral freedom to make choices from their deepest conscience or their highest self. These are some of the main topics interwoven throughout the chapters of this book.

If you wonder whether I am passionate about ethics – I am! If you think I have a lot to say on business ethics – I do! If you think there is nothing new to be learned – there always is!

It is my sincere and fervent hope that this book will, if nothing else, inspire you to "stay inside yourself." This will help you to love what you do and do what you love. Because it is all about love really – it is as simple as that!

Annabel Beerel
Senior Returns Checker
Fipso Bottling Company
Doornforntein, South Africa, 1958
Ireland/Boston 2019.

# Acknowledgments

There have been a multitude of people who over the years have helped guide and shape my ideas on business, ethics, and leadership. It would be impossible to try to attempt to even name many of them. I thank you all for our engagement over the years. I wish to express my thanks to my corporate clients and colleagues, my academic friends, and my many students.

There are four people I would especially like to acknowledge for their feedback and ideas as I wrote this book.

Alphabetically, I would begin with John Clements, who I wish to thank for his input and support as the book evolved. John and I have reconnected after many years. He now lives in New Zealand and has worked internationally, more recently in Australia and Southeast Asia with different leadership teams. John provided some interesting insights into leadership and how people and leaders make ethical decisions and the mind traps they face.

My next appreciation goes to John Knights, who is the Chairman of Leader-Shape Global, a leadership organization that develops transpersonal leadership programs and works in partnership with organizations around the world. John has a wealth of experience in international business leadership. His leadership approach – leading beyond the ego – and his ability to bring theory into practice is always a great inspiration. Thank you John for your generous insights and feedback.

I wish specially to acknowledge Max Latona, my "ethics" colleague and philosophy sparring partner. Max, who is an associate professor of philosophy at Saint Anselm College and is the executive director of the Center for Ethics, Business and Governance, shares my love of ethics and philosophy. He and I have had some spirited discussions about ethics and morality and other things, and Max always brings thoughtful ideas to the table. Thank you Max.

Last and by no means least, my special appreciation to Tom Raffio, President and CEO of Northeast Delta Dental, who despite an intense work schedule, managed to read every chapter, and to give thoughtful advice and feedback. Tom and I go back many years, so Tom knows some of my quirks and helps me to navigate these more effectively!

Finally thank you to Rebecca Marsh and her team at Routledge. They have been wonderful to work with.

Annabel Beerel, PhD
August 2019

# Introduction

## Contents

## Ethics – the living question

This book is about ethics in the business context. You might call it a business ethics book. It is that and a lot more. It is a book about the world in which we currently live, and our challenges and struggles to live an ethical life in that world.

In fact, this book is a dialogue – or should be experienced as such. Its role and goal is to serve as a gadfly, buzzing around and dragging you into mindful attention as to the daily choices you make – whatever they might be.

You could choose to read this book like we do most business books. That is, rapidly, looking for interesting headings or chapters or quick lists of take-aways, and only sometimes being so present that the text speaks to us. Things get even better when we find that we are in conversation with the contents of the book and ourselves.

It is my hope to provide you with this type of book. A book that will lure you in rather than its contents being flicked away as we do to most gadflies.

The emphasis of this book lies in what you should question rather than in what you should do. This book, therefore, is largely a book about questions.

These are not easy questions, and are questions, as Rilke advised the young poet, where one can only gradually live into the answers.[1] Ethics is all about "living" questions, and about *living* those questions.

Contrary to what most people think, ethics is not about telling people what to do. It is about wrestling with the truth. And we can only learn the truth face to face. We cannot learn the truth through the lens of a lie. That means that we need to polish our own lenses, and the way to do that is through self-examination and growth in self-awareness. As I shall stress to almost the same degree as that of the real gadfly, Socrates, the heart of ethics is self-examination and self-awareness. One of the best ways to do that is to live questions. Another is to adopt a mindfulness and meditation practice — something I explain in detail in the last chapter.

## Practicing ethics

Another hope I am entertaining is that, if you do not do so already, after reading this book or parts of it you will begin to practice ethics. By that I mean, you will explicitly make ethical questions part and parcel of daily life. As you make choices, some significant ones and others less so, asking yourself what ethical motivation lies behind those decisions, and what you intend by making them will make an enormous difference to your life. You will find that you will slow down, reflect and begin to choose more wisely. You will also grow in self-awareness.

Practicing ethics will naturally advance your ethical competency. If you want to be a good golfer — you practice golf. You want to be a good attorney — you practice the law. If you want your executives or managers to be good ethical leaders and managers — you get them to practice ethics! The great Greek philosopher, Aristotle, said, "We are what we repeatedly do. Excellence, is not an act, but a habit."[2]

In the pages that follow, I have a great deal to say about ethical competence. I also stress the importance of knowing the language of ethics as it not only greatly helps one's cognitive and emotional maturity but improves one's ability to define and articulate ethical problems and to share and communicate ideas.

Ethical competence is also an essential requirement — in my book — of any leader, manager, executive, caretaker or steward. For without an innate ethical awareness and sensitivity, how can they possibly — or better still, how dare they — make decisions that influence and affect people's lives? Alas, many people lack this competence or any innate check and balance and alas, we are witnessing the ramifications of these deficiencies in our ailing world at this time.

## Business leaders: the new stewards of the planet

In modern times, where across the globe the towers of industry defiantly proclaim their conquest of almost all human domains, like it or not, they are now saddled with the responsibilities of stewardship of the planet.[3] Large corporations dominate almost all human activities and devour the Earth's resources while doing so. Well, they cannot have it all their way! There is no free lunch.

The impact of business corporations on every aspect of communal and personal life has reached new limits. No corner of existence escapes the tentacles of the business machine ever alert for attractive commercial opportunities. Every aspect of human life has been brought into the economic arena, where it is transformed into a commodity to be exchanged for some value in the marketplace. Everything is sucked into the capitalist cauldron, be it our social relationships, our private data, our ideas, and even our genes or DNA. Everything is commoditized, assigned a price and made available for sale.

Increased international trade has exposed even the most remote countries to the political reforming power of economics. The role of multi-national business corporations in shaping new economies and altering the fabric of social life is prolifically documented. I discuss this in detail in various chapters, so I will not expand further here.[4]

Due to these deep structural changes in society, where more domains have become directly dependent on the modern business corporation and its management, the price that corporate leaders must now pay for their predominance is stewardship responsibilities. A large question that lays before all of us is will they do so soon and with integrity?

### Need for ethical competence

Prior to the Enlightenment, when biblical themes punctuated public dialogue, both the moral authority of the Catholic Church and public religious sentiment provided some form of ethical check and balance on the behavior of the person in his or her community.

The secularizing influence of the Enlightenment spirit, however, challenged the authority of the Church and decried the role of religion as one that stifled human freedom and fostered superstition and inhibition. Especially in the realm of business, the liberated individualistic spirit turned the already slowly evolving gap between ethics (what I ought to do) and morality (what I actually do), into a rapidly growing chasm.[5] This chasm is what we are dealing with today and speaks to why there is an urgent need for ethical competence, in every realm, but most importantly now in businesses.

On this front we have a multitude of challenges. For one, our once public discourse of ethics has become a private one. And for many, there is no discourse at all. One of the consequences is that we have lost any ability to discuss ethical issues. The language of ethics has all but disappeared. Ethical discussions are either dumped into a legal brief or comprise assertions about what we approve of and what we don't. Our personalist tendencies have chased away the idea of any objective ethical principles or ideals.

While ethical theories always tend to lag new technological developments, with the speed of innovation, this lag has increased. Added to that, many new developments usher in new human circumstances previously not dreamed of. Consider cloning; genetically modified foods; self-driving cars; gene editing; robotics, artificial intelligence (AI), and so on. (I often wonder what my deceased grandmother would think if I told her I spend most of my waking life in front of a screen on which I write or interact with a mouse! I cannot imagine what she would think about cloning or robots or heaven forbid, gene editing!)

As our technologies get more sophisticated, so are their ethical impacts. For many scientists understandably enthralled with the possibilities as they break through new scientific frontiers, ethical considerations become an afterthought. And quite literally, once the genie is out of the bottle – remember what happened to Frankenstein – there is no way of getting it back in again!

Without a competence in ethics, and without ethical checks and balances, our new stewards of the planet are unlikely to do a "good" job, where "good" means ethical.

## The fragmentation of business ethics

Let's get down to discussing business ethics. As I said at the beginning, business ethics is about ethics in the context of business. Now some people, in the spirit of moral relativism, declare that because business is a whole other culture, it demands, or commands its own special brand of ethical theory. Now, as you know, I have been in business since I was five years of age. That is a long time ago, and I cannot agree with this assertion at all.

There are also other authors and ethicists who claim there is no such a thing as business ethics, and that a corporation simply develops its ethics in direct response to the issues it confronts in pursuit of its business objectives. In a way, this group has a point since many businesses seem to do just that. Whether this expedient behavior is a "new theory" and falls under the rubric of ethics, might be a point for discussion.

The well-known, now deceased, management guru, Peter Drucker, insisted that business ethics did not exist at all. Only ethics exists, he insisted.[6] He claimed that ethics rests in the individual and not in the business as an institution. This is a position I wholeheartedly support and that is reflected in the chapters that follow.

There is another matter that I think detracts from the study and understanding of business ethics as ethics, and that is it has been carved out as a special, almost independent discipline. Regrettably, the modern tendency to create specializations within specializations, thus fragmenting knowledge into ever smaller digestible building blocks, goes counter to gaining a coherent understanding of the whole. The increasing fragmentation of disciplines has a price.

We live in a unified world. This unity both encompasses and exists in every domain, not just physical, but intellectual, emotional and spiritual. By splitting off parts from the whole, we sacrifice a depth of understanding and a perspicacity or wise insight into the myriad connections that make things what they are. The larger the universe that we can grasp and integrate into our understanding, the wiser and more thoughtful we become. Alas, we have devolved into a materialist world that is preoccupied with manifold particulars that are isolated or split-off from the whole. It is in this low-level world, where we take minimal interest in the bigger picture, and where we spend our lives arguing which particulars or which fragments of knowledge have the greatest importance.

For reasons open to debate, we have lost interest in universal concepts and principles often citing them to be impractical theories. We tend to ignore Kurt Lewin (1890–1947), the founding father of social psychology's profound comment: "There is nothing as practical as good theory, because good theory guides effective action by turning knowledge into wisdom."[7] So with business ethics. It has become an almost isolated sub-discipline devoted to analyzing the morality of organizations by reference to a potpourri of ethical principles and injunctions. Along the way it provides a mixture of both theoretical and pragmatic guidelines as to what is morally praise-worthy behavior.

What the study of business ethics most often fails to incorporate in any depth is the greater macrocosm in which businesses operate. This omission is akin to the biologist studying the frog while giving minimum attention to the pond and its encompassing environment.

In Chapter 2, I discuss systems thinking and its relevance to business ethics at the macro and micro level. There I point out in some detail how systems are embedded in systems and how the macro environment impacts all sub-systems within its sway. I contend that without a profound understanding of the macro-environment one cannot really grasp the ethical behavior of businesses.

## Global capitalism

You will notice that in this book we discuss capitalism from several vantage points. While the major perspective presented is that of the US, many, if not most of the issues discussed are likely to resonate with what is experienced in many other countries.

The picture of global capitalism painted throughout these pages is not a rosy one. I think it is important, therefore, that I put my cards on the table at the outset lest any misunderstanding should arise. I am in favor of capitalism as a socio-economic paradigm. I have been an entrepreneur most of my life, as was my father and mother and their respective parents before them. I agree with many, that capitalism, if practiced with the innate checks and balances originally envisaged by its architects, is the most favorable socio-economic system devised so far. It speaks to the best of our creativity, motivation, freedom and possibility for self-fulfillment. The problem is, that at this time, the system has lost its way. Or let me be more precise, we have lost our way. Capitalism is simply a socio-economic paradigm. We are the ones that enact it and give it life. We are the ones that can either adopt it as is, or adjust, amend or distort it. We have done the latter. So there is no fixing capitalism. The only thing that can be "fixed" is ourselves.

As this book explores and explains, "fixing" ourselves and thus changing our paradigm of behavior is an ethical task. And, this task begins with each one of us. We who want to have our cake and eat it. We, who want pension plans, retirement annuities, mutual funds or whatever, growing as fast as possible where we fire the broker or fund manager if they fail our expectations, cannot expect "someone else" to be paying attention and money to the poor and needy, or the immigrants, or the environment.

We, who look to short-term measures for success (the daily stock listings and our savings accounts), cannot expect someone else to carry the cost of the longer-term view. It takes all of us. Besides self-awareness, a fundamental principle of ethics is self-accountability.

At no point in this text do I suggest that we need to reject capitalism and return to some version of communism or socialism. We simply need to get back to moderation and limits. We need to pull back the greedy arms of corruption and excess, and hopefully then we can return to a managed capitalism that provides a reasonably level playing field where all can benefit – including the environment.

What we do need to stop doing is pretending that we are victims; victims of a system that is outside of our control. We must begin at once to cease personifying the system. The system is not run by ghosts, and if it is, **we** are those evanescent, diaphanous wisps of spirit, not consciously present, but reveling in those aspects of capitalist behavior that suits our taste or our pocket, and decrying "the system" when it does not.

### The globalizing spurt

Distinctive patterns of globalization can be traced to the pre-modern period. However, the extent and intensity of globalizing forces, and the pervasive penetration of globalization's impact makes the present epoch unique. International trade has grown at unprecedented levels. This has resulted in a meshing of economies with one another, and the emergence of a new division of labor in the production of goods. Businesses slice up the stages of the production process and locate them in different countries, especially in developing and emerging economies. Countries worldwide consume an increasing number of goods from abroad, and their own production processes grow significantly dependent on components produced overseas.

Competition has intensified, and while national economies have gained from increased trade, the distribution of those gains has been uneven. It has certainly not been a win–win situation.

World financial flows have grown exponentially over the last ten years, and most countries are in some way plugged into the global financial markets. Where once financial markets operated to finance trade and long-term investment, now speculation dominates most current activity. The annual turnover of foreign exchange markets stands at a staggering one hundred times the value of world trade. These high levels of speculative activity tend to induce rapid and volatile movements in asset prices, which increase risks not only to the financial institutions but also to entire economies.

Increased industrialization has had an enormously negative impact on the environment. Pollution and degradation of the atmosphere and oceans, not to mention the diffusion of wastes and polluting products around the globe, have placed the ecology of the entire planet at risk.

By comparison with previous periods, for the first time in human history, anything can be made almost anywhere and sold everywhere. This means making each component and performing each activity at the place on the globe where it can be most cheaply done and selling the resulting products and services wherever prices and profits are highest. Profit maximization, the heart of the capitalist model, relies on minimizing costs and maximizing revenues. The social and economic consequences of this global drive for revenues and profits, are significant and will be explored throughout the chapters of this book.

The pressures within organizations have also escalated. Managers are pressed to ensure that their organizations continue to earn above average returns. Global investors trawl the globe eager to identify those organizations that are taking strategic advantage of local country operating disparities. Operating disparities include low labor costs (pay as little as possible for long work hours), low taxes, minimal safety and pollution standards, poor regulation irregularly implemented, and low material costs due to bargaining with naïve farmers or landowners.

The increasing ethical pressures for managers, lies in how to act as global citizens by eliminating some of the disparities that were to their competitive advantage and which provided the very justification for their global activities. How might they achieve this and how might this affect those positive net present value calculations that had investors salivating? A big question for all businesses is how does one act as an ethical global citizen?

The last great crash of 2008, arguably the worst ever, has not provided the usual re-correction. Au contraire. Global capitalism spurred on by the speculative fervor of untrammeled finance capital that knows no loyalties and no limits, has stolen the reins of moderation once more. Some critics say capitalism is now as bad, if not worse, than the worst of the other socio-economic systems we have tried due to its global pervasiveness. It is in this world that we are studying business ethics. It is in this world that businesses are challenged to act with integrity. It is in this world that you and I must find our ethical center and strive to role model ethical leadership.

## Ethics in perspective

### *Ethics is about choices*

Broadly defined, ethics concerns principles that guide our choices. And, everything we do in life concerns choices. There is no choice-free day, hour or even moment. As long as we breathe and are conscious, we are making choices. As we know, even not making a choice is a choice. There is no escape. As philosopher, Jean Paul Sartre pointed out, the flip side of our freedom to choose is that we must choose; we have no choice. We are condemned to be free! (Sartre, 1993).

Does that mean that ethics in some ways underpins all our choices? The answer depends on who you ask. The great Catholic theologian, Thomas

Aquinas would say yes. All our choices – whether we brush our teeth, wear a red shirt, or arrive on time – have an ethical implication or consequence. Everything has an ethical import!

If we were to talk to some of our more contemporary, personalist ethical theorists, for example David Hume (everything depends on our senses), Joseph Fletcher (situational ethicist) or Richard Niebuhr (act responsibly) they would say "no." Ethical guidelines are only appropriate where there are specific ethical dilemmas.

Whichever stance you take, ethics, which concerns choices, is about how we live our lives. As we grow up and develop and as soon as we can reason, ethics comes into play. Ethics is somewhere embedded in everything we think, say or do. It is inherently part and parcel of everyday life. By simply living, we "do ethics" whether we know it or not! (I expand on this in Chapter 5.)

The motivation for making ethics an object of study is to help us be more reflective, and to make wiser decisions which lead to more thoughtful actions. The early Greeks would add that ethics is essential in that it helps shape our character, and that nothing is more important for a fully functioning citizen than to have an exemplary character. Interestingly we do not talk much about character these days except in a more derogatory manner when we are referring to odd people or buffoons.

Since business management is largely about decision-making, one would assume that ethics would dominate every curriculum of managerial study. Regrettably this is not the case. While most business schools have at least one mandatory course in business ethics, one mandatory course out of twenty or thirty courses in the curriculum is hardly likely to make a deep and lasting impact. As I argue in this text, corporate management needs to do some of the heavy lifting here.

### Ethics as the path to greater wisdom

Unfortunately, many people misunderstand what ethics is about. Over the years, as an ethics professor, I have heard people (both students and mature adults) volunteer all kinds of definitions or explanations for ethics. These range from "ethics tells you what is right or wrong" to "unethical people are evil," "ethics is for catching the bad guys," "they give us ethics codes so that we will behave" or "being ethical is about following the rules."

As you can, see most of these interpretations or understandings place ethics in a rather negative light. Regrettably, ethics is seen as something to be feared, or as something constraining, or something only applicable to bad guys.

Let me set the record straight. Ethics is not about snagging rogues or policing our lives. Ethics is there to guide our choices so that we might live life to its fullest. Ethics is an invitation to reflect, deliberate and discern. With each decision, the ethical impetus is there encouraging us to make wiser and better choices. Ethics serves to make us be more alert, more sensitive, and more thoughtful.

Ethics is expansive; inquiring, prompting, asking, calling us to maximize our human potential by making choices that help us realize our freedom to be all that we can be. Studying ethics helps us mature, grow, seek wisdom and live a thoughtful and intentional life.

Ethics is not an exact science. It is not a tidy discipline wrapped up in neat answers. It is about the messy particulars of life: our choices and their consequences. Ethics has to be lived, consciously, daily. It is a practice – not an abstract discipline, expedient crutch or capricious hobby.

An ethically sensitive person is not someone who knows all the "right" principles or theories or has all the "right" answers. An ethically sensitive person is someone who thinks about his or her values and the ethical principles by which he or she lives. An ethically sensitive person strives to live a principled life.

Ethics is about asking whether one has made the "right" choice; what "right" means in that specific circumstance, and what other options are available. One might say that by consciously and reflectively "doing" ethics, one is striving for wisdom and seeking to achieve "rightness."

What I emphasize repeatedly throughout this book is that the ethical life is a system; an integrated, systematic way of being and adapting to one's existence. It is not simply a series of so-called moral praiseworthy actions that lack an ethical foundation, although for many it has become simply that.

### *Business ethics and organizational behavior*

As I have said, business ethics is ethics within the business context. That means it is concerned with the myriad decisions that make up organizational life. It is not just about good or bad or right or wrong at work. It is far more than that. It is about people's fundamental disposition and behavior at work. It is about what motivates them, what their work ethic is like, their critical thinking skills, their ability to wrestle with complex decisions, their adaptability, their diligence and perseverance, and their ability to exercise leadership.

A truly ethical organization is a vibrant one; one that is oriented towards people's well-being, and one that places emphasis on good decision-making. Unfortunately, the frequent misunderstandings of the purpose of business ethics explains why infusing ethical thinking into many organizations is so often reduced to one-off remedial seminars (Starbucks, Wells Fargo!), codes and rule books rather than making it part of the oxygen of everyday work life that is filled with choices and decisions.

## The power of culture

Ethics is embedded in an organization's culture. It does not float above the daily lives of people like a hot air balloon. It is not an intellectual abstraction that can be taken up and put down. It concerns the intentions and the choices made by the individual and the group, by senior management and the lowest person on the totem pole. It is directly affected by the values, assumptions and expectations of people within the organization. Ethics is a lived experience through intention, motivation and action.

One cannot discuss business ethics without discussing culture. As I mentioned in the Preface, everyone knows what is going on in organizations either consciously or unconsciously. Just as cultures reward what is said or done, they reward what is unsaid or undone. I learned a long time ago, there are no secrets in systems. And as we shall discuss, this makes the collusion and bystander situation extremely demanding as true ignorance of corruption is rare.

While many people quote the late Peter Drucker's words that, "Culture eats strategy for breakfast," in my experience, few leaders and managers truly understand the power of culture.[8] What Drucker was pointing out is that culture is the power, the energy, the direction, the motivation behind all corporate action. Culture shapes behavior, conditions people and their responses, creates in and out groups, and either supports or radically fights change. Culture sets the tone and defines what is said and what is unsaid. Culture is the glue that holds the organization together.

If you want an ethical organization, ethics must be infused across the culture. Ethical awareness and discourse must be supported by policies, procedures, protocols, rewards systems and above all by management role modelling.

Different business managers in different organizations respond to the pressures to be more ethical in a variety of ways. While some recognize that ethics is intrinsic to all business behavior and thus see ethics as an end in and of itself, others see ethics merely as a means to an end whereby law cases can be avoided and/or beating the ethics drum is a public relations opportunity. Unfortunately, the latter perspective predominates in most organizations. We discuss culture at some length in Chapter 2.

## A guide to good practice

In a presentation at Bentley College (February 2014), the Executive Director of the Markkula Center for Applied Ethics at Santa Clara University, Kirk O. Hanson, reflected on the current state of business ethics in corporations and whether any progress had been made. According to him, the record is "spotty." Based on several measures, business behavior then was worse than it was in the early 1970s. Hanson attributes some of the declining ethical behavior to the impact of globalization, the pressure on attaining high quarterly earnings, and the temptation of huge executive salaries.

Despite the introduction of the Federal Sentencing Guidelines in 1987 and 1991, which authorized federal prosecutors and judges to give more favorable legal treatment to organizations if they had an ethics program in place, Hanson reported that little progress has been made. Ethics programs have focused on compliance with rules and the law, rather than the promotion of ethics. Along with that, senior corporate managers still believe that ethics means obeying the law and avoiding behavior that offends customers or attracts negative public opinion. This outlook, he claimed, promotes self-interest rather that reflecting a commitment to ethical behavior.

Overall Hanson's assessment is that despite many efforts over the past 30 or 40 years, there has been minimal success in integrating ethics into corporate management and business. He asserts that the future of an ethical organization is dependent upon the development of ethical managers. He argues that the final determinant of ethical behavior comes down to the individual integrity and character of managers and their employees. The approach to ethics that he advocates is that as professionals, all employees should put their professional values to work.

I wonder what Hanson is saying now.

## Goals of this book

This book is a practical guide to leaders and managers as to how to put their own and their employees' ethics and professional values to work.

A prime goal of this book is to invite leaders and managers to get to know themselves, and to better understand their own ethical dispositions and valences. It is a call to them to actively practice ethics, with interest, vitality and perseverance. They are also encouraged to monitor, coach and mentor their employees so that they have the confidence to express their values and their ethics.

Another important goal is to guide leaders and managers in becoming more ethically competent. They need to understand the nature of ethics and they also need to have some competency in the language of ethics and morals. As with any discipline, ethics has its own vocabulary. Mastering some of the key terms assists the ethically competent manager in promoting clear ethical thinking and facilitating ethical discussions. Using ethical language helps depersonalize issues thereby moving them to discussions concerning noble and practical principles to be followed rather than leading to a contest around preferences.

The ethically competent leader or manager also needs to understand the systemic issues within organizations that inhibit good behavior. He or she needs to know how to navigate these and motivate the workforce to feel morally free to act out of their highest selves.

Another goal is to prompt leaders and managers to place ethical considerations on the front burner of the organization's decision-making processes. They need to know how to identify and then how to work their way through a moral dilemma. To this end, I have provided the Moral Reasoning Framework in Chapter 9.

Finally, the ethical leader or manager needs courage. How does one develop courage? Through practice; practicing ethics. Ethics and courage walk hand in hand. Both evolve and bloom into courageous wisdom when directed by well-intentioned and guided practice. A prime goal of this book is to advance that practice.

## Reflection, deliberation, choice and action

The discussions in this book are formulated around three critical ethical and decision-making foundations: reflection, deliberation, choice and action.

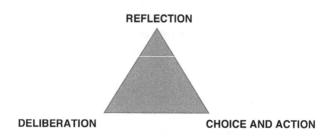

*Figure 0.1* Reflection, deliberation, choice and action

### Reflection

- What does it mean to be an ethical person? How does reflection on one's values and critical thinking make one more ethical?
- What is the importance of self-examination and self-awareness to ethics? To me?
- How does moral development influence one's making of choices? How can one influence and shape one's moral development? What do I do?
- How does one consciously develop one's character? What do I do?
- What kind of decision-maker am I? What ethical principles influence my choices?
- Do I bring my whole self to my decisions; do I worry about my actions; do I worry about the consequences?
- Do I make wise choices? How do I know?
- How do I understand the notion of justice?
- Do I make wise choices regarding others? How do I know?
- Am I my brother or sister's keeper?
- Do I have a moral imagination?
- Do I have empathy for others?

### Deliberation

- How do I frame a moral dilemma?
- What is my personal stake and what are the value conflicts I am experiencing?
- What are the systemic issues I am wrestling with?
- How do I overcome the ethical barriers within the organization?
- What would a GOOD manager do?
- What does good corporate citizenship expect of me?
- How do different or competing ethical guidelines inform by decision?

### Choice and action

*Choice*

- Which option is optimal and why? How do I justify my choice? What key criteria did I use?

- Do I have the moral courage to take the unpopular option or the high road?
- Can I follow through on my intentions with well thought through strategies for effective impact?

*Action*

- Can I overcome the organizational barriers to being an ethical person?
- How can I develop my moral courage?
- How might I strategize and navigate the corporate terrain so that I might effectively give voice to my principled conscience and ethics and stay alive?
- How do I promote global corporate citizenship? What mindset do I need?
- How do I articulate my position?
- How do I manage stakeholder conflicts?

## How to engage with this book

As I mentioned in the opening paragraph, I hope this book will lure you in and invite you to make ethics an ongoing conversation in your life.

The book has two parts. Part I comprises five chapters. These chapters describe the external and internal business pressures that organizations face and the ethical pressures these tensions create. These chapters lay out the macro and micro factors that inhibit people from "doing the good they wish to do."

Part II comprises a further five chapters that provide some guidelines as to how one can navigate one's way given the external and internal pressures outlined in Part I.

I have also organized the chapters in a manner that I hope is useful to a variety of readers in the following manner:

This text readily serves as a business ethics text that can be used as the foundation of a curriculum. Here one could begin at Chapter 1 and diligently work one's way to Chapter 10.

For those who like frameworks and models, one could begin at Chapter 9, The Moral Reasoning Framework, and then read different chapters as they relate to the framework.

This is also an ideal book for human resource professionals who are interested in among other things, organizational behavior, culture development and reward systems. They may elect to focus on Part I and the last chapters in Part II.

The executive, leader or manager who would rather not work their way through the progression of the book, can readily "jump" around as each chapter stands on its own and is clearly cross-referenced to other chapters as appropriate.

I would suggest that Chapter 1, 5, 8 and 10 are a must for everyone!

## Comments on cases

All the cases provided are true stories. They occurred at different times in several different countries. The names, dates, and details have been changed to preserve the anonymity and privacy of the people and organizations concerned.

I encourage you to share the cases with others and to discuss the questions posed throughout the text with colleagues and friends. You will be amazed at what will surface and what you will learn!

## Key terms

| | |
|---|---|
| Character   8 | Mindfulness and meditation   2 |
| Enlightenment   3 | Self-examination   2 |
| Ethical competence   2 | Self-awareness   2 |
| Excellence   2 | Truth   2 |
| Gadfly   1 | |

## Notes

1 This is spelled out in charming detail in Rainer Maria Rilke's *Letter to a Young Poet*. Novato, CA: New World Library, 2000.
2 Aristotle, *Nicomachean Ethics*, 1999.
3 Discussed by Max Stackhouse and others in *On Moral Business: Classical and Contemporary Resources for Ethics in Economic Life*. Grand Rapids, Michigan: William B. Eerdmans Publishing Company, 1995.
4 I discuss this in detail in Chapter 1 on capitalism and Chapter 8 where I discuss the impact of businesses on the environment.
5 The distinction between ethics and morality will be explored in detail in Chapters 3 and 4. Also see RH Tawney's *Religion and the Rise of Capitalism*. New York: Harcourt, Brace & World, Inc., 1962.
6 Peter Drucker. *Management*. Abingdon, UK: Routledge, 2015.
7 Kurt Lewin. *The Conceptual Representation and the Measurement of Psychological Forces*. New York: Marino Fine Books, 2013.
8 Peter Drucker. *The Practice of Management*. New York: HarperBusiness, reprint 2006.

## References

Drucker, Peter. *Management: Tasks, Responsibility, Practice*. Abingdon, UK: Routledge, 2015.
Lewin, Kurt. *The Conceptual Representation and the Measurement of Psychological Forces*. New York: Marino Fine Books, 2013.
Sartre, Jean Paul. *Being and Nothingness*. Washington, DC: Washington Square Press, 1993.

# Part 1

# The external and internal ethical pressures businesses face

# 1   Capitalism – the macro environment

## Contents

### Am I my brother's keeper?

You are thrilled. You have just been appointed the manager of the sub-prime mortgage division of Carefree Bank & Trust Co. This was a rapid promotion as you have only been with the bank for six months since you graduated from the Wharton MBA program. Boy was that exhilarating but also expensive!

It is July of 2005. The economy appears to be booming. House prices are still soaring after a seemingly never endless three-year upward spiral. You have five people who report to you, and you have budget responsibility for your department. With this promotion, you earn a good salary which will help repay those student loans and help you finance the down payment on your new house you and your fiancée are planning to buy. You are also on a bonus scheme based on the value of sub-prime mortgages you manage to close. If you meet this year's target, this will bring your own personal remuneration to a delightful $350,000 p.a. Not bad for a rookie mortgage broker! Life is good!

You have been fortunate in that you have a very amenable boss who believes in promoting his staff. He is also demanding in that he wants results in return. That is only fair. You feel especially fortunate in that he has taken a liking to you and is clearly giving you a big break. You are determined you will not let him down as there are many others waiting in the wings to get the break you did. Your future wife is also in financial services and she, too, is ambitious. She is very proud of you and how quickly you seem to be climbing the corporate ladder.

It is Monday morning and your first mortgage customer of the week is sitting opposite you. He is a carpenter who wishes to purchase a new house. He wants a big one as he works out of his home. He needs a large garage to accommodate his carpentry work. He too is excited, as he has identified, what he calls, a beautiful new home in Sudbury, Massachusetts, that fits his needs. The price is $750,000.

You settle down to ask him the usual routine questions. What is his annual income? He claims it is around $40,000 gross. Does he have a lot of debt? He says not much. You then work with him on identifying his expenses and, based on a rough calculation, you figure out that the monthly mortgage if he makes a down payment of $30,000 (that is all he says his mother will lend him), will be about $6,000 per month. You have done some juggling with the numbers to get the best rates. You also tell him that he can choose a variable rate mortgage where he only pays the interest and none of the principal for a period of three years. If he chooses this option, the monthly payment will go down to $2,500 per month. After the three years, the special introduction interest rate will go from the current 3.5% to 23%, plus he will have to begin paying back some of the principal.

You explain very carefully that his mortgage payments in three years will increase to around $10,000 per month. Does he believe that in three years he will earn this kind of money? He nods confidently. He has all kinds of plans to expand his business and to bring in new partners that will radically increase his income. You point out that there will always be another opportunity to refinance if things don't go exactly as planned. He smiles and asks how soon he can have the money as he does not want to lose the house.

You fill out the appropriate forms and ask him to read them carefully so that he fully understands the implications of his decision. He duly signs with gusto. You know the bank's underwriters will pass this one, as they have other similar ones, so you feel confident that this is another done deal. You rub your hands with glee as your mental calculator rings up the new total of your bonus. Life really is good.

### Questions

- Caveat subscriptor means let the buyer beware. By invoking this principle in the case presented, where the buyer was clearly apprised of his rights and obligations under the mortgage contract, has one fully performed one's ethical duty?
- When one has made a decision that is defensible by law but not from an ethical stand point, which principle should rule – the law or ethics?
- If you were the mortgage broker in this case, what would you have done?

## Capitalism – the macro-environment

> *Capitalism is the astounding belief that the most wickedest of men will do the most wickedest of things for the greatest good of everyone.*
>
> John Maynard Keynes

## Business ethics and capitalism

In the introductory chapter, I critiqued the discipline of business ethics and how it has become this fragmented and isolated topic of study. While most textbooks provide many paragraphs on various philosophers, ideas and ethical theories – as do I – what I think is missing, is a discussion of the interconnectedness of the multiplicity of disciplines that have a direct impact on the nature of business ethics. Without attention to this larger vista, one cannot truly understand the various influences, especially global capitalism, on organizational and individual ethical behavior.

In this chapter, I focus on the macrocosm, namely global capitalism, which serves as the key driver for the growing free-market impetus that is transforming ethical and economic behavior across the world. Capitalism, as it is currently practiced, is facing adverse reactions from many corners of the globe. The popular argument that growth is good; capitalism spurs growth and thereby raises the tide for all boats, is now seriously under question.

In this chapter, I provide some insights into how we got here and what that implies for business ethics as well as ethics for you and me.

To really understand capitalism as a system, we need to understand its evolution and founding principles. As we shall see, capitalism does not simply fall under the subject of economics but spans several different domains. With some consideration of these multiple domains, we gain important insights into how we got into our current situation, and maybe how we might get out of it.

Let us begin by clarifying what is meant by the term capitalism and its basic theoretical principles.

## Capitalist economics 101

### Defining capitalism

> Capitalism is a socio-economic system based on private property and the competition of the free market. The capitalist system is also known as the free market system. In a capitalistic system, businesses, or individuals, offer consumers products and services that meet their wants, and the prices are set by free, voluntary agreements to buy and sell.[1]

Let us unpack this definition and its underlying assumptions.

**Firstly**, when we refer to "private property" we mean that the "means of production and distribution" (land, labor, equipment, and money) are owned either by private individuals or corporations. The owners of the means of production and distribution earn profits on their "property," where profits represent the difference between the cost of production and distribution and the sale of products and services produced and distributed. The accumulated property (means of production and distribution plus the profits earned on their sale) is called "capital" and the owners are called "capitalists."

The owners of corporations are known as the shareholders (or stockholders). Shareholders exercise a level of control over the organization and receive a share of the profits in return for their investment. Workers by contrast, sell their labor to the corporation for a wage. Labor is thus a commodity like any other.

**Secondly**, competition in the free market refers to many individuals and businesses operating in markets free from governmental interference and regulation. This rarely happens in practice as we shall discuss later in this chapter.

Capitalist philosophy holds that totally free markets result in the most efficient and socially optimal allocation of resources. Competitive behavior is greatly encouraged as it increases efficiency in markets by keeping prices down and meeting evolving consumer needs.

**Thirdly**, in a capitalist system producers (sellers) and buyers can enter and leave the market quite freely. Sellers endeavor to meet consumer desires and consumers are free to choose that which they wish to consume. Prices are set based on supply and demand where neither the buyer nor the seller has an absolute power advantage over the other. This implies that there is a level playing field for all participants.

## The four stages of capitalism

### Mercantilism

The first emergence of a form of capitalism known as mercantilism, can be traced back to the 15th–16th centuries. This was a time when European traders began exploring new worlds which they found to be brimming with cheap and exotic resources. Within no time these lands were annexed to the mother country as foreign colonies who were soon forbidden to trade with any country. The mother country profited significantly by selling their new-found resources to other countries which also helped secure a positive balance of trade. The banks and governments that financed these overseas ventures received shares and profits in return for their investments.

### Classical capitalism

The next stage, resembles the capitalism of today. Here entire countries organize on free market principles. This form of capitalism was advocated by Adam Smith (1723–1790), who provided the original blueprint in his *Inquiry into the Nature and Causes of the Wealth of Nations* (1776). Smith, often dubbed the father of modern capitalism as discussed in more detail under Adam Smith and Free Markets on page 26, prescribed a market economy where the market place regulates itself based on self-interest, competition, free response to supply and demand and with minimal, if any, interference from government.

Classical capitalism gave rise to the capital markets (financial markets) that set prices for shares in companies, financial instruments and currencies of exchange. The main idea of classical or laissez-faire capitalism, as it is sometimes referred to, is that markets self-regulate.

### Keynesian stage

The third stage of capitalism is often defined as the Keynesian stage after John Maynard Keynes (1883–1946). Following the devastating stock market crash of 1929, the question raised – a question which remains paramount to this day – is whether markets can in fact self-regulate. Influenced by Keynes, most nations have deployed government intervention as a way of regulating the excesses of monopolies and maintaining a level playing field for smaller businesses. Again, thanks to Keynes, governments were encouraged to intervene by investing directly in the economy to ensure full employment even at the expense of increasing the national debt or negatively impacting the performance of the financial markets. Policies were introduced to protect national industries from overseas competition and to provide for the elderly and disabled who could no longer sell their labor.

### Global capitalism

Global capitalism, known as the fourth stage of capitalism, is defined as capitalism that transcends national borders. It is based on the same ideology as classical capitalism, only now the holders of the means of production extend their reach globally. The Keynesian approach to protecting national economies and industries has been dissipated in favor of international free trade. Added to this, financial investment flows move in and out of countries pursuing the best investment returns. International agreements that support the free movement of trade and goods have increased the flexibility of where and how organizations wish to operate and have made it more difficult to monitor or hold them to account for ethical infractions.

Key components of global capitalism include:

- Production takes place on a global stage
- Labor can be sourced around the world
- Financial flows operate globally
- Corporations now have transnational power
- No global system for adjudicating corporate governance exists

## The main ideas and movements that shaped capitalism

### Capitalism – the new spirituality

To understand some of the underlying existential motivations for capitalism, it is important to delve a little into religious history. The reason for beginning here is that most Caucasians, who find their genetic roots in the Western hemisphere, have deep within their DNA the effects of the profound influence of the controlling decrees of the Catholic Church (the Church).

Europe, in the middle ages and early modern period, was dominated by the Church that dictated what was to be valued and what was condonable behavior in every conceivable dimension of life. The individual and the collective found much of its daily motivation determined by obedience to the dogma of the Church which proclaimed "Her" to be God's representative and instrument on Earth. Daily living occurred within the shadow of the nearest steeple.

Biblical themes shaped the attitudes of society toward stewardship, poverty, the concept of dominion, and the principles of social justice. Both the Old and the New Testament embrace a recurring theme, one that criticizes the pursuit of wealth and the behavior of the rich while upholding the virtue of poverty. Repeatedly the sacred texts recount the failings of the rich and extol the benefits of being both poor in spirit and in pocket. These themes were given as requisite daily fodder to the masses.

Martin Luther (1483–1546), and his Reformation, served as a radical end to the Church's omnipresence and omnipotence. As we shall see, pivotal changes around ethics and morality took place at this time and these changes provided the seedbed for capitalism and business ethics.

### Martin Luther and the Reformation

Martin Luther's Protestant Reformation shifted the focus of ethics and morality from one communicated and mediated by the Church and its priestly agents, to one where the individual deals directly with God and develops his or her own ethical conscience. Salvation could no longer be acquired through good works, obsequious attention to dogma or regular confession. Followers of the Protestant movement had to enter into a direct relationship with God, and via his or her own conscience, resolve the existential angst around salvation alone. No priestly intermediary could advocate on one's behalf or assure one of one's heavenly reward.

Luther's approach, adopted by both John Calvin (1509–1564), and the Pietists, also placed religion squarely in the personal domain. Ethics, stripped of abstract and universal principles, became a highly personal struggle in deciding what was good and right. Contrary to the Catholic Church, Luther exalted work by claiming it a "calling" from God. Calvin argued that only a life of good works could provide the conviction of a person's own salvation. This meant bringing all actions, including economic ones, under relentless control and scrutiny as reflections on personal conduct. Economic motives were no longer considered alien to a life of the spirit. The capitalist was no longer distrusted as one who had grown rich off the misfortunes of his neighbor. Now it was not the accumulation of riches but rather their misuse for the purposes of self-indulgence that became the enemy of the God-oriented life. With self-discipline and sober behavior, money-making could be carried out for the greater glory of God. In the Calvinist schema, economic life became endowed with a new sanctification.

Another Protestant movement, Methodism, under its leader John Wesley (1703–1791), took on a strong emotional character while also supporting the idea of work as a calling. Assurance of salvation came from the forgiveness derived from the spirit evident in ecstasies and trances. Wesley exhorted his followers to gain all they could, save all they could, and do works of mercy. Strict self-control and diligence in work provided self-assurance of a heavenly afterlife.

By the mid-eighteenth century, religious fervor was no longer directed at the Church and its demands but was now injected into economic life. This too was being shaped by the rapidly advancing Industrial Revolution which ushered in a new class of capitalists. This emerging class, inspired by the Protestant ethic of ascetic and thrifty behavior, began to accumulate vast amounts of capital. This intense worldly activity counteracted the feelings of religious anxiety previously ameliorated by the Church and the sacraments.

## The Enlightenment

The next period of great influence in the changing self-understanding of humankind was the Enlightenment (17th–18th centuries). Known as the Age of Reason, this period heralded liberation from magic, myth and magesteriums, where human reason was raised to a new, highly elevated status.

The Enlightenment era stimulated the scientific approach to all disciplines. It dismissed the insights of the liberal arts and humanities and instead initiated the branch of study known as the social sciences, where the behavior of human beings was now to be studied using the scientific deductive and inductive methods. The new spirit of unfettered and unlimited reason fostered the belief that, given an objective, value-free, social scientific approach to the study of all phenomena, all the world could be made intelligible. Mystics, mysteries and sacramental rituals were to be poo-pooed and rejected, as they deflected human beings from their primary and superior faculty of reason.

Grounded in cause-and-effect thinking, the Enlightenment mechanistic worldview created a reality which added unbridled encouragement to control the world, analyze it, understand it and dominate it. Individual rights to life, liberty and property (see discussion on John Locke further in this chapter) reigned supreme. Morality became more a question of individual conscience (inspired by the Reformation as discussed earlier), than concern for the common good. Ethical theory became action rather than character focused. Arguments in favor of moral relativism (discussed in Chapter 3), grew in number.

The Enlightenment philosophy, that placed every aspect of life in the hands of reason, also fostered a spirit of unrestrained individualism. This individualism, already sparked by the Protestant movement, paved the way for even further feelings of independence, alienation and the lonely pursuit of salvation.

## The iron cage

The combination of the Reformation and Enlightenment movements that gave rise to the capitalist spirit is well documented in sociologist Max Weber's (1864–1920) classic, *The Protestant Ethic and the Spirit of Capitalism* (1996). In this book, Weber explains in detail how and why the Protestant ethic, described briefly earlier, inspired more capitalistic enterprises than did Catholicism, and how religious zeal redirected into economic life legitimated capitalistic behavior.

Weber concluded his seminal work on a dismal note, however. He anticipated that the pursuit of wealth, stripped of the religious and ethical meaning that Protestantism tried to give it, would result in a pre-occupation with external goods (materialism). The pursuit of wealth, he believed, would no longer lie on the "saint's shoulders like a light cloak, freely thrown aside at any moment," but would become an "iron cage."

### Capitalism and the Jews

In his book titled, *Capitalism and the Jews*, (2010), Catholic University of America Professor of History, Jerry Z. Muller tackles a very sensitive subject with great diplomacy. He explains how Jews have been conspicuous in their presence in the history of capitalism, and their success has been both a source of pride and embarrassment.

Anti-capitalists have blamed the Jews for their domination and anti-Semites have condemned capitalism as a form of Jewish exploitation. Jews have conveniently become a lightning rod for discontent.

There is no question that Jews excel at capitalist activity. This should come as no surprise, Muller explains, as Jews have been associated with trade and the lending of money throughout recorded history. To understand why this is so, requires a brief review of the history of the Jews as a diasporic minority. Like other diasporic merchant minorities, such as the Armenians, Greeks and Chinese, they have the cultural dispositions and skills that are conducive to trade. A large part of their economic competence derives as a compensation for their political powerlessness.

### The long shadow of usury

Jews have always been associated with lending money with interest. Prior to the Enlightenment period, this was a highly stigmatized activity within many cultures. Usury was branded with the illegitimacy of economic gain not derived from physical labor.

Usury was also highly condemned by the Catholic Church, reviled as a process of making money from money. Money was to be used in exchange and not to increase with interest. The Church denounced this activity as sinful, and Catholics were forbidden to lend to one another at interest. Lending at interest to foreigners, however, was permitted.

As Europe expanded, the economic function of money lending became more important. During the Renaissance, the Catholic Church needed to borrow money to finance its new basilicas and fine art collections. The Jews, not forbidden by Catholic canon law, and condemned to perpetual damnation in any event because of their repudiation of Christ, came in very handy. They were assigned the "dirty work" of raising finance and lending the Church large tracts of money for which they earned tidy sums in interest.

As commercial contracts expanded, and states and governments began to need money to finance foreign exploration, the Jews became indispensable to political authorities while becoming increasingly odious to pious Christians. The Jews were used for their financial savvy and at the same time condemned for being the usurer and economic parasite. It suited the system perfectly!

### Lack of economic and political power

The history of the Jews is one of expulsion and displacement. Once they left Israel and formed a diasporic minority in a foreign land, they were frequently deprived of economic and political privileges. They were forbidden to own land, to take up certain political positions or engage in certain professions. To survive they learned to become master traders. They developed a competence in arbitrage by converting everything to a monetary value and excelling in trading across markets. They knew how to exploit opportunities to buy low and sell high.

Due to social deprivation, money came to take a central role in their lives. It was a way of survival. Whereas barter had been the method of trading, the Jews ushered in the concept of both credit and monetary exchange. Over the centuries, this financial trading competence became part of their DNA. They understood commerce better than most and excelled at evaluating risks and market fundamentals. They also knew how to convert almost anything into a tradeable commodity.

### Success

Having provided the background to the Jewish success story, Muller explains how and why Jews dominate capitalism today. It is not just their centuries of financial trading expertise that explains their disproportionate representation at the helm of large capitalist organizations especially in the financial service industry, but their almost fanatical dedication to education.

Initially Jews were not allowed to attend certain universities, but once they opened their doors, Jewish students flocked in. Muller explains how Jewish parents will sacrifice everything for their children's education, making that a major family commitment and goal of family life.

Nowadays Jews dominate almost all professional fields and they collect proportionally more Nobel prizes than any other ethnicity.

Anti-semites, says Muller, still blame the excesses and distortions created by capitalism on the Jews. They are criticized for their excessive focus on money, and the greed, excess and corruption that now plagues the financial markets in particular.

As in the past, Jews have become convenient scapegoats for the system.

### Adam Smith and free markets

#### Who was Adam Smith?

Adam Smith was a Scottish economist, philosopher, author, moral philosopher and a key figure during the Scottish Enlightenment. His two major treatises were *The Theory of Moral Sentiments* (1817), and *An Inquiry into the Nature and Causes of the Wealth of Nations* (*Wealth of Nations*, 1776). In his work, Smith eagerly adopted and applied the Enlightenment principles of liberty and rationality to his ideas of the economy.

### The idea of self-interest

> *Self-interest equates to interest in the other.*
>
> Adam Smith (1776)

Before we look at Smith's economic views and his frequently quoted "invisible hand" argument, it is worthwhile noting that Smith, the moral philosopher, placed great emphasis on the sentiment of sympathy. In fact, his *Theory of Moral Sentiments*, is an exploration into how the fortune of others and their happiness is of special interest to each one of us. In his *Moral Sentiments* – by no means a brief text – Smith points out how it is in our own "self-interest" to care about how others fare as our welfare is inextricably linked with theirs. Self-interest thus equates to interest in the other. This fundamental notion of "sympathy" as he termed it, underpinned his theories of the free markets and how to promote the wealth of nations.

### Smith's free market principles

> *It is not from the benevolence of the butcher, the brewer or the baker that we expect our dinner, but from their regard to their own interest.*
>
> Adam Smith (1904)

In his *Wealth of Nations*, Smith laid out several foundational principles of the free market (capitalist) system as he envisaged it.

**First**, he envisioned a free market economy that would consist of small buyers and sellers, none of whom would be sufficiently large to influence the market price. This level economic playing field, with its equality of distribution of power, Smith believed, was essential to the effective operation of a free i.e., perfectly competitive market.

**Second**, Smith advocated that the owners of capital should remain directly involved in its management. In other words, the owners should be the organizational managers. He believed that the owners of capital make far better decisions regarding its allocation than do non-owner managers who are simply its stewards. Owners tend to take factors other than short term profits into account.

**Third**, Smith argued that in market transactions, an economic actor intends his own gain and is "led by an invisible hand to promote an end that is no part of his intention." This quote has been used almost indiscriminately to support individualistic self-interested behavior in the free market propagating that somehow the corrective forces of the market will ensure economic well-being for all. What is ignored or conveniently forgotten is Smith's definition of self-interest which means interest in the well-being of others.

In the box below, I cite the exact paragraph in the *Wealth of Nations* that includes the invisible hand phrase. Providing its context illuminates Smith's intended meaning which is quite different to when it is used context free.

---

### The invisible hand argument

> The annual revenue of every society is always precisely equal to the exchangeable value of the whole annual produce its industry, or rather is precisely the same thing with that exchangeable value. As every individual, therefore, endeavors as much as he can both to employ his capital in support of domestic industry, and so to direct that industry that its produce may be of greatest value; every individual necessarily labors to render the annual revenue of the society as great as he can. He generally, indeed, neither intends to promote the public interest, nor knows how much he is promoting it. By preferring the support of domestic to that of foreign industry, he intends only his own security; and by directing that industry in such a manner as its produce may be of the greatest value, *he intends only his own gain, and he is in this, as in many other cases, led by an invisible hand to promote an end which was no part of his intention . . .* (emphasis mine). By pursuing his own interest, he frequently promotes that of the society more effectually than when he really intends to promote it.
>
> (*Wealth of Nations*, 1904, p. 477–478)

A careful reading of this paragraph reveals the following:

Smith assumes that the total production of a nation will equal the total national output. He does not factor in income from capital – an important consideration when it comes to income equality as we discuss later in this chapter. Smith also assumes that by supporting domestic industry everyone will gain as national income will increase. He does acknowledge that it would be foolish for an individual or a nation to produce goods that can be procured more cheaply internationally.

---

**Fourth,** Smith insisted that capital that flowed from trade should be nationally rooted.

**Fifth,** he supported a sound framework of public policy and law enforcement that served to keep the market in check and that prosecuted those who cheated or misapplied the rules. He held that market participants who did not behave responsibly or morally should be actively restrained.

Smith argued energetically in favor of the virtues of the free market system, but he also acknowledged its limitations. He recognized that the institution of private property and the free market virtually assures inequalities and might even create enmity between the few rich and the relatively poor. He hoped, however, that this enmity would be countered by sympathy between the parties and a sense of prevailing justice within society. He presupposed a strong sense of community that would provide the "invisible hand" of correction, as he believed there can be no justice based on prosperity alone.

*Summary of Smith's free market checks and balances*

> *No society can surely be flourishing and happy of which the far greater part of the members are poor and miserable.*
>
> Adam Smith (1904)

- The free market will only work where sellers and buyers have equal power.
- The owners of capital should be the managers of that capital.
- Financial capital from trade should remain with national borders.
- Government should intervene appropriately to ensure that monopolies do not take over.
- The basic virtue of human beings is justice. People have within them a sense of sympathy and a need for approval from their fellow citizens. These forces serve as a check on or a corrective to excessive behavior. The invisible hand works because, and only when, people operate with restrained self-interest in co-operation with others under the precepts of justice.

### David Ricardo and the law of comparative advantage

David Ricardo (1772–1823), an English Enlightenment philosopher, also supported the idea of free markets and particularly that of international free trade. His thesis was that it is in the best interest of all nations to produce goods and services in those industries in which they have a "comparative advantage." He argued that capital, however, must not be allowed to cross borders from a high-wage to a low-wage country. He also stipulated that participating countries must balance the trade between them and that each country must have full employment (Korten, 2015).

### John Locke, property and moral worth

John Locke (1632–1704), another English Enlightenment philosopher, was a key proponent of the idea of human rights as opposed to the divine right of kings and the feudal structures of the time. He insisted that all humans have the right to life, liberty and property.

Locke came up with, what was then a revolutionary idea, that the land people live on and grow things on only has a material value once it has been transformed by being worked or tended. He advocated that those who did this work on the land should own the land, and not the king or feudal lords, and that the value of a property should be based on the labor put into it. My property was therefore "proper to me."

Under what was known as the labor theory of value, morally speaking, Locke argued, the price of a good or service should equal the total amount of labor value (wages) required to produce it.

As part of his political philosophy, Locke also supported revolution by the people, insisting that they can overthrow the government if it does not duly protect their rights and their private property. The government is there to serve the people and not vice versa. (In Chapter 6 on Ethical Principles, this is explained further.)

Locke's claim that humans are entitled to life, liberty and property is said to have influenced Thomas Jefferson's writing of the US Declaration of Independence on the 4th of July, 1776 (along the way, property was changed to the pursuit of happiness), and has most surely firmly captured the mindset of the American people.

### Property means happiness

Locke's influence resulted in property becoming an extension of the individual. It works something like this: The more time and work invested in a property, the more it says something about the owner. The more property one has, the more conscientious one must be and certainly the happier one must be. (Remember the new Protestant spirit!)

We can see how this emphasis on placing value on property, along with the entitlement to the unbridled amount of property, led to an expression of personal moral worth. Owning property has become a way of sustaining ourselves, expressing our freedom, and through free exchange, experiencing our happiness (see Milton Friedman in the next section). If we combine this new understanding with the emerging idea of free markets and the free exchange of property, we can see how this creates happiness for everyone. Wealth equates to happiness which is morally praiseworthy.

As we shall note in the chapter on ethical theories, these too were experiencing evolution in line with the changing social consciousness of the times. Jeremy Bentham (1748–1832), an English philosopher, held to be the founder of modern utilitarianism, advocated that the "greatest happiness for the greatest number is the measure of right or wrong." This has become a persuasive ethical theory that supports the capitalist spirit. More on this in Chapter 6 where we discuss ethical theories.

### Milton Friedman and the social responsibility of business

Milton Friedman (1912–2006), an American economist and Nobel prize winner, is best known for his enthusiastic support of free market principles and the pursuit of profits. Friedman was opposed to the ideas of Keynes insisting rather that government should stay out of the markets unless the safety and survival of the citizens are at stake.

Friedman is also known for eschewing the idea of corporate social responsibility insisting that the companies' only responsibility is to make as much profits as they can.

If you recall our discussion of Locke and property becoming an indicator of happiness and the utilitarian ethic of moral worthiness, Friedman's position becomes somewhat understandable. Everyone is happier once a free exchange has taken place. Buyers get what they want at the price they want it, and sellers gets the price they want so they can make a profit. The more profit, the more free exchanges have taken place, the more happy people there are, and the more morally praiseworthy behavior has taken place. Money is now part of the moral equation. Wealthy people are happy because they have property and lots of money and they are therefore morally worthy. As mentioned before, happiness is based on material wealth and is a measure of moral worth. Redirecting or giving money away and thus robbing people of the opportunity for free exchange is not, in this framework, morally praiseworthy.

Friedman was insistent, however, that corporations should play by the rules, should be open and not deceptive, and that monopolies should be curbed (Friedman, 1962).

The Friedman mindset is still alive and active although many may not be consciously aware of the implicit assumptions and reasoning that supports this outlook. We know because we have studied the evolution of capitalism!

## The multi-disciplinary nature of capitalism

We have now reviewed some key ideas and instrumental movements that have shaped the system of capitalism. What we can learn from this review is capitalism's complicated evolution and its penetrating and intricate influence on the evolving social consciousness of human beings.

Let us view this evolution through a few different lenses.

**Philosophical/ethical** questions include "Who are we?" "How should we live?" and "What makes for a good life?" Many would answer that capitalism provides an answer through its principles of liberty, freedom and the unbridled pursuit of private property made possible through free markets resulting in a sense of well-being, elevated status and happiness.

**Theology** delves into the metaphysical questions of who or what is God and how can we relate to this God? What is salvation and where do we find it? According to the few theorists we have covered, capitalism and the intense materialism that has ensued in its wake, in some way alleviates our existential anxiety of engaging directly with God and ensuring our salvation.

An important point to bear in mind is that the search for salvation is an existential need. We all seek deliverance from harm, ruin, loss and of course a dark death. How we look for and find salvation is an important ethical question.

**Religion** is the study of systems of faith and worship. In reviewing the evolution of capitalism, we gain some insight into how faith and worship through appeasement of God through righteous living was projected into economic behavior.

**Sociology** is concerned with the development, structure and function of society as well as with social issues that arise. The ownership of private property along with capitalism changed the nature of society and societal relations from a community oriented one to one focused on the individual and personal happiness.

**Economics** is the study of production, consumption and wealth. The capitalistic system clearly sits squarely in this domain

**Political science** concerns government, politics and power and how these inter-relate and manifest themselves in society. Capitalism is a new form of political economy in that its operations affects political policies. Aristotle, the great ethicist who we shall meet in Chapter 3, also wrote the first formal treatise on politics called *Politics* (1984), no less, discusses how politics and ethics are inter-related. More on ethics and power later.

**Psychology** is the scientific study of the human mind, behavior and motivation. Human motivation regarding salvation, liberty, ownership and happiness underpins the capitalist endeavor.

### Faith and ultimate concern

The renowned German-American Protestant existentialist, philosopher, and theologian, Paul Tillich (1886–1965), is best known for his two books, *The Courage to Be* (1952), and *The Dynamics of Faith* (1957).

Tillich believed that everyone, religious or atheist, has some object in life that serves as his or her ultimate concern. This object of concern is deemed sacred or holy. Everything else pales in comparison. This ultimate concern claims ultimacy in life whereby other concerns are sacrificed in favor of the sanctified object. Even for those who deny God, says Tillich, there is some god who claims this primary allegiance and attention (Tillich, 1957).

In our postmodern existence we can readily relate to this idea in that for many the hallowed Temple of life to which they devote significant time and attention is their iPhone, Facebook, Macys, video games or a Twitter account. Responding to the materialist capitalist endeavor in the form of consumerism is now for many their ultimate concern.

What we observe from the above summary, which is perforce brief, is that capitalism has not only influenced what people do and how they do it, but the very nature of their being – how they live; the idea of a good life; the relationship to God or the gods; the search for salvation; where to find happiness; the primacy of freedom as liberty, and the exchange of the spiritual life for the materialist one. This is the expansive terrain in which business ethics is embedded. This is the world we want to understand and influence constructively. This is innate in our consciousness. It is our socio-economic and political system and our daily lived experience.

# The early criticisms of capitalism

## *The ghost of Karl Marx (1818–1883)*

Karl Marx is an unpopular name in most Western democracies and frequently minimal attention is given to his many insightful writings' theories. He is blamed for the insidious version of Communism, the rise of which we saw in the 20th century. It is thus challenging perhaps to learn that Karl Marx's perspicacious insights into the dynamics of capitalism highlighted many of its inherent shortcomings. Please withhold your dislike of all that is Marxian, if you can, and read on.

## *Capitalists versus the proletariat*

Marx saw history as driven forward by the constant conflict between those who control the forces of production (the bourgeoisie, i.e., the capitalists) and those who do not (the proletariat, i.e., the labor class). Through his lens, the history of class struggles between the two. He predicted that a free-for-all capitalistic spirit would lead to this struggle between capital and labor which we are now so clearly witnessing as some element of the so-called populist movement. He, like Adam Smith, foresaw the resulting inequalities of wealth and power between the capitalists and the labor class, or as we call it, the growing divide between the rich and the poor.

In *The Communist Manifesto* (1848), Marx made some interesting predictions regarding the social and economic implications of capitalism. He anticipated that technological progress would increase the gap between productive capacity and realistic demand. He understood that technical innovation results in higher yields for less inputs, and that the question becomes how to dispose of this surplus. You can make more things, but can you sell them? (Ever wondered who was going to buy all those cars or clothes stacked in warehouse lots?) He predicted that the modernizing process would make supply problems ever worse, and the scramble to avoid holding surpluses, combined with the effect of competition and falling prices would pressure businesses to reduce costs (1992, pp. 6–8).

Marx understood how the revolutionary spiral of technology continues as long as corporations produce attractive profits thereby attracting more capital that inspires further technological innovation. Technological innovation leads to increased supply and other efficiencies resulting in falling prices and hence falling profit margins. This places firms' rates of return on capital in jeopardy. Marx referred to this as the "epidemic of over-production" (1992, p. 9). Contrary to economic orthodoxy, he did not agree that supply would shrink to meet demand and that in this way the over-supply problem would solve itself. If and when a correction did occur in the market, Marx argued, the proletariat would always be the ones to suffer the most. Marx did not believe in any "invisible hand" of correction. "The bourgeoisie cannot exist without constantly revolutionizing the instrument of production, and thereby the relations of production, and with them the whole relations of society" (Ibid.).

Marx anticipated that capitalism would need to become a globalizing force in order to be self-sustaining. He foresaw that the attempt to solve the oversupply problem would create a need for constantly expanding markets for a firm's products, and to this end they would chase the ends of the globe. Or, as we are seeing it currently, engage in unethical behavior, like selling customer data, to advance that goal. The firm will do anything to gain larger markets and more market share. This activity would result in old established national industries being dislodged and destroyed by new industries whose introduction would soon become a life and death question (think coal and steel) for many traditional workers in the so called "developed" countries. He also predicted that the cost of labor would become subject to international arbitrage, where the supply of peasants in the less-developed countries would become the subject of a global jobs auction (Grieder, 1997, pp. 229–230).

Marx wrote prolifically about the social impact that capitalism would have on an international scale and how its allure of freedom and accessible wealth would seduce nations to forsake their own culture in order to participate in the promised spoils of a capitalistic society. According to him, the bourgeoisie through the rapid improvement of all instruments of production and by the immensely facilitated means of communication, would draw all, even the most "barbarian" nations, into civilization. Marx claimed,

> This activity compels all nations, on pain of extinction, to adopt the bourgeoisie mode of production; it compels them to introduce what it calls civilization into its midst, i.e., to become bourgeoisie themselves. In a word, it creates a world after its own image.
>
> (1992, p. 7)

Marx anticipated the future power of finance capital. He referred to it as the "Robespierre" of the capitalistic revolution. The sole motivation of finance is to maximize the return on capital without regard for national identity or political or social consequences. He saw finance capital as the enforcer of the imperative toward globalization, and the social and economic upheaval created by the technological revolution exacerbated by disloyal financiers interested only in their financial returns. He argued that free trade would foster the speedy migration of finance capital always in search of more lucrative financial propositions (Ibid., p. 25).

In response to these globalizing forces, Marx anticipated an army of Luddites assembling around the world intent on combating the globalizing forces that disempowered them. These forces, he believed, would continue the struggle of the classes and would challenge the power of the capitalists in a manner in that only the powerless can do-through revolution. This might be a reminder of what we saw in Seattle, Oregon, in 1999, followed soon after in Washington, DC, Prague and Genoa! (Now France! December 8, 2018). In response to the gatherings of the World Trade Organization (WTO), the protest movement against globalization broke out in full force. If globalization is supposed to benefit everyone by making their lives better off, many, many people are not experiencing it.

Marx summarizes the principle tenets of capitalism as follows: The corner-stone of the capitalist ideology is that economic growth is good. This growth rests on the exploitation of living labor engaged in the processes of production and the gap between what labor is paid and what it creates in monetary terms. Marx anticipated that capitalism would devour itself and that the proletariat would rise up in arms. Is he wrong?

### Thorstein Veblen and conspicuous consumption

The American economist and sociologist, Thorstein Veblen (1857–1929), intro-duced the term "conspicuous consumption" in 1899 in his book *The Theory of the Leisure Class: An Economic Study in the Evolution of Institutions.*

Veblen critiqued the emerging class of *nouveau riche* who arose as a result of capital accumulation during the Second Industrial Revolution (ca. 1860–1914). "Conspicuous consumption" was a term he applied to the behavior of the upper classes and the emerging rich who displayed their wealth through ostentatious consumption as a means of publicly manifesting their social power and prestige.

Veblen's book exposed the growth of consumerism and the mechanics of the growing consumer society who spent excessively on goods and services that were way beyond their needs or means. He ridiculed those who were motivated by the desire for prestige and the public display of social status, rather than by the intrinsic, practical utility of goods and services. He argued that people's wants were rapidly moving well beyond their needs.

Economic research reveals however, that conspicuous consumption is a socio-economic behavior more common to the poor social classes and in some of the countries with emerging economies. Among such people, displays of wealth are used to psychologically combat the impression of poverty and the various stigmas attached to that label.

In the US, consumerism fueled by a relentless advertising and marketing presence that dominates every form of communication media, blatantly encour-ages conspicuous consumption persuasively demonstrating how necessary it is to spend and look good. How else will organizations get rid of that excessive inventory that Marx anticipated would fuel the fight for market share and global markets?

### Capitalism and creative destruction

Economist Joseph Alois Schumpeter (1883–1950), who wrote the book *Capitalism, Socialism and Democracy* (1942), is best known for his cliché "creative destruction." He viewed capitalism as unique in history because of its ceaseless self-generating ability to both initiate innovative change and stimulate cycles of change. His inquiry into the dynamics of capitalism initially focused on why industrial growth in the capitalist model does not continue as a smooth and uninterrupted process. He decided that a stimulating event, most often a new technological invention, causes entrepreneurs to appear in clusters. The activity of these clusters moves industry forward in rapid spurts of growth. Think of robots.

As pioneers in their field, entrepreneurs address systemic problems, removing obstacles within their own industry as well as those of a similar nature in other industries. As a result, the challenging cycle of entrepreneurship has unintended effects beyond its immediate sphere of action. Schumpeter refers to this as a process of industrial "mutation" where entrepreneurship nourished by investment capital revolutionizes the economic structure from within by continuously destroying the existing industrial model and incessantly creating a new one. This perennial gale of creative destruction results in atomistic competition that begins as one small firm against another and ends up in a new world of competitive monopolies. Think iPhones or electric cars.

Schumpeter anticipated that large-scale industry would become the most powerful engine of progress driving the long-run expansion of total output always on the hunt for new markets. In a world dominated by large and powerful monopolies such as we see today, perfect competition is not only impossible but would vitiate the systemic nature of output-driven capitalism (remember Marx). According to him, competition, contrary to the ideal of Adam Smith, would perforce be uneven and unfair, especially to the smaller national firm that will potentially be driven out of business.

Yet creative destruction is only half of Schumpeter's message. Far less in vogue is his projection that entrepreneurs will disappear as innovation becomes mechanized in corporate labs and that ultimately the very success of capitalism will beget a new socialism. Something to consider as we observe the political landscape worldwide.

## Contemporary criticisms of capitalism

In the past two decades, growth in the criticism of global capitalism has risen to a crescendo. One of the flaming fires that fuels this criticism lies in the growing disparities between rich and poor. On a macro scale, one might say this is the most severe ethical challenge of the times. While the initial proponents of capitalism, for example Adam Smith, acknowledged the innate tendency of capitalism to reward the owners of capital at the expense of the workers, they believed that there would be checks and balances that would keep things in some balance and harmony. Alas, those checks and balances, have vaporized in almost every country it seems.

Below I have selected extracts from some of the current literature on the failures of global capitalism as it is currently practiced. I present these failures so as to provide the macrocosmic backdrop to the discussions of business ethics that follow.

As we shall discuss ethics at length in Chapter 6, ethics is first and foremost about the concept of limits. Moderation is a key ethical principle and a personal virtue. As we review global capitalism from a multitude of perspectives, it seems we live in a world that has become in total disregard of any form of moderation or limits. This reality is the crux of our major problems today.

Let us look at some of capitalisms critics.

### Capitalism – the social disruptor

William Greider, A journalist for the *Washington Post*, has written extensively on the social, political and economic tensions that global capitalism has introduced into the twenty-first century world. Greider writes about the huge social transformation that capitalism has launched and how this has changed relations both within and between societies. While global capitalism has liberated masses of people from socially ingrained class structures, it has not replaced those structures with any coherent system to which the new emerging classes may turn. According to him, social relations are over-turned and are often in disarray resulting in new forms of human exploitation (1997).

### Capitalism – the path to hedonism

A strong criticism of capitalism provides the focus of Daniel Bell's book, *The Cultural Contradictions of Capitalism* (1996). Bell claims that the three realms – the economy, the polity and the culture – are ruled by contrary axial principles: for the economy, efficiency; for the polity, equality; and for the culture, self-gratification. According to him, the resulting disjunctions of these three realms have framed the tensions and social conflicts of Western society in the past 150 years. He states that once capitalism lost its transcendental ethics, the cultural justification of capitalism became a turn toward hedonism (1996, p. 293).

### The power of finance capital

George Soros, the internationally renowned investment fund manager, philanthropist and founder of Open Society Foundations, considers the global capitalistic system to be characterized not only by free trade but more specifically by the free movement of capital.

In his book, *The Crisis of Global Capitalism* (1998), Soros explains the causes for the inherent instability in the financial markets and challenges the widespread belief that markets self-correct as a dangerous misnomer. He claims that, "Since capital is more mobile than any other factor of production, and financial capital is more mobile than direct investment, financial capital can move swiftly to where investors receive the highest returns" (1998, p. 101). Return-hungry investors can thus patrol the globe, rewarding those economies where labor costs remain low and where productive growth potential exists while punishing those who fail to deliver competitively acceptable returns. Hoping to improve their economies, often to the detriment of the local cultural and social infrastructure, individual countries compete aggressively to attract finance capital that the capitalist system so actively promotes as the harbinger of prosperity. Competition for investment capital takes the form of granting generous tax breaks, enhanced rights to capital mobility, access to coveted tracts of land, requirements to meet lower standards of pollution than in other countries, and a variety of distribution and labor rights.

In the wake of these drivers, Soros argues that no individual state can resist the power of global financial markets, and no institutions have the power for rule making on a global scale. He foresaw in 1998, that the future world market would be dominated even more by publicly owned international companies that will dictate the terms of trade to nation states. Part of the picture, he claims, will be a further deterioration in political and moral values (Soros, 1998).

### The dangers of unregulated financial innovation

Paul Krugman, the Nobel prize winning economist, in his *The Return of Depression Economics and the Crisis of 2008*(2009), summarizes how the once triumphant capitalism, that brought hope and better livelihoods, has brought the global economic system to its knees. He describes the crash of 2007–2008 as the worst economic crash ever and places the blame squarely on the lack of sound government policies, the lack of transparency in the capital markets, unregulated financial innovation and the free flow of capital.

Krugman, a Keynesian in outlook, advocates that the public sector must take up the slack when economies are pressured. He believes in the importance of timely government intervention and the importance of ensuring full employment as the primary political-economic concern. He criticizes the American government and the Federal Reserve for being more concerned with the well-being of the financial markets than the people.

Krugman, along with many others, marks the repeal of the Glass-Steagall Act of 1933, which separated investment and commercial banking activities, as the beginning of the unleashing of unregulated rapacious finance capital.

The 1929 Great Crash, as it has been described until 2008, was considered the result of overzealous commercial bank involvement in stock market investment, where commercial banks took on far greater risks than was clearly prudent. The Glass-Steagall Act was put in place to prevent this from happening again. The Act was repealed in 1999 by then US President Bill Clinton, some say to endear himself and the Democratic party to Wall Street.

In his book, Krugman describes the fragility of the global economic system, the implications of the overcapacity of supply as anticipated by Marx, and the deregulated market of complex financial instruments that no-one understands or knows how to account for. He claims that the securitization of home mortgages and the exuberant market of credit default swaps served as the tipping point for the entire financial system. The question Krugman poses toward the end of the book is, "what have we learned since then?"

## The curved world of finance

David Smick, the hedge fund manager and author in his *The World is Curved. Hidden Dangers to the World Economy* (2008), decries the greedy behavior of private equity firms and hedge funds. They may have mastered the rules of leverage, he asserts, but they certainly do not understand risk. Their hunger for high returns fuels entrepreneurship but does not help entrepreneurs turn their ideas into substance. They hide exposures to risk, but worst of all they hide that they do not really know what their exposure is. (see my personal reflections). Mark to market calculations are the widest guesses in the world as any thoughtful accountant will attest. (I have been there and can attest!) And the financial industry, which is purely a scavenger industry that rides on the backs of others, is not related to real assets but fictitious numbers that no-one can really verify.

Smick also criticizes governments for being in cahoots with the financial sector based on some pact that neither party understands. He writes that as long as they grease the palms of one another, this myopic situation will persist.

Smick claims the world is not flat (referring to Thomas Friedman's book on globalization), but is curved as our sights are limited, and we cannot see very far. We also don't see what we don't want to see so we keep repeating the same mistakes. When will it end?

## Personal reflections

### The Big Bang

In 1986, I was appointed director of a well-known investment bank in London, UK. The Big Bang was the name given to the deregulation of the financial markets in the UK at that time. During this period, a flood of US investment bankers moved into Old Broad Street (the main street in the City of London), and began beguiling everyone with the new financial instruments they had devised called swaps, futures and options. No-one really knew or understood these arcane instruments especially not the accountants or regulators. My main task at the time was to try to implement systems that the bank could use to track their accounts and their exposures. It was an impossible task. Even though I reported directly to the CEO and the Chairman of the Bank, I could not get anything implemented. No one adhered to policies. The bankers wrote deals on the back of envelopes and then changed the numbers to suit their commissions. Credit limits were exceeded. Risk thresholds were ignored. Mark to market calculations (refer my earlier reference), were continuously manipulated to ensure positive outcomes. Huge paper profits were made based on fallacious accounting, exposures not placed on the Balance Sheet, and all other kinds of conjuring tricks. After eight frantic months of trying to implement controls that were directly and blatantly violated by the CEO himself, I quit. The bank was ignominiously placed in bankruptcy two years later after one of the most well-known trials in UK banking history. In the end the bank paid a hefty fine, but no-one was personally prosecuted. Now, thirty years later, what has changed?

## MBA aspirations

Whenever I teach MBA students, I like to learn what motivates them.

Over the years I have gained some interesting insights as to why they pursue an MBA. One question I always ask is, why they want an MBA. What do they hope to do with their education? Interestingly, the US students overwhelming respond that they wish to become millionaires. They don't talk much about the good they are going to do for businesses but mostly about the large stock options they plan to secure. Also, a high majority of the students wish to be in banking or software. Most seem disdainful of manufacturing and industry in general.

By contrast, international students are less blatant in their desires. Some talk of growing their companies to make a difference, to be innovative and do on. Overall, less that 20% of them talk about financial gains as being their prime motivator. This includes students from India, Hong Kong, Singapore, Portugal and the UK.

## My word is my bond

It was 1992. I was living and working in London. One of my clients was one of the largest UK banks for whom I was developing an AI system that would help evaluate strategic risks. The person I was working directly with, let us call him Alan White, was head of the International Division and of global strategic planning. He had been in banking for decades and had seen many crazy market eruptions. This one particular day, we were discussing the change in the banking landscape over the previous five years. With tears in his eyes, Alan bemoaned what was happening to the banking industry. He spoke of how banking used to be a noble profession. It was an honor to be a banker, he said, and to uphold that noble commitment that "my word is my bond." Now, he said, "we bankers have become greedy thugs in it just for the money instead for the honor of serving the community."

Over the years I have lost touch with Alan. However, when I visit London, I enjoy going to the pubs in the old part of the City of London where one can see napkins and envelopes appended to the pub wall, some of them dated two hundred years ago, on which lending and borrowing contracts were scribbled in a sentence or two. Simply on the back of an envelope people contracted for thousands of pounds based on "my word is my bond."

I wonder what Alan is thinking now.

## Global capitalism gone adrift

Robert Kuttner, founder of the Economic Policy Institute and Chair of the Heller School for Social Policy and Management at Brandeis University, in his book, *Can Democracy Survive Global Capitalism?* (2018), describes the dismantling of the political-economic checks and balances put in place after the crash of 1929 and World War II and the resurgence of the speculative power of private finance. He writes that what was once managed capitalism has become a laissez-faire nightmare based on the fallacious belief in the corrective hand of the market.

Kuttner documents how financial deregulation accelerated during the Thatcher-Reagan era and how it was soon embraced by the International Monetary Fund (IMF) and the World Bank. In 1988, the European Council approved a formal directive whereby all member states of the European community were instructed to abolish all remaining controls on capital movements. The Maastricht Treaty of 1992, that cemented European integration, continued to bury the last vestiges of any capital controls.

According to Kuttner, the US excesses regarding laissez-faire capitalism and the power of the financial markets far exceed those of other countries, yet many of them too have succumbed to the allure of global capitalism's promises. He provides a brief political-economic history not only of the US, but of the UK, France and Germany. He discusses the downfall of the social democrats and the revolving door between politics and Wall Street. He points out how Bill Clinton, Tony Blair and Gerhard Schroder shifted steadily from the left by embracing more conservative economic policies and happily cozied up to business corporations for which all three were handsomely personally enriched.

Kuttner points out how the pull of global capitalism and the need to be internationally competitive according to global capitalism's rules has even impacted the socially and welfare oriented Scandinavian countries. He describes how China has managed to have its cake and eat it when it comes to international trade, partly as it has the huge financial resources to purchase the US Treasury's debt.

Kuttner's analysis covers the seemingly unlimited and unstoppable power of the financial markets, and how governments appear to be afraid of challenging the financial services industry and the huge corporations. He says that finance is no longer servant and that market forces have become disembedded from society. The consequence is that nation states can no longer manage their own fiscal policies in pursuit of full employment. The rules are now structured to favor corporations and banks at expense of workers and citizens.

After the corporate scandals of the late 1990s and the early 2000s, the Sarbanes Oxley Act made scant impact. Even the Dodd-Frank Act of 2010 that was supposed to address the massive cost of misdemeanors by the financial service industry left private equity firms and hedge funds and bond-rating agencies alone. One must surely ask – Why? Banks have become too big and too powerful to fail! They can hide their exposures off balance sheets without any recourse. Why this is tolerated has yet to be explained.

**Flashpoint 1.1**

- Banks that were too big to fail in 2008 have experienced the greatest growth during the recovery boasting record profits in the billions.
- The Wall Street banks that were too big for the US government to allow failure in 2008 are now collectively 37% larger than they were before the crash.
- After the crash of 2008, the wealthy top 1% captured 95% of income and wealth accumulation gains.
- In 1995 there were 365 billionaires worldwide with a net worth of $892 billion. In 2014 there were 1,645 billionaires with an aggregate net worth of $6.4 trillion.
- The world's richest 0.7% hold 44% of global wealth and the top 10% hold 87% of global wealth.
- By 2014 the Bank for International Settlements reported that the global value of derivatives contracts (those arcane financial instruments that Warren Buffett calls weapons of mass destruction) had reached $710 trillion, 20% more than before the derivatives-driven financial crash of 2008.

(Korten, 2015, pp. 27–33)

In conclusion, Kuttner argues that capitalism has become anti-democratic. The loss of negotiating power of the working class, the astronomical divide between rich and poor, the lurching international crises due to hot-money and the political hegemony of finance, has broken the social contract. No wonder there is a rising populist movement!

### The structural inequities caused by private property

*The poor you will always have with you.*

Matthew 26:11

Thomas Piketty's book, *Capital in the Twenty-First Century* (2014), tracks the historical evolution of income equality. He explains the dynamics of private capital accumulation and how it leads to the concentration of wealth in a few hands. His central thesis is that the causes of divergence of wealth between rich and poor rests on the ability to own unlimited private property which results in deep structural inequalities.

Piketty's main argument is that the rate of return on capital can be significantly higher for longer periods of time than the rate of growth of national income and output. This means that wealth accumulated in the past grows more rapidly than output and wages. Capital reproduces itself faster than output increases. If this situation persists for a sustained period, large imbalances in wealth result. This dynamic, Piketty explains, has nothing to do with the free market us such, but rather with government policies regarding wealth accumulation, distribution and taxes. Inequality, he says, is a political matter.

One factor that dilutes the power of the inherited wealthy is high national growth rates. Growth rates include population growth and per capita growth. So where population growth is slow, this increases the impact of capital accumulated by previous generations. The downside of high national growth rates (beside the environmental sustainability issue which we discuss in Chapter 8), is that the new entrepreneurial classes become the new rich and create a new cycle of growth in wealth and in time, their children become the new inherited class. He points out that except for the emerging countries, it is unlikely that more developed countries at the boundary of technological innovation, will have high growth rates.

Part of his analysis includes the ability for top managers in large companies, especially the financial services sector, to set their own remuneration with no relation to productivity or merit. This, he argues, adds to structural imbalances as merit has no longer become a value.

Piketty ends his book by decrying the domination of economists who rely on theoretical speculations without concern for the political implications. Like Reich, who we discuss next, he denounces the divorce of economics from the political economy. Unfortunately, our overly rational, materialist culture tends to hide behind rationalistic calculations and ignores the true meaning of wealth and prosperity – my comment.

---

### The Bernanke bailout fallout

Bernard Bernanke, Chair of the Federal Reserve from 2006–2014, initiated the idea of "quantitative easing," which meant exchanging bad loans on banks' balance sheets with good new money underpinned by negative interest rates. For a few years, property prices continued to fall while thousands of people lost their jobs. Banks, who learned they have nothing to lose, returned to speculation and investment. Property prices began to creep upwards in price while wages remained stagnant and even declined. This added to the wedge between those who depend on rents and dividends for their income and those who depend on wages. When asset prices rise faster than wages, the average person falls further behind. No wonder, everyone wants to own property in the hope of getting ahead of the game. This demand for property fuels asset prices, and so the circle continues – see Systems Thinking in Chapter 2.

## Saving capitalism

Robert Reich, the political commentator and professor, in his book, *Saving Capitalism* (2016), takes a comprehensive look at the weave and woof of capitalism as practiced in the US today. Without mincing his words, he declares the free market notion to be a myth and he excoriates the financial elite for their corrupt ways and for their sense of entitlement to unlimited wealth plus their blatant disregard for any checks and balances in the system. His major argument is that there can be no economic system without certain governing rules and an impartial government prepared to implement those rules. The rules, he states, refer primarily to:

- Property and what can be owned,
- Monopoly and the degree of market power that should be permissible,
- Contracts as to what can be bought and sold and on what terms,
- Bankruptcy and the consequences for purchasers who cannot pay up, and
- Enforcement that ensures that people do not cheat.

Reich provides astounding evidence for how these governing rules fail in multiple ways in the US economic system. He further discusses at great length the lamentable collusion between the government, Wall Street, and most devastating of all, the US Judiciary. Surely the American founding fathers, who went to such great lengths to create a coherent system of governance with clear checks and balances, must be weeping.

Reich, who was Secretary of Labor for the Bill Clinton government, lays the current disappointing state of affairs at the feet of all politicians, Republican and Democrat alike. Like Kuttner, he bemoans the treatment of the unions and the decline of the middle classes. He states that Wall Street

## Flashpoint 1.2

- In 2010 The Supreme Court of the US decided that corporations are people under the First Amendment, entitled to freedom of speech. Corporations can thus act as individuals and are no longer limited in their spending on political advertisements.
- US health costs are the highest in the world by a factor of almost 2.
- US drug companies are permitted to prolong their patents by paying generic producers to delay producing lower cost versions.
- The purpose of business to maximize profits is a fallacy – it exists nowhere in the law.
- Intellectual property rights and patents are snapped up by the large corporations thus eliminating competition and dominating innovation.
- The law allows pharmaceutical companies to pay doctors for prescribing their drugs.

- Millions are spent by the mega-corporations in lobbying to fight against anti-trust laws. For example, in 2015, Amazon spent $ 3.5million, Facebook $6.4million, Microsoft $10.5million and Google $15.8 million.
- Between 1980 and 2014, the financial sector grew six times as fast as the US economy overall.
- The ratio of CEO to average worker pay was over 300 to 1 in 2015.
- In 2013, shortly after the crash, Wall Street bankers pocketed $26.7 billion in bonuses.
- Wall Street accounts for a significant portion of political campaign donations to both the Republican and the Democratic parties.

Extracts from Reich (2016)

now owns the country and that the creation of behemoth organizations such as Amazon, Google, Microsoft, Facebook and Comcast, continuously surrounded by a platoon of lawyers to ensure their dominance, has wiped out any possibility of market fair play. According to him all the heralded benefits of capitalism have been eviscerated. People are underpaid their worth, except for the bankers whose earnings defy rationalization.

Reich tries to end his devastating critique on an upbeat note that the spirit of the American people will not fail them. On how this is going to pan out, he is rather vague.

### The Federal Reserve and Goldman Sachs

In 2011, banking lawyer Carmen Segarra took a job with the Federal Reserve Bank of New York where she was appointed supervisor of Goldman Sachs. In her book, *Non-Compliant: A Lone Whistleblower Exposes the Giants of Wall Street*, 2018, she documents in painstaking detail the collusion between Federal Bank employees and the executives at Goldman. During her seven months, before being laid off for refusing to alter her notes and redact her evidence of non-compliance, she discovered that Goldman blatantly ignored banking rules and regulations, failed on many risk assessment ratings, had no conflict of interest policy, ignored rules relating to foreign transactions, and did not have safety nets in place to protect people's investments, to mention a few transgressions.

These failings were known to the Federal Reserve (FED) and they jokingly would poke at Goldman using the motto, we will "let them hurt, but not too much." Time and again when Segarra tried to make progress on any compliance matter, the employees at Goldman stalled and she, Segarra, was cautioned by her superiors to go lightly.

After being laid off in 2012, Segarra sued the FED for wrongful dismissal and due to some small technicality, her case was dismissed. Since being laid off, nothing has changed. The same people run Goldman Sachs and some of the players Segarra wrestled with have been promoted. She has some interesting reflections on YouTube.

(See the Whistleblower's Dilemma in Chapter 5)

## Growth at all costs

An idea deeply embedded in modern economic and political culture is that economic growth is the key to everything (remember Marx!). It will alleviate poverty, it will usher in new opportunities, it will result in a growth in jobs and pay packets, it is the way to solve our over-supply problem, and everyone will be better off. However, the rise in population and this relentless pursuit for growth is, among other things, devastating the environment. Growth requires energy, and fossil fuel consumption in the US, according to the Energy Information Administration (EIA), will reach record levels in 2019. As we know fossil fuel emissions are devastating to our environment.

The pursuit for growth and the squeezing out of the small butchers and bakers in the villages, is one contributor to the burgeoning size of cities. At this time (2018), it is estimated that nearly 70% of the world's population lives in urban areas. As a result, consider the enormous demand for water, sanitation, energy, food and other natural resources. Many rural people have been evicted to make way for large landowners who monopolize food production to meet the growing needs of the urban populace.

According to David Korten, capitalism's most critical collateral damage is its destruction of the Earth's living system. The Earth is its own living system (See Chapters 2 and 8), and while we might focus on certain areas such as climate change, the very vibrancy and health of the entire system is at risk. Climate change in and of itself wreaks havoc on other micro systems. We hear of the melting of glaciers, rising sea levels, ocean acidification, reduction of fish stocks, and the disappearance or reduction in numbers of important animals and insects that influence the health of our eco-system.

Corporations have yet to truly embrace the Triple Bottom Line, something we discuss in Chapter 2. Known as externalities, many corporations still do not carry the burden of their production footprint as they have conveniently transferred it to another country that does not have such rigorous standards as say in the European Union (EU). Alas, as I mentioned under the power of finance capital, on page 25, many countries in a desperate attempt to attract foreign direct investment or finance capital will reduce their environmental standards so as to attract industry. But that is changing – see following. Once again, Korten says, corporations rule the world when growth becomes the organizing principle of public policies.

**Waste not – want not**

*CNN July 18, 2019*

Cambodia has become the latest Asian country to reject shipments of waste sent to its shores by Western companies for processing.

Cambodian officials announced Wednesday that they were sending 1,600 tons of trash back to their source – the United States and Canada.

A total of eighty-three shipping containers of plastic waste were found on Tuesday at the major southwestern port of Sihanoukville, reported the Secretary of State and spokesman to the Ministry of Environment. The containers, opened by customs and excise officials, were labeled as "recyclable products."

The Cambodian customs ministry is now conducting an investigation into how the containers ended up in Cambodia and which companies or groups are behind the import. If discovered, they will be fined and brought to court. Meanwhile, the federal government will begin the process of sending back the trash to the US and Canada.

"Cambodia is not a dustbin where foreign countries can dispose of out-of-date e-waste, and the government also opposes any import of plastic waste and lubricants to be recycled in this country," said the state spokesman.

## The eighth wonder of the world – the power of compounding

We are always chasing growth. Whether it is our own salary, our personal wealth or that of our company or nation. There is a fixation with growth – and we know why. Marx and others explained the capitalist dynamics.

The benchmark for national well-being is not health or personal happiness but rather growth, commonly measured as GDP (gross domestic product).

- Let us look at the compounding impact of growth. We are inclined to think that 1% per year is very low. However over five years that amounts to 5.1% growth.
- Now let us take a growth rate of 1.5% per year, which would still be considered low. 1.015 compounded over five years = 7.735% growth.
- If we take 2% compounded over five years this equates to 10.41% growth.
- What we really want, or are told, is that we need 5% per year or more – which over five years equates to 27.63% growth.

Now these numbers may seem small for our own wealth since asset prices can grow so radically as pointed out by Pinker above, but for the Earth's resources, our ecological footprint growing at a rate of 2% or more incessantly is devastating. Even in biblical times, the fields were left fallow periodically to give them a chance to nourish and regenerate themselves. We just want more and more because our economists and financiers say that is what will make us wealthy or, it is a panacea for all economic ills.

## The gap between the ideal and the practice

If we compare the founding ideas of capitalism and the cautions provided by its early proponents with the capitalism currently practiced today, we find the following:

1   Smith's major assumptions regarding morality, justice, and self-restraint do not hold. We do not have markets consisting of many small buyers and sellers with equal power. On the contrary, large corporations and e-commerce have all but wiped out the small market participant. This reality is not only evident in the more developed countries but is beginning to impact the emerging economies.
2   Smith also advocated that the owners of capital should be the managers of the businesses in which they invest. This too is not practiced much with the exception of very small or medium sized family firms. Instead, we have armies of MBAs or professional managers clamoring to be in charge and to earn outrageous salaries wherever possible.
3   The invisible hand of correction, whereby self-interest means interest of the other, remains largely invisible! Self-interest has come to mean, selfish, self-centered, deceptive and entitled.
4   Many of capitalisms proponents advocated that capital from trade should remain nationally rooted. Ricardo claimed that capital should not be allowed to move from high wage countries to low wage countries thus creating an arbitrage on labor. This idea has been not only dismissed but labor cost arbitrage across countries has been the backbone of multinational competitiveness. The labor theory of value has been totally discarded as the only thing that matters is competitive efficiency and not a decent wage. Marx too warned us against this trend.
5   At the time of Adam Smith, and even into the mid-twentieth century, the idea that financial instruments would trade on their own without any relation to material goods, was outside of anyone's imagination. This has of course created a large part of our current problems where other people's money is used by bankers for speculative purposes.
6   Capitalism was supposedly to be grounded in a sense of communal justice supported by a system of justice regulated by the government. It seems that regulation is either non-existent or arbitrary. Self-regulation has been tried and clearly does not work. As Reich explains in his book, many

bills intended to be a means of correction to market irregularities are passed and are then not given the funding to ensure their implementation. It is simply smoke and mirrors. Government interference is minimal and only there to serve its own political agenda or to appease Wall Street.

7    The financial sector that brought down Wall Street in 1929, and the world in 2008, reigns supreme. Maybe Marx was right. It is the Robespierre of capitalism that has ushered in a "reign of terror" which has corporations quaking in their boots as to how they will survive. I discuss the "culture of fear" in the next chapter.

8    According to Friedman, the free market spirit was to be supported, however corporations were expected to play by the rules; to be decent, to be transparent, and to be curbed from becoming excessively large and powerful. Sadly, in many cases this behavior does not exist, and any laws intended to curb the size of corporations clearly have no teeth.

## Some ethical questions posed by capitalism

From a business ethics viewpoint, what might we conclude from this rather dismal picture of global capitalism? How can one have an ethics discussion when so many ethical violations are rampant across the socio-political-economic system? How does one inspire ethical behavior when corruption, deception, the abuse of power, and widespread conflicts of interest are condoned?

Global capitalism as currently practiced surely raises several significant ethical questions, such as:

• In the capitalistic system one can own as much private property – savings accounts, stocks, real estate, commodities, cash and so on – as one can provided it has been obtained by legally defensible means. This idea of unlimited anything challenges the ethical notion of moderation and the concept of limits. When is enough, enough?

• The process of buying and selling requires negotiations, accordingly those most skillful or with the most power get to dictate terms. Is this really a free market?

• Capitalism encourages the accumulation of wealth and results in an uneven distribution of wealth, something that has become a significant issue around the world, especially in the US. Is this just? Should wealth be limited or redistributed?

• Proponents of capitalism argue that it promotes freedom in every aspect of its activities. Transactions between buyers and sellers are voluntary. Employees can work for anyone they choose. Dissatisfied employees can leave at any time and work for other firms or create business of their own. Does capitalism deliver on these freedoms?

• Capitalism encourages competition. Global capitalism intensifies competition especially for labor at lowest cost and for funding sources. Does this breed hostile behaviors exacerbated by the high stakes involved?

- The growth of mega corporations like Google, Facebook and Amazon are now being challenged particularly in the UK and Europe for the mass of data they have accumulated and their marketing power to influence both supply and demand and how it affects free market forces. Is the playing field fair for both consumers and suppliers or does might make right?
- All the architects of the capitalist system insisted that finance should be nationally rooted and not allowed for arbitrage purposes. Why are unchecked international financial flows condoned and even encouraged?
- The unrestrained pursuit of growth has enormous consequences for the sustainability of the Earth and the environment. Do we not have an ethical obligation to the planet?

---

### Corruption – a worldwide problem

**Australia:** Australia banking inquiry: Scathing report calls for industry overhaul. www.bbc.com/news/world-australia-47112040

**Canada:** Allegations involving Prime Minister Trudeau that officials inappropriately pressured former Justice Minister Jody Wilson-Raybould to help major construction company SNC-Lavalin Group Inc (SNC.TO) avoid a corruption trial.

**Denmark:** In 2018, Danske Bank CEO Thomas Borgen was ousted for the bank's involvement in one of worst money laundering scandals in European history. Following an investigation into payments of around €200 billion at its Estonian branch, Danske Bank conceded that a "significant" number of the payments were suspicious.

**Germany:** In 2017, Deutsche Bank was fined a total of $630 million by US and UK financial authorities over accusations of having laundered money out of Russia. According to US and British regulators, Deutsche Bank's anti-money laundering control mechanisms failed to spot sham trades with a value of up to $10 billion, not knowing who the customers involved in the trades were and where their money came from.

**Malaysia:** Malaysia's state-owned investment fund, 1MDB, was supposed to attract foreign investment. Instead, it spurred criminal and regulatory investigations around the world as a result of financial deal-making, election spending and political patronage under former Prime Minister Najib Razak. The figures are mind-boggling: A Malaysian parliamentary committee identified at least $4.2 billion in irregular transactions related to 1MDB. Bankers in ten countries around the world were in one way or another involved in the mis-appropriation of funds.

**US College Admissions Scandal:** The 2019 college admissions bribery scandal, nicknamed Operation Varsity Blues, exposed a criminal conspiracy to influence undergraduate admissions decisions at several top

American universities. It was disclosed on March 12, 2019, by United States federal prosecutors, that at least fifty-one people are alleged to have been part of it, a number of whom have pled guilty or agreed to plead guilty. Thirty-three parents of college applicants are accused of paying more than $25 million between 2011 and 2018 to William Rick Singer, organizer of the scheme, who used part of the money to fraudulently inflate entrance exam test scores and bribe college officials.

## Executive summary

This chapter described the macro-economic environment in which businesses operate and the dynamics which directly impact their behavior.

The overall purpose of this chapter is to raise awareness of the under-currents in the macro-environment and to invite questioning, debate and reflection on how these currents and tensions influence people's ethics at work.

Here are some of the key points discussed:

- Capitalism has evolved over many centuries to what it is today.
- Global capitalism provides the backdrop in which business organizations currently compete.
- By tracking the evolution of capitalism, we realize that it is not simply an economic system but that it affects many aspects of human individual and social behavior.
- The evolution of people's self-understanding and social consciousness that sparked the idea of liberty provided the seedbed for the capitalist endeavor.
- Capitalism fostered the growing spirit of individuality initiated by the Reformation and work became infused with new meaning and purpose as a surrogate form of salvation.
- The idea of the right to owning unlimited private property acquired by legal means has radically altered social structures and relations as well as the meaning of morality.
- The founders of capitalism offered a blueprint that provided a cohesive socio-economic system. Critics of capitalism illustrate how far the current reality has strayed from the original design.
- Capitalism has several inherent dynamics one of which is to depend on persistent growth and to create growing disparities between the rich and the poor.
- Many critics claim that global financial flows are one of the most detrimental aspects of global capitalism.
- While capitalism can provide many benefits, the fact that it has become excessive in practice and has lost its moral underpinning, we are now experiencing its shadow side.

## Questions for reflection

- Do you think the details of the opening case are influenced by the global capitalist spirit?
- Has capitalism become an iron cage – see page 24.
- What do you think is the greatest ethical challenge presented by capitalism?
- Does your organization feel the pressures of global capitalism as described in this chapter? If yes – in what way?
- Do you support the idea of unlimited private property?
- How does one create an ethical business culture if the political-economic system itself is unethical? Suggestions?

## Key terms

Age of Reason   24
Arbitrage   26
Classical capitalism   21
Common good   24
Comparative advantage   29
Consumerism   32
Creative destruction   35
Enlightenment   24
Free markets   20
Invisible hand   27
Keynesian capitalism   21

Labor theory of value   30
Laissez-faire   21
Liberty   24
Materialism   24
Mercantilism   21
Methodism   23
Proletariat   33
Property   20
Reformation   23
Self-interest   21
Sympathy   27

## The dissolution of the political economy

The political economy is the study of production and trade and their relations with the law, moral conventions and government and with the distribution of national income and wealth. As a discipline, it used to be part of moral philosophy where one studied the "household" management of the state. In the late 19th century, the term economics began to replace political economy as mathematical modelling took over as a method of analysis and measurement. It thus moved from the liberal arts to the sciences. Nowadays economics refers to the narrow study of the economy which excludes political and social considerations. Some contemporary economists take a more inter-disciplinary approach, whereby they examine how political forces and policies affect socio-economic policies and the resultant distribution of income; however, the bias still seems to be around mathematical modelling and assumptions of perfect rationality.

## Note

1 Thomas I. White. *Business Ethics: A Philosophical Reader*. New York: Macmillan Publishing Company, 1993, p. 12.

# References

Bell, Daniel. *The Cultural Contradictions of Capitalism.* New York: Basic Books, 1996.

Friedman, Milton. *Capitalism and Freedom.* Chicago, Illinois: University of Chicago Press, 1962.

Grieder, William. *One World, Ready or Not: The Manic Logic of Global Capitalism.* New York: Touchstone, 1997.

Korten, David C. *When Corporations Rule the World.* Oakland, CA: Berrett-Koehler Publishers Inc., 2015.

Krugman, Paul. *The Return of Depression Economics and the Crisis of 2008.* New York: W.W. Norton & Company, 2009.

Kuttner, Robert. *Can Democracy Survive Global Capitalism?* New York: W. W. Norton & Company, 2018.

Marx, Karl. *The Communist Manifesto (1848).* CreateSpace independent Publishing Paltform, reprint 2014.

Marx, Karl. *Das Kapital.* New York: Penguin Classics, 1992.

Muller, Jerry Z. *Capitalism and the Jews.* Princeton, NJ: Princeton University Press, 2010.

Picketty, Thomas. *Capital in the Twenty-First Century.* Cambridge, MA: Belknap Press, 2014.

Reich, Robert B. *Saving Capitalism: For the Many, Not the Few.* New York: Vintage Books, 2016.

Smick, David M. *The World is Curved: Hidden Dangers to the Global Economy.* New York: Penguin Group, 2008.

Smith, Adam. *An Inquiry Into the Nature and Causes of the Wealth of Nations.* London, UK: Methuen & Co., Ltd., 1904.

Smith, Adam. *Theory of Moral Sentiments.* Boston, MA: Wells and Lilly, 1817.

Soros, George. *The Crisis of Global Capitalism.* New York: Public Affairs, 1998.

Tillich, Paul. *The Courage to Be.* New Haven, CT: Yale University Press, 1952.

Tillich, Paul. *Dynamics of Faith.* New York: HarperOne, 2009.

Weber, Max. *The Protestant Ethic and the Spirit of Capitalism.* Los Angeles, CA: Roxbury Publishing Company, 1996.

# 2    Ethical barriers at work

## Contents

## The jet is ready!

Susanna Johnson (VP of Finance and Administration), along with the other vice presidents of Palermo Inc. had taken their usual seats around the table in the President's office. The morning was to be devoted to the preparation of the President's presentation of the recent quarter's financial results to the board and shareholders.

President Don Peruchi was in an upbeat mood. He opened discussions with a recount of his early morning telephone conversation with the chair of the board, Elizabeth Pigeonthatch, an energetic female septuagenarian, who sat on at least a dozen different boards. The president spent 20 minutes emphasizing Elizabeth Pigeonthatch's support for the management team and her request that he communicate to them her appreciation of their work that resulted in Palermo Inc. achieving its forecasts despite a difficult economy. The president effusively thanked the management team for their sterling efforts and their loyalty to him as president during these challenging times. He went so far as to say that they were the best team that he had ever worked with and hoped that their association would be a long and happy one.

When the president briefly halted his soliloquy to take a breath, Catherine Cantell, the Vice President of Human Resources, leapt from her seat to turn on a fan. The stifling heat in the room augmented by the hot air exuding from the president, despite the thundering efforts of the air conditioner to cool the environment, had caused a rapid opening of collars and general de-robing of excess garments.

Oblivious of the discomfort and general commotion that ensued in the wake of Catherine's actions, Don Peruchi moved on with his agenda. He continued:

> Given the current economic climate and the obvious recent successes of my management team, I know that we will be able to convince the board and the shareholders that we will meet our goals and that they have nothing to worry about. I know that I can count on you for your support.

Peruchi followed this last comment with an attempt to make eye contact with everyone seated at the table. Used to his intimidating style, members of the management team adopted various strategies to avoid his challenging stare. Some examined their fingernails, others pretended to make notes on their writing pads, and others seemed deeply in thought while staring out the window or inspecting the newly installed plush brown carpet.

Vice President of Information Technology Scott Trevino tried to alleviate the palpable tension by smiling carefully and commented, "We will do what we can." Scott believed that, although he was irritated by Don Peruchi's style and hated the culture of the company, he owed the organization an allegiance. His duty, as he saw it, was to do as he was told and to uphold the image of the company as best he could. He was not the president, and he would never want that job or responsibility. In exchange he would do his duty and be as loyal as possible. Life was good, he earned well, had great share options, and his son with special needs was attending the best school of its kind in the state. He was not going to rock the boat, no sir!

Vice President of Marketing and Communications Lee-Anne Kilroy was less subtle. She did not like the president's style or values and challenged him regularly on these issues. Unfortunately, he riled her so that she lost her cool, often becoming so emotionally upset that she would lose support from the rest of the group, who did not want to be associated with "that emotional woman." At this juncture she exclaimed: "Marketing can only go so far. At some stage we are going to have to deliver the real goods. Then what will we do? Sales are down, orders are down, and our competition is doing a better marketing job than we are. I told you that slashing the marketing budget will have severe repercussions and here we are trying to pretend that nothing has happened. Well it has, and the downward trend will continue until we can reorient our strategy – something I have been insisting on since I joined this organization over two years ago! Don, we have some major work to do here. Why do you keep resisting it?"

Obviously annoyed, Don stared at Lee-Anne, his face changing from a forced smile to a badly concealed grimace. Vice President of Human Resources Catherine Cantell intervened swiftly. Catherine had been with the organization nearly twenty years. She had seen it grow from its entrepreneurial roots into a serious public organization. Her husband was a retired executive of Palermo Inc., whose technical skill in electronics and whose entrepreneurial style had helped place the organization on the technological map. Catherine's skill lay in mediating between rival organizational stakeholders and defusing their anger. Previously a trade union negotiator and now part of management she could play both sides of the game. She was a great believer in astrological signs and their interpretations and would readily intervene in management meetings with comments such as "the line-up of the planets indicate that today is an unsuitable day to make decisions," or "the positioning of the moon last night means we should not try to resolve conflicts on a day like today." While ridiculed behind her back for allegedly crazy insights, few dared to challenge her assertions head on. Renowned for her need to get her own way, most people deferred to her interventions, preferring to take the path of least resistance.

Raising her head from her notebook filled with astrological graphics and jottings, Catherine proclaimed:

> Don, I understand what you are trying to do here. I agree that it is in the best interests of the organization if we uphold stakeholder and especially employee morale. We know that we have some serious strategic work to do but there is no point in making that public. That is our in-house business. Overall the greatest benefit to the greatest number will accrue if we keep a cool outward exterior and not let people know the difficulties we are really facing. They wouldn't know what to do with the information so why trouble them unnecessarily? Let's keep the analysts satisfied and hopefully they will support holding the share price steady, thus preventing us from having to take drastic action too quickly.

John Martin, the Vice President of Operations, looked up from his inspection of the new carpet. A technical man through and through, he hated these management meetings. He preferred short discussions that resulted in immediate action. John believed that not much positive resulted from all this talk. He believed that performance, delivery and industry benchmark achievements were the hallmarks of success.

A highly numbers-driven executive, John arrived at every meeting well prepared. According to him statistics do not lie and his tenacity for hunting down numbers to support any and every decision irritated some of the other executives. He did his homework and was always up to date with the latest events in the operating divisions. His style was combative, and he was one of the few people who dared challenge some of the president's often hasty decisions.

Although generally surly, and often quite a bully in order to get his way, John considered himself a "ladies'" man. He was known for having had affairs with several of his administrative support staff and this negatively affected the influence he might otherwise have had. Some felt he deserved severe reprimand for his philandering while others believed he should be demoted from the position of vice president. Despite his poor popularity at the management level, the people in his division remained loyal to him as he had a reputation for getting things done and looking after his own. Catherine Cantell had held several serious discussions with John warning him about the consequences of sexual harassment, but to no avail. John continued to try to seduce whomever he could. In general, people were afraid of his position and his power and so turned a blind eye to his inappropriate behavior. Usually the women with whom he had affairs left the organization shortly after the relationship terminated.

John exclaimed:

> Don, we will of course do the best we can, but I think we need to lean on the low performing divisions more. Employees have seen significant salary increases over the past few years and I think it is time now to cash in on the goodwill that we as a management team have created. I suggest that we implement a hiring freeze immediately and review those divisions whose performance is lacking. According to my figures, the Research Department remains overstaffed and the Component Division continues to underperform. I think it is time we read the riot act to the manager of the division, Martha Katz, and tell her that we are going to merge her division with the Electronics Division unless she can convince us of an immediate turnaround.

The only one who challenged John on a regular basis was Susanna Johnson. She disliked his bullying manner and his obvious arrogance. Susanna too could play the numbers game and learned quickly that John managed to amass those numbers or statistics that supported his agenda. Repeatedly she found that closer scrutiny would reveal omissions and inaccuracies that the less well-prepared members of the management team would not detect. She also had learned from the grapevine that Martha Katz had ignored John's frequent passes at her and had reported his behavior to Catherine Cantell.

John and Susanna came head to head frequently during many of the discussions. Unfortunately for Susanna, the President was not that adept at numbers, operating more by instinct than logic and so sided with whomever he felt more personally aligned at any given time. This decision-making style resulted in many stop-go decisions and frequent policy-making inconsistencies.

Susanna Johnson sat at the meeting depressed. She realized that no-one wanted to face the truth regarding the company's deteriorating financial position. The competition in the industry was vicious and, by saving money at the wrong time in the wrong places, plus the growing cost base, Palermo had forsaken the technological lead that it once held.

Susanna recognized the impossibility of repeatedly extracting the imaginary rabbit from the hat. She asked herself why she had allowed the CEO to railroad her into diluting the truth regarding the organization's finances. She knew that she had a lot of credibility with the management team, however, they were so used to concealing the truth from one another they did not even want to hear it from her. They preferred to cling to their belief in miracles and their insatiable appetite for larger salaries and increased perks. How could she confront the CEO and challenge his truth and yet not frighten off the others thereby disempowering herself? Despite her professional role as chief financial officer, usually considered to be the ultimate utilitarian, Susanna longed to live a truthful and meaningful life. These political power plays exhausted her and made her feel that she was losing her soul. Susanna jumped in:

> John, I am not sure of the source of your figures, but my analysis reveals a very different picture. In calculating your numbers have you taken into consideration the transfer pricing that occurs between especially the Components Division and the other divisions? If so, I am curious to know what rates you used and how you apportioned overheads. I suggest that before we make any decisions on this issue, you and I revisit our calculations together to see where they differ.

"Good idea," exclaimed Don, relieved that he did not have to take the conversation any further. He liked Martha Katz and had recently given her an enormous salary increase plus further share options. He had not discussed this action with any other member of his management team and would not like it to come out now that she was underperforming.

The Vice President for Research, Olive James, leapt into the conversation. Olive, one of the first female African American doctors in the field of specialized electronics, usually spoke in slow, somewhat hushed, and deliberate tones. "I never cease to be amazed," she said,

> at John's need to always point the finger at someone else. What is more, since when is the Vice President of Operations responsible for evaluating

the financial performance of other divisions? I would personally appreciate it if he saw to the performance of his own divisions and didn't interfere in those areas where he has limited knowledge of what really goes on. Further, having been pushed into this position, I report reluctantly of course, that the Research Department has been getting very little co-operation from some of John's departments. I would have never brought this up at this meeting but would have approached John myself had he not decided to go on a rampage against other divisions that do not report to him. This is an unfortunate way for us to operate as a management team by publicly denigrating one another. I suggest Don, that you as CEO, put a stop to it.

At this point Miguel Gonsalves, the Vice President of Overseas Divisions, butted in. "I hate to change the topic at this point, but I know Don that you are going to have to leave just now and I need a few minutes to talk with you about the latest contract that I am working on in Peru. I need some decisions before you go. Can we hold this other conversation over until we meet next week?"

At that moment Louise, the president's administrative assistant stuck her head in the door. "The jet is ready Don – how long will you be?"

## Questions for reflection

- How would you describe the group dynamics among the management team?
- To what extent does fear play a role in the management team's behavior?
- Do people have a good understanding of what is going on at Palermo?
- Does the group share a culture of trust?
- What indicators do you detect of ethical sensitivities among the management team?

I imagine this story prompts a few thoughts and possibly a familiarity with some of the characters. I will use this story as our referent point as we reflect on the internal dynamics of organizations and how these impact people's ethical behavior.

## A systems perspective

In Chapter 1, we looked at global capitalism as the macrocosmic environment within which business organizations operate. You will recall that to appreciate the complexity and nuances of the capitalist system, we could not simply take a unidimensional perspective. We needed a more holistic, or what I refer to as a systems perspective. This more encompassing view shed light on the fact that capitalism impacts not only our economic life, but our personal, religious, social, and political life too. We saw that capitalism profoundly influences, and is influenced by, our motivations, behaviors, worldviews, relationships with one another, and our definition of what constitutes happiness or a good life.

Having an appreciation of global capitalism, we now turn to businesses and how they function internally. What I wish to illustrate is that internal business pressures can conspire to derail personal value systems and ethical standards by providing a veritable set-up for dishonest behavior. However, before we progress any further, I wish to clarify what systems thinking is and what it means to view things systemically. We may not be consciously aware of it, but the Palermo Inc. story at the beginning of this chapter has already primed our mental systems pump.

### Definition of a system

A system is a regularly interacting and interdependent group of parts, items or people, that form a unified whole with the purpose of establishing a goal (Beerel, 2009). There are numerous types of systems. There are biological systems (the respiratory system), mechanical systems (air-conditioning systems), ecological systems (plant life), social systems (groups and communities), and economic systems (business organizations).

By studying systems as a whole as opposed to treating them as an aggregation of parts, we can find out certain things about them, like their strengths and weaknesses, and how they behave under certain conditions. Think of the way we observe and analyze teams. We can assess a team by looking at its performance without needing to analyze the actions of each player. Similarly, with organizations we can assess an organizational culture as a system without having to analyze each person and his or her contribution to that culture.

### A glance at systems theory

Systems thinking emerged in Europe in the 1920s. It was pioneered by biologists who saw living organisms as integrated wholes, i.e., as systems. To understand the behavior of a living organism, they argued, one cannot simply study the parts. Rather, one must study the organizing relations or patterns of relationships immanent within the organism. By studying these relations, one gains the real understanding of that organism. Systems thinking, therefore, takes the approach of studying a system as an integrated whole whose essential properties arise from the relationships between the parts. In a nutshell, systems thinking focuses on the connectedness, patterns, relationships and context of the system (Capra, 2014).

### Systemic properties

By adopting a systems approach, we come to see that the relationships among the parts of a system have certain characteristics that together manifest irreducible characteristics of the system itself. In other words, all systems have properties of their own that are not reducible to the parts of the system. For example, think about groups or group dynamics. I am sure you have observed that a group has its own distinguishable character that exists apart from the aggregate characteristics of its members.

## Reflection

How might you describe Palermo Inc., as a group system?

*Interdependence*

Another important insight is that everything is a system. Nothing is independent, and all systems affect one another even where parts of the system appear distant from one another. Let's take an example: Women across the world form a system, and women in China form a sub-system of that system. Due to the nature of systems, therefore, whatever impacts Chinese women will in some way impact women across the world – and vice versa.

*Infinite embeddedness*

A system is also always embedded in other systems. This means that any system is always a combination of systems and sub-systems. Arthur Koestler coined the term "holon" to refer to that which is whole in one context and simultaneously a part in another (Koestler, 1967). Holons are nested within each other. Each holon is nested within the next level of holon which establishes their interconnectedness and inter-dependence.

Take the United States. The United States is a system, and corporate America is sub-system of that system. A company is both a sub-system of corporate America and a system in its own right. The board of directors are a sub-system of the company, and so on. If you think about it, the number and interconnectedness of systems is infinite.

*Simple and complex*

Systems range from simple to complex. The more complex the system, the greater the number of sub-systems, and the more intricate their operations.

Sub-systems are arranged in some form of hierarchy that facilitates achieving the sub-system's goal, which is in service to the larger system's goal. Think of the many systems in our bodies and how they each function in service of their own tasks as well as for the overall bodily system of health, growth and well-being.

Hierarchy is central to the systems theory in that it is the theory of wholeness. Hierarchy describes an order of increasing holons representing an increasing wholeness and integrative capacity (Waddock, 2006).

*System boundaries are porous*

Each sub-system in a hierarchy has its own boundary that contains within it inputs, processes, outputs and feedback loops that contribute to the overall system performance and goal (Senge, 1990). Through the system boundary, systems import all kinds of elements from the other systems of which they are part. For example, if the larger system is unhealthy or insecure and experiencing fear, the sub-systems will import these emotions into their environment too. If the larger system is at war, the sub-systems will become warlike too. It follows that if racism or sexual harassment is a feature of the system at large, the smaller systems will reflect these features too. If a company as a whole behaves like a bully, it is likely that most of its divisions and departments will mirror this type of behavior. (See the discussion on the macrocosm-microcosm principle later in this chapter.)

### The goal of living systems

Not surprisingly, the primary goal of all living systems is survival. This survival is not just physical survival, but includes psychological, emotional, economic, social and political survival. No matter how survival is defined, survival is the primary and most immediate goal of all living systems. When a system's survival is under threat, for example, in the case of intense competition, or poor financial results, the system will default to a "fight for survival" mode, which may take many forms – as we discuss below under Managing Fear. Think about the behavior of the people in Palermo Inc.

Realistically, most living systems do not just want to survive; they want to be healthy, to thrive and prosper. In a healthy system, all the sub-systems contribute to this health or well-being. The contribution each sub-system makes might differ, but the goal is always the same, to foster health and well-being. For example, if we have healthy family systems, we have a healthy community system. If we have healthy community systems, we have healthy counties or states, and we have a healthy national system. The opposite is naturally also true. If we have an unhealthy national system, we will have unhealthy states, communities and families. Everything is interdependent. There may be pockets that counter the trend, however these are likely to be small, isolated and struggling to hold their own against the tide.

For systems to remain healthy and survive, they need to be open to external forces and be adaptive to change. Closed or maladaptive systems rarely survive for any extended period.

### Systems theory summary

In general, systems theory provides us with the following insights:

* Everything is a system.
* All systems are embedded in other systems.
* All systems are interdependent.
* All systems strive for survival.
* Systems exist within a hierarchy.
* Systems need to be open and adaptive to survive.
* Systems have irreducible characteristics that belong to the system as a whole.
* Sub-systems contribute to the survival of the larger system.
* System behavior depends on system structure.

- The patterns inherent in the system are the configured relationships that are characteristic of each system. If the pattern is destroyed, the system dies.
- All patterns in systems form a network. When we look at life, we look at networks.
- These networks are in continuous communication.
- Feedback is intimately connected with the network pattern.
- All networks self-organize into patterns.
- Systems live in dynamic tension between order and chaos Capra and Luisi (2014).

### *The macrocosm–microcosm principle*

An integral part of systems theory is the macrocosm–microcosm principle. This principle states that in a living system the characteristics and force-fields that exist in the whole system are in some way recapitulated in every part of its sub-systems. A well-known example is our DNA. The DNA that is the genetic code of the human body is contained in every cell. Scientists need only a scrap of skin or a drop of bodily fluid to determine the genetic make-up of the entire body. The microcosm reflects the macrocosm and vice versa.

If we transport this idea into business organizations, we observe the same phenomenon. The values, attitudes and behaviors of for example, an industry, are reflected in the organizations that make-up that industry. An easy example is the financial services industry. Think of how the competitive, money-driven culture is reflected in so many individual organizations in that sector.

The macrocosm–microcosm principle can be very helpful as we consider the nature of business ethics. With systems thinking, we get an idea of the patterns of ethical behaviors that are the DNA of a system and what that means for creating an ethical culture in the system and its sub-systems. As we now know, ethics does not operate in isolation, nor is it independent of other factors or just dependent on one human being. Systemic pressures can be huge, palpable, often over-whelming and frequently places the system or a person's survival in question. Therein lies one of our personal big challenges: is it better to survive or to be ethical? History is replete with countervailing arguments!

---

**Your turn – systems thinking**

What patterns and relationships do you see between –

- The US stock market boom and mass shootings?
- Climate change and obesity?
- AI and the worldwide refugee crisis?

Maybe you can discuss this with your management team. You will be surprised what comes up!

---

## Systems thinking and business ethics

Now one might say this systems theory is all well and good, but how does one apply it to organizations? My response is that while one wants individuals to be ethical, one cannot assess or influence their ethicality unless one understands the context, the relationships and the patterns of value and behavior in which the person (who is also a system) is embedded. There is also the very real challenge that this book is majorly pre-occupied with, which is: How does one constructively influence people to be ethical if the environment is inimical to ethical behavior?

## The nature of business ethics

### The field of study

Business ethics is concerned with the ethical deliberations, decisions and moral behavior that people exhibit at work. Since decision-making usually requires balancing conflicting values and/or dealing with various decision trade-offs, ethics, which provides guiding principles for decision-making, is concerned with the conditions in which decision-making takes place. Ethics is also concerned with the justification of the principles brought to bear in resolving conflicts of values as well as with the moral action that is in fact taken.

### The goal of business ethics

The goal of business ethics is to enhance ethical behavior throughout the organization by fostering a culture of mutual trust, transparency and personal moral accountability. Clearly, this is easier said than done. To create an organizational atmosphere and culture that encourages ethical thinking and behavior requires a good understanding of the business dynamics and moral pressure points managers and employees experience.

### The Triple Bottom Line

Broadly speaking, we could summarize the moral pressure points that business organizations face as arising from the efforts to simultaneously satisfy three high-level ends. These are the sustainable profitability of the business (a reflection of economic value), the sustained welfare of the people or stakeholders impacted by business operations (a reflection of social responsibility), and the environment (a reflection of the impact on the environment). These three aims are often referred to as **People, Planet and Profit** or the Triple Bottom Line. (I discuss this further in Chapter 8.)

  While ideally these ends should not create value conflicts, frequently they do. The senior management team is thus constantly making decisions that try to balance achieving these aims. This balancing act requires good decision-making skills along with thoughtful moral reasoning strategies. One might argue that handling this complexity effectively gives managers some right (perhaps) to claim large salaries. Unfortunately, too many ineffective managers get the big bucks without being able (or even bothering) to deliver on these crucial goals.

## Never say never

In the early 2000s, we experienced the free fall of Enron, Worldcom, Global Crossing, Tyco and others. These business corruption horror stories, among several others, resulted in the Sarbanes-Oxley Act (SOX, 2002). At that time the regulators argued that the implementation of SOX would end corruption, and that the devastation of people's financial lives could-would never happen again! Well – wrong! Usher in 2007–2008 – now we had the corruption and bankruptcies of AIG, Lehman Bros., Fannie-Mac, Fannie-Mae, Countrywide, Bernie Madoff . . . and so on. The fallout was on a far huger scale than the earlier one. The impact across the US was astronomical. Within a very short space of time, the sleeve unraveled further as many of the largest European banks hit the dust. The impact on Europe in general has been devastating, and arguably, many of its economies are still struggling to recover fully. In response to this crash to beat all crashes, in 2010 the US enacted the Dodd-Frank Wall Street Reform and Consumer Protection Act. This Act was held to be the most comprehensive Act since the Glass-Steagall Act of 1933 (repealed in 1999 – see Chapter 1). This Act was going to ensure that consumers were never again going to be subject to predatory mortgage lending, that Wall Street would not take undue risks, that banks were not going to get too big to fail, and that the Federal Reserve (FED) would monitor hedge funds and other high-risk activities directly. Well, in 2018, the US Congress rolled back many of the Dodd-Frank reforms. At the time of writing (February 2019), President Donald Trump has repealing the Act in its entirety high on his Agenda.

Now fast forward a decade since 2008 and on the current ethical corruption sheet (2018), we see names such as Barclays Bank, Bank of America, Petrobas, JP Morgan, SAC Capital, Volkswagen, Walmart, Wells Fargo, Goldman Sachs, Uber, Deutsche Bank, Danske Bank, Facebook, Google, McKinsey and Carlos Ghosn and the Renault-Nissan affair . . . and of course, many more. And then there is the prevalence of sexual harassment across many organizations and institutions, and most regrettably, the US college enrollment scandals.

Ethical scandals continue unabated. How is this possible?

---

### Flashpoint 2.1

The drivers behind deceit and greed in the large corporations according to Frank Partnoy in his book, *Infectious Greed* (2003) include:

- Extortionate bonuses including stock options
- No downside for financial investors or traders
- No regulation of important sectors of the market
- Inefficacy of regulators
- Collusion of public accountants
- Extreme focus on short term results
- Reluctance on behalf of the Justice system to punish corporate executives

*What about corporate governance?*

Despite a lot of huffing and puffing about corporate governance, with many books, articles and conferences on the topic, corporate governance standards are generally low and lack rigor. Conflicts of interest among directors, and "you scratch my back – I scratch yours" deals proliferate.

Corporate governance refers to the checks and balances that keep business managers in line and within legal and ethical limits. Every organization is supposed to have some form of corporate governance structure which includes a minimum of two directors for private companies. Public companies are expected to have more than two and to include some outside or non-executive directors. The corporate governance system specifies the rights and responsibilities of key members in the organization and spells out the rules and procedures for making decisions on corporate affairs. All public companies are also supposed to have an audit, compensation, finance and executive committee of the board. These committees are charged with oversight and due diligence reviews of the respective functions within the organization.

Boards meet regularly, and in most public companies board members are paid handsomely (on average $200,000 p.a. in the US) for attending three to four meetings a year to which many travel in private jets and stay at premier hotels. To top it all, some board of directors are given stock options. Obviously, the fact that board directors are paid compromises their independence. It is always difficult to bite the hand that feeds one especially if the food is yummy!

The method of nominating directors to the board is also a matter for concern. Most board directors are invited into the position by the CEO to whom he or she then reports. This of course raises all kinds of conflicts and creates a mutual back-scratching atmosphere evident in so many boards.

How do the corporate shenanigans continue when there is supposedly this independent oversight? Well, sadly collusion, loss of arms length relationships, conflicts of interest, loss of transparency and of course all kinds of opportunities to dip one's finger in the honey jar has vitiated many attempts to tidy up the corporate governance arena. Bear in mind, corporate governance is a subsystem of the organization and will thus reflect the same ethical DNA as the corporation – and vice versa!

(I say more about corporate governance in Chapter 8.)

## Personal reflection: we did not know!

A few years ago, I was recruited to be the change consultant for two large organizations that had recently merged. I did not participate in any of the pre-merger discussions nor was I privy to any of the pre-merger due diligence or other documentation. My task was to help with integration of the newly merged entity. Let us call it Muddled Inc.

It did not take long for me to find out that contrary to this being a willing merger, in fact it was a de facto takeover and the smaller organization was angry, upset and in total disarray. Its systems were in a mess, people were confused and lacked clear roles and responsibilities, and there was no accountability anywhere.

I was told there had been a due diligence of sorts, yet no-one could say who was involved, when it was carried out and where the documentation was to be found. It was claimed that the auditors of both firms and the boards of both organizations had participated.

Two months into my assignment, I found the following:

- The bank statements had not been reconciled for over eight months including over a financial year end, yet somehow the auditors had signed off the accounts.
- Inventory to the tune of $160,000 had been stolen and the CFO was aware of this loss. The inventory manager reported to the CFO who had not reconciled the inventory with the books for over six months. The inventory manager was still in charge of all warehouses and partook in the inventory count to identify the loss. He was asked to rectify the records with the revised count.
- Staff were working at other organizations during the time they had clocked in at their present official employment.
- The CFO submitted the monthly accounts to the board and finance committee on a spreadsheet without producing a balance sheet. I reviewed several of these and found that the books did not balance.
- Major assets had not been depreciated for at least three years.
- Accounts receivable included a significant percentage of debts due over one year.
- There was evidence of sexual harassment in the smaller organization. These had been reported to human resources, yet no-one had taken any action.

At the end of the two months, at my request, I met with the newly combined board and reported my findings. The board that met monthly and the finance committee of the board were both present. As I reported on the above (and there was much more), they looked at me in consternation. I ended my presentation and the response from the board chair was a simple shrug – "We did not know!"

Question: How would you explain these severe ethical lapses?

### *Where are the auditors?*

As you can imagine, this question is personal for me in that my first career was as a public accountant. I used to be very proud of being a member of the then highly regarded profession. Now, I am simply astounded at the lack of vigilance by many company auditors, along with their lack of competence and interest in upholding the highest standards of rigor and oversight.

Every company requires an annual set of audited financial statements signed off by a Certified Public accountant (CPA). An audit sign-off indicates that a public accounting firm has carried out an audit in accordance with Generally Accepted Auditing Standards (GAAS) and that it has investigated all significant transactions that might affect the health of the company either positively or negatively, most especially negatively.

In terms of GAAS, all material amounts need to be investigated and authenticated. In the case of organizations with thousands of transactions, Auditors use various forms of sampling methods to test the integrity of the amounts and the account allocation.

In signing off the audited financial accounts, the auditor also insures that Generally Accepted Accounting Principles (GAAP) have been used to reflect the financial figures. The GAAP underscore four important concepts:

- The going concern concept which means that based on the figures presented in the financial accounts, the organization will survive as a going concern in the foreseeable future, i.e., at least one year. The idea is to give the users of audited accounts, such as the shareholder, banker and creditor some assurance that the organization is not on the brink of imminent collapse.
- The materiality concept which means that all material or significant items have been duly accounted for in the audited financial statements.
- The consistency concept which means that all like items have been accounted for similarly in the current accounts and compared with prior years.
- The concept of prudence which underpins all others. Prudence means that the auditor has been conservative in recognizing liabilities and in valuing assets. Prudence also means that all expenses have been duly accounted for and that there are no off-balance sheet items lurking somewhere . . . Recall our bankers in Chapter 1.

So where were the auditors when Carillion plc suddenly went bust? Where were the auditors when billions of dollars were embezzled over several years from the power plant, ESKOM in South Africa? Where were the auditors when Kraft Heinz suddenly revealed massive losses and write-offs? Where were the auditors when Well Fargo's employees were generating thousands of fictitious accounts? Where were the auditors when Deutsche Bank "suddenly" had to write off billions of dollars? And on and on . . . Where were the auditors?

---

**Flashpoint 2.2**

KPMG, the smallest of the large four accounting firms is under investigation for (at least) the following four cases:

- The sign-off of Carillion plc accounts when Carillion was going bust.
- Misconduct in relations with Ted Baker Clothing.
- Work related to the Gupta family and their massive corruption schemes in South Africa.
- The sign-off of the private equity audit of the firm Abraaj that has gone into liquidation.

# The shadow side of organizational life

How are we to understand this abysmal state of affairs? How does corruption continue unabated and, one might argue, even more blatantly than before? Is global capitalism to blame? What is happening within organizations? The people who run them and who work in them are ordinary people. They might be our next-door neighbors. What is it about institutional life that makes being ethical such a challenge? And where has all the hype about business ethics got us? And what about the ethics officers or internal ethics committees, who are supposed to monitor ethical behavior within organizations and serve as helplines to ethically challenged people? Where are they?

Self-regulation has not worked. Draconian regulation, such as SOX, has not worked. Many of the watchdogs have partnered with the thieves. Whatever legislation is left has little teeth. Whistleblowers who have had the courage to blow their whistles have invariably paid a far greater price than the perpetrators. It seems it pays to be "bad!" How are we to make sense of this all? And how are we going to help shape an ethical organization?

Armed with our systems thinking toolkit, let us now look at some of the inherent system dynamics within organizations.

## *The power of culture*

The culture of any system is its most powerful organizing force. Culture dictates many things. It determines whether an organization is adaptive, innovative, responsive, efficient or ethical.

The organization's culture has a profound impact on every individual that is not to be underestimated. Employees experience strong pressure to fit in, and failure to do so is usually met with all kinds of censure. Being made an "outsider" to the system is a dangerous place to be. Outsiders are frequently ostracized, side-lined and often scapegoated when organizational tensions run high.

## *Culture as the glue of the organization*

Culture is the embodied values, principles and practices underlying the social fabric of an organization. Culture underpins the organization's actions and reactions and connects stakeholders to each other and to the company's purpose and processes. Culture is the glue that holds an organization together and unites people around shared assumptions, beliefs, and practices.

Who shapes the culture of the organization? Everyone, yet none more so than the CEO and his or her senior leadership team. If the CEO is also the founder of the organization, his or her values play an even more significant role.

## Components of culture

### The physical aspect of culture

This includes the phenomena one sees, hears and feels. For example, the architecture of the buildings, the layout of the offices, the technology in use, the décor or aesthetic impact, the clothing and attire of employees, and observable behaviors such as eating at desks or walking around without shoes.

### Values

This includes attention to learning, people development, and expectations around participation and involvement. Here we also include customs and rituals, myths, legends and stories depicting the organization's heroes or villains. Then there are the espoused ethics and values along with performance standards and etiquette that are appended to mission statements, included on websites, and plastered on walls.

### Shared assumptions

These are the most important elements of culture and their impact cannot be overestimated. Shared assumptions include both the written and unwritten rules of the game, of which the latter typically predominate. Then there are group norms around engagement, acceptance, language and shared meanings. There are also rules as to what makes a person a group insider or outsider.

Levels of competency are usually spelled out in job descriptions; however, actual competency is often measured by unwritten yet commonly agreed upon criteria.

Employees tend to have mental models of the organization and how it does and should do its work. There are both clear, overt rules for rewards and punishment, and equally clear, yet covert rules. Everyone soon gets to know what really gets rewarded or punished and by whom. The same goes for power and status. What is shown on the organization chart frequently has little to do with where the real power lies.

Among shared assumptions are the culture's typical way of responding to changes in the environment. Then there are assumptions about what time means and how it can or cannot be used. People have ideas about what is reality and what is the official story line. They know who they believe and who they don't, and how public to be about their opinions.

There are also overt and covert assumptions about what is a promotable activity and what will get one fired. There are unwritten codes or assumptions about who can be recruited and who can be laid off. Some people will never be recruited and some never laid off, whatever the cause. Play and humor is also a key cultural determinant.

*Connectivity and no secrets*

Recall the reconnaissance example I shared with you in the Preface. If something is going on in the organization, everyone knows even if they do not verbalize it. Some people may know more than others, some people may be actual protagonists, while others may be the silent observers. Whatever their role, at some level, cognitively, emotionally or psychically, people have a good sense of what is going on in their system. As I described under systems theory, this inter-connectedness and inter-dependence is intrinsic to all systems.

I am sure you have heard it said: "There are no secrets." Well, within a system there are no secrets. Recall, systems are networks in continuous communication. And in the case of those people who claim ignorance, the likelihood is that their ignorance serves as a defense against their suspicions. In truth, at some level, they know. (See I don't want to know – in Chapter 3.)

With regard to communication itself, the cultural system dictates what can be shared with or divulged to whom and what cannot. The culture colludes in all matters, consciously and unconsciously, to ensure that all important factor – survival!

**Reflection**

What values, shared assumptions and secrets did you detect in the Palermo Inc. case?

*Communication*

A very important element of culture is that of communication. This includes what gets communicated and to whom. Things such as transparency, clarity and accuracy of information are important telltale factors of how the organization does or does not get effective work done.

Is communication carried out in silos or is there a healthy cross-functional communication? Do bosses communicate with their staff or do they just bark out orders? Does staff willingly communicate upwards?

And then there is the question of how things are communicated. Is everything by email or in meetings? Do people actually talk with one another? How do they talk – furtively or openly; sparsely or frequently; with vigor or with reluctance?

As you can imagine one can pose a million questions here. The important point is to note the color or tone of the culture's communication style and whether it is open, respectful and truthful. I have yet to come across an organization where the people claim they have superb communication at work.

Wearing our systems thinking and ethical hats, communication is all about information being carried along the organization's systems network. Both what is said or conveyed or not said or not conveyed is information, and the system conveys it all! There are no secrets. Everything is hidden in plain sight to those who are paying attention. (Remember the Preface.)

## Reflection

How would you describe the communication among the Palermo management team?

### *Accountability and consequences*

Ethics and accountability go hand in hand. An accountable culture, where people are given clear, distinct, SMART goals,[1] and then are regularly and consistently held to those goals, is more likely to be an ethical culture than one that does not promote accountability.

Accountability means that people are evaluated and rigorously held to their goals. If they fail to meet these goals, unless there are truly exceptional or extenuating circumstances, there are consequences. Accountability without consequences is no accountability. It is simply a charade.

Unfortunately, too many organizations do not have a culture of accountability. Work commitments and deadlines are allowed to slip, people are not asked to account for their goals regularly or consistently, goals are muddy or non-consistent and/or supervisors shy away from difficult conversations. Under these conditions, when consequences do eventually take place, it is often long after the fact as an excuse for some other unrelated reason, or because someone needs to be blamed for problems – see Those Evasive Bureaucrats in this chapter.

Lack of accountability is a seedbed for unethical behavior. Those who cannot help themselves will take advantage of the system and the slippery slope will soon show its hand. Lack of discipline, self-accountability, rigor and a desire for excellence provides the murky dark corners in which the cockroaches can do their business – see How to Exterminate Cockroaches in this chapter.

### *Reward systems*

Reward systems are a huge determinant of culture. As we know, there are both explicit reward systems and implicit ones. Both result in some form of material benefit.

An example of an implicit reward system is one where, for example, those people who stay late or show up on Saturday mornings are treated more favorably by their demanding bosses. Another example is the benefits that accrue to lackeys and sycophants in terms of being assigned special projects or given special bonuses.

Then there are the more explicit reward systems determined by pay scales. Research has shown that the cultures of organizations that have high remuneration packages are more aggressive and tend to be more unethical than others. It appears that the emphasis on material rewards fosters our self-serving and ignoble motivations.

It is also important to note that organizations that have very low wage scales, where people are almost at minimum wage or a little above it, also encourages unethical behavior. Here the unethical behavior is less overtly aggressive and more passive aggressive. For example, employees skirt safety standards, cheat on their time sheets, or deliver sub-standard work.

Reward systems are a strong form of communication. Every thoughtful leader or manager should pay due attention to both the implicit and explicit reward systems and what it is they convey to employees. This includes looking at the size of their own pay packages in relation to that of others. If the gap is huge – it speaks oceans! If leaders and managers don't care – that speaks oceans too!

### The madness of groups

Madness, said philosopher Frederick Nietzsche, is the exception in individuals, but the rule in groups. Psychoanalyst, Sigmund Freud agreed. He saw people participating in groups regress to an infantile state. According to his observations, the more a group has in common and the higher the degree of mental homogeneity, the stronger the evidence of the "group mind." When the group mind goes into action the individual gives up his or her own autonomy and sense of self and sacrifices these in service of the group or the group's leader.

The famous psychologist, Carl Jung, held some very strong views about group pressure. According to him –

> Every man is, in a certain sense, unconsciously a worse man when he is in society than when acting alone . . . Any large company of wholly admirable persons has the morality and intelligence of an unwieldy, stupid, and violent animal. The bigger the organization, the more unavoidable is its immorality and blind stupidity . . . Society, by automatically stressing all the collective qualities in its individual representatives, puts a premium on mediocrity, on everything that settles down to vegetate in an easy, irresponsible way. Individuality will inevitably be driven to the wall.[2]

Jung's strong views on the unethical behavior of groups is one among many. In general, human behavioral researchers hold the view that individuals are endowed by nature with qualities of sympathy and consideration (remember Adam Smith). These sentiments provide them with a capacity for justice, caring and even altruism. Depending on the circumstance, they can at times even be objective about matters that involve their own interests. However, the collective egoism of the group rapidly destroys these more noble sentiments. In the face of group pressure, individuals succumb to the group's overriding interests. These interests are most often more about establishing the group's power or who has power within the group, than how to make ethical or wise decisions.

Many philosophers, sociologists and psychologists have written about the impact of group pressure on individual behavior. Almost without exception, they conclude that individuals tend to lose their sense of autonomy and personal authority when they are part of group activities or participate in group decision-making. As we discuss in Chapter 3 on moral development, individuals have great concern about belonging and being accepted by the group. Breaking away from the group is for most people a terrifying prospect. Groups and teams offer a shared sense of self that gives people a sense of definition and a reality in the world. Challenging the group or breaking away from group or team membership requires a strong personal ego and well-developed sense of self. It can also be a dangerous move as the group tends to turn on and scapegoat detractors.

Groups do not only share common understandings and outlooks they also share secrets and defense mechanisms. Working together they learn to see things the same way. They also learn together how **not** to see what they do not want to see. They have self-deceptions in common. The power of the collective pact impacts thoughts, oughts, and moral behaviors. If the group does not want to see unethical behavior, it will not. It also has the potential to "kill" anyone who breaks this unconscious agreement. Collaboration at all levels is the name of the game and the passport to safety.

Increasing the size of the group increases the difficulties of achieving a group self-consciousness. The larger the group the less inclined to ethical behavior, and the more people are held sway to the coercive pressures within the group. Depending on the circumstances, individuals in the group either silence themselves totally or uphold the group ego. In the worst cases, they will forsake themselves totally and become part of an unruly mob!

The idea that groups diminish the moral agency of individuals is an alarming one. I imagine that many of us have witnessed how group dynamics alters the self-differentiating power of the individual. The pressure to conform to group pressure in business organizations is enormous. Frequently I hear phrases such as: "I try not to rock the boat," "you have to play by the rules," "you cannot fight the system." One need only attend a group meeting to see many of these dynamics at work.

When we note that many organizational activities are carried out by committees or teams, we need to be cognizant of the group effect. The smaller the team the less likely the group dynamic will impact the ethical and self-defining capacities of the individual. The larger the team or the group, the more likely individual autonomy and agency will be squelched. Similarly, the more bonded and united the group the greater the common mind, and the less likely anyone will step out of the explicit and implicit rules for keeping the group intact.

One important strategy when assigning teams is to keep on changing the membership. This limits the development of too much bonding and too much of a group mind. Understandably, managers are often reluctant to do this as the team seems to be working so well together and they often resist the idea of embracing new members. Depending on the purpose of the team or group, the price of letting a group mind develop may be too high not to intervene.

So is there any counter to this rather pessimistic view of groups? Well, one psychology researcher, James Sorowiecki, in his book, *The Wisdom of Crowds*, argues that overall, crowds are more intelligent, more attuned and more savvy than individuals. In his book he cites innumerable examples that seem to indicate that groups of people outthink individuals every single time. There are two important caveats that he includes when drawing his conclusions. The first is that the crowd includes diversity. This means that the people offering their ideas, opinions and recommendations come from diverse backgrounds. The second is that the individuals who make up the crowd are independent of mind. This means that these individuals arrive at their conclusions, suggestions and so on relatively free from the fear of group pressure or a loss of moral freedom. He claims that the best collective decisions are the product of disagreement and contest, not consensus and compromise.

Sorowiecki explains crowd or group mind behavior as arising out of individuals being uncertain about what to do. They may be uncertain because they do not have the facts, the dilemma or challenge in question is outside of their experience, or they are overwhelmed by conflicting tensions. Whatever the reason, the individual feels that the crowd must know something they do not know, or know best, so they defer to crowd opinion. This important point we take up again in Chapter 3 under Impact of the Situation.

These are interesting and plausible explanations for many individuals' behavior. Bear in mind that what Sorowiecki points out very clearly is that to get the benefit from the wisdom of crowds or groups, an essential feature is that each individual in the group is capable of arriving at independent conclusions. This means there is no (or minimal) group pressure, no fear of being an outlier, and no group think or group bias. In an organizational setting, where culture very quickly gets a hold of the group mind, finding opportunities for the individual to think and act from this place of independence is extremely difficult.

## Reflection

In the Palermo Inc. case what evidence did you detect of:

- The group mind at work,
- The power dynamics in the group,
- Individuals' need to belong to the group and not violate norms,
- Unconscious agreements, and
- Independent thinking?

### *Managing fear*

As we consider the barriers to ethical behavior within organizations, an important factor we must tackle head on is the issue of fear. If we study the details of some of the corporate scandal stories, we find evidence of the group's need to conform and the cultural pressure that silences many employees. What we can readily infer is that a culture of fear prevails. And where fear exists, moral decision-making is always compromised in one way or another.

The matter of fear is not talked about much because the topic is a sensitive one and of course brings up our own feelings of fear. Yet, to be effective in organizations, one needs to appreciate the significant role of fear in organizational life. (See Some Research Results in Chapter 10.)

*Containers of fear*

All organizations are containers of fear. This is a natural phenomenon and not specific to any one type of organization, although some organizations, due to their culture and internal dynamics, have higher fear levels than others. Here are some components of the fear element ever present in organizational life:

- People bring with them their existential fear about living and dying.
- They fear being overwhelmed by the group.
- They fear whether they are actually good enough to be part of the group.
- They fear whether they will meet organizational goals and performance standards.
- They fear whether other people in the organization will like them even when they insist they do not care.
- They fear whether the job they have is really going to take them where they want to be.
- They fear the power of their superiors who can radically influence their future. (Fear of authority is discussed in Chapter 4.)
- They fear being laid off when it does not suit them.
- They fear being their full selves at work lest this challenges cultural norms.

The list goes on . . . Now most people do not experience all these fears at once, nor are their fears excessive. In general, peoples' fears are contained below the surface in a chronic sort of way and only rise above the surface when certain events cause them to escalate. These events can take many forms. One big event is when the organization is not doing well financially or when competition is intense.

When people experience heightened fear they tend to panic and often shut down. They lose touch with their intuitions and forget who they are. They lose confidence. They often feel victimized, left out, side-lined or abandoned. Sometimes they feel short-changed, worthless and unloved. Their sense of inadequacy is triggered which fuels even more fear. These feelings are scary and highly unwelcome. So how do people try to escape or deny these feelings? Here are some of their strategies:

- They disassociate to keep out the panic.
- They become literal because their heart and intuitions have shut down.
- They act out of character because they have lost their center.
- They get unduly angry because they feel only their weaknesses and experience being faced with everyone else's strengths.
- They become blamers.
- They get aggressive to shore up their self-confidence.
- They become passive-aggressive to get back at feeling victimized.
- They interfere and invade other people's territory so as to not feel left out.
- They strut their stuff to try to feel competent.

- They become arrogant and irritable to show they don't need anyone else, and anyway no-one is good enough for them.
- They grab all they can get to reassure themselves that they have things and they can get more if they need to.
- They become greedy to counteract their feelings of lack of self-worth.
- They show contempt for others to conceal their own feelings of unworthiness.
- They hide behind the group.
- They become overly entitled.

From this "little" list, one can see that people deploy all kinds of strategies to deal with their fears. Because of these many defensive behaviors, it is often difficult to tell that someone is acting from a place of fear.

So what is the lesson for us here? Group and organizational life raises the ante when it comes to fear. It is hard to be ethical when one is experiencing fear, and even more so when one is in denial that one is in fear. Fear prompts the survival instinct which is about self-preservation at all costs. From a business ethics point of view then, one major challenge is how to create a climate and culture that reduces levels of fear in a system and how to keep tabs on the fear thermometer.

### Reflection

- What evidence of fear did you detect in the Palermo Inc. case?
- What defenses against fear did you notice among the management team members?
- Would you say that Palermo Inc. has a fearful culture?

### The Wells Fargo saga

During and after the financial crisis of 2008, Wells Fargo seemed to be beating the odds. It had become the third-largest US bank, and a few years later its growing revenue and soaring stock price brought the company's value to nearly $300 billion. But behind this success was a company culture that drove employees to open fraudulent accounts in attempt to reach lofty sales goals. Between 2011 and 2015, company employees opened more than 1.5 million bank accounts and applied for over 565,000 credit cards in customers' names that, in many cases, were not authorized.

As early as 2010, Wells Fargo imposed extremely aggressive sales goals on its employees. They were instructed to sell at least eight accounts to every customer, compared with an average of three accounts ten years earlier. Supervisors threatened salespeople who failed to meet targets. One former employee reported, "I had managers in my face yelling at me. The sales pressure from management was unbearable."

Another former employee related, "We were constantly told we would end up working for McDonald's . . . If we did not make the sales quotas . . . we had to stay for what felt like after-school detention or report to a call session on Saturdays." A lawsuit against Wells Fargo alleges that "employees who failed to resort to illegal tactics were either demoted or fired as a result."

As early as 2011, the Wells Fargo board was informed about reports of ethics violations. The cheating continued, leading Wells Fargo to fire at least 1,000 people per year in 2011, 2012 and 2013. Let's face it, any company that fires 1,000 people for the same type of cheating, should know that situational factors are contributing to the cheating.

Many former employees reported that company sales goals were impossible to meet, and incentives for compensation and ongoing employment encouraged gaming the system. Wells Fargo pressured employees to cross-sell, offering customers with one type of product, such as checking or savings accounts, to also buy other types of products, such as credit cards and loans. One former employee described it as a "grind-house," with co-workers "cracking under pressure." Another former employee reported, "If you don't meet your solutions, you're not a team player. If you bring down the team, you will be fired, and it will be on your permanent record."

Apparently, in mid-2014, Wells Fargo attempted to curb fraudulent activity with an ethics workshop that warned employees not to create fake accounts in customers' names. Wells Fargo also modified its compensation structure to place less emphasis on sales goals. But clearly these efforts were not enough as in 2015 fake accounts were still being created.

One former employee described his brief time at Wells Fargo as "the lowest point of my life." He encouraged an elderly woman to sign up for a credit card she did not want by telling her "it was confirmation that she stopped by to update her address." This made him sick to his stomach. He reported, "But it was a tough economy, and I was worried; if I lost this job, I would be in a tough financial situation." Deceptive practices such as this were widespread across the company, and many former employees reported that their managers knew about them.

Jonathan Delshad, a lawyer working on behalf of former employees, said, "The better they did at sales, the more they advanced, so it got spread across the company. An entire generation of managers thrived in the culture, got rewarded for it, and are now in positions of power." One former employee said she could not meet sales goals in any ethical way and called the Wells Fargo's ethics hotline. She was fired.

In 2016, Wells Fargo was fined US $185 million for fraudulent activity, and CEO John Stumpf resigned. Between 2011 and 2016, approximately 5,300 employees were fired for fraudulent sales practices. Sales quotas were eliminated effective January 1, 2017 (https://ethicsunwrapped.utexas.edu/video/wells-fargo-fraud).

### Questions for reflection

- What was happening in the Wells Fargo system?
- How would you describe the influence of culture at Wells Fargo?

- What role did fear play?
- How would you explain the apparent inept corporate governance system?
- Where were the auditors?
- Do you think that an ethics workshop was an appropriate response to the vast amount of cheating? What alternative would you propose?
- To what extent do you think the CEO, John Stumpf, should be held accountable? (P.S. He had to repay $41million in stock options that had not yet vested, i.e., he repaid nothing. You could say he forfeited potential income. He blamed Carrie Tolstedt, the head of sales, for the cheating saga.)
- What would you have done if you were earning $12 per hour (as many people at Wells Fargo were), and you were battling to make ends meet?

### Those Evasive Bureaucrats

Sociologist Max Weber wrote a great deal on bureaucracy and its impact on people's behavior. Several years ago, business researcher Robert Jackall built on Weber's work and wrote a book entitled: *Moral Mazes* (2009), wherein he discusses the results of his research into people's behaviors within bureaucracies. Jackall was particularly interested in the way in which bureaucracy, defined as the impersonal routinization of work, shapes moral consciousness. In his book, he argues quite clearly that the bureaucratic system diminishes people's authenticity and moral agency. He emphasizes the negative effects of the power dynamics within large organizations in particular and how issues of fealty and loyalty serve to eclipse people's feelings of responsibility or respect for honesty.

Jackall describes managers' rules for success as being at the heart of the bureaucratic ethic. Success in a bureaucracy is socially defined and socially distributed. Failure is also socially defined. A person's usefulness to the organization depends on the person's versatility. Appearances mean everything in this world. The arduous details of work are pushed down, and the credit pushed up. The "higher-up" people expect successful results without complications from their underlings.

Jackall likens bureaucracy to a series of moral mazes. According to his research findings, bureaucracies erode both internal and external standards of morality. Bureaucracies are built on pyramidal politics and subordinates owe fealty to their boss. Bureaucratization provides a structure founded on patron power that systematically diffuses responsibility. Middle managers only transmit good news to protect their bosses and themselves. The real key to managerial success becomes the outrunning of mistakes. What matters is not a willingness to stand by actions but an agility in avoiding blame; not what a person believes or says, but how well he or she has mastered the ideologies that serve the corporation; not what he or she stands for, but whom he or she stands with in the labyrinths of the organization.

If we think for a moment about some of the corporate scandals we are reminded of the bureaucracies of Enron, WorldCom, Tyco, Arthur Andersen, the New York Stock Exchange, Barclays Bank, Goldman Sachs, Wells Fargo,

Volkswagen, and so on. Bureaucracy and its impact on moral behavior is readily apparent in many of the organizations now facing the horrendous consequences of managers having run amuck with the hierarchical power accorded them.

Bureaucracies, by definition, result in the division of labor that leads to fragmentation of authority and accountability. It encourages people to define their responsibilities narrowly and limits available information. Fragmentation also buffers people from the consequences of their actions. At worst, people feel little sense of personal responsibility or view themselves as cogs in a machine over which they have no control. In situations where people feel out of control, they feel more vulnerable to those in authority who appear to have the control they feel they lack. In those corporations where management does not foster a corporate ethical climate, and where they emphasize fragmentation and authoritarian control, employees will not raise ethically challenging issues. They would be crazy to try!

Another aspect of bureaucracy is that institutions originally created as means to ends have now become ends in themselves. The idea of formally structuring the roles, responsibilities, and activities of groups of people began when people realized their individual and combined interests could be better served through a group organization. Institutionalization of society has now become a moral and motivational problem. An attitude of subservience to the institution has evolved where individuals feel robbed of personal agency, self-determination, and true accountability. As institutions have grown, distinctions between owners-managers-workers have exacerbated the situation. Individuals feel depersonalized and unable to bring their full selves to work. A sense of alienation and the sense of loss in self-determination result in diminished personal moral responsibility.

People, by and large, need to work for psychological and economic reasons. Having work gives them identity and dignity and a place to go to. It is what society expects one to do, and it is what one's friends typically do. Unless one owns large amounts of capital whereby one "owns" the labor of others, the "organization" can snatch away one's social and work identity at any time. The hundreds of thousands of people who lost their jobs during the 2008–2009 downturn, bear testimony to the work-identity vulnerabilities of business employees.

A last comment on bureaucracy refers to the issue of means and ends. In Chapter 6, we discuss Immanuel Kant's moral philosophy that holds that the dignity of human beings gives them a worth that is absolute and invaluable and, as such, incomparable with political or economic values. According to him, moral behavior implies that humans should be treated as ends and not merely as means to ends. In his moral system, all human action should be directed towards the end of furthering the welfare of all humans. This Kant saw as the roots of rational behavior, and rational behavior in many ethical systems, always means moral behavior.

The constant assertion by many senior executives that achieving the prime goal of the organization means making as much profit as possible (or maximizing wealth) for shareholders creates one of the primary tensions in business corporations. The end, profit at all costs, results in treating people merely as a means to that end. If people within the company are made to feel as pure means to ends, a sense of personal moral agency will be missing and will undoubtedly have a negative effect on the ethical climate of the corporation.

The new business ethic of People, Planet, Profits is supposed to eliminate the "profit as the only end" mentality. In practice, when organizations are doing well, i.e., they are growing, profits are good, prospects look promising, the focus on people and the planet usually improves. Once profits or the share price comes under pressure, however, people and the planet are once again relegated to the end of the line. Maybe your organization is exceptional. Bravo if that holds true!

## Reflection

In the Palermo Inc. case what did you notice regarding –

- Fealty and loyalty,
- The importance of appearances,
- Agility by management members to avoid blame,
- Fragmentation of knowledge and responsibility,
- Evidence of personal accountability, and
- People being treated as a means to an end?

## In the Wells Fargo case

- What role do you think bureaucracy played enabling the unethical behavior to continue for so long?
- How did fragmentation of authority add to the problems?
- Did the need to survive trump being ethical?

### *Let's be honest*

Whenever I ask people to name or list their most important ethical principles, invariably one of the first principles volunteered is honesty. There are other times when I challenge a group or seminar participants as to whether anyone does not think that honesty is a critical ethical principle. Never in my experience has anyone pushed back and said "no – honesty is not a valuable ethical principle."

This discussion frequently then leads me to ask the group whether we could have an ethical pact in the room. This pact would mean that for the remainder of our time together, we would agree to be openly and frankly honest with one another. No matter what, we would be transparent and honest. (At the commencement of any class or seminar we establish ground rules in which confidentiality is a big one. Namely, what is discussed "in the room, stays in the room." Everyone agrees they will not reveal stories, anecdotes, complaints or whatever to anyone once the class or seminar is over.)

Back to the honesty issue: When I extend this invitation to the group, I then ask people to raise their hands in agreement with this pact. Rarely do more than one or two people raise their hands. Usually, mine is the only hand raised.

So what happened to our commitment to honesty? Of course, as people look around the room they smile and laugh and nod their heads knowingly. The issue about honesty is, "I want YOU to be honest so that I know where I stand. I will decide whether it is safe enough or worth my while to reveal my own honest thoughts, feelings, ideas and actions. Honesty is really about you and not me!"

How does an organization deal with this reality? Well, first managers must appreciate that people will only be honest up to a point. That point depends on the culture and whether there is some trust and belief that supervisors are fair and trust-worthy. Even if there is a high degree of trust, honesty will still only be "relative." In other words, people's honest responses will in most cases "depend" on something.

Regrettably many managers do not know or even reflect on this reality and assume that because there are rules, codes, and maybe consequences for certain actions, that people will feel obliged or better still, be eager to be honest. True honesty is precious. It is like a beautiful, fragile flower that needs to be coaxed, nourished, fed and reassured so that it can come into full bloom. The only way to begin and perpetuate this process is for senior management to lead by being totally honest and openly vulnerable in everything they do. That is no easy mat-ter, and in my experience rarely accomplished. How might one achieve this?

### Reflection

In the Palermo Inc. case, what evidence did you see of honesty? Of dishonesty?

## Professional roles versus personal morality

Harvard professor Arthur Isak Applbaum approaches the challenges of being ethical from a different perspective. He explores the ethics associated with professional roles. In his book, *Ethics for Adversaries* (1999), he asks if profes-sional roles can provide moral permission to harm in ways that, if not for the role, would be considered wrong. The adversary legal system presents a vivid example. Lawyers are permitted, within the rules, to make the case for what they know to be false and to advance causes they know to be unjust. Many other practices invoke similar adversary arguments for their justification. Applbaum discusses the problem of hired hands as an instance of a general moral problem. How can acts that ordinarily are morally forbidden – violence, injustice, decep-tion, coercion – be rendered morally permissible when performed by one who occupies a professional or public role?

### *Professional roles and moral standards*

In order to make his point Applbaum sets the debate between private and profes-sional morality by describing the activities of Charles-Henri Sanson, appointed an executioner by Louis XVI, during the *ancien regime*.

Throughout Sanson's career he ministered with professional detachment to his morbid duties. His claims regarding the recognition of his profession as having legitimate standards resemble the claims made by politicians, lawyers, journalists and business executives to justify their commitments to their professional roles when those roles ask them to act in ways ordinarily considered morally wrong.

The Sanson discussion with a man called Mercier centers on whether personal or professional values should prevail. In the debate between the two what arises is that roles sometimes may direct one to ignore moral reasons for actions that others, outside the role, may not ignore. A defense attorney, for example, has a role-relative reason to argue for the acquittal of a factually guilty client. In addition, the defense attorney, in his or her moral deliberations, does not consider the social consequences of setting a dangerous criminal free. The many cases of OJ Simpson in the US come to mind.

Now one might argue that a business executive has a role-relative reason to maximize the profits of his or her company, and that he or she need not count the miseries of unemployment as a reason not to close an unprofitable factory. Maximizing shareholder value may constitute the criterion for being a good manager, but being a good manager does not mean one is a good person.

While it is quite a leap to compare the business professional with the professional executioner (although given the sad consequences for thousands of people impacted by many of the corporate scandals, maybe not!), the professional role-personal morality discussion confronts us with several critical questions. For example: Do roles have independent moral force or independent moral grounding? Can an action that is otherwise morally impermissible become permissible when performed within a role? Think of the issue of confidentiality. Under what conditions can or should one break it? Or the withholding of medical information? (See Chapter 9 for a further discussion on this issue.)

### Detachment and impartiality

Another matter is that of professional detachment and impartiality. As a professional, it is held that emotions should be suppressed, decisions should be based on rational analysis devoid of personal bias, and performance should be diligent and fastidious. Do these actions reflect moral integrity? What do you think?

The issues of emotions in ethical theory has always been troublesome. Throughout Western philosophical and religious thinking, only reason's mastery has been considered trustworthy moral guidance. A more modern view that challenges the hegemony of reason or rationality in the ethical domain is that just as reason guides and monitors emotion, so, too, can our emotions guide reason. Our emotions can prevent us from giving assent to coldly rational actions. Lack of anxiety, guilt, empathy or love can devastate moral functioning leading us to disregard moral rules or arguments without a qualm.

Further, it can be argued that emotions energize the ethical quest. A person must be emotionally interested enough and care enough about discerning the truth to persevere with attachment rather than detachment. Emotional intelligence, something all well-functioning professionals are supposed to have, means the appropriate deployment of emotions, not denying or suppressing them. (See Chapter 4 for further discussion here.)

If we return to the question of whether personal bias or judgment should prevail when one holds a professional role, then the legal, economic, or medical system would be subject to the vagaries of personal bias and persuasion. In the business context, once a person lets his or her personal views influence his or her professional duties, the business organization would become subject to the capriciousness and whims of each business manager. Confusion would reign and a severe dose of moral relativism would set in. (See Chapter 9 for an expansion on this dilemma.)

### The pitfall of diligence

As for a professional being diligent and fastidious, this presents less of a moral dilemma and more of a moral alert. Implicit in this professional expectation is that diligence refers to careful and obedient execution of the rules of the organization or attention to the expectations of its cultural code. Diligence does usually not encourage inquiry or conflict. Diligent people typically are not those who question or challenge moral consciousness. Diligent people conform.

### Reflection

In response to the questions posed above, where do you stand? What is the moral duty of a professional? When should personal ethics prevail – if ever?

---

### Your turn – professional role versus personal ethics

You are VP of Human Resources of Honesty Trust, plc. The economy has been tough, competition is intense, and sales have dropped radically. The senior management team has decided to lay off several members of staff and to close a division. This is a big blow to the organization, as they have touted being a trustworthy culture that does not layoff staff. All layoff discussions are top secret as the PR machine is working on how to relay the news to the stock analysts.

You know that Julie Bridge is one of the people who will be laid off. She has been with the company for many years, is a single mother with three children, and is in the process of buying a small house. Excitedly she had discussed this with you as she was contemplating her year-end bonus. You are torn. In your role as VP of Human Resources and a senior member of management, you are bound by confidentiality. Yet, Julie, who is a diligent, loyal worker is highly exposed. What are you going to do? Tell her to hold tight before committing to the new house? Or are you going to keep things confidential as you are duty bound to do? What principles or rationale will you use to support your decision?

And if you tell her, are you not duty bound to tell everyone else? – see Justice in Chapter 7.

## Ethics and decision-making

As human beings we are perpetual decision-makers. That is what we do from morning to night – make decisions. Some decisions are big and significant, and some are tiny and almost irrelevant. Yet, all day, as long as we are conscious, we are making decisions: decisions about what to do, where to go, who to see, how to respond, what to wear, what to think, which feelings to allow into our consciousness, and what to suppress. Decisions . . . decisions.

In business organizations we are expected to make decisions and to make good ones. Good decisions are measured mostly by their outcomes. A good decision advances the mission of the firm, allocates resources optimally, results in an acceptable ROI (return on investment), motivates people, and is thoughtful and even creative. As managers, we are judged by the quality of our decisions. People who demonstrate good decision-making get rewarded (in most cases), and those who do not are ignored, reprimanded or asked to leave.

Almost all decisions have some ethical component to them. Whether it is who to place in a team (respect, empathy, care); who to promote or demote (justice); how to deal with customers (respect, transparency); how to handle suppliers (respect, honesty); what to pay people (justice, transparency); which new products to launch (competence, safety, social responsibility). There is barely a decision that does not involve some ethical consideration. Thoughtful managers make this consideration explicit. That means ethical deliberation is part and parcel of all decision-making criteria. Thoughtless managers do not make this an explicit and so people just muddle through.

Since ethical considerations are inherent in all decisions, why do we not normally treat them as such? Why is ethics this "separate concern" that only comes to people's attention when someone is found with their hands in the cookie jar or a customer lodges a complaint? Why is the focus of ethics reactive, largely focused on repairing harm, rather than proactive where it informs decision-making up front? Anyone who engages in a serious ethical misdemeanor places the organization at risk. This means that it is a bad decision! Bad decisions invariably result in negative consequences, if not immediately, then later. Good decisions, on the other hand, are invariably grounded in sound ethical thinking where the consequences for the organization are positive, not only in the short term, but in the longer term too.

If ethics is not seen as an intrinsic part of decision-making and doing business, its inclusion will not be part of the corporate culture; its absence will. Ethics will simply be considered a watchdog activity aimed at catching people who break the rules.

## Reflection

In the case of Palermo Inc., did you notice any explicit recognition of ethical considerations? Does ethics seem to be part of Palermo's decision-making culture?

## How to exterminate cockroaches?

The continuous unfolding of new stories of immoral behavior of business executives and employees provides a clarion call to all of us. As we are assailed with the never-ending stories of dishonesty and deceit, we must ask ourselves how and why seemingly ordinary people get caught up in fraudulent and dishonorable behavior. How did the man or woman next door, whom we have known for years and with whom we sometimes share gossip over the fence, get themselves into these situations? How can we insure that we do not get into similar situations?

Saul Gellerman (1989), in his article, "Why 'Good' Managers Make Bad Ethical Choices," suggests four rationalizations that people have always relied on to justify questionable moral conduct. These are: "believing that the activity is not 'really' illegal or immoral; that it is in the individual or the corporation's best interest; that, the unethical activity will never be found out; or that, because it helps the company the company will condone it."

Gellerman then proposes some practical rules that can "control" managers from getting into trouble. His practical rules in essence suggest checking that managers are not rewarded for immoral behavior and increasing the level of spot checks, audits and other inspections. At the end of his suggestions, however, he adds "For the hard truth is that corporate misconduct, like the lowly cockroach, is a plague that we can suppress but never exterminate" (Ibid., p. 18).

Well none of us want to be one of those cockroaches. Neither do we want to be associated with nor do we want to work in a company of cockroaches! But what can we do to ensure that we do not become one of the cockroaches? Practice ethics!

### Reflection

In the case of Palermo Inc., do you see evidence of cockroaches?

### A culture of fear?

As we reflect on our globally stressed world, global capitalism, the competitive zeal that plagues almost all companies, the demanding terms of global finance, and the tumultuous internal dynamics of organizations – especially large ones – how would we describe the over-arching culture or environment? It seems we are living largely in a culture of fear?

We fear terrorists; we fear the growth in violence in our schools; we fear Alzheimer's; we fear impotency; we fear we can never keep up with the changing world. It is a tragedy, but many not only fear death, they fear life.

People in business fear bankruptcy, fear a takeover, fear losing their jobs, fear the next stock market crash and fear the costs of getting old. Young people are now so fearful and in such despair that they are turning to opioids and suicide as a way out.

It seems we live largely within a ubiquitous web of fear. And wherever fear predominates, distorted power dynamics follow. Fear and abusive power go hand in hand. Power represents control. When people are in fear, people fight desperately for control. People in fear turn to fear-based solutions in a vain attempt to rid themselves of their fear.

For example:

> Afraid of crime? Hire more police and build more prisons.
> Afraid of AIDS? Don't have sex.
> Afraid of immigrants? Keep them out especially by building large walls!
> Afraid of foreigners? Bomb them.
> Afraid of terrorism? Restrict civil liberties.
> Afraid of incompetence? Blame others for stealing yours.
> Afraid of freedom? Insist on the value of your narcissism.

The developed countries – so-called – face a profound socio-psychological question. How might we diminish the power of the culture of fear? America, especially, needs to ask itself this question. How can a country born out of the adventurous and entrepreneurial spirit of hosts of immigrants arriving on her shores, have developed such an extreme brand of xenophobia? As a nation its response to almost all challenges is to declare "war." The war of terrorism, the war on AIDS, the war on drugs, the war on obesity, the war on crime and immigrants, the war on impotence, the war on . . . The American language is that of war and hence the psychology of warfare predominates – think systems.

What we are concerned with in this book is how the "fear factor" influences business ethics. Because the whole of America is at war, it is not surprising that this is also true of corporations. In fact, the US based multi-national conglomerates that dominate world trade are the ultimate twenty-first century war machines. These war machines are fighting the "new crusades" by striving to penetrate every nation and every culture where they can dominate or crush local industry. The power now granted – or taken – by multi-national organizations, dictates the rules of the new global war and adds to the pervasive culture of fear in those economies and industries who are destined for a radical death.

How does one inspire ethics in people when many breathe in this toxic, fear-based atmosphere?

## Our moral calling

So is it all an enormous set up? Are we victims caught up in impossible circumstances and in an impossible world or system? Is global capitalism the main culprit forcing us to be ultra-competitive where survival lies in growing big, powerful and wealthy? Or is it the way organizations are set-up? Are we simply pawns in this huge complex network of systems and inter-relations?

It seems we are at a crossroads. Do we succumb or do we claim our own autonomy and moral agency? Can we develop our ethical mindsets and find the moral courage to look beyond our fears and the pressures of our cultures and communities? Can we define our own ethical principles that we have arrived at through honest deliberation, open conversation and mature discernment? Surely, we have a duty to leave a sustainable world as our legacy after we are mere compost for future worlds.

In the next chapters we discuss how we can take a moral stand amidst a sea of troubles, and how we can let our ethical character shine through. Even though at times we may yield to moral infractions, at other times we find the strength and moral courage to take the high road. Even though others may set an unethical agenda – overtly or covertly – we can resist and can prevail if we so choose. I am not suggesting that it is easy, on the contrary, standing up to overwhelming pressures where one's life or livelihood might be at stake is very difficult, but it can be done. Our willingness to keep trying, and even to fail and try again, is what defines us. It is this moral resilience that provides the light and life of our world.

**Executive summary**

This chapter explored the many dynamics that exist within organizations that have a significant impact on people's ethical behavior. The following key points were covered:

- Systems theory is briefly explained where I pointed out that all organizations are part of systems and themselves comprise many sub-systems.
- Systems both export and import their behavioral dynamics to systems in their network. The implication here is that systemic pressures are immense and often ignored, mis-interpreted or underrated.
- Corruption continues unabated despite the financial fallout of 2008–2009. Legislation, corporate governance, and the audit function is clearly not providing the ethical oversight or correction with which it has been charged.
- The power of culture in the organizational system cannot be over-estimated. Cultural pressure is often a determinant of individual behavior.
- A culture that does not uphold individual accountability provides a seedbed for unethical behavior.
- Group dynamics rarely improve the ethical behavior of people, and in fact most often result in group egoism and a fight for power rather than the pursuit of integrity.
- The undercurrent membership requirement of the group is to honor both the written and unwritten pact as to what can be said or done or not said and not done. The group depends on and survives due to this collusion. People who do not conform are ostracized.
- All institutions are containers of fear and depending on the leadership and culture, this can be either excessive or modest to minimal.
- Bureaucracies tend to heighten the tendency for unethical behavior due to the demeaning environment, the fragmentation of authority, and the blame game that predominates. Accountability is muddied and avoided wherever possible.

- Honesty is highly conditional and is usually about you and not me!
- A tension exists between professional roles and personal morality and how to view what is morally acceptable within a role that would not otherwise be morally acceptable. The question is: Can one be immoral under the cover of a role?
- All decisions in some way or another include an ethical dimension. We tend not to realize this and respond to ethical issues reactively rather than proactively.
- One might say that currently many of the developed countries, especially the US is living in a climate of fear. This atmosphere is not conducive to ethical thinking or moral behavior.
- Despite the systemic challenges we face, we are called to live a life of self-examination and personal moral agency. This theme will be developed in the next chapters.

## Questions for reflection

- If you were appointed the ethics consultant to Palermo Inc., where would you begin addressing change?
- From an ethical perspective, what do you think is the most constraining part of a culture or group dynamics?
- On the fear spectrum, how would you rate your organization and its culture as observed by the behavior of employees?
- Does your organization have a culture of accountability?
- What do you think was going on at Muddled Inc.?
- What stood out most for you in this chapter?

## Key terms

Adaptive   62
Bureaucracy   79
Corporate governance   66
Culture   55
Fear   59
Generally Accepted Auditing
   Standards – GAAS   67
Generally Accepted Accounting
   Principles – GAAP   68

Hierarchy   61
Holons   61
Macrocosm-microcosm   62
Organisms   60
Organizing relations   60
Patterns   60
Systems thinking   60

## Notes

1 SMART goals stand for Specific; Measurable; Achievable; Relevant; Timely.
2 Carl J. Jung. *The Archetypes and the Collective Unconscious.* New York: Princeton University Press, 1959, p. 240.

## References

Applbaum, Arthur Isak. *Ethics for Adversaries*. Princeton, NJ: Princeton University Press, 1999.

Beerel, Annabel. *Leadership and Change Management*. London, UK: Sage Publications, 2009.

Capra, Fritjof and Pier Luigi Luisi. *The Systems View of Life: A Unifying Vision*. New York: Cambridge University Press, 2014.

Gellerman, Saul W. Why "Good" Managers Make Bad Ethical Choices. *Harvard Business Review: Ethics in Practice: Managing the Moral Corporation*. Edited by Kenneth Andrews. Boston: Harvard Business School Press, 1989, pp. 18–35.

Jackall, Robert. *Moral Mazes*. New York: Harvard University Press, 2009.

Koestler, Arthur. *The Ghost in the Machine*. New York: Hutchinson, 1967.

Partnoy, Frank. *Infectious Greed*. New York: Times Books, 2003.

Sarbanes-Oxley Act passed by US Congress in 2002.

Senge, Peter. *The Fifth Discipline*. New York: Image Books, 1990.

Soroweicki, James. *The Wisdom of Crowds*. New York: Anchor Books, 2005.

Waddock, Sandra. *Leading Corporate Citizens: Vision, Values and Value Added*. New York: McGraw-Hill/Irwin, 2006.

# 3   Am I an ethical person?

## Contents

> I do not understand my own actions. For I do not do what I want, but I do the very thing
> I hate . . . I can will what is right, but I cannot do it. For I do not do the good I want, but
> the evil I do not want is what I do.
>
> Romans 7:15 NRSV

## For I do not do the good I want . . .

Your job requires you to review employee time records. In this capacity, you are privy to seeing when people clock in and out each day. This past week, as you were reviewing several time cards in order to check the overtime charged, you realized that someone had tampered with the records. You notice that three people who came in the previous Saturday to sort out a computer system failure had their overtime hours struck off their cards. The only other person who has access to the cards other than you, is your boss. You highly suspect it was him. You know he has been told by head office to reduce every possible expense as the quarterly results look poor.

You have spent hours deliberating on how to deal with your discovery. You know it is hugely unfair to the people involved who have worked extra hours in good faith, hoping to earn extra money. As you see it, this is clearly an act of injustice and a blatant abuse of power. You decide to discuss the situation with your partner who agrees that something must be said. This matter should not be ignored or passed over. You rehearse what you are going to say to your boss the next day. You organize your thoughts; you summon up your courage, and you march confidently to work. And then . . . confronted by your boss you suddenly get cold feet. He is grumpy, disengaged and clearly in a bad mood. You feel afraid. In this climate of layoffs, he could turn on you. The consequences could be bad. Better to keep your mouth shut. Just go along this time and pretend you did not notice. Next time you will say something!

If this example does not fit with one of your experiences, perhaps you can replace it with a similar story of your own. Consider a time when you have been unable to follow through on your own ethical principles (what I ought to do) so that they resulted in the moral action you intended (what I actually do).

Does this failure make you a bad person? Surely not. Being able to consistently follow through with feet on the ground action, on our most thoughtful and prudent ethical deliberations, is a lifelong challenge. What is important, however, is that we are aware of our lack of follow through and that we persist in trying to overcome the variety of obstacles that thwart our best intentions.

The ethical challenge to follow through on our highest ideals and values is something most of us struggle with more frequently than we might care to admit. Like St. Paul in the opening quotation, we experience what I call the "ethics-morality gap." Ethics refers to what my principled thinking guides me to do – "the good I want," while morality is what I actually do – the specific actions I take. This distinction will be explained shortly.

Before we tackle the ethics-morality gap, however, we need to examine some of the foundational thinking that underpins the domain we refer to as ethics. In these next few pages, I provide a glimpse of some of the most influential ideas and thoughts that have evolved over the ages and that have brought us to where we are now, in our postmodern world. You will notice, that a great deal of these ideas are based on propositions put forward by the two Greek notables, Plato and Aristotle.

As I mentioned in the Introduction, to make reading about ethics interesting and effective, I recommend that you use the text as a mirror for your own thoughts and behaviors. In this chapter in particular, I ask you to participate in your own self-examination. Remember ethics is not just about others. It begins right at home with us.

## Know thyself!

*The unexamined life is not worth living.*

Socrates (Apologia)

### Ethics begins with self-examination

According to the annals of Western civilization, it was around 600 BCE that the Greeks began asking questions such as: Who are we? Why are we here? How should we live? What does it mean to live a good life? What does "good" mean? This self-inquiry was prompted by a growing self-awareness that human beings have a conscious mind and can exercise conscious choice (Tarnas, 1991). It is these sorts of questions that set the wheels of Western philosophy in motion.

Carved on the forecourt of the Temple of Apollo at Delphi and reiterated endlessly by the Greek philosopher Socrates (469 BCE–399 BCE) throughout his life, is the injunction that the most important of all human engagement is self-examination. This self-examination is to be directed at how one lives one's life and what kind of person, or character, one is becoming. Character development was at the heart of Greek ethics.

The word ethics, is derived from the Greek word *ethikos*, meaning character or disposition.

A key premise for the Greeks was that what humans desire above all else, is happiness, and that the only way this can be achieved is by living a life that is good for the soul (Tarnas, 1991). A good life for the soul, according to the Greek philosophers, Socrates, Plato and Aristotle, is attained by making virtuous choices, which means choices guided by certain ethical principles, moderation being a key one.

Self-examination is the exercise of evaluating whether one is making these virtuous choices and thereby living a good life. The activity of self-examination itself, which requires introspection and spending time with one's soul, augments one's sense of inner peace and contentment and ushers in happiness. Simply put, healthy self-examination contributes to our experience of happiness. (Note the current growing mindfulness movement that postulates similar ideas – see Chapter 10.)

### Some key concepts

In the discussion of self-examination, we notice an important connection between five concepts namely, happiness, the soul, virtuous choices, ethical principles and a good life. I refer to these concepts many times in the next chapters, so I think now is a good time to clarify what they mean. As you read about these concepts, you might like to consider their general relevance today, in our twenty-first century world, and to yourself personally.

Let's begin our discussion with happiness; that thing, claimed Aristotle, to which all things aim (Aristotle, 1999).

*Happiness*

> *The mass of men lead lives of quiet desperation.*
>
> Henry Thoreau, *Walden* (1854)

As we rapidly move towards the close of another decade in the twenty-first century, one thing that stands out is how the longing for happiness has become big business. Speakers, artists, writers and TV hosts provide all kinds of advice on how to quell our fears, find our true selves and realize that illusive dream – happiness. Self-help books that provide the ten steps to Happiness adorn many bookshelves. By contrast, the Greeks kept it simple. They said the answer to happiness lies in living a life of self-examination, moderation, taking care of our souls and acting virtuously. Happiness, in Greek *eudaimonia*, which also means prosperity, flourishing or well-being, will follow.

HISTORICAL PERSPECTIVES

Plato (428 BCE–328 BCE), maintained that happiness, or well-being, is the highest aim of moral thought and conduct, and that one attains this by practicing the virtues (referred to as *aretê* meaning excellence). Aristotle (384 BCE–322 BCE), Plato's student, who we discuss in some length in Chapter 6, held that happiness, being an inward state of contentment, is attained largely by living a life of moderation.

Jesus and the Buddha would probably say that happiness results from a rejection of worldly attachments and is attained by a life spent in compassionate engagement and service to others. The great Catholic theologian, Thomas Aquinas, said that happiness is attaining or knowing God. The brilliant French mathematician and philosopher, Blaise Pascal (1623–1662), in his book *Pensees*, comments on humanity's existential discontent. He says that "man's unhappiness springs from one thing alone, his incapacity to stay quietly in one room." (*Pensees* #168). Pascale also had a great deal to say about the negative influences of distractions and diversions on humankind's contentment. Imagine what he would say today!

Immanuel Kant (1724–1804), who will feature a great deal in our discussions when it comes to ethical principles, did not think happiness is a core value to be pursued. He said that contentment was to be found in the rigor of living life according to the dictates of pure rationality and doing one's duty.

MODERN PERSPECTIVES

We now turn to some of the postmodern philosophers, for example, John Stuart Mill (1806–1873), who we also met in Chapter 1.

Mill considered happiness to be the result of an equation. If pleasure exceeded pain, ergo, one was happy. Henry David Thoreau (1817–1862), the naturalist, poet and philosopher, discovered that happiness resulted by reconnecting with our inner selves. The German philosopher, Friedrich Nietzsche (1844–1900), said happiness was striving toward ever greater self-realization without recourse to anything outside of oneself.

Leo Tolstoy (1828–1910), the Russian writer, deemed one of the greatest authors of all time, had a great deal to say about happiness. Many of his characters were caught up in a feverish pursuit of happiness in one way or another, and few, if any, found what they were looking for. The more frantically they searched for it, the more it eluded them. Tolstoy's sad personal story was also one of trying to find happiness and inner peace. Towards the end of his life, he gains the insight that the pursuit of one's own happiness brings narcissism and enslavement to chaotic desires which in turn lead to disharmony, frustration, conflicts and unhappiness. What is far more worthwhile is to pursue peace, kindness, and justice and to have a transcendent purpose in life.

The great British philosopher, Bertrand Russell (1872–1970), in his classic *The Conquest of Happiness* (2013), provided a down-to-earth guide on what ails us and how we can attain happiness. He suggests a cure for unhappiness which he claims arises largely from people's self-preoccupation. He also writes about the perniciousness of our insatiable desire for success and our fear of boredom. He says we are caught up in self-deceptions regarding our importance and the extent of our merits, not to mention our addiction to approval from others. The secret to happiness, according to him, is to have many wide interests, to invest in causes that lie beyond our selves, and to cultivate an inner zest for life. Love and affection are very important provided one does not project or force this on others. We need to open the windows of our minds, to resign ourselves to things beyond our control, to practice moderation and to be able to enjoy a quiet life – a little like Pascal's ability to stay quietly in one room (Russell, 2013).

TWENTY-FIRST-CENTURY HAPPINESS

As we reflect on these insights, how do we experience happiness today in a culture addicted to conspicuous consumption? In Chapter 1 we discussed the "pursuit of happiness" and its relation to property ownership and wealth, where more wealth supposedly led to more happiness. Instead, rather than having great wealth, many people are drowning in debt, are unhealthy, depressed, anxious regarding their future, feel alienated at work, stressed by their family commitments and worry about retirement.

A high percentage of young people are scared, lost and feel hopeless. Suicide statistics worldwide are the highest ever and rising. In the US for the first time in two generations, the projected lifespan of adult men is decreasing due to mental illnesses and suicides. Despair is everywhere. So where is this happiness? Regrettably few people realize how much their soul hungers to be reconnected with nature, with a community, and most of all, with their true inner selves. Many people do not seem to realize one cannot consume one's way to happiness, nor will a million likes on Facebook obliterate the emptiness that rings inside. No matter how many videos one watches on how to overcome one's fears and sense of inadequacy, this alone will not satisfy the yearnings of our true natures.

A key insight here, raised by Plato and reiterated by others, is that happiness itself cannot be pursued. If anything, its pursuit leads to a greater sense of frustration, failure and unhappiness. It is by doing other things, such as living a virtuous life, helping others, and especially nurturing our souls that happiness results. Happiness is an outcome of other wholesome activities. (A Google search shows over 660 million entries for "How to find happiness.")

## The soul

> *Trailing Clouds of Glory*
>
> William Wordsworth, *Intimations of Immortality* (1804)

### THE GREEK SOUL

According to Plato, humans have a body that is inseparably bound to the senses and is subject to the same fate as everything else in the world – namely death. Humans also have an immortal soul. This immortal soul existed originally in a world of ideal Forms or Ideas before it inhabited the body. These Forms or Ideas are eternal and immutable (Plato's, *The Timaeus*).

Plato contended that once the soul finds itself inhabiting a body, which is like a prison, it forgets these ideal Forms. As the individual lives in the world of natural phenomena, which are merely shadows or fragments of the eternal Forms or Ideas, a vague recollection of the (perfect) world it came from stirs in the soul. This recollection creates a yearning by the soul to escape from the body and return to its true realm. This yearning, Plato calls *Eros* which means love, and this love is an ardent desire to be rejoined with the Forms.

Once the recollection begins, the human experiences the sensory world as insignificant by comparison and longs to return to its real home of the Forms. Unfortunately, says Plato, most people are not philosophers who, by putting the love of wisdom above all else, work at returning to their real home. Instead they are content with a life among the fragments or shadows, never realizing that they are in fact in the shadows which they misplace for reality (Plato's discussion of the Cave in the *Republic, Book IV VII*).

Aristotle took a different tack. He taught that a soul is to be found wherever there is life. Since life exists throughout nature, the soul exists throughout nature. The soul makes something function according to its nature. So when it comes to humans, the soul is that which governs the life functions of the human. The human soul is also higher than the soul in nature in that it can reason.

### THE MODERN SOUL

While the Enlightenment philosophers, who we met in the previous chapter, tended to dispense with anything close to the metaphysical or mystical in favor of rationalism and science, the Romantic movement (end of the 18th Century), with well-known personalities such as Victor Hugo, Samuel Taylor Coleridge, Ralph Waldo Emerson, William Wordsworth, Henry David Thoreau and John

Keats, sought to re-enchant the world. They used poetry, prose and new forms of art to reinforce the natural goodness of human beings. They emphasized a return to nature, affection for relics of the past, an appreciation of sense and sensuality, and stressed the value of emotions and intuition. For the Romanticists, the soul was an important element of our experiencing of life. It was the inner home of our sense of beauty, pathos, love, spirituality and sense of the sublime.

If we proceed to our current era, we encounter Thomas Moore's highly popular book, *Care of the Soul* (1992), which clearly speaks to the needs of the times. Moore speaks of the soul as something that lies between understanding and unconsciousness. The soul, he says, is not a thing, but a quality or a dimension of experiencing life and ourselves (1992, p. 5).

The main thesis of his book is that we give scant attention to the soul except when it complains through various pathologies such as illness, aches and pains, depression, emptiness, a sense of meaninglessness and a loss of values. He points out that care for the soul is not a self-improvement project or a means to living more comfortably. Caring for the soul, he claims, has its own purpose and end. The soul warrants care simply because it is our soul, the deepest core of who we are.

Jungian Psychologist James Hillman in his book, *The Soul's Code: In Search of Character and Calling* (1996), builds his discussion of soul on Plato's *Myth of Er*, which comes at the end of Plato's *Republic*. The story goes that the soul each of us is given has assigned to it a unique daimon (guiding spirit) before we are born. The soul has selected an image or pattern, a sort of blueprint, that we will live out on this Earth. The daimon guides us to the Earth, but once we get here, we forget everything. The daimon, however, does not forget everything and continues to try to carry out our destiny as set out in the blueprint. If we attend carefully to our inner voice, i.e., our soul speaking, we will catch glimpses of our daimon in action and we will work with it to live out our calling. This daimon then acts as our soul on Earth needing nourishment, beauty, time, recognition and love (Hillman, 1996).

The highly acclaimed psychologist and writer, Ken Wilber, writes about the soul that can be found within the deepest part of ourselves. He says there is in the infinite silence of our interior being the soul that is whispering about love, bliss, and peace. The soul is that intersection between time and the timeless. It is to be found when we have shifted beyond our normal ego consciousness into the transpersonal realm where the soul is our bridge to eternity and the pure spirit in which we participate (Wilber, 2000, p. 106).

It might be fair to say that, almost all the philosophers and theologians that follow in the wake of the Greeks claim that a human soul exists and that it has divine qualities or features. It is generally held that the soul is some part of us that connects us both to the deepest part of ourselves and to our divinity or to an eternal transcendent or ultimate principle.

*Virtuous choices*

Again, the idea of the virtues stem from the Greeks. Plato's virtues are the skills and dispositions that guide the choices that lead to happiness or well-being. In the *Republic, Book 4*, Plato discusses four chief or cardinal virtues. (He has identified others elsewhere, but these are the main ones.) The four are wisdom, courage or fortitude, temperance or moderation and justice. Wisdom refers to the rational part of the soul; the ability to know good and evil and what is good for a person. Courage refers to the spirited part of the person, that part that gets angry at injustices or loves to overcome challenges, while temperance refers to both the spirited part and the appetites, appetites being a person's passions and desires. Justice is the virtue that ensures that every part of the soul performs its task in harmony (Copleston, Vol 1, 1993).

Aristotle too has a great deal to say about the virtues. There is a highest good which is happiness, and in order to attain happiness, one must exercise the virtues which is a rational activity. He divides the virtues into two classes – intellectual virtue and moral virtue. We will focus on the moral virtues here which Aristotle names as courage, temperance and justice with the crowning virtue inherent in all others, being prudence (being practical wisdom, *Phronesis*).

Aristotle makes a big thing about habit. He claims that we become just by doing just actions, we become courageous by doing acts of courage and so on. Self-examination lets us see what our habits are and how we habitually respond to people and situations. Over time our habits coagulate and shape our character. Aristotle stresses that we are what we habitually do.

The central question for Aristotle is not what the right action is to perform but rather what sort of human being we aspire to be. What do our thoughts or reactions say about us, about who we are, how we live our lives, and the habits that are part of our daily living? Moral virtue then, derives from the choices we make that reflect our character and our habitual attention to the virtues mentioned above.

The concept and even the language of virtue in our postmodern world smacks of anachronism. While we readily talk about excellence it is mostly in reference to operational or technical matters as in "best practice." People talk about personal excellence in their profession perhaps or with reference to the sports field. Excellence or virtue as a habitual practice of self-mastery, self-discipline and measured, noble behavior is neither routinely explicitly cultivated nor held up as an educational ideal. In business organizations people are encouraged to be excellent in their jobs and outside of that, few really care. People are rarely hired for nobility of character but rather for their technological or marketing smarts. Maybe this lack of attention to virtue is something that fuels our troubled world.

### The good life

According to Plato, a life predominated by reason is the highest good for humankind. However, while a person has reason, they also have feelings, desires and appetites (passions). A good life is one where all these factors are realized (expressed) in perfect harmony, and where reason rules and the other factors obey. Thus, a life balanced between reason and the passions results in a good life which is also a happy life.

For Aristotle, full self-realization is the highest good – the *summum bonum*. How does one attain this self-realization? Through exercising reason in practicing the virtues. Aristotle believed that all things naturally tend towards *entelechy*, which means achieving one's potential. When the soul attains this innate perfection or *entelechy*, as a result of virtuous choices, then a person experiences happiness.

Epictetus (50 AD–135 AD), was a Greek Stoic philosopher who too believed that a happy life and a virtuous life are synonymous. He was most concerned with the steps one needs to take in the pursuit of moral excellence. His notion of a good life is where we bring our actions and desires into harmony with nature. The prime goal is to achieve inner serenity and so gain personal freedom. His prescription for the good life centered on three main themes: mastering your desires, performing your duties, and learning to think clearly about yourself and your relations with the rest of humanity. What matters most in life, is what sort of person you are becoming and how you are living (Epictetus, 1995).

If we move away from the early philosophers to the influence of the Western religions, we find that in general the good is obedience to a deity and the good life is submission and obedience to the sacred writings of the priesthood.

The period of the Renaissance and early Humanism (1300–1650) shifted things somewhat by inspiring a new recognition of the dignity of humankind and who or what was to define the good and the good life. One notable philosopher of the times was an Italian nobleman by the name of Giovanni Pico della Mirandola (1463–1494), who argued in his *Oration of the Dignity of Man* (1486), that man contains all things within himself and has the potential to become anything he desires. Man is now a free, self-creating agent. Pico was a forerunner of the Existentialist movement, something we discuss in Chapter 6.

If we fast forward a few hundred years to the Enlightenment, we meet David Hume (1711–1776), the Scottish Enlightenment philosopher, who held that it is human moral sense that determines what we think is good. Hume discounts the idea of objective moral truths to be discovered by reason alone, but that feeling, and sentiment is what gives them their validity.

Our friend, Immanuel Kant, took an opposing view in that for him reason was ultimate. This reason governs the will, which, when it obeys the inner (divine) law of duty, expresses the highest good there can be, which is freedom. Thus, the good or the good life is about doing one's duty and doing one's duty gives one a sense of freedom. Free-willed beings, said Kant, are the most valuable things in the world. They are ends in themselves (Grayling, 2003).

The postmodern philosophers bring in some different ideas about the good life although most agree that happiness is the key goal of life. If one is happy, one is supposedly living a good life. Good equates to personal happiness.

What we observe about modern thinking is that happiness is based on what pleases a person. While reason and rationality are not totally jettisoned as an important method of making choices, the modern path to happiness is far less structured and more personally relativistic, i.e., no objective standards or guidelines such as the virtues are prescribed. Everything has become more and more "up to me." Some postmodern philosophers emphasize what is good for the group and some for what is good for the individual, but the royal road to happiness is less and less paved with objective standards, rigor or self-accountability.

Happiness has become an object to be acquired rather than an inner state of mind to be personally developed. Self-mastery or the idea of self-discipline has been swept aside as Puritan or unnecessarily self-punitive in favor of "being me" or "expressing my true self." As we discuss in the next chapters, these predominant themes have a direct impact on our ethics and of course business ethics.

## Ethical principles

Ethical principles are those rational guiding propositions or injunctions that suggest, propose, direct and provide guidelines regarding our choices. These principles are objective, rational, non-situational "oughts" that are presented to us as guides to our choices. For the Greeks, these ethical principles were spelled out in the virtues. Aristotle's famous taxonomy of ethics is described in detail in his *Nicomachean Ethics* (1999).

We will say more about his ethics in the next chapters, but what is important to note is that the virtue ethics approach is often referred to as character-based ethics.

Since the Greeks and their virtue approach, many ethical principles have evolved in response to changing social circumstances, e.g., the growth of cities, war, and shifts in human consciousness, for example, the Renaissance, the Enlightenment and the Romantic movement and of course postmodernism.

Chapters 6 and 7 chart some of the key ethical principles that have evolved over time including many that we are familiar with as we use them in daily life.

## Why be ethical?

I would hope that at this point the value of striving to be ethical (or virtuous) is obvious: It leads to a good life and happiness. I would like to take this argument one step further by invoking the mighty Plato again. In his *Republic, Book II*, he pens a discussion between Socrates and his brother, Glaucon. They are discussing the matter of Justice (one of the cardinal virtues) – something we explore in Chapter 7.

In this story, Glaucon is challenging Socrates by claiming that being ethical is basically a pain. He uses a story to illustrate his point. The story concerns the Ring of Gyges.

Gyges is a poor shepherd who finds a ring in a fissure opened by an earthquake. The ring makes its wearer invisible, so that he or she can go anywhere and do anything undetected. Gyges is an unscrupulous fellow and realizes that the ring can be put to great personal advantage. He ostensibly uses the ring to gain entry to the royal palace where he seduces the queen. In no time at all he becomes King of the land and an abusive one at that.

Glaucon challenges Socrates by saying, now imagine two rings – one given to a person of virtue and one given to a rogue. How might they behave? The rogue will take advantage of the cloak of invisibility, where he can do whatever he pleases without getting caught. He will not recognize any inner moral constraints. How will the virtuous person behave? Glaucon says he will do no better than the rogue – no one has the strength of mind or character if he can take what he wants without consequences. Once there is no reprisal why would someone not do what is best for himself? In fact, they would be stupid not to make the ring work to their advantage.

The discussion then moves to whether being ethical has any value for its own sake or whether we do it because we want others to treat us well or we do not want to get caught – namely based on our need for reciprocity or to escape punishment.

Socrates develops a long circuitous argument which we will not go into here, but that culminates in his saying that being ethical or just is an intrinsic good. It is good because of its inherent value. It is not an instrumental good that should be pursued for the sake of something else. (We discuss this distinction later in this chapter under Grounding Values.) So being virtuous or just is inherently good for us. That's it. We don't need anything more – the good life and happiness that follows are bonus and should not be pursued for their own sake. Live rightly – striving for virtue, goodness and justice and the rest shall follow.

---

### Your turn – what would you do with the ring?

Now it is your turn; What would you do if you found this miraculous ring? Do you agree with Glaucon that you would be a fool not to use it to your advantage? Or, would you still be the upright, virtuous person you aspire to be? Imagine – you could get away with anything!

Now: One step further. What do you think about people say, investment bankers who get away with everything – no consequences! Wouldn't they be stupid not to continue doing what they are doing?

What does your best friend, partner, management team think?

---

### Summary and implications

It is time to take stock of where we are and to consider the relevance of our discussions to business ethics.

We began the chapter with an example of the ethics-morality gap in action. In evaluating our own tendencies to fail to follow through on our noble principles or to take the "moral high" road as we call it, calls for self-examination. Now what will this self-examination do for us? According to the early philosophers and among other things, the growing mindfulness movement, self-examination gets us to reflect on who we are, the choices we make, whether we are living a good life and whether we are achieving what we want to achieve, which is happiness.

In summary –

• Self-examination is the most important of all human engagement. It is the key to being ethical. It helps us grow in self-awareness and develop our character. It helps us be more self-accountable and personally responsible for our choices. It leads to happiness.

- Happiness is what everyone longs for. It is our ultimate and prime end or purpose in life. It is an inner experience and not an outer objective. This experience is attained through living a life of reason, being virtuous and taking care of our souls.
- Caring for the soul is important because it is the deepest core of who we are. It is our innate character and holds the key to the destiny to which we are called. It is the path to self-transcendence – something many philosophers and psychologists say is our innate calling – see Transpersonal Leadership in Chapter 10.
- Virtuous choices are those made by using our reason and living a life of moderation in harmony with ourselves and others.
- The good life is a happy one where one practices self-mastery and makes virtuous choices. More recently we have come to believe that the good life is one that pleases us and makes us feel good about ourselves.
- Ethical principles are guidelines that help us make virtuous or good choices. Good choices are those that are rational, objective and result from prudent deliberation.
- Being ethical has intrinsic value. Our intention should be directed in doing what is ethical for its own sake and to let the other things follow in due course.

As you can see these ethical ideals have great relevance to both individual and group life. They sum up some of the deep motivations that drive human behavior. Organizations attempt to address these issues by, for example, sending people for coaching to become more self-aware, and offering emotional intelligence programs to heighten awareness and relationship management. Attempts are made at pleasing the soul with soothing colors on the wall or evidence of fountains and plants. Corporate ethics codes are created to guide decision-making. Making these attempts effective, however, requires them to be part of a coherent system rather than a collection of fragmented and unconnected efforts. The Greeks gave us a coherent system. Now we need to develop our own.

Finally, if you wish to be ethical or shape an ethical organization, everything begins with self-examination. There is no escape!

### I don't want to know

Ever had this conversation or some version of it?

> *I don't want to know!*
> *You don't want to know what?*
> *What is going on. Leave me out of it.*
> *Why don't you want to know?*
> *Because if there is anything fishy going on, the less I know the better.*

*What if there is nothing fishy going on?*
*Then fine. I still don't want to know.*
*Why don't you want to know?*
*I just feel better not knowing.*
*So, you are afraid you suspect something?*
*I told you, it is not my concern. I have lots of other things to worry about.*
*Do you think that suspecting something but not knowing for sure leaves you*
*    blameless?*
*Yes – I do not want to be involved. Leave me out of it!*

There are several important points that stand out from this interchange.

First, ask yourself whether you sometimes take this stance of not wanting to know so as not to be implicated. Well, guess what? Only true, genuine, appropriate ignorance excuses you. Once you suspect that something is amiss in any way and you do nothing, you become what is known as a "bystander."

Second, the ethical behavior of the organization is directly affected by everyone's behavior not just the direct perpetrators of any dark or nefarious deeds. Collusion by silence, feigned ignorance or a distancing by not wanting to be involved is tantamount to being complicit. When something is going on in the company, everyone knows, even if it is just a suspicion. (Recall my opening story in the Preface and discussed again in the previous chapter.)

What philosopher Hannah Arendt pointed out to us, is that real evil lies in ignorance and complacency (Arendt, 2006). Without ignorance, complacency and a reluctance to be involved, far less corrupt or evil deeds would be wrought. Not wanting to be involved does not let one off the hook. What avoidance demonstrates is a failure in moral courage. And moral courage lies at the heart of character, moral competence, effective leadership and good citizenship.

Third, every time we agree to collude in silence, we reinforce and condone further misbehaviors.

Fourth, every time we silence our inner murmurings, we are denying our self-awareness at a deep cost to our personal integrity and our soul.

Being ethical is tough. It makes a deep moral claim on us. We cannot escape choosing, and choices have moral implications.

When challenged with the question: Am I an ethical person? I must factor into my response recognition that knowledge of something always lays some kind of ethical claim on me.

## Grounding values

Self-examination and self-awareness activities reveal to us our deeply held values. Many of these values were shaped by the influence of our families and our early childhood experiences.

We find there are many values. They might include creativity, beauty, peace, punctuality, kindness, honesty, loyalty, respect, fairness, love of money and so on. Not all values are necessarily "good" or ethical ones.

Over time we find that the values we live by are tested. As a result, we discard some, and from time to time we might add new ones. Alternatively, we might reprioritize our list. By the time we are in our mid-twenties, researchers tell us, we have an almost intractable set of values on which we base our assumptions, shape our opinions, and direct our choices and decisions (Rokeach, 1979).

Our values help us find focus and orientation. They inspire our motivation. They also tend to make us judgmental. We are inclined to approve of people who have the same or similar values and disapprove of those with different values. Pretty much everything we do or think in some way bumps up against our values. We are value driven! Values lie at the heart of everything.

Values can be divided into two types, terminal and instrumental. Some things we value for their own sake. They have intrinsic value – like being ethical. These are known as terminal or end values. For example, the values of happiness, peace, deep friendship, love and safety have inherent value; values we hold above all else.

By contrast the values of say, honesty or respect, are known as instrumental values. These are values we hold because they lead to something else. They are instrumental to attaining something beyond them. For example, if everyone is honest then the world is a trustworthy place and people are safe. Honesty is instrumental to the terminal (end) value of safety. Another example is respect. If everyone is respectful, then no-one will harm another and there will be peace. Desiring respect is instrumental to creating a place of peace.

Again, researchers tell us that most of us have very similar instrumental and end values, yet the way we prioritize them may be different (Ibid). You may place peace and honesty high on your list, while I place closeness to God and family loyalty as tops on mine. Whatever our lists and however we prioritize them, they shape how we see and live in the world. At the end of the day, we select the values we believe reflect who we are and that make us happy. Our values drive all our decisions in our hope that they will result in our happiness. As we know, happiness is the ultimate end value we all desire! We all want to be happy and the purpose of values is to get us what we want. How each of us hopes to attain happiness may differ, however, our ultimate goal or end value, is to be happy. Our values are there to take care of number one – namely, us!

## Exercise 1 – values

- Jot down a list of your values.
- Now prioritize the list by placing the values most important to you at the top of the list and those with lower priority lower down the list.
- Mark (I) for instrumental and (E) for end value next to your list.
- With the instrumental values, try to see which end values they are seeking to satisfy.
- Which of these values, if any, have been present in influencing your decisions today or this week? Can you provide clear and explicit examples?
- Write down what you have learned from this exercise.

Ask your spouse, partner, friend, co-worker to do the same exercise.

Now compare lists and discuss together what you have learned.

## Value tension

An interesting discussion about values often arises. It goes something like this:

> I am furious with Karen. Who does she think she is? How dare she speak to me that way, and in front of the whole accounting department! It was so disrespectful! She humiliated me. It was totally unnecessary. I value respecting others. I would never do a thing like that!

The problem with this outburst is that the person in this example is the one who values respecting others. It would appear Karen does not. One cannot project one's values onto others. They have theirs or they choose to live their values in their way. It is not for each one of us to expect others to either have our values or live them the way we do. Our task is to make clear what values are essential to us and what we will or will not tolerate from others. We cannot change them. We can simply set our boundaries. This requires a very direct conversation that is not about whose values are better, but rather which behaviors are tolerable to the parties involved so that a certain harmony can be achieved. What helps in the values discussion is identifying the end value/s which both parties are likely to agree upon. (According to Rokeach, in general we agree more readily on end values than instrumental ones. We tend to want the same ends but have different means for getting there.) For example, even though Karen might be disrespectful, she is likely to want peace. Few people do not want peace! So addressing Karen by asking her how all parties might promote peace and harmony might get better results than deriding her for her lack of respectfulness. We take up strategies for articulating one's ethics and values in Chapter 9, where we discuss this under Having the Difficult Conversation.

## Value confusion

Many organizations and many leaders lay great claim to the fact they are value driven. They think this makes them ethical. However, this statement misses the boat entirely. We are all value-driven! We cannot live life without having values. It is like saying one is someone who needs food.

No matter who we are, our values underpin our worldviews, our assumptions, attitudes and behaviors. So to claim you are a value-driven person, or a value-driven organization, does not on the face of it mean much. Even the Mafia has values! What really matters is: What are those values? How are they expressed? Do those values contribute to life-giving and constructive decisions? Do those values guide decisions that reflect wisdom, compassion, harmony and a desire to live according to the truth? Furthermore, are those values applied consistently? For example, is honesty applied only to certain people or in certain situations or always, no matter what? Is respect freely given without thought of race, color, creed, religion and so on?

The key question is how our values tie into out ethical principles and how they influence our decisions.

Now that we have clarified some important terms and the background to ethics, it is time to wrestle with the distinction between ethics and morality and the ethics–morality gap raised in the opening case.

## Understanding ethics

> *Learning how to live takes a whole life.*
>
> Seneca

### The ethical quest

Let me begin by setting out some definitions of ethics. Ethics is the rational and systematic reflection on what makes something good, bad, right or wrong and how one justifies one's choice of action. Ethics analyzes concepts such as "right," "wrong," "ought," "good," and "evil" in their moral contexts. Ethics seeks to establish principles of behavior that may serve as action guides for individuals and groups (White, 1993).

Ethics, as a discipline, includes a range of principles and ethical terms that form its subject matter (Messerly, 1995). Ethics used to be called moral philosophy which was the philosophical study of morality (Sterba, 1998).

A question posed earlier in this chapter was: Why be ethical? Why should one bother? Besides Plato (1989) and his Ring of Gyges discussion, philosophers, sages, theologians and social thinkers since the beginning of recorded history agree on the answer to this question. Living an ethical life advances human well-being – or leads to the good life and happiness as we discussed earlier. Nowadays we go further by acknowledging that ethical behavior advances the well-being of all life, not just that of humans, and it makes us healthier.

Pursuing an ethical life (the Greeks called it a virtuous life) leads to a good life. What is a good life? As we discussed in some detail, a good life is one filled with a sense of fulfilment, flourishing, harmony, well-being and happiness. A good life means living and acting justly. A good life results from careful reflection and discernment that leads to the making of wise choices and good decisions.

We can sum up the ethical quest as the striving to make wiser choices. By increasing one's self-awareness and engaging in continuous examination of how one lives one's life, one tends to make wiser and more considered choices. In looking at one's decisions, one analyzes the type of decisions one has made and questions how one arrived at those decisions. One reflects on the values, assumptions, inferences, personal biases and preferences, fears and hopes, knowledge and expectations that led one to select one decision choice over another. Ethics is thus about **reflection and examination**.

Ethics is also about **deliberation**. Deliberation occurs as one asks oneself what factors one is taking into account in making a certain decision. One questions what choice would lead to a good decision – bearing in mind the definition of good above – as opposed to a not so good one. What, in fact, renders a decision a good or a bad one? What criteria should be used? Wherein lie the differences? Which ethical principles seem most appropriate to guide which type of decisions? What makes them appropriate? How does one justify using one ethical principle rather than another? What factors should be considered? These deliberations are often referred to as **moral reasoning**, something we discuss in detail in the next chapters.

Ethics is about **questioning**. It is concerned with the interpretation of ethical principles. Should certain ethical principles be interpreted differently? Has the meaning of flourishing or well-being or justice changed due to time or circumstances? Are there new interpretations or new principles that one should consider? What ethical principles do we need to guide us now? How would that change the decision under consideration? How does one justify certain rules and roles in certain circumstances?

The issue of slavery provides a good example regarding ethical deliberation and questioning. The idea that people should be treated equally goes back 2,500 years. The problem with this ethical principle was that at the time it applied only to "equal" people, i.e., only equal people were to be treated equally. In other words, those not considered "equal"; women, children and slaves for example, did not fall within the ambit of this principle. It has taken thousands of years for ethics to catch up with the idea that all people, by virtue of their humanity, are equal and therefore, all people, without exception, should be treated equally. (Realistically we are not there yet as regrettably we still discriminate and do not treat all people equally.)

---

### Definition of ethics

Ethics is concerned with the principles of right conduct and the systematic endeavor to understand moral concepts and to justify moral principles. Ethics analyzes concepts such as "right," "wrong," "permissible," "ought," "good," and "evil" in their moral contexts. Ethics seeks to establish principles of right behavior that may serve as action guides for individuals and groups. It investigates which values and virtues are paramount to the worthwhile life of society (White, 1993).

---

Ethics critiques moral behavior. It contemplates the critical awareness of the tensions and opposing values that exist in the world. Ethics searches for foundational principles that transcend the relative historical particularities of specific situations without becoming so abstract as to be ambiguous or impractical.

Overall the field of ethics covers activities required to sustain a cohesive society; to ameliorate human suffering; to promote human flourishing; to promote justice at both the societal and individual level, and to foster and nourish the well-being of the Earth and its present and future inhabitants.

### To sum up

Ethics is the rational endeavor to pursue a good life and experience happiness. This is achieved through –

- Continuous reflection and examination
- deliberation
- Questioning
- Re-interpreting ethical principles where appropriate
- Promoting justice and harmony
- Evaluating moral actions taken

### Ethical principles

In order to live an ethical life, we can turn to many ethical principles to guide us. These principles have evolved over the centuries. They take the form of theories and injunctions proposed by philosophers, theologians, social activists and others. Many of these theories and injunctions have been incorporated into our thinking as we have grown up. They have become part and parcel of our decision-making tools. The Golden Rule provides a well-known example: "Do unto others as you would have them do unto you." Other frequently used principles include, "You should do your duty," or "Every person should be treated equally" or "We need to do what is best for the majority."

Ethics, as a discipline, is **continuously evolving**. This means that as our social consciousness changes, and as new dilemmas arise, we devise new, or reinterpret existing ethical principles. As a result, contrary to say 500 years ago, we now have business ethics, bioethics, and environmental ethics. If we take one specific example, in the mid-1900s we suddenly awoke to the fact that the well-being of the planet is as important as our own personal well-being. There will be no human flourishing if we do not take care of the planet. (Native people have known this and paid attention to this fact for eons.) As a result, we now have new ethical principles that focus on sustainability and avoidance of harm to the natural habitat and to the Earth.

Ethics has a **developmental** aspect. Ethics invites us to engage with the principles that may require re-interpretation. Ethics does not provide clear cut answers. It involves searching, seeking and striving. Searching for the most appropriate interpretation; seeking for the optimal consideration of possibilities; striving to uphold goodness, harmony and well-being.

Ethical thinking draws us into greater **cognitive maturity**. The ability to engage in ethical thinking as opposed to simply following norms or rules reflects greater engagement in the dynamics of life and greater personal responsibility for the well-being of humankind. (We discuss this in the next chapter under Moral Development.)

Because ethics concerns principles rather than rules, we need to intellectually engage with them. We need to consider how the principles should be interpreted; how they relate to particular circumstances; how to deal with conflicting principles, and how applying different principles makes a personal statement about us.

As we note when we discuss Moral Development in Chapter 4, the majority of people prefer to conform to rules, norms and conventions rather than grapple with ethical principles that require intellectual and often emotional engagement for their application. People who strive to be ethical are far more thoughtful than those who do not, for the simple reason that ethics requires judgment and discernment rather than obedience. Exercising judgment and discernment entails more risk than simply obeying. Being ethical is risky and requires courage. There will be more discussion on courage in Chapter 10.

Now let us look at the term "morality."

## Morality

Morality refers essentially to people's behavior; what it is they actually do. A person's behavior is deemed moral or immoral depending on whether it conforms to the commonly accepted rules of conduct and customs of the group or society to which the person belongs (McCollough, 1991).

An example of a moral norm is monogamy. Anyone who chooses to have more than one spouse in a monogamous culture or society would be considered immoral.

---

### Definition of morality

Morality refers to the norms, customs and mores approved by a particular group, society or nation as values and standards perceived to be good and right for that group, society or nation.

---

Moral norms or customs are established by people to facilitate their coexistence in a manner they believe to be optimal. Moral norms and customs act together with laws to keep people's self-interested behavior in check. They serve as a form of disciplinary control over group members.

The moral norms of a group or society are usually established by those in power (those in power make the rules), or those in the majority. Custom or tradition frequently plays a strong part in setting the standard or tone for expected moral behavior as people are often reluctant to overturn deeply embedded cultural norms.

Just as new ethical principles evolve due to questioning and probing, moral norms also change. This might arise as a result of pressure from newly accepted ethical principles or because there is a changing of the guard. Think about the ethical debate concerning healthcare that yo-yos back and forth depending which political party has the power. Another example is the environment and sustainability. As a result, recycling has (almost) become a new moral norm (Table 3.1).

*Table 3.1* Ethics – morality summary

| ETHICS | MORALITY |
| --- | --- |
| Cognitive | Behavioral |
| Reference to ethical principles | Dictated by moral norms and customs |
| Examination and reflection | Conformance and obedience |
| Deliberation and continuous questioning | Adaptation to changing cultural pressures |
| Evidence of moral reasoning | Evidence of actual behavior |
| Refer to striving for goodness | Refer to right or wrong behavior |
| Emphasis: the person's choice in freedom | Emphasis: the person's action in conformance |

As we can see ethics and morality are different concepts. Ethics concerns reflection and judgment, continual questioning and analysis, and is forever evolving. We also note that ethics is about the theory that holds up an ideal, while morality is about the messy, real world of behavior and action. Ethics is the discipline, while morality is the subject under study. One could say that ethics is the theory and morality is ethics when applied in specific contexts.

Ethics acts as the ongoing critical analysis of morality. As the theory evolves so it challenges the practice. Furthermore, in ethics we are primarily concerned with intention, motivation and deliberation, i.e., why is it that we intend to do something? With morality, the prime concern is with what we actually do regardless of our intentions or deliberations. The motivation is of less interest.

If we refer to the opening quotation from St. Paul, his ethics guide him as to what he should do; what he wills or really wants to do. However, when it comes to his actual actions, he does not follow through on his will or intention. He ends up doing the very thing he does not want to do. Here we see the **ethics-morality** gap or tension in action. Ideally, we would like to see our ethical principles followed through in our actions. There are of course reasons why we do not. But then the axe murderer had his reasons too. Self-examination helps us see how and why these "reasons" impacted our behavior and what we might learn from them.

The opening case is an example of how this ethics-morality gap occurs in real life. How many times has it happened in your world this week?

Once again:

Ethics – what ought we to do? – this concerns our thinking, deliberating, questioning, reasoning about what is good or bad, right or wrong conduct with the goal of advancing goodness by making a wise choice.

Morality – our actual behavior – are we applying the rules/norms/customs that govern what people do in the practice of life with the goal of conformance to expected norms or adherence to the rules?

# Moral relativism

## *When in Rome, do as the Romans do*

Moral relativism refers to the principle that moral claims are relativistic, and that there are no universal absolutes that should always apply regardless of circumstance (Messerly, 1995). This means that no overarching guiding ethical principles, norms or customs exist. Each group, society or nation should be entitled to live according to its own customs, norms and laws that the citizens or group members believe creates the harmony and order that suits them best. There should be no interference from external powers or sources.

Due to globalization, the issue of moral relativism has become increasingly significant. As companies set up networks in different countries, they are challenged by the questions of which values and ethical principles to apply when setting standards of corporate behavior. Should the norms be that of the home country or should organizations support and condone local moral practices? For example, is it ok to say that in the United States discrimination between race and gender will not be tolerated but, due to the local country norms, organizational subsidiaries, branches or networks will adhere to the local customs and policies where these prejudices do apply? Simply put, the moral relativism question asks whether each culture or society should be entitled to have their own social norms which decide people's morality and that these should prevail.

Let us return to the slavery example. Prior to the Civil War in the United States, in the Northern states, slave owners were held to be both unethical and immoral. In the Southern states, however, owning slaves was considered a completely moral endeavor and the abolitionists were those seen as immoral. Here we see "moral relativism" at work. Who is correct? Is that even the question? Should all societies be able to create their own local norms without any check and balance? And, can there even be a final arbiter who can state what should be the moral ideal?

We explore the moral relativism question in greater depth in Chapter 8 where we discuss the challenge to organizations to act as global citizens. There we raise the question: When do we do as the Romans do and when don't we? How do we justify this difference? In Chapter 9, we look at our struggles around moral language

Now a last point on moral relativism: If you think about it carefully, you could argue that morality is itself relativistic. Remember we said morality is proscribed by a culture, nation or group. In Islam more than one wife is acceptable. In Christianity or in the United States, not so. Therefore, morality itself is relativistic. It is contextually dependent and there are no absolutes. Or are there? What do you think?

# The value–ethics–morality framework

I have created a framework shown in Figure 3.1 to illustrate the relationships between values-ethics-morality-law-professional codes. Moving from values to professional codes we see that the scope is reduced and that we drop into more

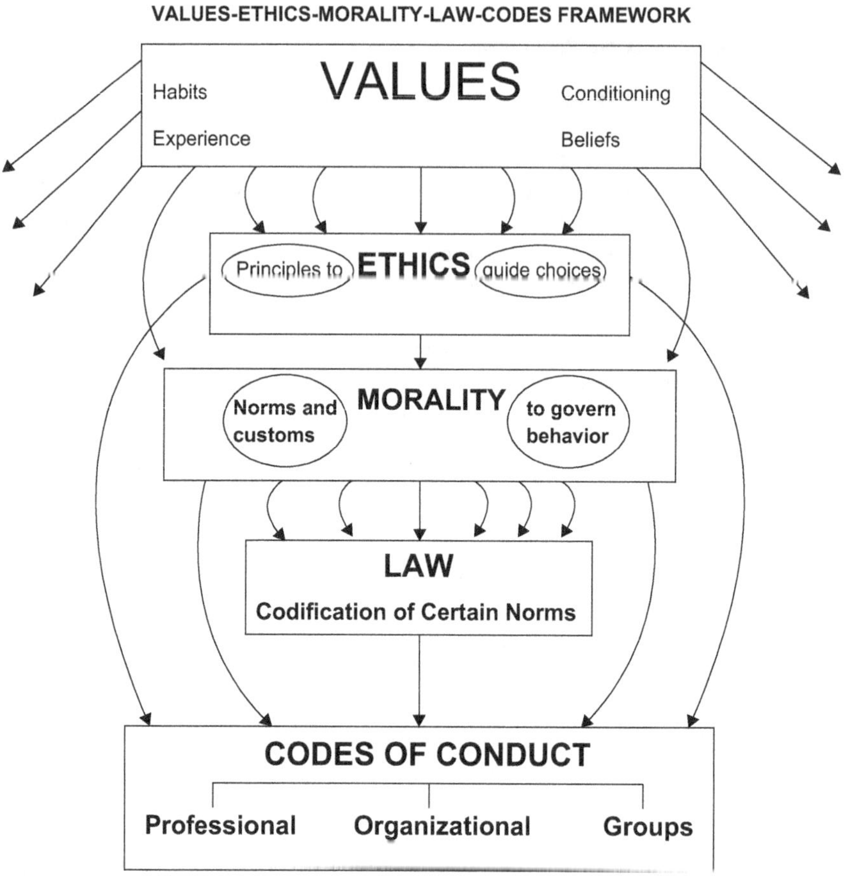

**VALUES-ETHICS-MORALITY-LAW-CODES FRAMEWORK**

*Figure 3.1* Values framework

specific contexts. It is also important to note that for example, the law is only a codification of some ethical principles such as avoid harm, and not others, for example be faithful to those you love.

**Explanation of diagram**

   **VALUES:** Have the broadest ambit in that they influence everything we do and think from not stealing something we covet to loving chocolate cake. Focus: How can I/we get what I/we want to make us happy?
   **ETHICS:** Ethics has a smaller ambit than values. Ethics refers to the principles that guide our choices/decisions influenced by our values. Focus: How to live a good life based on wise decisions.
   **MORALITY:** A narrower range than ethics. This includes selected ethical principles plus cultural norms and customs combined to create a "moral code" for a group, society or nation. Focus: Harmony, reciprocity and order.

**LAW:** The narrowest range. This includes the codification of selected moral norms and customs. Selection is based on who is in power and the strength of rhetoric of a group or party. Focus: Justice and order.

**CODES OF CONDUCT:** Selected ethical principles; moral conventions and legal rules used to create moral conformance and behavioral norms for a specific organization or group. Focus: Control of behaviors, setting of standards that can be expected.

## Case: a little matter of safety

The case below was presented to a group of managers at a small community hospital. They were asked to step out of their shoes as manager – something hard to do – and to read and respond to the case as if they were an employee not in a managerial role. The case is true. As with all the cases presented, the facts and names have been altered for the sake of confidentiality.

### Case

You work in a hospital in Plant Services. It has been very busy of late and in the past few months, due to high volume and a shortage in staff, you have had to put in quite a bit of overtime. You do not mind that too much as your kids are in college and the expenses are mounting.

You have been working at the hospital for quite some time and know many of the staff. Some of them are also your personal friends.

In the past few weeks, what has come to your attention is that Clive, a member of the Safety group, is frequently not showing up on time. You have noticed this due to your extra time at work and your being around in the early morning and late evenings. Plant Services works hand in hand with Safety, and there have been times when you needed to talk with Clive about an issue and he was nowhere to be found. Lately whenever you have seen Clive, he appears agitated and tired.

Although you have tentatively asked questions about Clive, not wanting to appear too nosey or too interfering, no-one seems willing to discuss the issue. The people in the Safety Department assure you that everything is ok and that Clive is just taking a little added time. It also appears that someone is clocking in for Clive so that his lateness is not being reported to his supervisor. Once or twice you have overheard mutterings, but you have not been able to put your finger on what is really going on.

Last week matters came to a head. You were working extra time by standing in for John who was on sick leave. It was late in the afternoon when everyone was ready to go home when Plant Services received a call from the clinic, a building a little down the road. Apparently, someone had slipped on the sidewalk where little sections of ice remained even though the weather was thawing. The people calling Plant Services were looking for someone in Safety to come down and to respond to the issue. Apparently no-one from that department could be found so Plant Services was the back-up. You knew that snow removal and road access to the hospital was specifically Clive's responsibility.

You decide to speak with Jerry and Leo who are also personal friends of Clive to see if you can get to understand what is going on. They tell you that Clive is in bad shape. His marriage is falling apart; he has left home and he is in financial difficulty. Furthermore, he has just learned that his father is critically ill. Those who know these details do not want to make Clive's life more miserable and therefore they are giving him some space to sort himself out. They tell you that they take turns covering for Clive and for clocking him in so that he does not lose pay for not being present for the full shift. They also call him on his cell phone when they sense he is going to be late.

You are astounded to learn Clive's story and the associated intrigue.

Questions posed to group of managers:

- What are you going to do, if anything?
- What is your moral reasoning?

The case itself is not simple. Various perspectives need to be taken as there are many stakeholders.

## Questions

A)  From an ethical perspective what "ought" you to do?

  The ethical perspective invites one to engage in moral reasoning (discussed at length in Chapter 9). Moral reasoning is that reflective and judgmental activity one engages in to understand an ethical dilemma, to reason through it, to decide on the wisest choice of action and then to decide how to proceed.

B)  From a moral perspective what do you feel obliged to do?

  The moral perspective focuses on the norms, rules and conventions of the hospital. What is expected behavior at this instance. Who and how are people conforming or violating norms? How does one keep order and respect for rules, roles and conventions?

---

### Personal exercise 1

- Are you an ethical person? If so, how do you support your answer?
- Are you a moral person? If so, why do you choose to be moral?
- When you last had a moral dilemma, which ethical principle or moral rule guided your choice of action? In hindsight, would you have done anything differently?
- Think of a person you know who exercises leadership? Does he or she demonstrate clear ethical principles in his or her choices? How do you know?
- When did you last behave immorally? Why?

## Being an ethical manager

Managers are the key decision-makers in the organization. Managers are expected to make good decisions and to implement them effectively. This effectiveness determines the future of the organization. If good decisions are being made, that is half the battle. Follow through and implementation is the next critical step.

Since most decisions, especially significant ones, have an ethical dimension to them, it is important that managers invest time in developing some ethical wisdom and that they use every opportunity to practice ethics – something we discuss in Chapter 9.

A key point raised in this chapter is that ethical wisdom lies in reflection and deliberation. This means that ethically sensitive managers need to engage in self-examination and developing their own self-awareness. They need to reflect on the kinds of people they are, their value systems and the types of decisions they make. They need to be open to self-development and change and should seek out opportunities for personal growth and challenge.

Ethically sensitive managers thrive on asking new and different questions. They do not hide behind rules and laws. While they know the rules and laws, they should be prepared to challenge them if they believe they do not enhance goodness, well-being and life-giving opportunities. Ethically sensitive managers are prepared to take risks to uphold or advance an ethical culture.

Ethical managers are concerned with ethical principles and consciously wrestle with finding the most appropriate principle to guide a specific decision. Ethical managers are concerned with justice (discussed in detail in Chapter 7). They understand the importance of deliberation and judgment. They also appreciate that fostering ethical thinking in others is a developmental activity that fits in well with a transformational as opposed to a transactional leadership style.

Regrettably many managers claim they have no time to be ethical; that there is no time to reflect and deliberate as the hurly-burly speed of work life expects them to make speedy decisions that keep things moving. They sometimes argue that the organization does not want them to be ethical. They are expected to follow the company line and to execute according to standard operating procedures and rules. Some say that by the time they get home they are too tired and/or have other pressures waiting for them there. They claim that reflecting on the day's decisions or the ethical implications of certain actions requires more energy than they have available due to other calls on their attention.

A combination of humility and open-mindedness among managers provides the fertile ground needed for an ethical organization to grow and flourish. Without these dispositions, managers will not create that ethically vibrant organization that brings out the best performance of its managers or its employees.

As we shall see in our next chapters, where we discuss moral development, if managers do not extend themselves to become ethical managers, there is a direct impact on the organization's creative potential. An ethical mindset is one that is alive with questions; with new ideas; with the intention to stretch one's potential. Having ethical managers who direct the organization will result in enhanced creativity, a spirit alive with newness, diminished fear, and overall a more successful business.

## Exercise 2 – am I an ethical manager?

- Based on the discussions in this chapter, do you consider yourself an ethical manager?
- If yes – Can you provide an explicit example where you acted ethically?
- If no – What do you find as the greatest obstacle to ethical behavior?
- Does the organization you work for have an ethical or a moral culture?
- Can you think of an example where you have experienced the ethics-morality gap?

## The Volkswagen emission scandal

Martin Winterkorn, who took over as Volkswagen's CEO in 2007, planned to transform his company into the world's largest automaker by snatching first place from Toyota. Winterkorn saw the neglected US market as a path to success, though the company would need to triple its car sales in the US to meet its goal. Upping sales meant its engineers had to conjure up a near miracle – create powerful, fuel efficient diesel cars whose emissions passed the test of America's increasingly stringent pollution regulations.

Volkswagen had dismissed the idea of competing in the hybrid market, instead electing to build diesel cars, which held just 5% of the US auto market in 2007. Winterkorn believed that diesel promised high fuel efficiency without sacrificing power. However, diesel cars generate significantly more pollutants than gas-powered cars.

The company's leadership set aggressive goals. Former employees described a workplace in which they were bullied and feared contradicting their superiors. Failure was not tolerated. One senior executive bragged that he forced superior performance by "terrifying his engineers" and at times fired engineers or executives who displeased him. CEO Winterkorn didn't like bad news. "Before anyone reports to him, they make sure they have good news," said one industry analyst.

Volkswagen engineers solved the challenge by installing cheating software in cars exported to the US. The software would recognize when a car was being tested for emissions in a lab because only two of its four wheels were used. In these cases, emissions-controlling devices would be activated that would ensure the cars met US emission standards. On the road, where the defeat device automatically turned off, testing in some cases showed emissions 35 times higher than allowed.

In 2014 the defeat devices were discovered by researchers curious about why diesel technologies appeared cleaner in the US than in Europe. The fallout was enormous. Regulators across the world opened investigations and VW halted sales of its 2015 models. Between 2009 and 2015, 480,000 diesel vehicles that did not meet emission standards had been sold. Winterkorn resigned amidst claims that he did not know what was going on, senior managers were suspended or put on leave, and VW's stock plunged. One senior engineer, out of approximately 40 engineers involved, became the fall guy in the US and was given a seven-year prison sentence. At the time of writing, Winterkorn is being sued in both Germany and the US for "massive fraud."

What happened here? Do we see similar patterns as in the Wells Fargo saga? Our discussions in Chapters 1 and 2 provide some insights into how an ethical misdemeanor of this magnitude arose.

In the case of VW, there was of course the global pressure to increase sales and profits and gain market share. Winterkorn was "a win at all costs" leader. Autocratic leadership that reinforced a culture of fear inhibited people's sense of personal moral agency and integrity. People knew what was going on but colluded in silence. The bureaucratic nature of VW (the seventh largest company in the world in 2017, according to *Fortune* magazine, August 2018) led to a lack of accountability, fragmentation of responsibility and personal alienation. People were treated as mere means to ends and lost all sense of personal pride.

We may also remind ourselves of Saul Gellerman's rationalizations used for questionable moral conduct (see Chapter 2 – How to exterminate cockroaches), namely:

- believing the activity is not really illegal or immoral
- it is in the corporation's best interest
- the unethical activity will not be discovered
- because it helps the company, the company will condone it

Well, the rationalizations only worked for a while. Volkswagen is still paying the price of this huge fraud.

## Executive summary

This chapter began our more detailed discussions on the roots of ethics and morality. The emphasis here is no longer on the broader landscape of capitalism and the internal dynamics of organizations, but on the individual. It is in this chapter that we begin to explore our own ethical propensities by delving into the terms, ethics and morality.

This chapter emphasizes the essentiality of self-examination and reflection if we wish to be ethical people and desire to keep an inner compass that strives to honor our better selves.

Here are the key points:

- There is a difference between the concept ethics and that of morality. Ethics provides us with high-level rational principles or guidelines, while morality refers to our actions or behaviors.
- Frequently we experience an ethics-morality gap where our ethical intentions do not translate into action. There are of course reasons for this which we should explore through self-reflection as a basis for personal growth.

- If we are in any way suspect of unethical behaviors and we do not act in some way, we are bystanders. We are complicit.
- Being value driven does not mean we are ethical. Everyone lives by what they value.
- The root of ethics lies in self-examination and self-awareness.
- The path to happiness is attained by living a virtuous life and by paying attention to our soul through self-examination.
- Behaving ethically has intrinsic value.
- Moral relativism refers to the notion that there are no universal, objective principles of behavior that are context independent.
- It is only by practicing ethics that we can claim to be an ethical manager.

## Questions for reflection

- What role does self-examination play in your own reflections on your behaviors?
- Do you agree that ethics has intrinsic value, i.e., it is valuable for its own sake?
- What do you think of the moral relativism argument?
- What similarities do you see between the Wells Fargo saga and that of Volkswagen?

## Key terms

Courage   92
Character   93
Daimon   97
Deliberation   92
Entelechy   99
Eros – love   96
Ethical principles   92
Ethics – *Ethikos*   108
Ethics–morality gap   92
Eudaimonia   94
Forms   96
Good life   93
Goodness   97
Happiness   93
Justice   92

Moderation   93
Moral relativism   111
Moral philosophy   111
Reflection   106
Prudence – *Phronesis*   98
Reason   96
Romantic movement   96
Self-examination   92
Self-awareness   93
soul   93
Values   92
Virtue ethics   100
Virtue   94
Wisdom   96

## References

Arendt, Hannah. *Between the Past and the Future*. New York: Penguin Books, 2006.
Aristotle. *Nicomachean Ethics*. Cambridge, Massachusetts: Hackett Publishing Company, inc., 1999.

Copleston, Frederick. *A History of Philosophy*, Vol. 1. New York: Image, 1993.

Della Mirandola, Giovanni Pico. *Oration on the Dignity of Man*. Washington, DC: Regnery Publishing Inc., 1956 (originally 1486).

Epictetus. Interpreted by Sharon Lebell. *The Art of Living*. San Francisco, CA: HarperSanFranciso, 1995.

Grayling, Anthony Clifford *What is Good?* London, United Kingdom: Phoenix, 2003.

Hillman, James. *The Soul's Code: In Search of Character and Calling*. New York: Warner Books, 1996.

McCollough, Thomas E. *The Moral Imagination and Public Life*. NJ: Chatham House Publishers Inc.,1991.

Messerly, John G. *An Introduction to Ethical Theories*. Lanham, MD: University Press of America, 1995.

Moore, Thomas. *Care of the Soul*. New York: HarperCollins Publishers, 1992.

Pascal, Blaise, translator Honor Levi. *Pensees and Other Writings*. New York: Oxford University Press, 2008.

Plato. *The Collected Dialogues*. Edited by Edith Hamilton and Huntington Cairns. Bollingen Series LXXI. NJ: Princeton University Press, 1989.

Rokeach, Milton. *Understanding Human Values*. New York: The Free Press, 1979.

Russell, Bertrand. *The Conquest of Happiness*. New York: Liveright, 2013.

Tarnas, Richard. *The Passion of the Western Mind*. New York: Ballantine Books, 1991.

Thoreau, Henry David. *Walden* (1854). Reprint Createspace Independent Publishing Platform, 2018.

White, Thomas I. *Business Ethics: A Philosophical Reader*. New York: Macmillan Publishing Company, 1993.

Wilber, Ken. *Integral Psychology: Consciousness, Spirit, Psychology, Therapy*. Boston, Massachusetts: Shambhala, 2000.

Wordsworth, William. *Intimations of Immortality (1804), Selected Poetry of William Wordsworth*. New York: The Modern Library, 2002.

# 4 Ethics and moral development

## Contents

## Ethics in action

Imagine you have just been hired into a new job. You are relieved as you have been out of work for six depressing months. The job is not exactly what you wanted but is good enough and will help pay the bills. You know you sold yourself well at the interview and that you have quite a bit of work to do to get up to snuff on the computer systems that you led your interviewers to believe you have mastered. You find yourself putting in some late hours and some weekend time to gain that mastery.

One Saturday afternoon, as you are sitting at your desk, working on your computer, you hear your boss enter his office next door. Other than the two of you, you are reasonably certain that the building, or at least your floor, is empty. You do not know whether your boss is aware that you are there. You hear him make a phone call. Without other people around it seems the walls are paper thin. You do not intend to listen; however, you cannot help but overhear him talking to what seems like a customer. It sounds as if your boss is agreeing to the delivery of some of the firm's products directly to a port – you are not sure which one. It sounds like Boston. You then hear some discussion about payment, and you realize that your boss is having the payment transferred directly into his personal account. You hear him spell his name and give the account details of some bank in the Cayman Islands. He thanks the person on the other side of the phone and says cheerfully "I think we have a good thing going here. Good to do business with you!" You are shattered. Surely you misheard . . . there must be some mistake. Fearful that your boss will find out that you are there, you tiptoe out of your office and flee down the rear fire escape.

## Drat those moral dilemmas!

Many moral dilemmas land in our laps quite unexpectedly. We were just minding our own business, doing our work, keeping our nose clean, when wham, we are suddenly plunged in the middle of a nasty or unfortunate situation. Drat!!! We did not ask for this trouble or inconvenience, yet for some reason there it is, and now we must respond in one way or another. Why can't life be simple?

### Inconvenient

Besides the element of surprise, many moral dilemmas arrive at the most inconvenient time. They occur just as we think we are getting on top of things or when we are getting ourselves organized. In the case above, you are just getting settled into a new job and gaining some credibility with your boss. Now, you are placed in a quandary. Did you really hear what you thought you heard?

Was it truly nefarious or did you miss something important that would explain everything?

### Out of our comfort zone

Moral dilemmas frequently place us in a situation we have not experienced before. They take us out of our comfort zone and challenge us in uncomfortable ways that can cause confusion and a sense of vulnerability.

The twist in this case is that you overheard something and did not make your presence known. Did your boss know you were there? It would seem not. But maybe he did. How are you going to find out? You can hardly ask him and then explain that you ran away. Oh, why did you flee down the fire escape? Why did you not saunter into his office or better still stay quietly at your desk? What were you afraid of? It is all so complicated now.

### Time is a factor

With many moral dilemmas time is a factor. You only have so long to react or the dilemma will take a course of its own. In this case the time pressure is on as to whether you tell someone, confront your boss or decide to do nothing. If you leave any response too long, and something was amiss in the transaction you overheard, might you be considered as someone complicit with the dark deed?

### Many stakeholders

Moral dilemmas always impact more stakeholders than one first realizes. It is also likely that several of these stakeholders have competing interests. If competing interests exist, this adds further complexity to the dilemma in question.

Taking the case cited above, the stakeholders affected in this case include you, your boss, the management team, members of the firm, the customer and members of his or her firm, the shareholders, possibly your family, the boss's family . . . and so on. If one carried out a detailed analysis it would be surprising to see how many people would be affected by, what seems on the face of it, a simple case.

### Dilemmas versus problems

Solutions to moral dilemmas are rarely clear cut. That is why they are referred to as dilemmas and not problems. Problems can be solved. With dilemmas at best one can optimize a result given many trade-offs. Invariably there are compromises.

In the case of the overheard telephone call, what are you going to do? Do you confront your boss? What if there is an explanation and you end up accusing him falsely or even insinuating something untoward? What if your boss fires you on the spot for eavesdropping? You will be back to pounding the pavement again. How will you explain why you were in the office and did not say hello to him? Why did you not make your presence known? You could have pretended you heard nothing. How would he know? Can he pick up that you know? Surely you can conceal it. What will you gain if you make an issue of this? Do you go to human resources? Do you slip an anonymous note under the CEO's door saying that an investigation should be made into deliveries to the Boston port? Or, do you letting sleeping dogs lie? Maybe you misheard and there really is an explanation and you should just get on with your job. You need it. Your family needs it. Just keep quiet. If you work after hours in the office again you will have music playing so that anyone else will know you are there. This was a one off – no big deal.

## Exercise 1 – Ethics in action

Referring to the case above:

- What do you feel obliged to do?
- Why are you going to do what you are going to do? What are your reasons?
- What guiding principle, rule, law, convention is behind your choice of action?
- What strategies are you going to adopt to voice your concerns?

## Moral development

Lawrence Kohlberg (1927–1987), a Harvard psychologist, was inspired by the ground-breaking work of the Swiss psychologist, Jean Piaget (1896–1980), who wrote the extremely influential book, *The Moral Judgment of the Child* (1997).

Kohlberg, considered the leading pioneer in moral development, carried out extensive research into the way people reason about what is right or wrong. He observed that as people mature, they move up higher levels of complexity in their deliberating process. Their progression reflects an increasing understanding of the concept of morality and, in some (far less common) cases, this evolves into a capacity to engage in ethical reasoning.

As we discussed in the previous chapter, ethical reasoning differs from moral behavior. Kohlberg's stages illustrate this by showing how engaging in ethical reasoning reflects a higher degree of moral development than simply responding morally or what he calls, reasoning at the conventional stage (Kohlberg, 1981).

As a result of years of research, where he investigated thousands of interviewees, Kohlberg observed how most people move from stages of total self-interest, to the appreciation of the existence of others, and then to acknowledgment of the demands of society that requires conformity to its moral values and norms. He found that some people, however, move beyond these stages to greater independence of mind where they have the potential for questioning, and challenging on ethical grounds, the validity and appropriateness of the norms, customs and laws of society. At these later stages, people are also less dependent on others for approval and acceptance, and care instead, that they are self-defining. Part of their self-definition is their ability to be more principled decision-makers.

Below is a summary of Kohlberg's findings. He concluded that three levels and six stages sum up a person's potential moral development as they grow-up and evolve to greater maturity. There is, however, no guarantee that every person will progress through all these stages. As we will also see, progression does not mean that we do not at times regress to lower stages. While Kohlberg provides some age guidelines in his schema, these do not necessarily hold, as we shall discuss.

## Kohlberg's stages of moral development

### Level one – pre-conventional stages – it is all about me!

In these stages the child is focused on him or herself and everything is based on self-interest.

Stage 1 – very young child

Obey or pay
Authority prevails – fear of punishment

Reasons for behavior are essentially to avoid punishment or hearing the word "no!" Fear of authority is paramount.

Stage 2 – slightly older child

Self-satisfaction
What's in it for me?

Reasons for behavior are expanded to include deferring to others' needs as part of strategy of getting one's own needs met.

### Level two – conventional stages – how do I fit in with others?

In these stages, the child begins to recognize the needs of others, the importance of conforming and belonging to a group, and the need for rules of social order and reciprocity.

Stage 3 – moving into teen years

Approval – meeting group norms
Loyalty – the need to belong

In this stage, the person has a limited appreciation of situations as viewed by others and assumes that everyone has a similar outlook. Approval from the group (family or peer group), is seen as essential, regardless of the consequences. The individual readily subordinates his or her own needs to that of the group.

Stage 4 – teenager onwards

Law and order
Duty to society

At this stage, the person understands that there is a social system that requires norms to ensure harmony and safety. These norms define roles and obligations that require respect and adherence. Lack of conformance has consequences, usually negative ones, such as punishment, non-approval or non-acceptance. It is at this stage that moral conventions and norms become ingrained.

### *Level three – post-conventional stages – becoming an ethical person*

At this level the person has moved beyond conformance and has internalized certain values and ethical principles that guide his or her life. These principles are universally acceptable and well-tested. Here the person does not simply accept group norms or moral rules and customs without questioning. He or she continuously inquires as to whether certain norms, rules and even laws advance flourishing of life and well-being. The person is concerned with whether the accepted norms or conventions uphold justice and compassion and whether they are relevant to current realities. This is the level at which the person moves towards becoming an ethical person as opposed to simply a moral person. People who have reached this stage ask questions about what is good or bad, right or wrong, regardless of outside or external pressures. They are concerned with making principled decisions from a place of inner freedom.

Stage 5 – adulthood

Standards of society – uphold and add to these standards
Social contract – recognition that things evolve, change, and require taking a higher perspective

A person at stage 5 recognizes that there are conflicting views and opinions, and that to uphold society in a fair manner requires consideration, adjustment and due process. He or she understands that a democratic society is based on a social contract and that toleration within limits should always be considered. He or she is still somewhat guided by the norms set by society even when these maybe in transition.

Stage 6 – mature adulthood

Decisions of conscience
Application of logical ethical principles

A person who reaches stage 6, lives their life according to well defined ethical principles. These principles refer to justice, society's welfare, human rights, and respect for the dignity of individual human beings. The stage 6 person uses these principles as a filter and guide for decision-making. The stage 6 person is not inhibited by the pressure of society or conventions.

### *Cognitive emphasis*

An important aspect of Kohlberg's moral development schema is that his focus lay on the reasoning process behind the resolution of moral dilemmas. In other

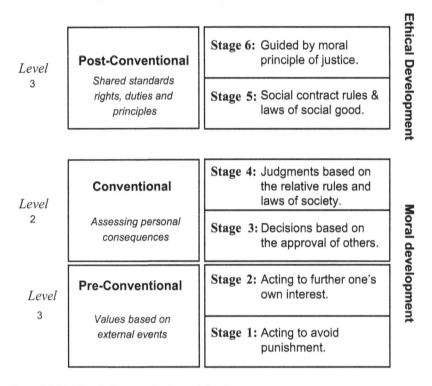

*Figure 4.1* Kohlberg's framework of moral development

Source: Down the right-hand side should read Level 3 – Ethical Development

words, moral development for him was determined by "why" people did what they did rather than what it is they actually did. From an overall ethics perspective, note that we are concerned with both the motivation (the why or the justification process), and the action itself.

Kohlberg's schema did not incorporate a discussion of the role of emotions, biases, previous experience or developed habits. Despite this limitation, his schema is useful when exploring people's rational justification for what they claim they would or did do (Figure 4.1).

### Testing Kohlberg

During the ethics bootcamps I have hosted for well over a decade, participants have an opportunity to discuss and debate many case studies. Of course, what people say they will do in a seminar setting, or when asked by others, may differ enormously from what they really will do in real life. One could thus challenge Kohlberg's methodology by saying that it does not capture the real-life situation.

Frequently, people are prompted by the seminar case to offer up a real-life example that they have in fact experienced. In those instances, we gain a better insight as to what level they really operate at. Either way, I have found that Kohlberg's schema can be helpful for discussions.

Another challenge to Kohlberg is that his schema is built on the "why" or the justification of our moral decisions. As we know we mostly reason after the fact. We tend to respond to events intuitively or emotionally, and then justify our actions in hindsight. So our real motivation at the time of action is not necessarily what our rational explanation makes of it. Some people argue that this makes Kohlberg's approach less valuable.

In Chapter 10, I discuss how our tendency to react with little or no space between stimulus and response can negatively impact our moral behavior and how Mindfulness can slow us down and thus improve our moral reasoning.

Another issue that people challenge with respect to Kohlberg's approach is that he assigned age groups to each stage of moral development. These are intended merely to act as indicators. As we look at our own moral behavior, we soon see that our justifications can vary widely – no matter what our age. Many mature adults operate frequently at stage 1 or 2 (recall The Jet is Ready case or the Wells Fargo saga.). What we also learn is that we are inconsistent. Depending on the type of dilemma and its emotional impact, we line up our moral ducks differently.

James Rest, former Research Director of the Center for the Study of Ethical Development, did some interesting work on the impact of the moral intensity of a dilemma and people's responses on the Kohlberg scale. In brief, his findings concluded that the higher the intensity, i.e., the emotional impact of a dilemma, the lower the stage from which people reasoned. Clearly emotional triggers play a key role in influencing people's justification for their actions and their consequent behavior. It is very difficult for most of us to take the moral high road when we fear imminent "death," the loss of our livelihood, or the intense disapproval or condemnation by a group.

While Kohlberg's schema is somewhat dated, it remains the most well-known framework for looking at moral development. Over the years, many researchers have challenged some of Kohlberg's methods and his results. Overall their findings have not proved to vary from his with any significance.[1] Interestingly, even cross-culturally his schema stands up to most research studies.

### Emotions in decision-making

In his book, *Descartes' Error: Emotion, Reason and the Human Brain* (first published in 1994), neuroscientist Antonio Damasio, describes one of his patients, Elliot, who had suffered damage to his ventromedial frontal lobe as a result of a tumor and the subsequent surgery for its removal.

Elliot had been a successful businessman, model father and husband. However, following his operation Elliot claimed that his life was falling apart. It became clear to Damasio that due to his surgery, Elliot had become totally dispassionate and was no longer capable of making decisions, especially when the decision involved personal or social matters. Even small decisions were fraught with endless deliberation: Making an appointment took 30 minutes, choosing where to eat lunch took all afternoon, even deciding which color pen to use to fill out a form was a chore. It turned out that Elliott's total lack of emotion paralyzed his decision-making capabilities.

In a later edition of *Descartes Error*, Damasio wrote that the general public still regards emotions as irrational impulses that tend to lead us astray. "When we describe someone as 'emotional,' it is usually a criticism suggesting poor judgment" (Damasio, 1994). Although neuroscience has built a strong body of evidence to demonstrate the direct link between reason, emotion and decision-making, most of mainstream culture still doesn't get it, he claims.

I concur in that in my experience many managers are still trained to keep emotion out of decision-making and are told that professionals leave their feelings at home when they are at work. Women frequently come under the hammer for being "emotional" as opposed to rational.

In his compelling book, *How We Decide* (2009), Jonah Lehrer makes the case that rationality depends on emotion. Motivation is driven by feeling, not intellect. Lehrer points out, "Emotion and motivation share the same Latin root, *movere*, which means to move. The world is full of things and it is our feelings that help us choose among them."

Our prevailing misconceptions about how the brain works keep us mired in obsolete ideas about the decision-making process. Many of us try to rule out the emotional side of decision-making only to find we become stuck in so-called analysis-paralysis. We often avoid making decisions or make them hastily because we want to skip the feeling part, which is not only unavoidable, it's short-sighted. The idea is not to exclude our emotions that may seem to pull us in the opposite direction, but to integrate them with our rationality, as Plato said, in a harmonious balance.

## Exercise 2 – Stage of moral development

If we return to the opening case on overhearing your boss, what are you going to do? Why are you going to do what you are going to do? What are the emotional factors at play and how are you going to rationalize them? Once you have thought this through, consider where you would place yourself according to Kohlberg's Stages of Moral Development.

## Ethics and morality again

Kohlberg's levels and stages further illuminate the difference between ethics and morality. His first two levels deal with a person's early learning and decision-making processes. As we saw, this begins with a totally self-centered view that over time evolves to one where there is recognition of others and a concern to adhere and conform to conventions. We can also see why Level Two is referred to as conventional morality as at this level we are cognizant of what it means to be moral, i.e., we have learned what society expects of us. It is important to note that at Levels One and Two, emotion such as fear of authority or fear of not being part of the in-crowd plays a significant part in moral motivation. When we operate at this level the "please disease" has us in its grip. (The please-disease is shorthand for a compulsion to act in a manner that is pleasing to others.)

At Level Three, the person moves "beyond morality." Here internalized principles anchor and guide the person's life. These internalized principles form the person's moral compass and shape his or her ethical sensitivity and conscience.

At Level Three, the person is inclined to apply his or her principles more consistently. At the earlier stages, this is less likely to be the case. It is at this Post-Conventional Level, too, that a person is also more likely to manage his or her emotions more carefully so that they are not the sole driving force behind actions. This is the level where people find a balance between reason and emotion (remember Plato), and can think and act ethically.

Many of us are of course interested to know which stages we reason from. In doing so there are several important things to note. As mentioned, the first is that many of us reason from a different stage depending upon the moral intensity factor. If we fear harm, bodily or otherwise, we will most likely respond from stage 1: fear. If we are deciding on how to fire someone at work, we will likely be guided by the law; stage 4. There will also be times when we might go beyond our normal moral duties and challenge and question a custom or convention. We might decide to operate outside of norms and insist on creating our own. Provided our arguments are logical and reasonable, and based on accepted universal principles, this would place us at stage 5 or even possibly at stage 6.

Based on Kohlberg's research, only a small percentage of people reason frequently from stage 5 (less than 15%), and an even smaller percentage from stage 6 (less than 5%). Reasoning from stage 6 is supposedly role modeled for us by Socrates, Jesus, Buddha, Martin Luther, and Gandhi and possibly someone like an Abraham Lincoln. I am not sure who I dare cite as a corporate leader in this category. Even the renowned Warren Buffett of Berkshire Hathaway, known for his independence, detachment and refusal to be co-opted or recruited by others, has had a few ethical blunders. Well, he is human too. Few, of us reach the stage where, like Sir Thomas More, we would rather succumb to death in the Tower of London, than violate our highly held principles.

From an organizational perspective, the low percentage of people who demonstrate ethical thinking presents an alarming picture. Organizations need ethical managers who are reflective, questioning and strive to be consistently principled. They need managers who will keep asking questions and who will move ethical behavior forward. They really need managers who strive not to be engulfed by the excesses that capitalism may offer, or the cockroach-like behavior possible in the unswept corners of the corporate culture.

If less than one in five people, on average, reason at Level Three, how can we be sure that our leaders and managers are some of these people? One possibility is that leaders and managers are hired because of their character and commitment to personal and organizational development. Another is to ensure that the corporate culture promotes and rewards ethical thinking and practicing ethics. More on both these points later.

## Behavioral ethics

Over the last decade a new field of ethics has emerged called Behavioral Ethics (BE). This subset discipline consists of an eclectic collection of psychological research topics. Its area of study is how people actually behave when confronted with ethical dilemmas. Study results are compared with generally accepted conventions or behavioral norms, i.e., it studies morality.

As we discussed above, research in BE finds that people are far from completely rational. Most ethical choices are made intuitively, by feeling, and not after having carefully analyzed the situation. Usually, people who make unethical decisions are unconsciously influenced by internal biases, like the self-serving bias, and by situational factors that they do not even notice. Many of the research findings confirm some of the other topics we have discussed, such as the power of the corporate culture, the pressure of groups, the impact of authority, feelings of self-alienation, the ethical tone of the organization, reward systems, and peer pressure.

An interesting aspect of the BE work is their investigation into cultural factors and how these play a role in moral behavior. Factors such as collectivism, moral identity and cultural biases are explored.

The key point that BE makes is that emotions and feelings play a large role in decision-making and that context is everything!

## Feminist ethics

Before we leave the Moral Stages of Development a further word on Kohlberg is essential.

Another Harvard psychologist, Carol Gilligan, challenged Kohlberg's research methodology and choice of research samples. She claimed that the emphasis both in the research and the samples used by Kohlberg was extremely male oriented and ignored the feminine approach to morality. Gilligan's issue with Kohlberg's conclusions was that it placed feminine moral reasoning lower on the scale than male reasoning (Gilligan, 1993).

The consequent debate she fostered resulted in an entire movement of psychologists, ethicists and social theorists engaged in attempting to distinguish male oriented from female oriented ethics. The debate centered on the male rational-impartial-justice approach to morality versus the female-relational-subjective-care-oriented approach to morality. We will not debate this matter here. Suffice it to say, that more recently, the debate has lost steam and that research results with samples of only women or that include both genders do not provide clear evidence that women reason distinctly different than men.

## My conscience is my guide

> *Thus conscience does make cowards of us all.*
>
> (Shakespeare, Hamlet 3:1)

I can think of no greater example of reflection on one's conscience than that of Hamlet, the beleaguered Prince of Denmark.

> *To be, or not to be, that is the question:*
> *Whether 'tis nobler in the mind to suffer*
> *The slings and arrows of outrageous fortune,*
> *Or to take arms against a sea of troubles*
> *And by opposing end them.*

In this famous soliloquy, Hamlet elegantly sets before us the ethics–morality gap that we have discussed and our struggles to take moral action or "arms against a sea of troubles" which frequently cost us dearly. Living a principled life – stage 6, where a well-developed conscience is truly our guide – is certainly not for the faint-hearted. In Hamlet's case, he is so fearful of following his conscience and the consequences of doing so, that he is contemplating suicide as an alternative!

It is also interesting to note that Hamlet does not say: "To do, or not to do?" He talks about being; "to be or not to be?" This ethical question concerns one's entire being; one's character. It is not simply a one-off action.

As we contemplate our own ethics – and more will become clear in Chapter 6 – the question of being as opposed to doing, is a significant one. Hamlet points towards the end of his ruminations the following:

> *Thus conscience does make cowards of us all,*
> *And thus the native hue of resolution*
> *Is sicklied o'er with the pale cast of thought,*
> *And enterprises of great pitch and moment*
> *With this regard their currents turn awry*
> *And lose the name of action.*

What Hamlet is now stressing is how our thoughts and doubts derail even our best and most energetic intentions by "turning their currents," i.e., diverting their momentum, and thereby resulting in a failure of the desired action. Our conscience tells us one thing, yet our actions reflect another.

### The impartial spectator

What in fact is a conscience? For some people, the voice of conscience is that of God or Allah or Yahweh. For others it arises as a prickle or a prodding. Some mention the sleep test, i.e., a bad conscience interferes with our sleep. Immanuel Kant held that our conscience was the moral law written on our hearts and recognizable through our faculty of reason. Others refer to their loyalties, duties, relationships or fidelity. According to the Scottish moralist and free market advocate, Adam Smith, our conscience calls us to love what is honorable and noble and reminds us of the dignity and superiority of our own characters (Smith, 1817, p. 180).

Whatever its formation, ideally our conscience should act as an impartial and well-informed spectator of our deliberations and actions. It is the judge within that challenges us to avoid inward disgrace, often expressed as "I could not live with myself." At the end of the day, we each must live with our own conscience that answers to our highest calling. And here we are again challenged as to whether our highest calling is at stages 3 or 4 or stages 5 and 6.

### Developing one's conscience

> *A conscience wise and steady,*
> *And forever ready;*
> *Not changing with events,*
> *Dealing in compliments . . .*

Henry David Thoreau (Cooke, 1970)

The development of our conscience is quite a complex matter. Over the years, it is shaped not only by our upbringing, values, beliefs and related group norms, but by our habits and experiences. Etched in our memories are lessons of either our own actions or those of others, that brought either praise or opprobrium. As we reflect on our conscience, we might find that it is frequently more influenced by a desire for praise and our deep aversion for blame than we realize or care to admit. Guilt (stage 1), a need to be considered praiseworthy or loyal (stage 3), or the desire to be deemed someone of merit (stage 2), impacts the higher ideals of the supposed impartial spectator. Developing a sound and wise conscience takes a lifetime of ethical work.

Ethical people ask whether their conscience serves as a reliable guide. They question whether they regularly extract their conscience from its "mental cupboard," look at it, shake it up a bit and refresh it. They question whether it is an informed conscience. They spend time reflecting on their moral dilemmas and how these were addressed, and the role conscience may have played.

A conscience is only as good as it is an alive, questioning presence in our life. If it has been mentally shelved as a container having all the answers, simply to be pulled out when needed, it is hardly one that assists the ethical life. As such it is simply a moribund faculty that frightens us into decisions to free us from moral guilt. This places us at Kohlberg's stage 1! If on the other hand our conscience is continually tested and ever evolving, then it might be instrumental in helping us to move towards stage 5 or even stage 6 in Kohlberg's schema. If our conscience is acute enough and attuned enough, it will not allow us to fall into lethargy or indifference by simply complying with expected norms and conventions. A well-developed conscience is grounded in sound ethical principles which have

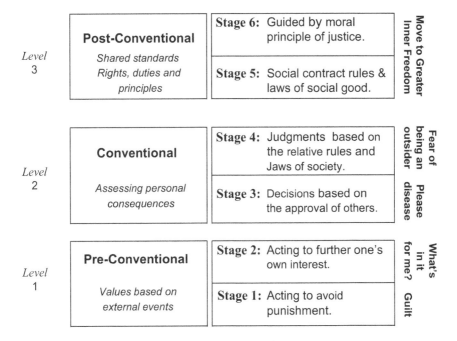

*Figure 4.2*

been tried and tested and anchor the person's ethical disposition. It has a great capacity for reasoning and reflection and stimulates inner moral courage. Having a grounded, principled conscience is a great gift to oneself and everyone else.

Developing our conscience needs to be an intentional activity. It does not develop on its own. It requires personal attention and time. It requires regular exercise. It needs to be challenged and stretched. Business managers are expected to exhibit and role model actions that reflect their own thoughtful and developed consciences. If the organization's managers do not take responsibility for the organization's conscience – who will? (Figure 4.2)

### Does, or should, a corporation have a conscience?

This question has been debated for decades. Some people argue positively saying corporations are units and as agents of society should behave morally. Others counter that people should be moral, but corporations are artificial persons and therefore it is inappropriate to expect moral behavior from them.

Those who argue in favor of corporate morality claim it should have moral sensitivity built into its management system and the corporation should demonstrate justice, care, honesty, transparency and duty just as people should. Just as people hold regimes accountable, such as the Nazi regime, and governments accountable, so should corporations be accountable. What do you think?

A big question this raises and to which we now turn is: Who or what is the corporation?

## Narcissism and the pathological corporation

### *Who is the corporation?*

Since time immemorial, humans have ascribed human characteristics to most everything they see or conceive of. The need to anthropomorphize (personify) helps us place all phenomena on the human plane. It is a way of cognizing the world. Since nothing is more important to us than ourselves and other human beings, it is not surprising that we fit the world into diverse human templates. We make the non-human world, humanlike. We select human-like models in order to understand experience. In this vein, our gods have human attributes. They are moody, capricious, loving and vengeful. We fill the night sky with human characters. We hear thunder as the voice of God. The flowering fields represent the fertility of Mother Earth, trees resemble our outstretched arms, and our motor vehicles are referred to as "she."

Our tendency to anthropomorphize extends to the institutions we have created to regulate our lives. There is Mother Church or the Mother Ship, the IRS as Uncle Sam, the Government as Big Brother and then of course business organizations as "The Corporation." The business corporation has even been enshrined as a separate *body* in the law. In the law's eyes, it is a legal *person* with rights, powers and responsibilities apart from the people who own and run the business.

Joel Balkan's *The Corporation* (2005) discusses how we project our psychological and emotional states into the corporation as a created being. As such, Balkan claims, The Corporation exhibits pathological behavior! It is self-interested, irresponsible, manipulative, grandiose, lacking in empathy with asocial tenden cies, does not concern itself with its victims, refuses to accept responsibility for its own actions, is unable to feel remorse, and displays unfailing arrogance.

What an awful indictment of The Corporation's character! Especially public corporations, Balkan claims, display these traits in abundance.

But who is The Corporation? What kind of being is this exactly and who gave it such incredible powers? What does it say about those who did?

We all know that The Corporation is the sum of all the individuals who own, manage, and participate in its organization. It is the combination of all individual and group energies, activities, and behaviors. Every individual without qualification partakes in its actions. Yet, we assign The Corporation a life of its own – How does this work?

## Thanks to the corporation

* The Company is paying for lunch today.
* The Company does not pay for overtime.
* I took one for the Company.

- The Company will deal with it.
- This Company makes me sick.
- The Company is doing well.
- Blame the Company!

---

## Flashpoint 4.1 – corporation as independent entity

In the US, corporations are deemed separate legal entities who may –

- Own property
- Contract with third parties
- Have the right to free speech
- May financially support political campaigns
- May initiate legal proceedings against others and defend their own actions as a corporation
- Can be held to moral account for their actions and pay a fine

---

## Flashpoint 4.2 – US corporate lobbying expenditures aimed at increasing corporations' power 2017–2018

| | | |
|---|---|---|
| Alphabet – parent of Google | $39.3 m | |
| Amazon | $27.4 m | |
| Facebook | $24.1 m | |
| Oracle | $20.1 m | |
| Microsoft | $18.3 m | |
| Qualcomm | $16.3 m | |
| Apple | $13.8 m | |
| Entertainment Software Association | $11.8 m | |
| IBM | $10.1 m | |
| Sub-total | $181.2 m | 82% |
| Total Spend all Companies 2018 | $221 m | 100%$ |
| Oil and gas companies | $125 m | |

**Source:** *Fortune* **Magazine, March 1, 2019**

**My Comment:** Total spend of US $346 million (221m + 125 m) divided by an average annual salary of $45,000 is equivalent to 7,690 jobs.

---

The Corporation is another example of our anthropomorphizing tendencies. The downside of this tendency lies in our disassociating from our responsibilities for its actions, especially the moral ones. It enables us to refer to The

Corporation as something that is other than us. "I only work here," is a common defense. But, at heart we know we are The Corporation. We are IT. We are implicated. We collude consciously and unconsciously. The Corporation is US.

### Hooked by our narcissism

In his book, *Narcissistic Process and Corporate Decay*, (1990) Howard Schwartz argues that peoples' narcissistic tendencies lead them to project their need for an *ego ideal* onto an organization resulting in often, seriously unwholesome consequences.

Using Freud as a basis for his thesis, Swartz explains the origin of narcissism and the concept of the *ego ideal*. According to Freud, our narcissistic tendencies are fostered in early infanthood when we find ourselves at the center of a loving world, where we are loved and protected. As we grow older, we find out that the world is not a loving place and that none of us are at the center of it. We find that we are never quite loved enough, we cannot be totally protected, and we come to realize our mortality. Our escape from this sobering reality is to create or find an *ego ideal*. From the Kohlberg perspective, this would be stage 1 behavior.

The Freudian term *ego ideal* represents an imagined image of ourselves if we could get rid of all things that cause us anxiety especially our feelings of being unloved, vulnerable and anxious about our mortality. Our defense against these depressing feelings is to attribute our anxiety to a person, or a place, or a group and we direct our aggression at this "bad stuff." We endeavor to create an image for ourselves of a "good world" devoid of this bad stuff.

This good world, reminiscent of early childhood, provides us with the possibility of returning to a state of narcissism. In this good world we can do whatever we want to do. The world has us as its reason for being. Everyone loves us, and we are free from all anxiety. Our anxiety drives us to pursue this *ego ideal* which involves rejecting who we are and how we really feel. Herein lies the key moral issue as we shall see.

### Ego ideal formation

Schwartz focuses on the case where the organization functions as the *ego ideal*. This dynamic he names as the *organizational ideal*. He explains how the creation of the *organizational ideal* provides an attempt to return to narcissism.

The organization as the ego ideal is the employee's projected idea of the organization. According to him or her, this is what the organization is supposed to be and would be except for the influence of the "bad stuff" in the world. The employee becomes committed to bringing about his or her ideas of what the organization should be. He or she assumes that others in the organization share the same interests and obligations to create this "perfect" idea of the organization. This assumed sharing eliminates conflict and along with it, all social anxiety. Schwartz draws the analogy to the tale of Narcissus, who falls in love with his own image in the pond. When the organization represents the ego ideal, the organization mirrors back the participant's love for the perfect image of him or herself.

Individuals who define themselves in terms of the organization, put themselves into an interesting relationship with others who have done the same. It becomes a relationship of idealized love and mutual responsibility to uphold the organizational ideal for others. In this situation, the organization's injunctions represent the ethical standard and individuals' relationships with one another is sanctioned by their mutual need to maintain their projected ideal. The consequence of these processes is that the individual rejects his or her spontaneous self and what he or she personally stands for in order to quell any anxiety that arises. Since anxiety can never be totally alleviated, her or she keeps striving and further denying his or her true self. Here you can think of the "company man or woman." Think also of our discussions of the organization as a container of fear in Chapter 2.

*Organizational totalitarianism*

Schwartz explains how this whole dynamic becomes a problem. The projection of the *organizational ideal* degenerates into organizational totalitarianism based on organizational power. Organizations have power over participating individuals. This power is entrenched through various layers of bureaucratic hierarchy. (We discussed this is Chapter 2). The more status one has in the hierarchy, the greater the perceived progress in the return to narcissism. The higher up the individual is on the corporate ladder, the more his or her actions are deemed the corporation's actions. Progress in the hierarchy is not only progress in the attainment of the organizational ideal for the individual but is considered progress for others as well.

Organizational totalitarianism, typical of corporate life, occurs where those in power can narcissistically impose their fantasy of their own perfection upon others as the organizational ideal. For the individual, acquiescing to the perfection of those in power becomes a moral obligation collectively enforced by others who have done so and with whom the individual defines him or herself. In turn, the powerful feel self-righteous believing they are of service to the community – which in a bizarre sense they are!

*The moral consequences of organizational totalitarianism*

The creation of the organizational ideal and the self-abandonment of the individual to the power of those higher up the hierarchy results in interesting moral consequences (individuals regress to Kohlberg's stage 1). The head of the organization specifies the *organizational ideal* and serves as the definer of reality. The subordinate is pressurized to see the world in the way that enhances the self-image of the leader rather than his or her own. He or she experiences uncertainty regarding which actions will correspond to the leader's whims and which will be morally acceptable since the leader defines what is morally worthwhile. As a result, the employee surrenders his or her own moral agency. (Eyes rolling and eyebrow raised "That's what the boss wants! Gotta keep him happy!")

What we find in this isolating world is not people engaged with one another, but roles in performance with one another. The bureaucratic power of the organization influences the individual's moral orientation to the world, essentially along the lines of Kohlberg's stages 1–3. The organization forms its own moral community based on its commitment to upholding the *organizational ideal*. Here we see the power of culture and its ability to silence, subdue and infantilize employees. For the individual to remain comfortably within the system, he or she must derive his or her identity from the organization. Any threat to the organization's existence is immediately personalized as a threat to the individual's existence. Defense of the organization equates with self-defense. The individual who is no longer the center of the world has placed the organization at the center of his or her world.

To those of you who might think that Schwartz and all this psychobabble is far-fetched, think of your organization and any other institution to which you might belong. Think of the hats, hoodies, uniforms and emblems employees are given as signs that "they belong!" This is "their company for them." Think of the company barbeques and parties that are intended to build community – and they do – by reinforcing the collusion and the power of the organization with which employees identify and give allegiance. Think of those people who don't show up and how they are questioned and even shunned. Think of the tickets to the baseball or soccer games or golf tournaments. All intended to solidify allegiance to the caring, understanding company. Care for the company and it may care for you. It is still the best bet in town.

For those who have read some of the plentiful literature inspired by the corporate scandals, you will be reminded of the themes of narcissism, organizational totalitarianism, self-abandonment and self-alienation that literally leap out of the pages.

This might be a good time to pause and to consider how we might project our ego ideal onto our organization: my company, our church, our baseball team, my not-for-profit. To what extent do we define ourselves by our organization? Who defines our moral reality for us? And those of us in positions of authority, what fantasies of our own perfection do we impose on others? Sobering considerations . . .

---

**Flashpoint 4.3**

Extract from *Financial Times*, February 23, 2019

The UK Serious Fraud Office (SFO) has closed investigations into Rolls Royce and GlaxoSmithKline, underlining "the agency's struggle to prosecute individuals whose companies have been linked to criminal activity." Some of the challenges lie with the awarding of DPAs.

Deferred Prosecution Agreements (DPAs) are a form of corporate plea bargain reached when a business that has uncovered bribery, fraud and other forms of financial crime among its employees and "self-reports" these crimes thereby agreeing to certain sanctions but avoiding prosecution.

My comment: So The Corporation pays the penalty and the employees get off scot free! What a wonderful way to be taken care of. No personal consequences!

*Moral justifying*

Our tendencies to anthropomorphize The Corporation, thus distancing ourselves from our role in its identity, plus our own narcissistic tendencies, provides a veritable set-up for moral irresponsibility. Added to this, often we succumb to the moral directives of our leaders or those in authority, believing them to be more competent and credible than we are. In no time, we accept the organization's moral culture as the norm of our world. ("That's how it works here!" . . . shrug . . .) If we don't fit in, we are soon ostracized, possibly encouraged to go or flee of our own accord.

We can look at Lay, Skilling, Fastow, Scrushy, Kozlowski, Ebbers, Winterkorn and hundreds of others who have abused their stewardship responsibilities regarding corporate resources with little if any guilt all done in the name of the organization. And stunningly, thousands of people colluded. The few whistleblowers, who found the courage to squeal, were soon evicted. More on that in the next chapter.

## Why good people do bad things

### *Personal reflection – a shadow tale*

For a period of five years, I worked with a most competent and dedicated CEO, let's call him Michael. Michael arrived at work at 5 a.m. daily and rarely left much before 7 p.m. He was a versatile CEO who was adept at finding new sources of finance and developing new programs for the organization that were invariably hugely successful. He was thoughtful about all projects and ensured they returned a satisfactory ROI. He was also always looking for ways to cut expenditures and improve the bottom line.

Besides his strategic touch and his careful money management, this same CEO was very caring of the employees. He paid them well and was always looking for opportunities to give them bonuses. On top of this amazing personality profile, he also had a wonderful sense of humor and could have people in stitches of laughter.

One day, while talking with the human resource director, I noticed she was very distracted. I asked her whether there was anything on her mind that she would like to share. After several minutes hesitation she got up, closed the door and sat down close to me adopting a confidential stance.

"I don't understand why Michael does it," she said. He earns well over $1 million a year and that does not include the benefits, but he cheats on his vacation leave and sick time." She then proceeded to explain to me that this intelligent, devoted, CEO would come in during the weekends, usually a Sunday, and alter the sheets that recorded any of his vacation or sick time. He would literally scrub out the entries and return them to zero so that he could get paid out these extra days at the end of the year. "Beats me!" she said.

> I have been wanting to talk to him about it for years but have not had the courage. It has been going on for as long as I have been here which is well

over fifteen years. Jack, the CFO knows about it too, but we have kept mum as his anger can be exceedingly unpleasant.

Why do people do things like that? Why does the politician denounce gay rights when he is gay himself? Why do people – your and my devoted Church attending neighbors – secretly watch pornography? Why does the caring therapist sleep with his patients? Why does the beloved classroom teacher steal money from her own children's college savings funds to feed the gambling habit of her lover? Why do rich people shoplift $5 items? Why, oh why?

All of these behaviors are ways in which the shadow shows its face. They reveal the discrepancies between the mask we hold up to the external world and our hidden, potentially destructive behaviors.

### Understanding the shadow

The idea of the shadow is not complicated. Yet understanding some of its facets and nuances can seem so. Carl G. Jung, the famous psychologist, claimed that the shadow is humankind's moral problem.

Most of us are not aware of our shadow and how it frequently shows up unbidden and sabotages our motivations, decisions and actions. This lack of awareness can have a devastating impact on us and others, as we shall explore.

### So – to explaining the idea of the shadow

The ego is what we consider ourselves to be and know about consciously. It is very important to us. We are deeply committed to our egos. We have invested a lot of effort, time, and money in developing it and it very much defines our identity. Over time, our ego becomes a firm structure within the psyche.

We begin developing this ego at a very young age when we start to discriminate between what we see as us and what we see as not us. We see ourselves as not angry, irritable, greedy, aggressive, envious, self-absorbed, controlling and so on. Bit by bit, as we grow up and develop, we create a sort of pantomime image – or persona – that we think presents the best face we can to the world and of course our own ego-constructed mirrors. In order to be seen as kind, courteous, intelligent, nice lookin, and so on, we push away, suppress and deny those qualities that do not fit the image that we think makes us acceptable, liked and successful. Here we see the power of conforming to moral norms and conventions in action. This is how we create our persona, the mask we present to the outside world so that we can fit in.

Our family, our society and culture, does a lot of this ego-shaping process. We are under a great deal of pressure to conform to what our culture expects of us. In fact, as we have discussed, it can be dangerous to go against cultural norms. So we adopt the cultural straight jacket and spend our time arguing about the size of its buttons rather than investigating what it has done to the person wearing it.

This ego-development process can also mean that we throw out some wonderful personal characteristics or potentials because they do not seem to fit into the conditioning pressures of our straight jacket tailors. For example, we might be creative or highly adventurous, or we might want to live in a hut in the Himalayas and meditate, but that is not what is expected of us. So all that longed for potential gets tossed into the shadow basement along with the other rejected items. Unfortunately, our hidden desires show up when we heavily criticize or are contemptuous of "those nonproductive art types" or those "hippies that want to do nothing but lollygag in some hut."

Simply put, what lies in the shadows is all those feelings, thoughts, and emotions that we have denied, suppressed, or repressed as not being part of us. They are attributes, emotions and behaviors that for some reason we do not accept as part of ourselves. For example, some of us try to look smart so that we can conceal our insecurities. Some of us pretend we are being thoughtful or contained, when in truth we are afraid to show our hand. And then some people are dedicated CEOs and cheat on their vacation time. We have all kinds of strategies to keep those shadows in place, but in one way or another they always show up.

### Fighting the shadows

Oscar Wilde wrote a wonderful tale about shadow issues called *The Picture of Dorian Gray*. Dorian was a beautiful, vain, young man who lived in nineteenth-century England. He was feted by many and spent much of his time preening himself so that people would admire him. A painter paints a picture of him that captures his strikingly handsome looks that have no blemish. Dorian, captivated by his own image – like Narcissus – desires to remain beautiful, handsome and perfect forever. He makes a pact with the devil that all signs of aging and degeneration, and any evidence of his greed and cruelty, of which he had a great deal and are described in the novel, would appear on the painting and not on his own face. The painting gets hidden in a wardrobe not to ever be seen by anyone. From time to time, Dorian's curiosity gets the better of him and he pulls the picture out of the darkness and takes a quick glance. He is shocked by his youthful face that is growing more and more hideous and distorted each time he peeks.

Like Dorian, many of us would rather not see the dark sides of ourselves. We blithely say ignorance is bliss. But most of us have come to learn that that is a fallacy. What it really means is that we do not want to do the work of really learning about ourselves. One part of that pseudo ignorance refers to our running away from our own shadows. We can shove our shadow in a drawer like Wendy in Peter Pan, or in a wardrobe like Dorian, but if you can visually picture running from your shadow, you will realize it is impossible!

By denying or repressing certain feelings and thoughts we alienate ourselves from reality and of course from our true selves. Distracting ourselves from shadow work, we feed on gossip, dramas, bad news, reality shows, zombie movies, hyped-up newscasts all in attempts to avoid looking clearly at the soap opera that is our own lives. These distractions allow us to see the shadows in others which we can vilify or laugh at and in some strange way it gives voice to our own shadows that are ready to pounce out of their hiding places.

In attempts to deny our shadows, some of us say it is easier just to be in life. Who in their right mind wants to waste time on all this introspective and reflective work that is the gobbledy-gook for the therapists? "I have many things to do," they say. "Things have to get done. I have enough to do to get on top of every day without distracting myself with all this self-inquiry."

Unfortunately, this ego talk often deludes us. Secretly we tell ourselves that we can fake it. Rarely is that true. The only ones we kid are ourselves. Others pick up our delusions and our shadows, sometimes unconsciously. We might think we are getting away with our behaviors, but little do we know what others are really seeing and perceiving. Our shadow behaviors are invariably regressive and lead us to behave in more immature ways – not to mention unethical – than we would consciously like. Shadow behavior usually takes us to the lower stages of Kohlberg's scale where we act out of fear, subservience or a desire not to break ranks with others. Avoiding our shadows deeply disempowers our authentic selves.

Our shadow is always very closely attached to us as we know all real shadows are. They are there in that sarcastic remark, the self-righteousness attitude, our addictive behavior, our contempt, and our sudden angry outbursts. Looking at these shadow behaviors is no fun. It makes us realize that this wonderful mask or persona we have created is not as perfect as we would like it to be. It challenges our egos where we are forced to recognize that we have some flaws and fissures and that we are definitely not all that cracked up we claim to be.

### Recognizing shadow issues

Identifying one's shadow issues is not easy because we defend against them. They challenge our egos, and that is frightening to us. Not only that, our shadows are elusive. They do not always come out in a clearly identifiable way. Sometimes we have to unpack them in layers to really get at the heart of what is lurking in the dark. And even when we think we have made progress, something new might suddenly emerge that shows us that we have some way to go. Shadow work never ends.

#### Defending and rationalizing

Indicator number one is: What do you defend or rationalize most about when it comes to your behavior? When do you insist that your thoughts, your approach or behavior is either exceptional, or it's the right one worthy of some incredible accolade or prize? When do you insist, passionately and with great energy, that you are justified in your behavior, or know better or you are smarter or whatever? What is behind that?

*Agitated energy*

Indicator two: Anything that sweeps you away with intense, almost agitated energy, is in some way a shadow issue. When you claim: "I know best" or "How can anyone be so stupid?" and your stomach heaves and churns in anger or contempt, you had better look deeply into your mirror to see what that is all about.

*Irritation and dislike*

Indicator three: What do you see or notice in other people that irritates, repels or downright annoys you in an unrelenting way? When do you find yourself in judgment, or contempt or irritated anger? She is such a smart-ass; he is so self-absorbed; she is an arrogant bitch; he is an incorrigible narcissist – I cannot stand her, him etc. Well guess what: You had better clean up that mirror in which you are preening your ego. Time for some straight talk or straight looking. This charged energy is the shadow calling for attention. What are these other people mirroring back to you?

*Unlived life*

Indicator four: What passions, desires, unlived interests or hopes have you had, or do you have, that do not get opportunities for expression? When do you find yourself dismissing other people or being contemptuous about them because they exhibit a freedom that you wish you had?

Our shadow is everything that we have denied ourselves from our original wholeness – both dark and light. It is in our shadow that we sometimes keep some amazing gift, capacity or ability that never or rarely is given an opportunity to flourish. Think of the saying, "she is a dark horse." The dark horse phenomenon refers to these surprising gifts that suddenly appear out of the shadows.

The above are some simple guidelines that we might bear in mind every day. We can also notice when we sometimes behave what we consider to be out of character for us. When we lose our temper on some poor unsuspecting soul. Or we act inappropriately at a meeting. Or we conveniently forget someone or undermine another person's efforts claiming quite innocently how sorry we were, it was a misunderstanding! These little, almost daily acts, have become our habitual, conditioned attitudes that are our own self-absorbed and often self-righteous garments – our own straitjackets – that distort our minds, harm other people, and limit our own possibilities. Our shadows are at large!

Shadow work is tough. It is rarely a one-shot deal. It takes personal strength and courage to peer into our own darkness. Sometimes, like Dorian Gray, we can only make little peeks at a time and then try to embrace what we have learned. And even when we think we have grasped a shadow issue, whatever it might be, and embraced it, it can still appear again in another guise at another time, to shake us up. There are many advantages to getting to know one's shadow, but it takes a great deal of courage to do that work. It can be quite horrible to learn about some of our actions and patterned behaviors that we just mechanically fall into.

The wonderful thing, however, about shadow work is that just the simple awareness and the willingness to look at these sides of ourselves and work on them as best we can makes us a better person with more character. Ethical people strive to grapple with their shadows.

### Buddhist attachment – shadows everywhere

An independent investigation into allegations against the Tibetan Buddhist teacher Sogyal Lakar (known widely as Sogyal Rinpoche), founder of the Rigpa community and author of the highly acclaimed book, *The Tibetan Book of Living and Dying*, has found that he committed acts of "serious physical, sexual, and emotional abuse."

The report by law firm Lewis Silkin details multiple allegations of physical, sexual, emotional and psychological abuse, as well as accounts of "living a lavish, gluttonous and sybaritic lifestyle," and "tainting the appreciation of the Dharma." The 50-page report found that "senior individuals within Rigpa . . . were aware of at least some of these issues and failed to address them, leaving others at risk."

The report details allegations that Sogyal Lakar "abused letter writers by slapping them, punching them, kicking them, pulling their ears, hitting them with a backscratcher, phones, cups and hangers." It is also alleged that a student was knocked unconscious and that monks and nuns were left "bloodied and scarred." Twenty-two witnesses provided evidence that they were aware of twenty more people who were regularly subjected to physical abuse, some on a daily basis.

The report also details allegations that Sogyal Lakar "used his role to gain access to young women and to coerce, intimidate and manipulate them into giving him sexual favors," for which there is "a significant weight of first-hand evidence."

Further, the report details allegations that Sogyal Lakar "instructed students to strip, show him their genitals, take photos of their genitals and show them to him, give him oral sex, have sex with their partners in his bed and describe sexual relationships to him, as well as lying to cover up relationships with him. He is alleged to have "groped students and asked one of his students to photograph attendants and girlfriends naked," as well as offered his attendants to other lamas for sex.

Extract from *Lion's Roar Magazine*, September 2018. Article by Lilly Greenblatt (https://www.lionsroar.com/independent-investigation-confirms-physical-sexual-emotional-abuse-by-sogyal-rinpoche/).

### Shadow work takes courage and humor

Doing shadow work takes a great deal of courage. This work challenges the persona we have created and the structure and strength of our egos. It can be scary work as Dorian Gray discovered. We get to see some sides of ourselves that we have trained ourselves to dislike and have happily projected onto others.

Peering into our shadows we might find ourselves in some dark corners as when we realize that we are full of envy, or when we feel pathetic, inadequate and weak and prop ourselves up behind bravado and self-righteousness. Even so, it is far more mature and self-accountable to acknowledge our shadows, to experience them consciously and to talk about them than to keep them buried in our inner dungeon, where they build up rot and odorous thoughts and behaviors ready to leak out at the most inopportune times.

Looking at our shadow brings to our awareness the kind of choices we make and the hidden agendas and ulterior motives that can overwhelm our good intentions. Wherever we go we carry out shadows with us. It is our personal duty to try to bring some of these unconscious complexes to our consciousness. If we do not, we will continue to hurt ourselves and others even when that is the last thing we wish to do.

Taking time to examine our motivations and our behaviors can be quite painful. It is hard to embrace attributes we have rejected because we despise them. Who wants to have a relationship with what one does not like or admire, in fact hates? And then when we find that these ogres remain part of us despite our denial, that is quite mind-blowing! We had hoped they would go away. They are someone else's problem or issue. Surely not ours!

It takes real courage to be in relationship with something we deplore. The question that often comes up is can we really do this work? Is our ego strong enough to see that some of it is built on shaky assumptions and that we have some pretty lousy characteristics that we were sure only others had? Here is where some humor can really help. Here is where we try not to take ourselves so seriously. Here is where we appreciate that we are not perfect and that actually we are quite a cartoon character with a big nose, long ears or whatever, and that we have some gross aspects. It is all in the mix of being a human, fully alive to everything.

Many people find it easier not to investigate their shadows and to continue to mechanically use them as part of their coping strategies. The problem with that approach is that they never get to the heart of who they really are. This means not working towards their own wholeness. Remember, one cannot have the light without the dark. Gandhi publicly demeaned his wife and sexually abused his nieces.[2] None of us get a free pass.

### Ethics and shadow work

Talking about faces, there is a story that Abraham Lincoln was going to the theater with a friend of his. He turned to his friend pointing to another man in the audience saying, "That man has such a terrible face!" Abraham's friend apparently queried, "But Mr. President how can you blame the man for his face?" Abraham Lincoln answered, "There comes a time in life when we are all responsible for our face!" (http://quoteseed.com/quotes/abraham-lincoln/abraham-lincoln-every-man-over-forty-is-responsible-for/)

There you have it! Straight from the president's mouth, we are responsible for crafting our face, our mask, our persona and the ego that stands behind it. Since the shaping of our face takes some time, and like Dorian, includes all the parts of us, we had better begin paying attention now!

We like to give lip service to the idea that we cannot lead others if we can't lead ourselves. Well, part of leading ourselves means continually developing our own self-awareness, our own character and our own ethical conscience. Shadow work is a big part of self-awareness that also develops our ethical capacity. It helps us see that we too have the potential to be evil and that we are in no way as courageous or as ethically clear headed as we think we are. Acceptance of our shadow leads to true ethical growth (Neumann, 1990). (See Chapter 10 for more on this.)

Shadow work means becoming attentive to our shadow behaviors and thinking about what lies behind them. What buried feelings or attitudes are leading us to act out in a particular way? What about ourselves can we learn from this message from the underground? The more we stay attentive and mindful to this open inquiry the more we will learn about our true selves, not just the one we have jammed into the straight jacket.

Once the shadows no longer own us from the inside, we can make different choices. We can curb their impetuousness and their showing up unconsciously. We can own them and thereby diminish their agitated energy. In time we will find that we do not make as many choices from Kohlberg's stages 1–3. We are less constrained and calmer as we do not have to use otherwise healthy energy to keep the monsters at bay. They are us and we are going to work with them as best we can, knowing that this work is a continual work in progress. The payoff will be greater inner confidence, a stronger ego in the best sense, and a more authentic and contained self that we can role model for others.

By looking at our shadows we discover what really helps us in life and what hurts. We find out what it means to be a decent individual and we see what takes away for that. We learn how our moral compass works and how suddenly it can be derailed. We also come to realize that at our core, there is a good part that has not been corrupted and that we can tap into and reclaim.

Being able to engage in shadow work is the sign of ethical maturity desperately needed both in personal and in corporate life.

---

### Your turn – me and my shadow

- List some of the traits that you most dislike in others. And then in yourself.
- Consider the last time you acted what you think was out of character for you.
- Nonjudgmentally ask yourself to what extent you need to please others and why.
- Reflect on what you might learn from these explicit observations.

## He is the boss!

Richard Evans is the Chief Controller for Paperweight Commercial Inc. (PCI). He has worked for the organization since he graduated with his accounting degree eight years ago. He likes working at the company and has made many friends there over the years. The other managers have seen him grow up and have been delighted with his technical progress. There was a huge company celebration party when he was appointed chief controller one year ago.

Richard has just made it through his first year in his new position. It has been a tough year where he has made many mistakes and learned a lot. Fortunately, his boss, the CFO, Mike Morris, is patient and has helped him sort out some of his mistakes. He is very grateful. It has also been a difficult year with a challenging economy and one where the company has not done that well. Paperweight Commercial Inc. has lost several major orders to cut-throat competitors and is currently experiencing a cash flow squeeze. The year end results need to portray a healthy picture as PCI is going to have to ask its bankers to extend its line of credit. As Richard reviews the proforma accounts, he is concerned that the financial picture does not looks as good as it needs to in order to satisfy the lending formulae of the banks. He wonders what to do and how the situation can be improved.

It is late Friday afternoon and Mike Morris enters Richard's office. He has just reviewed the proforma accounts and is clearly disturbed. He tells Richard that PCI will have to accelerate sending certain sales and maintenance invoices to clients so that they are captured in the current year as revenue. Without bolstering sales and accounts receivable, PCI will not get the credit line extension it needs. Mike says they can reverse the charges in the New Year, but for now they need to be processed immediately. Richard is nervous to comply with the request as it is clearly unethical and a violation of Generally Accepted Accounting Principles (GAAP). However, he is eager to please Mike. Also, he consoles himself; "He told me to do it and he is the boss! I must do what the boss tells me. I have no choice really!"

## I had no choice!

I think it would be hard to find a more prominent and insidious case of blaming the boss, than the public testimony given by Michael Cohen against President Donald Trump in early 2019. His six-hour elucidation of the multitude of devious deeds he performed in the name of his boss, or in attempts to curry favor with him, leave one dumbfounded. It seems inconceivable, to me at least, how one person can repeatedly and endlessly engage in so many nefarious dealings and so unashamedly hide behind the fact that he was told explicitly or subtlety, to do so. Cohen claimed that once one is in the system, in this case the Trump system, one obeys, or one is out. There is no choice!

From an ethics perspective, there is no such a thing as "I had no choice." Recall that ethics is about self-awareness that arises from reflection, deliberation, questioning and the desire or striving to make good and wise decisions. Once one abandons one's responsibility for the decisions one makes, one is no longer a free and fully functioning person. However, like Hamlet, our fears and doubts can readily overwhelm our moral sensibilities.

In truth we always have a choice. Sometimes the alternatives before us seem unpalatable. We wish that our problem or dilemma would simply disappear and relieve us of the agony to choose. At the time, we might feel that we cannot live with some of the consequences associated with a difficult choice. It might challenge our self-image, cost us our jobs, damage our status, or threaten our economic security. However, choose we must. Even if we decide to make someone else responsible for our decision, that is a choice. Sadly, that kind of choice places us in the role of victim. There can be no worse place for our ego or self-esteem than to be in the place of victim. As victims we are powerless, and that is really frightening! Being powerless we have no significance whatsoever. Now, there are of course circumstances where we are victimized. Those are tragic indeed. However, in most business scenarios, we do have a choice. Sometimes we take the low road because we cannot bear the consequences of doing something else. When that happens, the ethical thing is to own one's choice with a view to finding new alternatives and new courage in the future. It is also an opportunity for us to find strategies by which we may more easily be able to voice our concerns.

Finding our voice and freeing ourselves from the mental prison of no choice is an important part of our moral development.

What I emphasize in Part II of this book, is the importance of "doing or practicing ethics." Practicing ethics means availing of opportunities to dialogue, discuss and debate moral alternatives. I propose that ethical managers develop an adeptness at fostering these types of discussions. They should encourage employees to speak up about issues, especially those issues that might result in difficult conversations. Opportunities such as these, provide learning moments for all involved, and frequently reveal that more choices exist than are often realized.

### Exercise – I had no choice

- Have you found yourself in a situation where you have said "I have no choice?"
- Have you had a situation at work where you had to comply with your boss's wishes that went against your own values or ethical principles?
- Have you placed any of your subordinates in a position where they felt they had no choice?
- If you have had any of these experiences, what have you learned from them?
- What strategies might you adopt in the future to avoid finding yourself in the place where you feel that you have no choice?

## Moral freedom

*Man is born free but he is everywhere in chains.*

Jean-Jacques Rousseau

In the discipline of ethics, the matter of moral freedom is an important one. Moral freedom refers to the unrestricted and independent ability to make choices. If people cannot freely choose, then a strong moral argument exists that they cannot be deemed morally culpable for the consequences of their actions. The problem with the moral freedom argument is that, very few people, if any, are totally free. If this is true, does this mean that we can all escape moral responsibility for our actions?

The freedom argument is complex. The reason for this is that there are so many vantage points from which one might assess this thing called freedom. For example, there are anthropological, cultural, psychological, physical and economic perspectives. Although these perspectives are all interesting, we will keep things simple by only focusing on the economic perspective, namely, the question of economic freedom.

So what is economic freedom? Economic freedom pertains to the ability of a person to make choices without feeling that his or her economic survival is at risk. For example, it could be argued that starving people do not have moral freedom in an economic sense, and thus should be excused when they pilfer bread.

Since we are concerned with business ethics and the business context, the issue of economic freedom has great relevance. Employees depend on the salaries the corporation pays them to support themselves and their families. Losing a job is always traumatic and financially costly, even when other job alternatives exist. Usually people actively "fear" losing their jobs.

While people nowadays seem more job-mobile than say thirty years ago, people still fear being laid off. Employees want to be the one deciding when they leave a company and do not like being vulnerable to the corporation's ability to do so. Being vulnerable to corporate masters is scary. Given this factor, the issue of job security or the fear of being passed over for promotions, presents a major factor that affects the moral freedom of business employees.

Research shows that due to fear of losing one's job or being permanently side-lined, many employees conform, collude, abstain, ignore or regrettably get caught up in immoral behavior (Recall Wells Fargo and Volkswagen). "The boss told me to do it and he is the boss!" is a frequently cited excuse. Many people feel morally justified when they obey the boss, as they believe that the power of authority holds moral sway. If the boss told them to do it, they feel they are morally excused. Well, this is a dangerous place to be.

## The manager as moral authority

*King Lear:* Dost thou know me, fellow?
*Kent:* No, sir; but you have that in your countenance which I would fain call master.
*King Lear:* What is that?
*Kent:* Authority

(Shakespeare, King Lear, Act 1, scene 4)

Holding a position of authority raises several important issues for anyone, especially business leaders and managers.

Early childhood lessons taught us to obey authority as those in authority are "right." The person in authority knows the "right" thing to do and the "right" thing for us to do is to obey. Those in power make the rules! Obey has become associated with moral rightness. Obedience to authority, the boss, the president or the Fuehrer, is considered by many as doing one's moral duty. Authority also counts as rules or the law.

As we can learn from the famous Milgram and Stanford Prison experiments, and other atrocities that have taken place in the name of, among other things, religion and nationalism, people defer their reasoning to those in authority. There appears to be both a common belief and common practice that authority figures are to be obeyed not only for the power they wield but because obeying them is fulfilling one's moral duty.

Ethical managers need to be aware of this dynamic. Manipulating people's undue (and sometimes misplaced) sense of obedience, their desire to be dutiful and their fear of challenging authority is at best thoughtless, certainly self-serving, and at worst reprehensible. People who have earned positions of authority, either formal or informal ones, have an ethical responsibility to understand the emotionally regressive forces of authority on individual behavior and to avoid using those forces to their advantage.

## The Stanley Milgram experiments

People from the general public were invited to participate in a study of memory and learning. Some of the participants were designated "teachers" and some as "learners." The experimenter explained to participants that the study is concerned with the effects of punishment on learning. In the experiment, the learner is strapped to a chair and an electrode attached to his or her wrist. The learner is told he or she must learn a list of word pairs. Whenever an error is made, the teacher will administer shocks of increasing intensity.

The real focus of the experiment is on the teacher (the subject). After watching the learner being strapped into place, he or she is taken into an experimental room and seated before a shock generator. The shock generator has a line of thirty switches, ranging from 15 volts to 450 volts, in 15-volt increments. There are also indicators ranging from Slight Shock to Danger to Severe Shock. The experimenter explains to the teacher that he or she must administer the learning test to the person in the other room strapped to the chair. When the learner answers correctly, the teacher moves onto the next item. When the learner gives an incorrect answer, the teacher is to give him an electric shock. He or she must start at the lowest shock level of 15 volts and increase the level each time the man makes an error.

The teacher is a genuinely naïve participant in the experiment – a volunteer off the street. The learner is an actor who actually receives no shock at all. The goal of the experiment is to see how far a person will proceed in administering pain to a protesting victim when he or she is ordered to do so.

As the shocks escalate, the victim (actor) increases his protests until he demands to be released from the experiment. Conflict arises for the teacher who sees the suffering of the learner and is pressed to quit. The experimenter, the authority in this case, orders the teacher to continue. To extricate him or herself from the situation, the teacher must clearly challenge the authority and break off the engagement with him. The aim of the investigation is to see when and how people would defy authority by refusing to act.

The results of the Milgram experiments (several hundred people participated in a variety of similar experiments to that described), is literally "shocking" to say the least. Many "teachers" obeyed the experimenter no matter how vehement the pleading of the person being shocked, and no matter how painful or dangerous the shocks seemed to be. A significant percentage of participants (in some cases 65% of subjects) administered the highest level of shock possible (450 volts!), regardless of the consequences for the "learner" or victim. Few if any people did not agree to participate in the experiment once they learned that shocks had to be administered. The results for women did not deviate much from that of men. (Think back on our feminist ethics discussion.)

In his book describing these experiments, Milgram analyzes the behavior of and the rationalizations provided by the obedient participants. He describes how a variety of inhibitions against disobeying authority come into play preventing the person from breaking with authority and thus keeping his or her place in the experiment.

Here are some of Milgram's findings and interpretations of the results:

- In general, subjects found it difficult to break with the authority figure even though he (the experimenter) had little authority over them. The experimenter was simply a Yale professor engaged in an experiment. There were no consequences to the subject if he or she pulled out of the experiment.
- People justified their remaining in the experiment out of a sense of obligation or duty to the experimenter. They claimed they had a commitment to the experimenter, and it would be awkward to withdraw.
- People were unable to realize their values in action. They found themselves continuing in the experiment even though they disagreed with what they were doing.
- Some became so engaged in the technical task (pressing the correct switch), that it helped them ignore the larger consequences of their actions.
- Participants did not see themselves responsible for their own actions. They were doing what they were told to do. Some claimed, "I would not have done it by myself. It was what I was told to do."
- Women responded similarly to men. It seems they showed no signs of greater empathy or relational concern when they took on the role of teacher.
- Responsibility for the act and the consequences belonged to the authority.
- Moral concern for the victim was shifted to how well the subject was living up to expectations of authority. People looked to the experimenter for approval. Was he or she performing ok?
- The experiment acquired an impersonal momentum of its own. A mindset developed in the subject that "it has got to go on." The experiment became larger than the people in it.

- Some blamed the victim claiming the punishment he received was inevitable due to his deficiencies in intellect and character.
- The results of the experiment were worse when a third person, other than the teacher, administered the shock. Distancing the person from the effects of his actions resulted in even less concern for the victim.

As we think about the results of the Milgram experiments, we might ponder the make-up of human nature. The frighteningly powerful influence of authority and its enormous hold over our psyches must surely give us pause. Unfortunately, our education rarely provides us with opportunities to develop mature strategies for dealing with people who have authority over us. We are also woefully lacking in educating managers in how to be effective authority figures. Most ethics training excludes any attention to "working with authority."

The self-alienation factor revealed by Milgram's experiments, where a person renounces responsibility for his or her actions claiming, "I was told to do it," has severe implications for organizational behavior in general. Unfortunately, the Milgram experiments reinforce the reality that many people, in the face of authority, operate from Kohlberg's stage 1 – fear.

> What is most alarming is that similar "authority" experiments have been carried out in recent years, and the results are worse than those presented by the Milgram studies. People are nowadays even more inclined to succumb to authority than in the 1960s. So much for our evolution in consciousness and our growth in self-empowerment!

What Milgram's study of authority and obedience teaches us is that employees who demonstrate obedience are not necessarily –

- Supportive of an idea or initiative
- In agreement or assent of a proposal
- Loyal to their supervisor
- Committed to a course of action
- Understanding of the situation or themselves
- Respectful of those in authority
- In conformance with best practice
- Consistent in behavior
- Ethically disposed to a course of action

Obedient behavior simply conveys compliance. From an ethical perspective, this is important information. Getting people to obey, even with a smile on their face, does not mean they are taking ownership of their actions, adapting or learning. When people obey without feeling responsible, without taking personal ownership for their actions, and without a sense of having learned something from the activity they are engaged in, they are no better than robots. In fact, robots are better; they obey with no sense of self-alienation, they execute instructions consistently, and they sleep peacefully at night!

## The Stanford Prison experiment

The Stanford Prison experiment (1971), designed by Stanford psychologist Philip Zimbardo, was set up to explore the psychology of prison life and how specific situations affect people's behavior. Twenty-four out of seventy college-aged men were picked and randomly assigned either to be a guard or a prisoner. The experiment lasted only six days out of a planned two weeks when Zimbardo had to pull the plug. The mistreatment of the prisoners and the disturbing behavior of the guards escalated so alarmingly that the experiment had to be terminated.

For six days, half the study's participants endured cruel and dehumanizing abuse at the hands of their peers. At various times, they were taunted, stripped naked, deprived of sleep and forced to use plastic buckets as toilets. Some of them rebelled violently; others became hysterical or withdrew into despair. As the situation descended into chaos, the researchers stood by and watched.

Like the fake guards, Zimbardo himself got caught up in the study and started embodying the role of the prison's warden. It was thanks to his colleagues and his wife that he snapped out of it and ended the study.

In Zimbardo's book on his forty-year study of evil, he not only writes with regret about this experiment, but about the enormous power of systems and the unpredictable human response to situations (Zimbardo, 2007).

### *The ethical manager and authority*

Managers need to be educated to understand that many people obey authority out of fear: fear of losing the relationship with the authority; fear of the consequences of not obeying; fear of becoming an outsider; fear of having to take responsibility for one's own actions; and fear of not having an alternative action to engage in. Ethical managers understand this dynamic and do their best to work around it. They make every effort to diminish fear in the organizational system and they strive not to manage using fear-based strategies. (Recall managing fear in Chapter 2.)

Another matter for managers to consider is the issue of moral freedom. Does the organizational culture offer employees a sense of moral freedom? In my experience many employees feel they cannot be honest, nor can they challenge the boss on ethical matters, as there will be negative repercussions. "She will never forget once you challenge her!" is a phrase I have heard many times. Similarly, I am told frequently: "There is no way I would take a risk and try something new as you get punished around here if you make a mistake!"

These employee reactions are bad for business. It means that they do not feel morally free to act from a place of personal maturity and responsibility. It is obvious that the motivation for their behavior is Kohlberg's stage 1 – fear. Operating from this stage does not bring out anyone's sense of personal autonomy. It certainly does not advance an ethical climate. If anything, it encourages an atmosphere of skepticism and personal doubt. Moral development will be difficult to encourage if people feel unduly fearful or oppressed.

The third matter for our ethical manager to consider is that of conscience. While organizations cannot presume to supplant their conscience over that of the individual, managers must demonstrate that they have a conscience. How do they do this? They need to reinforce a corporate culture that upholds certain ethical principles and acceptable behaviors that are also rewarded. These principles should be explicitly written and articulated and, of course most of all, evidenced in practice. Far too many organizations have their principles and values plastered on walls where no-one really walks the talk.

The ethical manager has a huge part to play in his or her self-awareness as a person of authority and a shaper of culture. This calls for personal moral courage; an ability and interest in mentoring and coaching others, and a commitment to enabling employees to give voice to their moral sentiments and deeply held values. Employees need to be mentored and coached so that they can articulate their viewpoints without fear of personal, negative consequences. Regrettably, many managers say they do not have the time for personal development. This is where the CEO and the executive team needs to set some personal development standards. It is always a pity when things have to be mandated – and in truth, managers who are not prepared to engage in personal development should not be managers.

## Conclusion

What might we conclude from our review of the many factors that affect our ethical capacities and our moral development? Here is a recap:

As we can see, this ethics business is a complicated one. It is not a matter of simply learning attitudes or behaviors. As I pointed out in Chapter 1, our ethics is an entire system wrapped in and around our self-awareness, our ego identity, our worldviews, values and core assumptions, and our ability to be reflective and courageous. Ethics calls on our entire being as Hamlet well reminded us.

This chapter stresses that moral development is highly dependent on ego development, self-awareness, a recognition of our shadow and the courage to work with it, a sense of self-agency and determination, how we manage our fears and an ability to manage our vulnerabilities to authority.

## Executive summary

This chapter focuses on moral development and how we justify our behaviors. We review Kohlberg's moral development schema and consider its practical implications. Throughout the chapter we are invited to consider whether we consciously nourish our own moral development and along with that, develop a robust conscience that can weather outer and inner pressures and point us to that true north. We also review some of the factors that cause moral regression within organizations.

The main points covered in this chapter include:

- Moral dilemmas often arrive out of nowhere and usually take us out of our comfort zone.
- Moral dilemmas are in most cases just that: dilemmas. They are not problems that can be readily solved.
- Lawrence Kohlberg's 3 level–6 stage moral development schema is discussed along with the significance of each of the stages. Ethical, post-conventional as opposed to conventional behavior occurs in stages 5 and 6.
- Kohlberg's stages reflect rational justification and not necessarily the emotion that drove the behavior.
- Choices are invariably influenced by a combination of emotion and reason. Therefore, to consider ethics as simply a rational endeavor, short-changes the depth with which it touches us.
- While many have argued that women reason differently to men, research does not hold up that this is always true.
- Developing one's conscience is part of ethical maturity and is a complex matter. It also takes intention and attention.
- Many people project their needs to be loved and cared for onto the organization. In doing so they surrender their moral autonomy and submit to a form of organizational totalitarianism where those in charge define reality, and encourage a culture of subservience, group think, and collusion.
- A personal matter that we bring to daily life is our shadow. Lack of awareness of our shadow behaviors often lead us to think and act unethically. Part of ethical maturity is becoming more self-aware and in some control of our shadow tendencies.
- Our sense of personal freedom influences our moral behavior. If we feel frightened and under threat, we are more inclined to operate from Kohlberg's stage 1 – fear than from a place of accountable moral autonomy.
- The Milgram and Stanford Prison experiments brought to light our fear of authority. This is an important factor in organizational life. Ethical managers need to be aware of the power they have over others and how many people surrender their own agency in the face of authority.
- Developing our ethical capacities and growing in ethical maturity is a lifetimes' work and requires dedication and a committed desire to strive to be a noble person.

## Questions for reflection

- What was the last moral dilemma you faced? What made it a dilemma?
- As you think about this moral dilemma, what Kohlberg stages did you wrestle with?

- Do you know any people who would be considered stage 5 or stage 6 people? What makes them so?
- What mostly informs your conscience?
- Does your organization have a corporate conscience? If yes, how does it demonstrate it?
- What stages of reasoning does the culture of your organization encourage?
- What is your experience of the *organizational ideal*?
- Can you think of any time that your own shadow has tripped you up?
- How do you feel toward authority? Do you find it for the most part intimidating or do you feel you can hold your own? Think of examples as you provide an answer.
- Do you feel morally free at work?
- Is moral development part of personal development in your organization?

## Key terms

| | |
|---|---|
| Anthropomorphize  134 | Moral intensity  127 |
| Authority  124 | Narcissism  134 |
| Behavioral ethics  130 | Organizational ideal  136 |
| Conscience  125 | Organizational totalitarianism  137 |
| Ego ideal  136 | ROI – return on investment  175 |
| Feminist ethics  130 | Shadow  139 |
| Moral development  123 | Stakeholders  122 |

## Notes

1  See Annabel Beerel. *Dissertation: How the Power Dynamics and the Culture of Fear in Business Organizations Contribute to the Gap between Ethics and Morality in Business Practice.* Ann Arbor, Michigan: UMI Dissertation Services, 2003.
2  Reference – www.pri.org/stories/2016-01-30/gandhi-s-death-anniversary-not-everyone-grieving

> Gandhi's disgraceful treatment of women is a darker and lesser-known side of his story," historian Kusoom Vadgama said in an online petition she launched against the Parliament Square statue. Gandhi has been accused of sexual abuse of his grandnieces and psychological abuse of his wife. "That disgrace still continues today: his legacy is a culture that (like him) fails to empathize with the victims of sexual abuse.

And www.theguardian.com/commentisfree/2010/jan/27/mohandas-gandhi-women-india

## References

Bakan, Joel. *The Corporation: The Pathological Pursuit of Profit and Power.* New York: Free Press, 2005.

Beerel, Annabel. *Leadership and Change Management.* London, UK: Sage Publications, 2009.

Cooke, George Willis. *The Poets of Transcendentalism.* Philadelphia, Pennsylvania: B. Franklin, 1970.

Damasio, Antonio. *Descartes' Error: Emotion, Reason and the Human Brain.* New York: Avon Books, 1994.

Gilligan, Carol. *In a Different Voice.* Cambridge, MA: Harvard University Press, 1993.

Kohlberg, Lawrence. *Essays on Moral Development*, Volumes 1 and 2. San Francisco, CA: Harper Row, 1981.

Lehrer, Jonah. *How We Decide.* New York: Houghton Mifflin Harcourt, 2009.

Neumann, Eric. *Depth Psychology and a New Ethic.* Boston, Massachusetts: Shambhala, 1990.

Piaget, Jean. *The Moral Judgment of the Child.* New York: Free Press, 1997.

Schwartz, Howard S. *Narcissistic Process and Corporate Decay.* New York: New York University Press, 1990.

Shakespeare, William. *The Oxford Shakespeare: The Complete Works.* 2nd edition. Oxford, UK: Oxford University Press, 2005.

Zimbardo, Philip. *The Lucifer Effect: Understanding How Good People Turn Evil.* New York: Random House, 2007.

# 5  Ethical reflection – an interlude

## Contents

## Ethical reflection

This chapter is the last chapter in Part I. It provides us with a pause; a time for reflection on what we have covered so far. Part II covers the discipline of ethics and provides a framework for moral reasoning. We also discuss the critical ethical issue of the environment and I conclude with a mandate for ethical leadership.

By now I imagine you might be surprised at the vast terrain of human action in which ethics is a central node. I have had to be selective in deciding what to include when we look at the impact of both the macro, and the micro–environments, on human behavior. What is obvious, I hope, is that human beings are part of multiple forcefields which we need to 1) be aware of, and 2) to negotiate in order to make the best decisions we can and thus live a good life.

What I hope also becomes clearer as we continue our discussions of ethics and morality is that it is very personal. It is very much up to us. Every ethical question is aimed directly at us. Every choice has a potential ethical claim on us and as such ethics is personal work. It constitutes an intimate personal journey into greater self-awareness, other awareness and moral maturity. Ethical perfection – if one dare name such a thing – lies in good-hearted striving; striving to make good choices amidst a sea of troubles and, now and then, during some respite in gloriously calm waters.

Ethics is not just an abstract discipline but is the real on the ground discipline of everyday choices in everyday life, and those choices shape who we are and who we become.

And now to a brief summary of the previous four chapters plus some further commentary to aid your digestion of their contents.

## The ecology of global capitalism

As the media dishes up a never-ending banquet of juicy cases of corruption, deception, blatant conflicts of interest, lying, cheating and all other forms of sordid scandals, what are we to make of this all?

As described in Chapter 1, many decry capitalism for its cronyism, opportunism, unprincipled focus on private interests, and environmental degradation. Free trade that crisscrosses the globe, fueled by return hungry financial capital, fosters a competitive spirit that critics say is the breeding ground for unethical behavior. The fulcrum on which everything rests is unbridled materialism and greed. There are no self-imposed limits, or they are rare, governance at every level is a sham and smacks of conflicts of interest and incompetence, and behemoth corporations have more power than any one nation and certainly any governing body.

The whole notion of a "perfect market" is also bogus. The idea of a perfect market is that "all information is equally and freely available and that all prices reflect that information on a real time basis." This means that no-one has unfair advantages when it comes to obtaining information or has greater ability to act on that information. We know that this too is false. Insider trading abounds. Hedge fund managers and wealthy investors are privileged insiders who have access to an abundance of information that the person on the street is certainly not privy too.

Our fervent pursuit of growth, at the corporate and national level, is not only flooding our world with consumerist gadgets, but is destroying our ecosystem. To grow we need energy and infrastructure, and now the footprint of 7.7 billion people intent on the relentless extraction of our natural resources to satisfy these needs, is destroying the planet on which we depend. The Triple Bottom Line, coined by John Elkington in 1994, intended to promote sustainable practices, is frequently touted and, alas, less frequently practiced.

What the criticisms of capitalism illuminates is that the idea of a "free market" is a myth. It is no longer a place of equality where people freely exchange goods and services and where innate corrective forces temper excess and ensure the well-being of all. There are still many people, however, who counter that, even with its imperfections, capitalism remains the best system there is. It has brought millions out of poverty, it has fueled innovation, improved communications, enabled social mobility and provided opportunities that were until now, not possible. While this may be so, as we have already discussed, one of the key fundamental ethical principles is that of moderation. What we see in global capitalism is moderation wildly adrift taking with it the foundational principles of justice and sympathy, the two virtues which Adam Smith so ardently vested in our human nature.

In Chapter 1, we charted the evolution of capitalism and reviewed its current score sheet. At this point in time, it reflects a rather dismal picture. I also raised the question as to how one creates an ethical organization in an ecological environment that is so polluted and where seemingly many of the powers one might call on to cleanse the environment, are some of the greatest polluters. If we scour the globe, we see the problem of corruption painted in almost every corner. There are few countries that can claim clean score cards and, alas, the so-called developed countries, who should know better, have some of the weakest moral balance sheets of all. The capitalist-democracy debate raises some deep ethical questions such as freedom, moderation, justice, benevolence, transparency, integrity and trust. These questions get at the heart of who we are as humans, individuals, neighbors, parents and organizational leaders and managers.

So called "fixing capitalism," as with everything we wish to change, can only begin by changing ourselves.

## Ethical barriers at work

In Chapter 2, we discussed many of the dynamics of organizational life that serve to inhibit our moral sensibilities. Using a systems perspective, we were reminded of humans' ultimate need for survival and how, for both the system (the organization) and the individual, this is a matter of primary pre-occupation both consciously and unconsciously.

A snapshot of a day in the life of Palermo Inc. (The Jet is Ready case) revealed a not unfamiliar example of the power of culture and how people tend to behave like herd animals for safety sake. Many of us too have experienced how groups regress to a group mind, and how an unconscious pact exists as to what the group sees or does not see, and who is in and who is out.

Organizational life also raises the ante regarding our fears, for which we adopt individual and collective strategies so as to ameliorate or defuse those fears even at the price of our own moral agency or integrity.

The larger the bureaucracy, the greater the demand for fealty and loyalty and the greater the need for moral agility to avoid and escape blame. Bureaucracy also leads to fragmentation of authority and accountability, which distances the worker from his or her work and where people are simply treated as means to monetary ends. This alienation, between a person's work input and a meaningful recognition of its products, also adds to apathetic, disinterested and sometimes, blatantly ethical misbehaviors.

In the light of these inherent organizational dynamics, and of course enveloped in the currently polluted ecology of global capitalism, creating an ethical culture is clearly no easy matter. One might readily say, given all the dynamics outlined, it is almost impossible to do so. The system is too powerful, and we are too limited and confined to shift or change anything. Let's just hope we are no worse than the rest and better than most.

## The first commandment – know thyself

In Chapter 3, we begin the exploration into our own morality. We noted that ethics begins with self-examination where we openly and honestly peer into our own inner temples and question our ideologies, worldviews, and the assumptions that shape our choices. Through this self-examination we get to look at our values and our ability to use these to guide us toward a life of integrity (walking our talk) and inner truth. The mirror is also held up to us where we see our sense of impotence in the face of larger forces than our own and we observe our strategies for survival.

The roots of Western ethical thinking lie with the Greeks who provided us with a coherent program for ethical self-development. Their claim was that everyone's ultimate desire is for happiness. According to them, the path to this happiness is to live this life of self-examination, where the only thing we can know is that we know very little, and therefore we must have humility. We should also aim to live a virtuous life (exercising wisdom, courage, temperance and justice) which is good for the soul.

Our exploration into the world of ethics begins with a review of some of the principle concepts that provide the basis for our Western ethical mindset. These principles include the desire for happiness, the importance of the soul, the meaning of virtue, the concept of good and the good life, and the meaning of ethical principles as objective, rational guidelines that require interpretation for their practical application.

We also noted that our goal is to become someone who "practices ethics" through reflection, deliberation and discernment, rather than someone who conforms to consensus driven behavior proscribed by the prevailing culture. We are challenged to consider whether, in the challenging environment within which we currently live, we can take the ethical high road. How to do this is the underlying question of this book.

## Moral development

In Chapter 4, we used Kohlberg's well-known moral development schema as the basis for our discussions on moral development. We also noted how this framework helps to distinguish between morality and ethics. Behaving morally, where we blindly conform with cultural and societal conventions, places our moral development lower on Kohlberg's schema than when we use higher levels of reasoning.

Using Kohlberg's schema as our guiding framework, we investigated various motivational behaviors triggered by the work setting that influence our ability to act with moral maturity. We are also reminded that our shadows, those aspects of us we have decided are "not us" and have suppressed, tend to sabotage us often serving as the source of our moral misdemeanors. The intimidating power of authority is also explored as we reflect on the Milgram and Stanford Prison experiments, along with our own inhibitions with respect to authority.

What we learn from this reflection is that not only do we have external factors that inhibit our natural desires to be good people, but there are strong internal ones too. We also realize that being ethical takes work. Hard and courageous work. It is inner work; something that many people dislike. Our culture favors doing rather than being. But we must rise above cultural pressures and work on our Being. If people think a few ethics courses can sort this all out, think again!

## Blame the situation

Social psychologists, Ross and Nisbett, in their book *The Person and the Situation* (2011), point out the power of situational influences on our moral behavior. They claim that based on many research studies findings our predictions of how people will behave in certain circumstances are frequently wrong. They refer to this as the "fundamental attribution error" (Ibid, p. 4). This error occurs where we tend to privilege the person and discount the situation. This means that we rely on the characteristic behavior of someone, often giving them the benefit of the doubt, and do not take the subjective influences of the situation into account.

Ross and Nisbett explain how we all exist within field forces and that these forces are both impelling and restraining. This push-and-pull creates yet another tension between the individual and the social group within which they are surrounded. The powerful social pressures and constraints exerted by informal peer groups represent the potent restraining forces that must be overcome. A tragic example is that of the young woman publicly raped in Central Park, New York City while dozens of onlookers did nothing. Individuals questioned afterwards had all kinds of justifications, such as: "I was not qualified to do anything;" "No-one else seemed to do anything, so I was not sure that I should;" "I could not really judge what was going on"; "I was afraid they would turn on me"; . . . and so on. This case presents an example of bystander collusion where there is a ready diffusion of responsibility and no personal moral ownership.

Ross and Nisbett point out that situations are complex and so are people's interpretations of them as we never really know in the moment what the actor's individual construal of the situation will be. It seems that people experience a high pressure to conform to the erroneous majority even with arbitrarily constructed groups or groups that are total strangers. In general, they conclude that the presence of other people inhibits moral interventions. We are reminded of our discussions of the madness of groups in Chapter 2.

This is important information for ethical managers. Predicting how people will behave is more complex than we think. Ensuring that people understand the values and ethical principles that the organization wishes to inculcate requires careful thought and execution. We are dealing with highly subjective matters! It is also a wake-up call to each one of us. Just as we might think we can predict our own behavior and that we know our own moral stages, situations can unexpectedly change things. As always awareness and humility are important ethical reminders.

## Ethics and critical thinking

### Logic and rhetoric

It is no surprise that the early philosophers sandwiched the discipline of ethics between those of logic and rhetoric. If you think about it, to be an ethically sensitive person and to be able to perform sound moral reasoning requires an ability to think clearly and rationally through a situation (logic). Thereafter, you have to be able to assert or argue articulately in favor of a certain course of action (rhetoric). So logic and rhetoric are natural partners to ethics.

As we have discussed, ethics is concerned with what one ought to do. Ethics also includes the continuous questioning and exploration of how to refine the "what ought to be done" based on changes in known information and/or changes in the prevailing social consciousness. In the latter case, think of how the worldwide trend to recognize gay marriage has changed social consciousness and thereby social norms. Ethics is thus an alive discipline that invites continuous questioning and fine-tuning.

Due to changing circumstances and a continuously evolving social consciousness, every age prompts new ethical principles or a re-interpretation of existing ones. Even so, these principles tend to lag social, technical and scientific advances. This means that new ethical principles are always scrambling to keep up with the times. Bioethics, with DNA altering and gene-editing experiments, provides a pressing example. To be a critical thinker requires one to keep up with the times and the changing social currents. We cover this in greater detail in the next chapters.

### Components of critical thinking

An important element of ethical thinking is the ability to think critically. The concept of critical thinking comes from (you guessed it) the ancient Greeks. The word "critical" derives etymologically from two Greek roots: *kriticos* (meaning "discerning judgment"), and *kriterion* (meaning "standards"). The word critical thus means "discerning judgment based on standards."

Critical thinking has three dimensions: an analytic, an evaluative and a creative component. For example: What was said or done? (analytic); what are the merits and faults? (evaluative); what conclusion can be drawn? (creative).

We typically draw our conclusions from a combination of information, inferences and assumptions.

- Information includes observations, facts, sounds, smells, feelings.
- Inferences are mental jumps by which we conclude something to be true in light of something else being true. For example: If you wave a revolver in my direction, I will infer that you plan to shoot me.

- Assumptions are something we presuppose. They are part of our inherent system of beliefs and we use them to interpret the world around us. In the example above, the underlying assumption which led to my inference is that people who wave revolvers are dangerous and tend to shoot people.

Many of our assumptions are internalized and we are unaware of them. As a result, we fail to question them or even become aware of how they shape our reality. They have simply become ingrained and part of our way of being in the world. This lack of self-awareness – something we discuss under Ethics and Mindfulness in Chapter 10 – creates huge blind spots for us and frequently gets us into trouble. A key part of critical thinking is the making of our unconscious assumptions more conscious.

In decision-making, there are times when either or both our inferences or assumptions are inaccurate, illogical or unsound. From an ethical perspective, critical thinking requires us to be aware of our inferences and the assumptions on which they are based with a view to seeing how they influence our moral behavior.

To clarify, let us take two examples:

### Example 1

| *Person A* | *Person B* |
| --- | --- |
| Situation: A man is lying in the gutter | Situation: A man is lying in the gutter |
| Inference: That man is a drunken bum | Inference: That man is injured |
| Assumption: Only drunken bums lie in gutters. | Assumption: Anyone lying in the gutter needs help. |

### Example 2

| *Person A* | *Person B* |
| --- | --- |
| Situation: A friend tells you she is going to have an abortion | Situation: A friend tells you she going to have an abortion |
| Inference: She does not plan to marry her boyfriend | Inference: For health reasons the doctor advised her to do this |
| Assumption: Babies conceived out of wedlock are aborted. | Assumption: Pregnancies that threaten the mother's life are aborted. |

What we can infer from these two examples, is that Person A and Person B have very different ethical sensitivities. If they shared a moral dilemma, it is likely they would propose very different courses of action.

The point here is not who is right or wrong, but awareness. Critical thinking not only tests the rigor of our inferences based on our assumptions, but the validity of the assumptions themselves.

Based on the hundreds of people that have gone through my ethics bootcamps, we have a long way to go in the self-awareness department! Not only that, frequently our inferences do not line up with our assumptions.

Alas, critical thinking is not something we practice with rigor and thoughtfulness. And many decisions are made as a leap from feelings to action without regard for a clear progression of critical thought. In our highly personalist world, when one challenges these emotive leaps (as in my role of facilitator or instructor, I often do), one is accused of being a rationalist, an academic, someone overtly intellectual or someone without feelings. End of conversation!

## When is an issue a moral issue?

Often people ask how one knows when something is a moral issue. In those subtler cases, where an obvious misdemeanor or temptation is not under consideration, what indicators exist to put one on moral alert?

Here are five guidelines:

### *Indicator 1: concept of limits*

Ethics is inherently about the concepts of limits, i.e., it is concerned with excess and deficiency. Whenever something or some situation is excessive or deficient, an ethical principle comes into play.

Let us take an example that every board should be wrestling with: The average income of a CEO of the S&P Index companies in 2018 was $14.5 million – that equates to $39,726 per day based on 365 days per year, and $ 3,310 per hour based on a 12-hour day. If one were to allow for 25 days of vacation time, the pay shoots up to $42,647 per day and $3,554 per hour. Who is truly SO valuable as to earn in one day what perhaps two people on the low end of the scale earn in an entire year? What earth-shattering contribution to humanity does that one individual make?

Apparently, the average CEO income has increased by $5 million per year since the 2008 crash. I am totally flummoxed as to how one explains this increase.

From a concept of limits perspective, this level of CEO pay is excessive, and therefore unethical and immoral (https://aflcio.org › paywatch calculations mine).

How about people aspiring to be trillionaires or societies that make trillionaires possible? Is this morally acceptable? Your thoughts?

### *Indicator 2: relationships*

Ethics pertains to relationships – our relation to ourselves in the form of self-awareness, self-accountability and self-care, and our relationship to others and the way we care for them. Relating includes our capacity for empathy, sensitivity, kindness, reciprocity, loyalty, respect, confidentiality, fidelity, and love. Therefore, any situation or circumstance that has a relational element to it, has implied ethical responsibilities and raises moral issues.

How many encounters can you name that are not in some way relational?

### Indicator 3: reality

Ethics is concerned with how one encounters and engages reality. Reality refers to what is true, real, actual, exists as far as one can reasonably determine it. Whenever one is trying to establish reality, our moral obligation is to be as truthful, open and objective as our highest intentions will allow us. This means not engaging in fantasy, imagination, defensive dissembling, manipulation, sophistry, or obfuscation.

How often do you find yourself avoiding reality?

### Indicator 4: power

Wherever there is a power dynamic or power differential, moral accountability raises its head.

The issue of power is inherent in almost all relationships. Power is the force or energy needed to get things done. We use our power with others to achieve things. Power dynamics may arise when we tussle for who has the most power or who has been given formal power.

The shadow side of power is its potential abuse. We all know the saying "absolute power corrupts absolutely." Alas, that is only too true. We have seen it with the power of the financial services sector, the Church and the Boy Scouts.

Power differentials always exists as few people have equal power. Once one has power over others, one is morally obliged to act justly, empathetically and respectfully. One should be aware of abuse that may even be unwitting. In the good old days, there was the term, *noblesse oblige*. This means privilege entails responsibility – or nobility obliges.

In sum, any power issue should place us on moral alert.

Have you ever found yourself taking advantage in a situation where you have more power than the other person or persons?

### Indicator 5: possession

Potential moral issues arise around matters of possession. This does not only refer to tangible possessions, but intangibles such as a person's reputation or privacy. The data confidentiality issue that is currently of growing concern, is a distinctive moral issue.

Have you ever found yourself gossiping about other people's behavior? Guess what. Gossip tampers with their reputation which is their possession.

As we review these five indicators, we can see that all our actions and choices in some way have a moral undertow. This is another important reminder that ethics and morality are not simply disciplines to possibly engage in as mild, abstract pursuits in front of the winter evening fire. They are the fire of everyday life – sometimes simmering, sometimes glowing, and sometimes burning in voracious fury. Every choice carries the flame!

## The whistleblower's dilemma

Possibly the most celebrated and written about whistleblowers of all time were Sherron Watkins of Enron and Cynthia Cooper of WorldCom. They were both named "Persons of the Year 2002" by *Time* magazine. Described as "heroines on the scene," they were applauded for their courage to expose the shenanigans within their organizations that cost thousands of people their livelihoods. Within two years these highly vaunted women had both left their jobs (http://content.time.com/time/specials/packages/0,28757,2022164,00.html).

Research points out that most whistleblowers pay a very high price. Experts say that the public rarely hears of most whistleblowers and the repercussions they face. Whistleblowing is a tough decision that has incredible consequences. Some whistleblowers are fired – see the Carmen Segarra case in Chapter 1. Others are ostracized by fellow employees and subjected to management abuses that lead them to quit. Some whistleblowers have found even their families and communities turn against them. (There is the sad tale of the Unabomber's brother who revealed his brother's identity to the FBI and was then vilified and chased by the community from his home.)

Once the whistleblower has quit, they find they are blacklisted and cannot get a job in their field. Most of them are left to strike it out alone (https://www.newstatesman.com/culture/books/2016/04/blood-relations-how-live-killer-family).

Many whistleblowers who go to their boss believe their news will be well received. Alas, this is usually not the case. Most bosses do not want to hear bad news or something wrong with their organizations that might in any way incriminate or inconvenience them. Their first concern is first and foremost for themselves and their vulnerability. The messenger is thus usually shot.

## Flashpoint 5.1

The Securities and Exchange Comission (SEC) has created a cash for tips program. The SEC Office of the Whistleblower has paid more than $326 million to fifty-nine whistleblowers in seven years. The office is now overrun with tips and has a new problem: tip fraudsters, i.e., people who send in frivolous or bogus tips. A question that is now being raised concerns the size of the tip rewards. Some whistleblower payouts have exceeded $50 million!

A whole industry has now developed around providing and investigating tips including former FBI agents, attorneys specializing in whistleblower claims, accountants and consultants.

(*WSJ* – December 9, 2018)

While new legislation has been put in place to protect whistleblowers, the fact that they exposed company secrets makes them "damaged goods" and invariably attracts retaliation is some form or another. Sadly, human nature is such that we do not like tattle tales even when we know that what is going on is unethical and should be stopped. And we indifferently shrug off the fact that we are bystanders, colluders and thus complicit with any dark deeds.

## Flashpoint 5.2 Financial Times Reports – March 6, 2019

The best way to encourage whistleblowers is to reward them.

Ted Siedle, who spilled the beans on JP Morgan's misdemeanors was awarded $30 million by US regulators. JP Morgan paid $370 million in penalties.

Rewarding whistleblowers was made part of the 2008 reforms. According to the Dodd-Frank Act (2010), whistleblowers are eligible to receive a portion of any fine imposed. The result has been a rash of spurious entries and thousands of submissions. The fee idea is now being adopted around the world.

## It is damned difficult being a moral person

Here is a detailed real-life case that illustrates how challenging it is to be a moral person, never mind an ethical one! As we discussed briefly in Chapter 3, moral reasoning is the process by which we make our choices about how to behave or take action.

As we work this case, we look at the component parts of what it means to be a person who makes well-considered choices. A popular description for this is a person who knows "to do the right thing." This description is alas both superficial and misleading. First, there are relatively few cases where the absolute "right thing" is so obvious it cannot be contested. In other words, there are few absolutely "right things to do" in all circumstances. Second, who gets to decide that the "right thing" has been done? Is it the actor or the person on the receiving end of the action? If all parties agree that the right things were done, well and good. At least the world has one less dilemma to deal with. What if they do not agree? Is it the person who wields the most power who has the prerogative to decide? Often it seems so!

Let us now address the question regarding what it means to be a moral person by systematically working through the Moral Matrix set out below. As we work through the matrix a key question is: Do we need to get all six things "right" to qualify as a moral person? Let us wrestle with this vexing issue (Table 5.1).

*Table 5.1* The moral matrix

| Decision-making Aspect | Moral Language |
| --- | --- |
| How I see and recognize moral issues | Moral vision |
| Is there a moral claim on me? | Moral obligation – do I feel obliged to respond? |
| Why do I choose to respond to this claim? | Moral motivation – the cause behind my actions |
| What do I intend by responding to this claim? | Moral intention – I intend to or desire to . . . e.g. do my duty |
| What I actually do – execution of choice. | Moral courage – did I follow through on my intention? |
| The results of my actions. | Moral consequences – anticipated or unanticipated. |

*The Chicago gallery dilemma*

You work for a family owned gallery in Chicago. You have been the gallery manager for a little over a year. You have been a very effective gallery manager. Sales have soared due to your effective sales techniques and you have tidied up a chaotic administrative system.

Working in the gallery has been difficult. The family members are continuously at one another's throats regarding ownership and control of the gallery. At every opportunity they try to pull you into their battles by getting you caught up in competing loyalties. The owner of the gallery, Lesley Hardgate, who is the matriarch of the family system, is a manic–depressive personality. Often, she showers you with compliments and gifts, at other times she publicly demeans and abuses you. Worst of all, because many of the family members have access to the gallery check book, they draw funds out of the business frequently causing a cash flow crisis. Consequently, month after month your salary check bounces and you have to appeal to Lesley for another check. On occasion even the second and third replacement checks have bounced. This has cost you money and all kinds of embarrassment as in many cases after payday, you have issued checks on the assumption that your salary check would clear. You have had to explain your situation to the bank manager, who has not been at all understanding. He keeps telling you to get another job. But in the current climate that is not so easy. It took you six months to get this one. You have also spent hours on the telephone with the credit card companies who upped your credit card interest rates due to checks you have sent them bouncing when your salary check was not honored.

It is August. For the fourth time in a row, your salary check bounces. You return from vacation and find that a few checks you have issued have as a result bounced too. You are furious. Lesley knew you were going away and guaranteed that the funds were there to pay you. Angrily you speak with Lesley who tells you that "money has disappeared from the business" and that you have to wait two weeks for a replacement check.

A week later, Lesley gives you a replacement check. Then a further few days later, one Saturday evening, after a busy day at the gallery, she leaves you another replacement check, having seemingly forgotten that she had already given you one. So now you have two replacement checks to cover the one that was not honored when you went on holiday.

You know that Lesley's books of account are a total mess and that she is unlikely to ever detect the error. At best, the accountant may find the error at the end of the financial year. Even that is uncertain as Lesley is forever giving people checks without recording what they are for. You are furious with Lesley and feel she has treated you very badly especially since gallery sales have doubled since your arrival. You could hold onto the second check and keep is at back up for further checks bouncing. You could also keep the second check as reparation for all the costs and discomfort you have experienced over the last months. After all, it is only $2,500 (you earn $5,000 per month paid bi-weekly) and surely you deserve that as compensation for what you have been through.

The last year has been very difficult for you financially. Besides struggling to get a job, you have had to make major repairs to your house. The ongoing financial drama with Lesley has not helped at all. In fact, one of your repairmen has not come back to complete the work he promised to do for you due to a check you gave him not being honored by the bank. Even more embarrassing is that your bank manager has mentioned that your checking account is in jeopardy.

What should you do? Hold onto the check for a bit and keep it as back-up? Keep the check and consider it compensation for the distress you have experienced? Tell Lesley about her error and return it immediately?

### Let us apply the Moral Matrix to our dilemma

#### Moral vision

The first thing moral behavior depends upon is moral vision. This means that we recognize that there is a moral issue in the first place. We can use the five-indicator guideline provided earlier.

Sometimes a moral issue may not be immediately apparent but has the potential to manifest itself in the future. Questioning whether moral issues exist and anticipating future moral issues requires moral vision. Many genuinely unintended moral slip ups occur as a result of poor moral vision. This is particularly true in the corporate realm when charting new scientific or technical ground. For example, the discipline of bioethics begins with having the moral vision to anticipate the moral consequences of new scientific breakthroughs. Imagine all the moral issues that in-vitro fertilization raises that were difficult to predict in advance.

Moral vision is an important, if not essential attribute of the moral person. To hone one's moral vision requires active engagement in the world. It requires attentiveness and an inquiring mind. Moral vision is not something that can be taught by rules. On the contrary, if anything, moral vision is suppressed once people are managed by codes and rules. As we learn how globally interconnected we are, and as we struggle with the rapidity of change occurring on so many dimensions, moral vision is an essential requirement for the ethical manager and the responsible corporate citizen.

Let us take our case with Lesley and the gallery. This is not a complicated case and does not as such demand great moral vision to see that a moral dilemma exists. The moral issue relates to honesty and accountability. Lesley has made a mistake. The result of that mistake is that you have been paid twice for the same work period. The moral issue is that you are not entitled to this money at this time. Lesley is unaware of her error and you could take advantage of the situation.

*Moral obligation*

Having identified the moral issue, the next step is that a moral person acknowledges some obligation or call to respond. Without a sense of moral obligation, it is unlikely that any moral action will be taken. Of course, there might be enforcement by someone else and luck or coincidence that may play a part in executing moral actions. However, true moral behavior requires the conscious recognition of one's moral obligations.

In the case of the gallery, as the gallery manager you have the responsibility for accurate accountability of the gallery's assets and its money. You are an honest person; you recognize that you have a moral obligation to be honest and to reveal what has occurred. There is a moral claim on you to own up to the situation. The error has resulted in your having money that you have not actually earned at this time.

*Moral motivation*

The next step is that moral behavior requires some form of moral motivation. A moral person not only recognizes a moral claim on them but is motivated to respond. Motivation almost always requires emotional engagement. Emotional engagement means experiencing some feelings (anger, indignation, excitement, empathy) related to the moral issue. One thing we want in our organizations is emotionally engaged people.

Switched off and detached people are rarely highly motivated. Some people deliberately suppress emotional engagement because they find the realm of emotions unsafe. Sadly, they do not realize that detachment in the realm of morals can prove the far less morally responsible option. Acting without feelings may eliminate capricious behavior but at the same time eliminates personal commitment and investment in the outcome of one's actions.

Let us again look at the situation of the gallery and Lesley. In this case, why would you choose to respond to the moral claim on you? There are many understandable reasons for you saying

> I realize that I have a moral obligation here, but because I have been treated so disrespectfully, in this case I choose not to respond to this claim. In fact, I am entitled to the money to cover the financial losses and self-esteem costs that all these bounced checks have cost me!

You could have a clash between your professional obligations and personal values. What would morally motivate you to suppress your personal interest and take the moral high road? Would you be a dreadfully immoral person if you did not? Isn't recognizing the moral claim on you and justifying your response not to respond sufficient? Alternatively, you could say this moral claim requires a moral response and because you are a decent, honest person, you will not take your cue from Lesley. You will tell her about the error.

### Moral intention

Next, we consider moral intention. Moral intention is closely allied to moral motivation. It refers to what it is that a person desires to achieve by responding to his or her moral obligation; for example; the intention to do one's duty or to satisfy one's own interest.

In the case of Lesley and the gallery, your moral intention may be to act with integrity by doing your professional duty by calling her attention to her mistake. That is the kind of person you are. Alternatively, your moral intention may be to show Lesley up as a person who is incompetent and cannot keep track of the checks she writes.

### Moral courage and moral freedom

Moral intention usually precedes moral action. What can happen between intention and action though, is a failure of **moral courage**. Where there is a failure of moral courage, moral intention will not convert into action.

At this point, prior to our moral action, we need to consider the issue of moral freedom. Moral freedom as we discussed, affects the way we assess someone's moral culpability. What if a person is not morally free to act? Is lack of freedom an acceptable moral defense? Can one claim to be a moral person where one's moral motivation and intention remain merely a soliloquy in one's mind? Must it be followed by action? When we look at a few ethical guiding principles in the next chapter we will see what they have to say about the matter. The matter of moral freedom is played out in our law courts all the time. They are full of cases where the villain gets off under all kinds of extenuating circumstances that fall under the claim of loss of "moral freedom."

### Moral action

Returning to the Moral Matrix, when we consider moral action, we must acknowledge that at the end of the day moral action is the critical aspect of morality. To qualify as a moral person therefore, there must be some attempt at moral action.

Let us return to Lesley and the gallery dilemma. Let us assume you have recognized the moral issue and your moral obligation and that you know what your moral intention in taking action will be. Now you have to act. You intend to tell Lesley about her error. However, suddenly you get cold feet. Lesley is always irrational and excitable when it comes to things about money. It is a subject she avoids. Most of the time, she is in a financial mess herself and strikes out angrily at others whenever the topic of money comes up. What if she lets loose at you and tells you that you mislead her and that it is your fault she made the error?

What if she decides not to pay you your next salary as she has already paid you twice in her mind, even if you return the second check to her? What if both these replacement checks bounce and you are left again without your salary and have to start begging again for replacement checks? Your bank manager will not be so accommodating next time. He could close your account. Can you take that chance? Do you even have a choice here? Would it not be better just to let things lie? If she finds out, you can say you were confused with all the checks bouncing that you did not pick up the error. Maybe it will never come up and in time it will pass over. You have begun looking for a new job anyway. You mean well. You want to tell her, but dealing with her and money is a nightmare. You really do not need any further aggravation. You are a moral person. You do not steal or lie. You certainly do not want to steal from Lesley. You are the best gallery manager she ever had, and she has abused you repeatedly. You are as honest and scrupulous as the day is long. In this case it was a genuine error. Let sleeping dogs lie. It will sort itself out in the wash!

After all your deliberations in the face of Lesley's disgruntled, moody face on Monday morning, you do nothing.

According to the Moral Matrix where does this place you as a moral person? Is lack of courage the deciding factor? What about all your honest deliberations and concerns and all your moral actions at other times? Do they count for nothing? Do you need to get all six steps of the Moral Matrix "right" to count as a moral person? What about consequences?

*Moral consequences*

The last component of the Moral Matrix is consequences. Do the consequences of our actions have to be morally sound for us to qualify as moral individuals? That is another tricky question. There may be times when we got everything else "right," vision, motivation, courage and yet, the execution of our action fails our good intentions. Sometimes failure will reflect on our morality, for example in the case of lack of competence or care. At other times, unexpected events may occur that could genuinely not have been anticipated. In this case are we "excused?"

What we notice from working through these components of moral behavior is that it is not easy to be a moral person. Many things can derail our good intentions. We may have the best will in the world, but we may not be able to follow through on it in all cases. Does this make us immoral or bad people?

As we shall see as we review different ethical theories, based on whichever theory or principle we defer to, we would be judged differently. For utilitarians, only consequences matter. For Immanuel Kant, nothing else matters but our motivation and intention to do our duty. Aristotle would say that we cannot be judged based on one or two actions but rather on our character and the narrative of our lives. What kind of life do we reflect? How overall do our intentions and actions come together?

There are rarely easy answers to most moral dilemmas. This is what makes them dilemmas in the first place. Our problems do not end here. Now we face the next challenge: Will any moral action do? Here is where our ethical principles kick in.

## Exercise 1: Lesley and the gallery

- If you were working for Lesley, and this was your experience, what would you do?
- Why would you do what you would do? What are the factors that you would take into account?
- What stage of Kohlberg's framework would you find yourself operating from?

## Which ethical principle?

Once a moral issue has been identified, we must consider which ethical principle/s might best guide us in our choice of action. Here is where matters can get challenging. Should we appeal to scripture or wisdom writings? Should custom, mores, or tradition influence our decisions? Should we lean into personal beliefs or learned dogmas on the topic? Should we take the virtue ethics, utilitarian, or contracts approach? What should the role of experience or precedence play? In the case of duty, how should we choose between two competing moral claims? As you can imagine, these are simply a few of a myriad number of questions we might ask.

Choosing a guiding ethical principle can be most challenging if one needs to reconcile one's own values with those of the corporation. In these case one might line up one's moral ducks quite differently from that dictated by the corporate value system. Herein lies the moral struggle of whether to conform or claim one's own moral authority. Not an easy choice either way.

In a business setting, the corporate culture dictates how things are "done." Explicit and implicit corporate values receive recognition as do rewards from senior management. Issues such as precedence usually inhibit new interpretations or patterns of behavior. A strong culture of expectations sets the tone for what comprises good or acceptable practice, and senior management endorses these practices as benchmarks of expected or preferred behavior. Organizational reward systems usually further reinforce the value system underwritten by senior management. The tension between being a moral principal in one's own personal capacity versus being a moral agent in a corporate capacity can result in confusion regarding moral accountability. The question often becomes not which principles to apply but whose. This reality circles us back to the issue of power and ethics. Those in power make the rules – essentially the rules about how others should behave. So where can the ethical manager turn for guidance when facing a moral dilemma? This is a most challenging question. Maybe the next chapters can help us.

**Executive summary**

This chapter sums up our journey so far. It highlights the ethical pressures that exist at multiple levels and that test our ethical capacities and moral courage. What we also come to realize is that ethics or business ethics does not provide simple answers. Instead, we find we must navigate our own way between multiple tensions where we wrestle with various ethical guidelines and moral obligations along with the call of our conscience.

Here are some of this chapter's key points:

- Business ethics can only be understood and addressed when we understand the multiple layers of systemic complexity involved.
- Global capitalism based on the free market system has lost its way and in so doing has eroded the ethical foundations on which it was originally conceived.
- Organizations, as communities of people, have within them many characteristics that inhibit people's moral sensibilities.
- Ethical responsibility begins with self-examination. Becoming ethical rests on inner work and a focus on our personal being.
- Part of ethical development is working on our own moral development.
- The more we practice ethics, the more ethical we become.
- Situations can upend our ethical predictions – both of ourselves and of others.
- The ability to think critically is an important part of being ethical.
- Whistleblowers usually pay a huge personal price.
- Deciding which ethical principle should guide which moral dilemma, is a complex and challenging question. It is a major part of moral reasoning.

**Questions for reflection**

- If your company is a global one, does it monitor its suppliers and distributors work conditions for fair conditions and just behavior? How do you know?
- Which challenges to ethical behavior outlined so far do you find most personally inhibiting, e.g., survival at work; group pressure; challenging authority?
- Have you had a situation where you or others have behaved totally out of character? How did you understand this dynamic?
- How often do you test your assumptions? When did you last notice yourself doing so?

**Key terms**

Assumption   161
Bystander collusion   162
Concept of limits   165
Critical thinking   163
Ecology of capitalism   159
Ethical culture   160

## Reference

Ross, Lee and Richard E. Nisbett. *The Person and the Situation.* New York: McGraw-Hill, 2017.

Part 2

# Ethical strategies and practice guidelines on how to become an ethical leader

# 6 From Socrates to modernity

## Contents

## All is fair in love, war and business

Sally Ann Jones is the owner/manager of a successful marketing and communications company. She has slogged through the recession, recreated herself several times, and managed to emerge with an increasingly profitable client base.

Sally Ann is also a very active member of the community. She engages in a variety for volunteering activities; helps out at the local church and sits on the local school board. She is extremely extroverted; loves being out in the public and has a wide circle of friends.

Recently Sally Ann faced what she considered a serious ethical dilemma. One day she was approached by a prestigious organization to provide a quotation for a significant amount of marketing and public relations work. She was thrilled having harbored hope for many years that one day she might land a client of this significance. The one nagging issue that blighted her joy regarding the client's invitation is that a friend and colleague of hers had worked for this client for several years. When the client called her up and asked her to submit a proposal the client's representative had also talked disparagingly about her friend's company. While she was delighted to be considered for the new work, now she felt torn by considerations of loyalty to her friend. Should she take on this client knowing that this was an important source of income to her friend? Should she tell her friend that this client had approached her? What would this do to their relationship? Would her friend think that she was trying to steal her clients? They had shared discussions about both personal and work issues for years. Could she be as honest and straight forward about this new development now that it intersected both of their businesses?

Sally Ann fretted for several days about how she was going to handle this with her friend. At a dinner meeting with her friend shortly after the client's invitation, Sally Ann felt compelled to spill the beans – as she described it. She told her friend about the call from the client and tentatively alluded to the client's alleged disappointment with the performance of her friend's organization. Her friend was appalled. She suggested that she call the client and see whether she could make amends. Sally Ann pointed out that what she had divulged was no doubt confidential and that would not help matters. She claimed that she, Sally Ann, was going to put in a proposal and would promise to let her friend know the outcome. "I just thought you should know," she told her friend. Their evening ended on a distant note.

When Sally Ann related the details of the evening to her husband, he castigated her for mixing friendship and work. "You got the call; you have the possibility of the work. You need it. You have wanted this kind of client for so long. You have worked so hard and deserve it because of the quality of what you produce. Why did you screw it up? Now she is going to meddle and try to get her client back! Can't you see – all is fair in love, war and business!"

What do you think? Do you think all is fair in love, war and business? What do you believe the ethical approach is here? Is there even an ethical issue? Maybe this is just good old capitalism at work.

## Exercise 1

### Questions

- What are the ethical issues here?
- If you were in Sally Ann's position what would you do and why?
- What would be your guiding principle?

## Guidance for the ethical quest

> *We can easily forgive a child who is afraid of the dark, the real tragedy of life is when we are afraid of the light.*
>
> Plato

In Part I, we reflected on the many systemic pressures that make living an ethical life challenging.

In my experience, few people begin life intent on being malicious, corrupt or dishonest. However, humanity can be frail, and sometimes the conflicting pressures presented during life's journey can be enormous causing us to succumb to our darker sides.

As we have discussed, several common ethical challenges we face include power dynamics, fear of failure, pressure to produce results, too little time to think, stress, fear of losing our jobs, fear of authority, and wanting to be accepted and be part of the safety of the group.

Where can we turn for help, guidance and inspiration as we chart our way through these turbulent waters? How can we rise above our fears and claim our moral autonomy and agency? What can we do to ensure that we do not silence ourselves when we witness or suspect unethical behavior? How can we survive with our morality intact? How can we hold onto our power in the face of group moral pressures? Oh, so many questions!

This chapter provides us with some guidance in response to these questions but gives no absolute answers. Our first step is to examine several well-known ethical principles along with the thinking that gave rise to each principle.[1]

While reading this chapter, you may wish to consider which of these principles resonate with you and which principles don't.

As a note: This chapter does not cover the important and complex matter of justice as the entire next chapter is devoted to that topic.

## Oh no – philosophy!

Many people have a distaste of philosophy. They say philosophy is simply a mind game where one just plays with words and abstractions that seemingly go nowhere. On the other hand, they insist that their lives and their decisions deal with real issues and get down to making things happen. Philosophy is simply a waste of time!

As a someone who came to an appreciation of philosophy later in life, I can remember a time when I might have identified with these sentiments. Today I see this from an entirely different perspective. I have also found that once business executives or managers are given the time and space to wrestle with thinking about how they think, and why they think as they do, they experience a new appreciation of that dreaded word "philosophy" and actually come to enjoy exploring the insightful questioning it can provoke.

Ethical principles fall under the banner of philosophy. And since ethics is about choices and decision-making, and we are concerned with the ethical principles that drive our decisions, it behooves us to have some understanding of these principles by studying just a little philosophy.

## Insights provided by philosophical ethical principles

- Ethical principles can guide us when solving moral challenges by providing ways in which we might think about things.
- They provide us with the language of ethics and morals thereby enabling us to articulate our ethical position more eloquently.
- Understanding ethical theories can help us develop our moral reasoning skills.
- They serve as an opportunity to reflect on our own morals and see how we line up our moral ducks.
- For those in management positions, reviewing the range of ethical theories that inform people's reasoning serves as a helpful reminder that we live in a

pluralistic world where different people use different ethical principles and different value systems to inform their decisions.

- Using ethical principles in our discussions helps depersonalize issues thus removing some of the personal charge often triggered in difficult conversations.
- Wrestling with how to apply different ethical theories makes us more thoughtful people and better decision-makers.

### Am I a good person? Do I care about my character?

We begin our discussion of ethical theory with character-based or virtue ethics which I introduced briefly in Chapter 3. I have selected the main ideas and themes of four people who have shaped the character-based approach. These are: Socrates, Plato, Aristotle and Jesus.

#### Socrates (469 BCE–399 BCE)

As we recall from Chapter 3, Socrates advocated that people's primary concern should be centered on how they should live. He expounded the Delphic motto "Know Thyself," as he believed that only through self-examination and self-knowledge could one find genuine happiness. Happiness, according to Socrates, results from living a life grounded in the quest for the truth. That truth is that we never know as much as we think we do and our claims to knowledge are seldom justified. The wisest person, therefore, is one who has humility and who considers himself worthless in face of the divine or God.

Socrates was convinced that having knowledge leads to living a good life. He believed that once one knows the essence of "the good," one will necessarily seek to do what is good. What is good is that which is life giving, noble, and advances human flourishing. Not seeking to do the good is detrimental to oneself as unethical actions harm the person who performs those actions more than the people they victimize. Evil and moral depravity occur as a result of ignorance. So "the good" is good for us; it is worthy of pursuit. A reasonable person would therefore always choose the good.

According to Socrates, moral values should not be accepted based on religious or political authority, or social traditions, or as a result of emotions or feelings. They should only be accepted based on rational and logical examination of the concepts involved. Because humans have the capacity to reason, they should act reasonably.

In sum, Socrates recommended a life filled with self-awareness and self-examination with a high emphasis on exercising reason in deciding how to live. Through education and contemplation, a person recognizes "the good" (or what is good), and our faculty of reason directs us to choose the good. By choosing the good, we act virtuously, we live a moral life, and we achieve our desired end – happiness.

> **Ethical injunction**: *Take that action that reflects a life of striving for human excellence and wisdom.*

*Plato (428 BCE–348 BCE)*

Plato was engaged in the search for absolute reality. He wanted to counter the subjective, changing, inconsistent and inconstant of the everyday concrete world. According to him, the world of absolutes is the world of Ideas or Forms. These Forms are prior to and superior to the concrete world. They are the archetypes in which concrete reality participates. They are unchanging essences that we can only understand with the "mind's eye," i.e., with a refined intellect.

These ideal Forms represent ultimate reality, which is ethical, rational and aesthetic in nature. They are effectively the good, the true, and the beautiful united in a supreme creative principle. Through these forms, the universe is ruled by a wondrous, regulating intelligence.

Plato believed that without the concept of the Forms, our knowledge is based on perception and opinions which are arbitrary, personal and situationally contextualized. The reality that presents itself as concrete to our senses is merely a copy or shadow of some other intellectual or spiritual reality (The allegory of the cave refers to these shadow realities to which we are attached in Plato's *Republic Book IV)*. It is only once we grasp the nature or essence of something, for example, goodness, that we can assess and compare the goodness that is inherent in what we perceive or experience and describe its relativeness to the absolute. Without the Forms as grounding, we simply live in a world of sensory illusion.

Plato insisted that the archetypes are only discovered through pure, abstract and dialectical reasoning. However, the archetypal world is not an abstraction. It is the basis of reality. The pinnacle of reality is the form of the good which the soul pursues through its highest part which is the intellect. (Recall Chapter 3 where we discussed Plato's idea of the role of the soul. The soul within us carries the recollection of the Forms.)

Plato places a lot of emphasis on both universals as objective principles (the forms) and the intellect. It is through contemplation and disciplined education that our intellect is honed and illumined such that it can experience the Forms. Plato does not provide any systematic treatment of ethics from which norms of behavior or rules can be derived. He confines himself largely to what is good for the soul and as I stated earlier, this means honoring the virtues (wisdom, courage, temperance, justice), and the forms of which they are part, so that one can live a good life.

> **Ethical injunction:***Take that action that reflects a virtuous life in accordance with the dictates of reason.*

*Aristotle (384 BCE–322 BCE)*

Aristotle had a great impact on the development of character-based, or what is often referred to as, virtue ethics. His ideas and writings are extensive, and the simple summary included here does meager justice to his major contribution to our understanding of ethics.

REASON AND THE NATURAL LAW

Aristotle believed that all human beings are "wired," so to speak, with the natural law. Due to our rational nature, by exercising our reason, we can recognize and respond to this innate natural law. What Aristotle meant by this is that our reason will lead us to make natural i.e., reasonable choices that recognize our moral obligations. Aristotle, like Socrates and Plato, tied ethics to the "reasonable man" theory by equating reasonable or rational choices with ethical ones.

REACHING OUR POTENTIAL AS A MORAL IMPERATIVE

Aristotle also believed that all things have a purpose and a function that naturally drives them toward their fullness or ultimate potentiality. He called this fullness or ultimate potentiality, *teleology* from the Greek word *telos* meaning goal, end, purpose. He argued that the moral imperative for human beings is that they keep striving to attain their ultimate potential. In modern parlance we would say this means that a human being is morally obligated to do all he or she can to "be all that he or she can be" for that is life's true goal or purpose.

Aristotle underscored this further by claiming that human life consists of the pursuit of ends (goals). The ultimate end is happiness which is achieved by being all that one can be. Moral deliberation is taken up with determining the best means to achieve this end.

To sum up these ideas then, Aristotle believed that everything has a function. The function of humankind is to be rational and practical. Rational activity means keeping our passions in check by 1) making reasonable decisions and 2) striving to attain our full potential or end. By practicing these habits, we will not only be happy, but we will be fulfilling our ethical goal or quest.

THE GOLDEN MEAN

Another very important ethical concept introduced by Aristotle is the idea of the "golden mean." It is the golden mean that clarifies the notion of virtue or virtuous behavior.

Acting virtuously means choosing to keep our passions or desires in check. Excessive or defective behavior (meaning nonvirtuous behavior), demonstrates a "form of failure" in checking the passions, while the "intermediate," or the "mean," demonstrates a form of success. The golden mean is thus taking the "middle path" or acting with moderation; namely, not too much and not too little. Virtuous or ethical choices imply choosing in accordance with "the mean." A good moral character, meaning one filled with virtue, is someone who strives to choose the "mean" or to act with moderation.

Now this is not as easy as it sounds. Choosing the mean or acting with moderation, according to Aristotle, implies that the act must be done at the right time, with reference to the right object, made toward the right people, with the right motive, and carried out in the right way.

Let us take the example of courage to better understand what Aristotle is getting at here. One can view courage as the mean between feelings of fear and supreme confidence. Excessive fearfulness we call cowardice. Excessive confidence we call brashness. A courageous person is one who holds the middle ground. He or she fears the right things, at the right time, to the appropriate degree. A courageous action, according to Aristotle, is one exercised at the appropriate time, not before or after the moment when a courageous intervention is required. Being courageous also depends on what one is being courageous about, i.e., its object. For example, defending one's friend with a hatchet against a field mouse would hardly qualify as an act of courage.

So "the mean" is something that is exquisitely appropriate in its timing, referent point and execution. This analysis illustrates that being virtuous is not easy. In fact, virtuous actions that qualify in all aspects are rare. Something Aristotle clearly recognized. He states himself that "the mean" is hard to attain. He acknowledges that from time to time, because of our desires we invariably swing towards excess in either direction. Sometimes we do too little and sometimes too much. This is quite understandable for we are human. Aristotle asserts that if we can focus on limiting the extent of the swings, however, so that we approximate "the mean" we are striving to do the best we can. Awareness and proper intention are for Aristotle sound moral attributes (Aristotle, 1999).

THE CENTRALITY OF PRUDENCE

Aristotle (after Plato), is known for naming the chief moral attributes of the virtuous person as temperance, courage (fortitude), justice and prudence. Prudence he believes is the foremost or cardinal virtue in that it defines or determines the other virtues. Prudence helps us find "the mean." It helps us decide the defining line of courage in the face of fear and confidence for example. Prudence provides the guiding center of action and defines the limits. Prudence defines appropriateness, timing and methods of executing the other virtues. A prudent person, for Aristotle, is someone highly perceptive, and who has perfected this ability to read situations appropriately.

While being prudent in our world usually refers to being cautious and risk averse, Aristotle had a different interpretation. A prudent person in Aristotle's terms is one who radically searches and finds a new edge; who charters new waters, and who finds new solutions while wrestling creatively with the dynamic concept of the mean. The prudent person finds new sources and new practices of wisdom. He or she is morally pragmatic, accepting the messy particulars of life and the difficulties in always doing the right thing.

CHARACTER

Aristotle differed from Socrates in that he linked moral virtue to character and personality rather than solely to the intellect. His concept of moral virtue involves our hearts as well as our heads. It addresses us in the entirety of who we are. He believed that to be ethical we must mold our character, which he defined as the total of our habitual actions so that we consistently pursue the good and moral life. Moral virtue arises from habitual action akin to learning a technical skill. The way to become virtuous, therefore, requires practice. The payoff lies in that a life full of virtue means to live both a good one and a happy one.

MORAL FREEDOM

In Chapter 4, I discussed the issue of moral freedom. It was Aristotle who raised this matter in relation to an individual's ability to make choices. He argues in his *Nicomachean Ethics, Book III* (1999), that virtues and vices can only refer to voluntary actions, i.e., choices made freely. He defined nonvoluntary actions as those done out of compulsion or ignorance. Compulsion occurs when the agent is under the coercive powers of others. Deciding whether compulsion truly exists and the extent of it, requires careful assessment and deliberation. Aristotle also points out that proving true ignorance, short of madness, is difficult. One important test is whether the person feels pain and genuine regret for any harmful action he or she may have caused.

ETHICS AS OUR LIFE STORY

Aristotle's approach to ethics was highly pragmatic. He acknowledged that ethics was far from an exact science in that it dealt with the messy particulars of daily living. His emphasis lay on a person's striving to live a life that reflected reasonable choices and moderation. He understood that people frequently get it wrong. Virtue for him lay in the right reasoning, the right intention and the effort to live a good life. In his schema people could only be judged by their life story and not by the circumstances of one action.

From this (believe it or not) brief summary, we gain a glimpse of the many aspects in which Aristotle investigated the nature of ethics. Through the efforts of St. Thomas Aquinas, Aristotle's framework came to form a significant part of the moral philosophy of the Catholic Church. The post-Reformation philosophers, however, abandoned much of Aristotle's thinking preferring to focus on moral actions rather than the virtuous state of an individual or character. (Discussed in Chapter 1.)

> **Ethical injunction**: *Take that action that is thoughtful, reasonable and honest, and reflects the life you want to live.*

We conclude the discussion of virtue or character-based ethics with the contribution made by Jesus.

*Jesus (circa 4 BCE)*

My discussion of Jesus excludes the perspective that many people believe him to be the Son of God, the savior of humankind, and a supreme object of worship and devotion. By not focusing on the divinity of Jesus and the meaning of his resurrection, I do not intend to dispute any claims to the foregoing nor to offend any believers. Here I focus purely on his ethical teachings and how these have influenced our moral consciousness to this day.

Jesus, the Jew from Galilee, like Socrates and Aristotle before him, advocated a total life and total character approach to ethics. At the time of his teaching, the Jewish priestly elite had developed the idea of the Law of God into one that embraced over 670 prescriptions and regulations to which "good' Jews were expected to adhere (See Deontology later in the chapter). The Pharisees, the priestly elite of that time, used the intricacies of the Law and rituals to assert their power and to inflate their religious importance. Jesus openly challenged this approach to God and to living a good life.

His major contribution to the ethics of his day was to bring a new understanding of the nature of God and of God's relation to humanity. The God of Jesus is a God who is full of love and mercy and who has an appreciation of human frailty. His God is a highly relational God, who places great emphasis on how people treat themselves and one another.

Living a good life for Jesus meant living in right relationship with God. His preaching was centered on what that meant and how to practice it.

ETHICAL TEACHING

In the Gospel of Matthew, a section referred to as the *Sermon on the Mount* (Matthew 3:16), sometimes referred to as the *Beatitudes*, conveys the essence of Jesus' ethical teaching. The *Beatitudes* contain various admonitions to live by a higher standard than the Law (the Law of the Hebrew Bible) requires. Not only should people not kill, they should not be angry. Not only should they avoid adultery, they should not look at others with lust in their hearts. Not only should they not swear falsely, they should not take oaths at all. Far from retaliating when injured, they should "turn the other cheek." Finally, they should love not only their friends but also their enemies.

The love of neighbor theme endures as the height of the Christian ethic and is the basis of all moral conduct. The love command is decisive and central. It cannot be reduced to rules. It is practical and is a concrete call to service. It is a choice that must be faced and made. Love cannot be delayed; it requires an immediate response. True love is always kind and merciful.

Jesus does not say what one should do. Anyone who truly loves, knows what must be done and understands the primacy of love. Love should be the determining motive of every deed. According to Jesus, our morals are empty and pretentious if mercy does not have the last word. Jesus sums up his own perfectionist ethics in his command to "be perfect, as your heavenly Father is perfect." (Matt 5:48).

GOLDEN RULE

Jesus also proposes certain limits on behavior in proposing his Golden Rule. Here he advocates, "In everything do to others as you would have them do to you." By suggesting that one uses oneself as a benchmark, he implies that we will not be excessive nor fall short with others, as we do not like others to do this to us. We like things to be just right, i.e., not too much and not too little, and if we adopt this standard for ourselves, we should adopt it in our relationship with others.

In the Golden Rule, Jesus, in similar vein to Aristotle, introduces the concept of limits and the idea of striving to find the middle ground or to exercise moderation. It is interesting that both of their concepts are referred to as "golden" thereby implying not only the preciousness and great value they hold, but the difficulty in making these concepts a lived reality. People must experience an inner transformation in order to behave in this way.

It is important to note that the Golden Rule as one of the basic ethical precepts is not limited to the Christian tradition but is found in the sacred writings of all the major world religions. Jesus, who was a Jew, undoubtedly knew of the saying in the *Torah*, "Thou shalt not avenge, nor bear any grudge against the children of thy people, but thou shalt love thy neighbor as thyself: I am the Lord." (Leviticus 19:18).

Depending on the belief system of the other traditions where either the other is like me or part of me, the obvious idea is that the happiness and suffering of others is akin to mine, or in fact part of mine.

SELF-EXAMINATION

Jesus' ethics has similarities with Socrates and Aristotle. Throughout his teachings he repeatedly stresses the need for self-examination, attention to how one lives one's life and concern for others. One's disposition and one's intention matters as much as one's external actions. Love, mercy and humility are of paramount importance.

> **Ethical injunction:** *Take that action that reflects unconditional love (empathy and compassion) and is the way you would like to be treated out of love.*

## Key principles of character-based (virtue) ethics

A summary of the perspectives presented by Socrates, Plato, Aristotle and Jesus presents us with following principles:

* Character-based ethics is concerned with how one lives one's life – the story that one's life would depict.
* Reflection and self-examination helps one achieve inner transformation and builds character.
* Acting reasonably and moderately needs to be habitual and molds character.
* Dispositions, intentions and actions all count.
* The right motivation of striving to do good, showing humility and displaying love or benevolence is essential.
* Decision-making informed by character-based ethics focuses on how the choice made influences and shapes the narrative of a person's life and character.

- In character-based ethics, each moment is a defining moment in that each decision further adds and defines one's character. No one intention or action determines a person's morality. Only the story of one's life can show the extent to which "one's tree bears healthy fruit."

## Challenges presented by virtue ethics

Several challenges present themselves when trying to adopt a virtue ethics approach. These include:

- Virtue ethics provides general principles such as the virtues or the golden mean. These principles require interpretation within the context. There are no rules or specific guidelines.
- The interpretation of the principles is totally dependent on the moral maturity of the person. Here is where one would need to take Kohlberg's schema and some emotional intelligence guidance into consideration.
- The emphasis of this principle lies on character development and the ethical awareness and competence of the individual to reflect and deliberate (see the Moral Matrix discussion in Chapter 5).
- The virtue ethics approach emphasizes striving to seek the good, knowing that sometimes one will miss the mark. People who want rules and regulations are likely to find the virtue ethics approach too ambiguous and nebulous.

*Personal exercise – all is fair in love, war and business*

Using a character-based ethics approach, how would you respond to Sally Ann's dilemma in the opening case?

---

**Your turn – who am I?**

In his renowned novel published in 1862, *Les Misérables* (also now a well-known musical), Victor Hugo pens the story of a certain Valjean who was imprisoned for many years for pilfering bread for his sister's starving child. His cruel captor is Javert. Valjean manages to escape and as a result of kindness from a priest, becomes wealthy and devotes his life to acts of kindness. Over the years, a hard-hearted Javert never ceases searching for him.

Several years later, Valjean has by now a new name and a new identity. Javert tracks him down and reports him to the French authorities. However, he soon tells Valjean he must have been mistaken because the authorities have identified someone else as the real Jean Valjean. They have him in custody, and plan to try him the next day. Valjean is torn. Does he give up his life, his freedom, the factory on which many people now depend for a livelihood, and his foster care for a young woman by going to the authorities and admitting that he is the true Jean Valjean? Or does he let things be? It was many years ago and he has repented and redeemed himself repeatedly for his petty crime. The song in *Les Misérables* is called "Who Am I?"

What would you do? Would you give up your freedom and go back to jail for another unjust sentence? Or would you let the other person take the fall and chalk it up to providence being on your side at last? Why would you do whatever it is you choose to do?

## Am I a dutiful person? Do I follow the rules?

In this section we discuss duty or rule-based ethics, referred to as *deontology*. Deontology derives from the Greek word for duty, obligation or imperative.

The deontological approach means doing's one's duty regardless of the results. With deontology, ethics is found in honoring our obligation to do what we ought to do. The key ethical measure lies in our intention. Our intention is what matters, not the consequences or the attainment of any goal such as happiness.

Rule-based ethics dominates the field of business and especially the professions. America and most European countries host thousands of specialized consultants engaged in writing rule books and codes for different industries and for every possible type of profession. Professional ethics, that of lawyers, doctors and accountants, largely adopt a rule-based approach. Business ethics officers have attempted to emulate this method by introducing more and wider ranging rules in the hopes of improving the ethics of businesses.

### Divine command theory

Divine Command theory states that an action is right if it was decreed by God. Moral obligations arise from God and our duties arise from God's commands.

We can think of the Ten Commandments serving as the rules for moral obedience for the Hebrews fleeing Egypt approximately 3,200 years ago. Christian and Islamic fundamentalist thinking also supports Divine Command theory through the literal interpretation of sacred texts out of which they read or infer God's explicit injunctions.

One might argue that a form of Divine Command theory exists within business organizations. The employer-employee relationship is defined by authority. The word authority means the right or the power to command and enforce obedience. Are the commands of the boss not akin to divine commands? Is the employee not morally obliged to comply with whatever his or her employer/authority commands? Based on our discussions in Chapter 4 on the moral power of authority, this is not as far-fetched as it sounds. Is doing what the boss says an ethical principle you can live by? Does it have the force of a divine command? What do you think?

> **Ethical injunction:***Recognize your obligation to God and perform that action that adheres to God's commands.*

### Immanuel Kant (1724–1804)

We have already met Immanuel Kant a few times. As you may recall, he was a German Enlightenment philosopher who had ultimate faith in reason. Kant's philosophy is quite complex. In what follows I will endeavor to simplify and condense his major ethical principles and assertions.

#### The religion of reason

Kant had his own version of Divine Command theory. For him the supreme God is reason. Through reason we know the will of God engraved in our hearts (a little like Aristotle's natural law). He argued that the pure religion of reason exists in every person. This religion includes those God-given, moral principles, commands, and duties implicit within us.

Kant defines human duties as divine commands, and, that if we truly and sincerely search our reason, we will know how we should behave. Knowing and acting on our divinely directed duty, gives us a freedom that is beyond anything else (Wood, 2001).

#### Morality lies in the intention

To be a moral person for Kant meant having the right intention. The right intention is to respond to the moral duties implicit within our beings known to us by reason. One must perform one's duty for duty's sake, for one's own conscience holds the place of the highest moral tribunal. Doing our duty is the only moral goal. We should not be misled by the desire for happiness as happiness rests on our instincts and our passions. These are far too capricious, subjective and relative. We should do the right thing not because it makes us happy, but because it is our duty (Wood, 2001).

Ethics, according to Kant, needs to be objective, absolute and precise, and comparable with the other sciences. It must be based on impartial reason. Just do your duty and let the chips fall where they may.

#### The categorical imperative

How does one know that one is doing one's duty according to the moral law? Kant had an answer for that. Any law is characterized by its universal applicability. This universal applicability he referred to as the "the categorical imperative."

It states: "Act only according to that maxim by which you can at the same time will that it should become a universal law." Universalizing the maxim means asking the question: What if everybody did this? By testing the principles of our actions in this way, we can determine whether they are truly moral.

The categorical imperative commands human conduct independent of context. In other words, whenever you can readily say there can be a law that allows everyone to do something, then that must be the moral law regardless of the situation or circumstance.

## *Treat people as ends*

Another famous formulation of Kant's was "do not use people as means to your own ends: treat them as having ultimate value, i.e., as being an end in of themselves" (Wood, 2001). You may recall that one of the criticisms of bureaucracy is that people tend to be treated as means to ends which invariably results in moral alienation.

## *Categorizing duties*

Kant's ethics raises several troubling issues. First, Kant categorized duties into perfect duties (do not lie, do not kill innocent persons, and do not use people) and imperfect ones (help others, develop our talents, and treat others with respect). In the event of a conflict between which duty to follow, he claimed that perfect ones supersede imperfect ones. The duty not to lie, for example, precedes the duty to help others. In the case of a Jew hiding under one's bed, our moral duty, according to Kant, would be to tell the truth to the Nazis rather than protect the person being persecuted. (In this case, Kant suggests not responding to a command that might lead to the truth or a lie. Instead one should be vague or ambiguous and thus try to lead the interrogator in another direction.)

Kant's schema, however, did not address how to deal with conflicts that occur within the same class of duties, for example, do not lie versus do not use other people. If we transport this problem to the corporate world, the tussle between a duty of honesty and loyalty, often the whistleblower's dilemma, serves as a poignant example. As such, Kant's ethic does not help us much when it comes to role conflict and conflicting duties within those roles. For example: A person is a daughter and a senior manager. Should she go home and prepare dinner for her sick and ageing mother or work late and complete important, time sensitive contract documentation?

## **Concerns with deontology**

Kant's ethics is highly formal, somewhat abstract, and is not motivationally appealing. His approach to ethics denies the human element inherent in ethical dilemmas and the messy particulars of real-life situations. Simply following one's duty as the measure of one's moral life limits opportunities for people to use their moral imagination and to experience personal growth. Total disregard for the context in which a moral action occurs also denies the need to alter actions under different circumstances.

Because deontology ignores consequences this presents a further troubling issue. According to Kant, if we do our duty, we gain absolution from all responsibility for the consequences of our actions. Regrettably, history is laden with atrocities performed by people carrying out "their duty" regardless of the consequences. Using deontology's own standard of the categorical imperative: Imagine if everyone engaged in moral actions with no concern for the consequences?

Professions and organizations frequently prescribe codes of conduct. These codes dictate the behavioral norms and rules by which adherents need to comply. Failure to comply with these codes can result in punishment and/or ostracization. With codes, the main moral question lies in whether one has done one's professional duty. One could argue that simply complying with rules and codes robs the agent of a deeper, personal responsibility, such as to one's conscience.

> **Ethical injunction:** *Do your duty which requires that you always treat people with dignity, and that your action can be universalized as the moral law for all people in similar circumstances.*

### Reflection – all is fair in love, war and business

Using a rule-based ethics approach, how would you respond to Sally Ann's dilemma in the opening case?

---

### Your turn – which loyalty?

Sophocles' play, *Antigone* (ca 441 BCE), presents us with a classic Kantian dilemma.

Creon, the ruler of Thebes, has ushered an edict concerning his niece Antigone's two dead brothers. One of the brothers, Eteocles, who had been ruling Thebes, was buried with due ceremony. The other brother, Polyneices, who had challenged Eteocles for refusing to give up his throne to him at the end of the year as agreed, was forbidden any burial whatsoever. His corpse was to be abandoned outside the city to be devoured by scavenging animals. This was the ultimate disgrace for a Greek warrior and his family. Antigone disobeys her uncle declaring that her nobility, her obligation to her family and the gods of the dead demanded action regardless of the ruler's orders. Antigone succeeds in giving Polyneices a ritual burial and pays a huge personal price.

---

> **Question:** Antigone chose her duty to her brother over her duty to her uncle/ruler. Which duty would you have felt obliged to honor?

What do you think Kant would have proposed?

## The end justifies the means!

Contrary to the virtue ethics approach that focuses on the character of a person, and the rule-based approach that focuses on the intention behind a person's actions, consequentialist ethical theories focus on consequences. Moral worth is determined solely by the outcome or the results of one's actions.

The most widely known and applied consequentialist theory is referred to as utilitarianism. The utilitarian approach to morality views an action or practice morally praiseworthy if it leads to the greatest possible balance of good consequences, or to the least possible balance of bad consequences. Actions should culminate in good results and limit harmful ones. Utilitarianism, like virtue ethics, considers the pursuit of happiness as the ultimate goal of all our actions (Garvey and Stangroom, 2013).

An important matter to bear in mind is the changing understanding of "happiness," something I outlined in Chapter 3. There I described how happiness has evolved from something attained by living virtuously to a more subjective measure of satisfying an individual's personal feelings of well-being.

What happiness means from a utilitarian perspective is up for debate as we discuss shortly.

### Founders of utilitarianism

Jeremy Bentham (1748–1832), an agent for social reform in London during the Industrial Revolution, became the leader of a group of individuals, including James Mill (1773–1836) and his son John Stewart Mill (1806–1873), who are credited as being the founders of utilitarianism. The central question at the time was how to take care of a new and different social environment. What political decisions would lead to the greatest good for society given the impact of the Industrial Revolution? How should welfare be determined and how should social funds be assigned? These were the kinds of moral questions Bentham and the Mills sought to address.

### The moral equation

The primary aim of utilitarianism is to maximize utility or happiness. Utility measures the happiness or unhappiness that results from a particular action. Net utility is the difference between the happiness and unhappiness caused by an action. Happiness relates to the pleasure or good an action can bring, while unhappiness relates to pain and other harms.

Simplistically, utilitarians think of morality like an equation. They seek to perform those actions that attain the most positive net utility (more happiness produced than unhappiness). In other words, if the "measure" of happiness exceeds the "measure" of unhappiness then positive net utility has been achieved. When this occurs, utilitarians consider the actions that led to this result as morally right. (Recall Milton Friedman in Chapter 1.)

Our common parlance for achieving positive net utility is achieving the best for the majority. If the majority of people gain more happiness than harm, ergo the action was morally praiseworthy.

Now, for the utilitarian, my own happiness is no more important than that of others. This means I need to be strictly impartial when I evaluate or measure happiness. As one can imagine, this position might be inconvenient at times.

### Utilitarian terms

At this point we need to clarify a few utilitarian concepts, for example: What does "measure" mean, how does one define "happiness," and how does one determine the majority? Finally, there is also the question of time. What might be good consequences in the short-term, may not be so if one takes a longer-term view. We get to these issues in a moment.

Just to be clear, utilitarianism focuses entirely on the consequences of actions. A person's character or motivation for an action is considered morally irrelevant. Only the happiness and unhappiness produced by an action, counts. In words familiar to us, the end justifies the means. It does not matter what a person intends or how they act as long as the end result increases net utility or advances happiness for the majority.

### The quality of happiness

John Stuart Mill became the most eloquent spokesman for utilitarianism. In his classic work, *Utilitarianism* (2002), Mill tried to address the measure issue and the definition of happiness issue. He noted that utilitarianism and the principle of utility concentrated on the undiscriminating quantity of happiness (or pleasure) but did not address any qualitative differences in happiness. He feared that excessive emphasis on pleasure would reduce utilitarianism to hedonism, a doctrine he considered "worthy of swine."

Mill argued that some pleasures are qualitatively better than others and that mental pleasures are superior in quality to physical pleasures. In defining the happiness to be achieved, Mill therefore distinguished between intellectual satisfaction and physical satisfaction. He strongly favored the former. A practical interpretation of his preference would be to place a higher value on the investment in schools, universities, or help for philosophers than investing in entertainment centers, field games or supporting football players (Coppleston, Volume VIII, 1984).

### Measuring happiness

Since the impact of the Industrial Revolution on work and social life, we have been wrestling with ways to measure happiness. Over the years, economists have taken the lead by proposing all kinds of econometric data that ostensibly measures happiness. (Economists love the word utility!) A few examples of happiness measures include statistical data on poverty levels, the GINI coefficient (named after the Italian statistician, Corrado Gini) that measures the income distribution within countries, indices that measure the percentage of people owning their own homes, and so on. The corporate financiers have added their own concepts to the mix, such as discounted cash flows, net present value and the measurement of risk.

As we look at the evolution of measures over the past two centuries, it is not surprising that utilitarianism has become the backbone ethics for businesses. Business leaders like to reassure others that their decisions are largely based on creating utility, i.e., doing what is best for the majority. Most of us know of course that this is nuanced language for optimizing the bottom line. Be that as it may, "doing the best for the majority" is a well-known ethical principle. Whether it resonates with you or not, is another question.

### Defining the majority

Another challenge to the utilitarian ethical algorithm is how one determines the majority. If only half a dozen people are impacted by an action, then this may not be an issue. However, ethical dilemmas because they are systemic, usually have a ripple effect which means that far more clusters of interest groups, called stakeholders, are affected than one immediately realizes. These stakeholders can amount to hundreds of thousands of people or large parcels of nature or the environment.

Identifying these stakeholder groups and then interpreting their competing interests is usually fraught with difficulty. Deciding how to group these interests to determine who is part of the majority and who is not, can be exceedingly challenging and is frequently fraught with acrimonious misunderstandings. We discuss some of these challenges in our discussion of Justice in the next chapter.

### Short versus long term

A further salient issue that consequentialism raises is the time horizon that is included in the net utility equation. As we all have experienced, what might seem advantageous or pleasing in the short term, may not be so over a longer time period. We also know that human nature tends to go for the quick fix in the hopes that some saving element will eradicate negative longer term consequences. Our avoidance of tackling climate change is a significant example.

There is no absolute answer to this one. The more sober, wise view argues for looking to the benefits in the long term. But then, how long is long?

### Drawbacks to utilitarianism

There are several drawbacks to utilitarianism. For one it is an ethic that favors the majority, leaving the minority with little or no representation. Another matter, alluded to earlier, is how does one objectively measure such a subjective emotion as happiness and over what period of time? Who is going to decide the definitions and the benchmarks of happiness? In business organizations it is assumed that happiness is defined by profit growth or the share price. Is this really a fair interpretation of happiness?

Utilitarianism also evaluates moral conduct on consequences that often cannot be foretold in advance or with absolute certainty. So with utilitarian thinking, we anticipate the consequences of our actions as best we can and adjust our behavior accordingly.

The good or bad intentions of the agent are ignored. This is certainly a tough situation if the agent strived to do the right thing and situational circumstances worked against him or her. On the other hand, as long as the "greater good" has been attained, regardless of the means which could include lying or cheating, decision-makers have fulfilled their moral duty. What about those instances where business managers intentionally manipulated the cash flows to produce the results they wanted? Did the end justify the means? If the share price goes up based on false accounting results can one say the end justifies the means?

> **Ethical injunction:** *Take that action that results in the greatest happiness for the greatest number of people or minimizes the most harm.*

### Reflection – all is fair in love, war and business

Using a utilitarian approach, how would you respond to Sally Ann's dilemma in the opening case?

---

### Your turn – health at work

Carlos Mendes runs a very successful restaurant downtown. He began with a small café ten years ago. Now his restaurant serves healthy homey meals throughout the day. The business has flourished, and Carlos has added a lucrative take-out service to other businesses in the area.

Over the years, Carlos has come to learn that the most challenging element of running the business is managing the people. Personnel issues have proven to be more difficult than he expected and have become more so over the years. This past week was no exception. It was Tuesday afternoon, and Carlos was working at the counter when Frances Taylor, the ex-wife of his chef, Tom Walter, came into the restaurant. Carlos had not seen her for some time. After ordering some take-out, Frances took Carlos aside. She claimed she was there to warn Carlos that Tom had AIDS. She said she thought Carlos should know as he was Tom's employer. Carlos was astounded and of course alarmed. He thought he needed to think this dilemma through overnight. The next day he came to work and took a careful look at Tom. Maybe he did look a little thinner. He certainly looked tired but then things had been crazily busy. He seemed his usual upbeat self and was telling everyone about his five-year old daughter and the birthday party he was planning for her.

Tom had remarried and now had three stepchildren who he adored. Carlos wondered whether he should ask Tom about his health. Did he have a right to ask this? If he were Tom, he would take umbrage at such a question. It was none of his business. But Carlos was torn. It was his business. He had heard customers talk about a waiter at a local coffee shop who had AIDS and how people were now staying away. Carlos thought he could not take that chance. He had everything vested in the business. He did not believe that AIDS could be transferred through food especially with the intense hygiene standards he insisted on. But what if customers are uneducated and uninformed? What if they too heard a rumor or if Frances was telling others about Tom. And what if Frances was just stirring the pot. Should he warn her that what she was doing was a potentially criminal offense? But even if she is stirring the pot, what if it is true? What should he do? He has everything invested in his business. Even if the law says he can do nothing but give Tom support, what if his business fails?

Carlos knows it is illegal to fire Tom. And Tom, who had been working with him since the beginning, would not find a job easily. Then there were the other staff to consider. The town was small. Other work was not readily available. Who should he take care of? Himself and his family? Tom and his family? The staff and a possible knock-on impact? The customers who had come to depend on him over the years? How was he to figure all this out? Surely, he has to do what is the best for the majority. How to decide on the greater good?

What advice would you give Tom?

## Power is what matters

Niccolo Machiavelli (1469–1527), with his dubious power strategies, has a firm place in the development of Western ethical consciousness. Undoubtedly his ethics, or, as some would argue, lack thereof, has both defined and informed the behavior of many people in positions of power. Historians often refer to him as the high priest of untrammeled self-interest and duplicity.

Machiavelli saw ethics and politics as matters of practical knowledge and wisdom derived from hands on experience. He believed that successful leaders must see the world realistically. They must be aware of the hard realities of situations and especially the issues directly related to power.

Machiavelli's book *The Prince* (1997), was essentially a manual on how to attune oneself to the fundamental truth of the world. This truth included the reality that, according to Machiavelli, all people passionately love their lives and their comforts and that they will do anything to escape death and poverty. We pledge our allegiance easily, but when it comes to redeeming our pledges, he said, we cannot remember why we ever made them in the first place.

Machiavelli believed that anyone who forgets that humans are this way are destined to suffer the consequences of their naivete. He claimed that trickery, subterfuge, and immoral acts are necessary choices in some circumstances. He based his approach on a motto of personal survival in an intensely competitive and harsh world where one needs to play to win. He advocated that one should not tell anyone of one's plans unless and until the other person has no choice to either join one or die. He also advised that one never bring someone more powerful than oneself into one's quarrel, lest one lose one's independence.

### Power is virtue

Machiavelli's theories rest on the idea that power is not the main thing; it is the only thing! Those in power are expected to do everything they can to keep their power and this requires doing whatever is expedient at the time. He also claimed that those in power should do everything they can to keep others who do not have power in their position of powerlessness. He took the side of those ancients who argued in Plato's *Republic* that "justice is in the interest of the stronger." He supported the absolute primacy of self-interest and dictated that people establish values that help them to win.

Machiavelli equated virtue with power. He asked: Can anything be bad that leads one to prevail over others? For him the consequence of survival and remaining in power justified the means to that end. He argued that one must know how to color one's life well, and appear to be faithful and true while being entirely fickle if that suited one's cause.

### Fear

Machiavelli argued that humans are not moved by abstract understandings of good and evil but by their desires and fears. He believed that one gains the allegiance of others through fear rather than love. Fear, he claimed, has a stronger hold than love in that the fear of pain never abandons a person whereas love can and does.

He asserted that one should not uphold one's promises if the context has changed since one made them, and that by honoring one's promises one diminishes one's power.

### Face reality

A key question for Machiavelli was: What will work in the world as it is? What works, according to him, is what ought to be done. Despite the devious strategies he proposes, Machiavelli does not blindly endorse or praise sleazy or immoral behavior, and he in fact acknowledges that such behavior is wrong and dangerous. However, one of his convictions is that "He will be successful who directs his action to the spirit of the times . . ."

Finally he claimed:

> How one lives is so far distant from how one ought to live, and he who neglects what is done for what ought to have been done, sooner effects his

ruin that his preservation; for a man who wishes to act entirely up to his profession's virtue soon meets with what destroys him among so much that is evil.

(Ibid, Chapter XV)

Machiavelli advocated what is often called a *real* power politics. Despite his adamant injunctions and his convictions regarding the practical success of his approach, it did not serve him well during his few unsuccessful years as a diplomat and supporter of the Republican cause during the Italian wars of the period.

Regrettably, many in the modern world have adopted his fundamental teachings with enthusiasm! Machiavellianism is alive and well in the halls of all too many corporations.

**Ethical injunction:** *Take that action that ensures that you come out on top.*

*Reflection – all is fair in love, war and business*

Using Machiavelli's tactics, how would you respond to Sally Ann's dilemma in the opening case?

---

### Your turn – Machiavellianism at large

- Can you identify any people who appear to have adopted Machiavellian ethics? If yes, what behaviors do they display?
- What is your opinion about some of Machiavelli's claims regarding human nature, e.g., his comment on fear and love?

---

## What does the law say?

Thomas Hobbes (1588–1679), an English political philosopher, is known for his book *Leviathan* (Hobbes, 1982), where he describes the world as being in a "state of nature" which is a situation prior to the formation of society.[2] In this state of nature, akin to the world of wild animals, humans engage in fierce struggles over scarce resources. They attack, steal, destroy, and invade one another to both protect themselves and prove their status. Life in this world, is one filled with continuous fear of violence and death, and the "life of man is poor, brutish, and short." Compassion and kindness would be ideal if everyone would be compassionate and kind, but everyone won't be. People compete for property and status, and some people always take advantage of others.[3]

In *Leviathan*, Hobbes proposes that in order to restrain people and maintain peace within society, we need a social contract[4] where all must obey rules from a central authority that has the power to enforce those rules. With a social contract, humans sacrifice some of their natural right to liberty so as to be protected from one another. *Leviathan* is thus the mortal god, who as sovereign, has been given the authority to establish legitimate political power and enforce compliance to laws. In a democratic nation we think of that authority as the government, and those rules as the law.

Hobbes advocated that morality consists of agreed-upon, mutually advantageous conventions that, assuming others' compliance, makes society possible. These rules arise as a result of our contracts with one another and with the central authority that provides order by legislating and enforcing laws. There are no antecedent moral truths. Prior to the contract, neither morality nor immorality defines our actions. We are in survival mode. It is the contract that makes actions moral and immoral. Character, conscience, feelings, disposition, duty or even consequences have no part in his ethical theory. Abiding by the contract is what orders relationships between people and sets the moral compass.

### Limitations to the contracts approach

The contracts approach, as with the rule-based or utilitarian approaches, ignores the character or motivation of the moral agent. He or she simply complies with the law or the prevailing terms of the contract. No personal discernment or judgment is encouraged. While many people are proud of being "law-abiding" citizens, and this surely has certain merit, there are times when it is ethical to challenge the law. Think of how many laws have supported discrimination or questionable justice. Recall Chapter 2 where I laid out the difference between the law and ethics and how the law represents the minimal moral standards of society.

> **Ethical injunction:***Take that action that complies with the law or the prevailing contract.*

### Reflection – all is fair in love, war and business

Using a contracts approach, how would you respond to Sally Ann's dilemma in the opening case?

## This is my right!

We now turn to the English philosopher, John Locke, who we first met in Chapter 1 when we discussed private property. Locke also took a contracts approach to ethics albeit from a very different angle to that of Hobbes. I refer to his approach as the human rights approach to ethics.

Locke's political theory aimed, as we discussed, at challenging the divine right of kings. He is known for championing one of the most influential ideas in modern history, and that is that all human beings have inalienable natural rights that no government may justifiably eliminate. He argued that any violation of these natural rights was a deed so intolerable that it justified political revolution.

For Locke, morality was centered in rights, especially the natural rights of the individual. According to him, and other natural rights theorists, human freedom exists naturally before legal and political institutions intervene.

In contrast to Hobbes, Locke believed that people form the social order not to preserve their lives but to protect their rights. In the state of nature, all individuals exist morally free, equal, and independent. Since all human beings have a right to moral freedom and equality, any government created through the social contract, has the obligation to respect the moral law embodied in natural human rights.

Locke believed that individuals have the right to life, liberty, and unlimited property, and government has no right to limit or remove any property or interfere in anyone's life. The government has limitations set by individual rights and exists solely to protect those rights. Individuals have the right to live as they please without any duty to themselves or others as long as they respect the rights of others.

John Locke was a guiding inspiration of the American Declaration of Independence that argues for uninhibited life, liberty, and the pursuit of happiness thereby enshrining the morality of rights in the US Constitution.

It is interesting to reflect on the influence that Hobbes and Locke have had on the moral and legal climate in the United States. For one, Hobbes foresaw that a contracts approach would require a great deal of bargaining and negotiating in order to satisfy rival needs. Locke, on the other hand emphasized the rights of citizens but made little mention of our responsibilities. What are we left with? Well, as many know or have experienced, the United States is arguably the most litigious environment in the world where people are continuously arguing about contracts or their rights. It also has one of the highest, if not the highest, number of lawyers per capita in the world.

### Limitations to the rights approach

Under the rights approach there is no objective morality. It could be deemed a personalist approach to ethics – see later – in that the demand for one's rights is highly subjective and self-referential. Here the moral concern is with the individual retaining his or her liberty but not at the cost of someone else's. When someone has detrimentally impacted someone else's rights, the parties seek legal counsel or arbitration.

> **Ethical injunction:***Take any action you wish as long as you do not impinge on the agreed upon and accepted rights of others.*

### Reflection – all is fair in love, war and business

Using a rights-based approach, how would you respond to Sally Ann's dilemma in the opening case?

## Oh, that slippery slope!

We have discussed character-based ethics (also referred to as virtue ethics), duty or rule-based ethics (deontology), utilitarianism, Machiavellianism, the contracts approach and rights-based ethics. All six of these ethical approaches attempt to provide some objective standards or benchmarks against which we can reference our behavior.

Character-based ethics suggests we turn to wise people to mentor us to help us exercise the virtues. These mentors will provide us with feedback on our character, the decisions we are making and the way we are living our lives.

In deontology we rely on our reason and the categorical imperative to inform us of our duty. Performing our duty is the moral measure.

Utilitarians look to "happiness of the greatest number" as the objective ideal. Machiavellianism measures ethics by the ability to maintain one's power. The contracts approach looks to the law or to the contract to establish what is "morally" right, and rights-based ethics defines freedom (liberty) as the measure of a moral society. The moral reference is: "live and let live."

### Move to personal preferences

As ethical theory has evolved over time to cater for our so-called progress in history, more contemporary theories tend to have ditched the idea of having some objective standard or benchmark against which we might reference our moral behavior. The modern approach to morality is to use one's own personal preferences as one's guide. This is referred to as *personalist ethics*. The challenge that this presents is that without an objective benchmark or "ideal" one cannot objectively assess what is true, good or right. There is no external referent point against which we can compare or to which we can turn to provide a moral guiding light. Without ideals, truths or external guides we find ourselves in the land of moral relativism. (Discussed in Chapter 2.)

In the land of moral relativism not only is everything contingent on circumstance, but morality is determined by personal beliefs, opinions, attitudes, feelings, desires, inclinations, tastes and preferences. Moral standards are cloudy, negotiable, and to varying degrees, subjective. As a moral relativist, if I claim that you have done something wrong, I am conveying my disapproval or dislike of your behavior. If you counter and say that it is my behavior that is immoral and not yours, we are at an impasse. We cannot appeal to any higher truth. In the world of relativism, we can both claim to be right!

Moral relativism is a very difficult topic that quickly comes down to people's biases and preferences. As reasonable people, I think most of us believe that there should be some room for relativistic thinking, since situations and contexts do have a bearing on an appropriate moral response. However, we should question: How much room should one allow; when should moral relativism be denounced and when should absolutes be appealed to? And then another of those ethical conundrums: Who should decide?

> **Ethical injunction:** *Take that action that appeals to your personal preferences and biases since there are no overriding rules.*

# I know what is right!

In general, the personalist approach to ethics views morality as an expression of individual feeling, personal conscience, responsibility or love. Personalists resist the idea that morals can be legislated as abstract principles or codified as moral laws. The personalist approach emphasizes the individualistic and the situational aspect to moral situations.

Here are three well known personal ethics approaches. Maybe you can reflect on when you last used one of these principles as your decision-making guide.

## It depends on the situation

Joseph Fletcher (1905–1991) states that ethics is concerned with people. The key guiding principle is to demonstrate responsible, thoughtful and caring love in the situation. True love will know what is fitting. True love is not sentimental, but discerning and careful. Assessment of the situation will determine the loving action.

> **Decision-making approach** – *The situation called for a loving approach.*

## The goal is to act responsibly

Helmut Richard Niebuhr (1894–1962), advocated a very similar ethic to Fletcher. He advocated an ethics of responsibility. He agrees with Fletcher that the immediate needs of the situation should guide the response. According to him the moral response is always the most context-sensitive fitting approach.

> **Decision-making approach** – *I did what I believed was the most fitting and responsible thing to do.*

## I know the right thing to do!

Jean Paul Sartre (1905–1980), a well-known existentialist, claimed that human beings must create their own values. He said humans are akin to gods! They must believe in their true freedom and make moral decisions from that place. That is the sign of true morality![5]

Sartre believed that first people exist and then they use their freedom to shape who they are and how to reach their potential. He believed in what he termed the radical freedom of the person (Anderson, 1993).

Existentialists contend that ethical theories are simply abstractions. It is only human beings exercising their liberty to choose who can really know what the right thing is to do. Everything in life is contingent, subjective, concrete and interpreted by human experience. However, and this is the big catch, many do not get that their liberty or freedom resides in a true authentic, pre-conscious self. That is the consciousness that is empty of all the conditioning of the phenomenal aspects of the world. My free choices should come from this deep, pure freedom, and not just my banal, mundane conscious freedom to choose. It is out of this unfettered, unpolluted freedom that I can develop and be the character or person I choose to be.

While this is a personalist ethic, it is one that places enormous responsibility on the individual to be as fully human as possible. To invoke this principle with sincerity and integrity, requires a great deal of personal maturity.

> **Decision-making approach**: *Because of who I am and my inner freedom, I know the right thing to do.*

We notice by looking at these three examples of personalist ethics that they have different emphases. Situation ethics looks at intention and consequences. Responsibility ethics is more like duty-based ethics and focuses on the action rather than the decision maker or the consequences. Existentialist ethics focuses on the authenticity of the decision maker in living out of his or her deepest, inner freedom.

## Reflection – all is fair in love, war and ethics

Using a personalist ethics approach, how would you respond to Sally Ann's dilemma in the opening case?

- Based on the situation from a disposition of love?
- Based on what is fitting given the circumstances?
- Based on total freedom of choice? No must, ought, should or . . .?

How would you respond in each of these three circumstances?

## Me, me, me

Self-interest theory (egoism), holds that human beings are naturally inclined to act for their own benefit. Some forms of egoism even claim that it is impossible not to act in our own self-interest. We do everything for the benefit of "me." Even the most charitable action is motivated by a self-seeking impulse; for example, I make donations so that I can feel good about myself. From an egotistical perspective, my own happiness and well-being is what is most important in my life. Moreover, egoists believe that society is better off if each of us takes this stance and takes due care of ourselves instead of pursuing meaningless acts of self-sacrifice. The upside is that by taking care of ourselves we are not a burden on other people or society.

> **Ethical injunction**: *Take that action that ensures my own safety, welfare and interests.*

## Reflection – all is fair in love, war and ethics

Using the ethics of self-interest, how would you respond to Sally Ann's dilemma in the opening case?

## The woman's voice

Three women stand out for their research into gender ethics, these are Carol Gilligan, Nel Noddings and Rosemarie Tong.

Gilligan, Noddings and Tong all claim that humans only know through relationships, and that relationships serve as the identifying characteristic of human beings. They argue that the traditional, male-oriented, abstract, universal, impartial and rational approach to moral decision-making lacks the relationship element.

### *Carol Gilligan*

We begin with Carol Gilligan, who we met in Chapter 4 as the challenger to Lawrence Kohlberg and his Moral Development schema. Based on her research, Gilligan argued that males and females have distinctly different moral orientations. According to her, women conceptualize moral questions as problems of care involving empathy and compassion, while men conceptualize them as problems of rights.

Her key thesis is that women exhibit a relational ethic she calls "an ethic of care." She claims that female identity formation takes place in the context of ongoing relationships. She asserts that girls emerge with a basis of empathy built into their primary definition of themselves in a way that boys do not. She argued that women construct moral problems differently than men do. Women see morality as a problem of care and responsibility in relationships rather than one of duties, rights and rules.

Gilligan claims that the central moral insight of women is that they view the self and other as interdependent. In contrast, men experience the moral imperative as respect for the rights of others, and self-protection from interference to their autonomy and self-fulfillment (Gilligan, 1993).

### *Nel Noddings*

Nel Noddings adopts a similar argument to that of Gilligan. She claims that the feminine approach to ethics focuses on caring for the other, where the moral emphasis centers on empathy rather than moral judgment. She argues against the criticism that women tend to be deficient in abstract reasoning, emotionally over-reactive, and that they fall foul of moral relativism. The essence of the feminine approach, she says, is the caring for the other so as to preserve the uniqueness of human encounters. Since all moral dilemmas are experienced in relationship, she claims, they require a care-based approach (Noddings, 1984).

*Rosemarie Tong*

Rosemarie Tong's work includes the comparison of various ethical frameworks, both traditional and contemporary. She claims that traditional ethics is grounded very much in the tensions between the self and separation, where "autonomous man" guards his rights vigilantly. This ethical orientation stems from an attitude of defending one's own interests against those of others. Feminist ethics, in contrast, she argues focuses on responsibility and obligation as the primary moral notion.

Tong sums up the difference between traditional, essentially male-based ethics and feminist ethics as a difference between obligation and preoccupation with universal rules by the former, and concern for and preoccupation with specific situations by the latter. She argues that removing the emotional base from moral decisions takes away much of the associated moral meaning, which diminishes particularly the positive consequences of behaving morally (Tong, 1982).

> **Ethical injunction:** *Take that action that demonstrates care and that best honors, preserves and enhances existing relationships.*

## Reflection – is all fair in love, war and ethics?

Using a feminist ethics approach, how would you respond to Sally Ann's dilemma in the opening case?

In your experience, do you think men would handle Sally Ann's dilemma differently to that of women? Here is an opportunity for you to carry out some research of your own.

## An ethical observation

What are we do with all these ethical theories? How are we to respond when different theories guide us to take different courses of action? For example, do your duty versus pursue your rights, or, do what is best for the majority versus take care of the most important relationships.

In reviewing the different ethical theories, there are several important points to bear in mind.

Ethical principles are just that, principles. Principles require reflection, deliberation and discernment for their application. They are not rules. Principles require interpretation and contextualization to make them applicable. Recall the explanation of ethics in Chapters 3 and 4. This book is about ethical principles that can be applied to the business context. It is not a book on codes or rules.

We also need to take great care not to insist that the principles we use are unequivocally the best or correct ones. While at the time they may seem the very best to us, there is this phrase "time will tell." We need a certain humility to appreciate that only in time will we really know whether our decision was a wise one. We also need to appreciate that what we see always depends on where we stand. This means that we will never really know all the perspectives, all the stakeholders affected, and all the consequences, intended or unintended.

Lastly, there is also the consideration of the outcome of our decisions. While we might believe that the outcome was good, ideal or even perfect, this sentiment might not be shared by others. Does that matter? Naturally that depends on the significance of the decision and who else and to what extent they were affected.

Let us must remind ourselves that the overarching ethical goal is to advance goodness; to promote flourishing of life; and to honor and assist all and everything to achieve its potential – whatever the situation. While that is our goal or desire, it is not an easy one to achieve. Many factors come into play, some of them outside of our own control. The best we can do is be aware, reflect, deliberate and choose with a sound intention and our hearts open and striving for rightness.

## Personal reflection

At this point, you may be asking yourself: Do I belong to the virtue ethics school or am I more of a consequentialist? Or, do I defer more frequently to the personalist approach? What does that mean in my life and the way I live it? What about my family and friends? What kind of ethical principles do they seem to live by? What about my organization? What kind of ethical principles seem most valued there? How do they fit in with my own?

You might also wonder: Under what conditions do I justify different ethical principles? Do I feel morally free in the environments in which I make choices? Would I select different ethical principles if I were more, or less, free? When I don't feel free to make choices what inhibits my freedom and how?

To help with your reflections consider the questions below.

---

### Your turn – testing your ethical principles

*Example 1*

You receive counterfeit money as part of your change from a transaction. What would you do? Keep it and use it? Pass it on? Throw it away? Report it to the police?

Does your answer differ if it is $5, $50, $500 or $50,000?

Which ethical principle/s guided you here?

*Example 2*

Your boss is your father. You find out that he is giving bribes to overseas agents to secure work. The organization (the family business on which the

---

family depends), relies heavily on the orders that come in from many of these foreign agents.

What would you do? Which ethical principle/s will guide you?

### Example 3

You work as a controller for a small engineering company. During the annual audit you notice that the auditor, a young inexperienced CPA, has made an error in pricing the year end closing inventory. The error works in favor of the company by resulting in a higher profit to the tune of $500,000. While this is not huge it does make a significant difference to the overall year end results and of course those bonuses. It will certainly help negotiating the extension of the credit line that you and the CEO have been discussing.

What would you do? Which ethical principle/s will guide you in your response?

### Example 4

You notice that your sales manager, Ted, a tall, dapper, flirtatious guy, has an eye for your new data analytics manager, Sushmita. She is a beautiful young woman who has recently arrived from India. Ted seems to be always teasing her and making a point of talking with her or going into her office.

One day you overhear him inviting her for drinks after work. She declines and he keeps pressing, teasing her and telling her what she is missing by not agreeing to this wonderful opportunity to be with him.

Ted has recently emerged from a drawn out, acrimonious divorce after his wife found out that he was having an affair.

What will you do? Will you let them sort it out or might you have a word with Ted? Or with Sushmita? Which ethical response will guide you in your response?

## Being an ethically principled manager

### Different principles mean different perspectives

An ethically principled manager should have some knowledge about ethical principles and should also be aware which of those principles inform many or most of his or her own significant decisions. This knowledge helps the manager understand that he or she brings certain ethical perspective to most situations. The ethical manager needs to understand that this holds true for other people, too.

While we have covered many of the better-known ethical principles in our Western culture, we have not by any means covered all the ethical principles people might avail of. Different cultures formulate and articulate their ethical ideals differently. For example, religious people may follow their God's injunctions as spelled out in sacred texts, while people who hail from certain ethnic cultures might bring totally dissimilar or contrasting perspectives. The ethically principled manager needs to be aware and sensitive to these varying possibilities.

### Principles and codes of conduct[6]

Most organizations have some form of codes of conduct. The ethically principled manager needs to understand which ethical principles underpin these codes. He or she also needs to appreciate that strictly following codes or rules reflects a *deontological* or duty-based approach to problem solving. While this is not necessarily a negative thing, as with all ethical principles, trade-offs exist. One aspect to consider when an organization places heavy emphasis on codes of conduct is that employees may be inhibited from exercising moral vision or moral imagination and/or they may ignore the consequences of their actions.

The ethically principled manager is continuously engaged in an ethical balancing act. Judgment must be exercised which includes a fair dose of empathy. And then there is this matter of justice – to which we now turn.

## Summary of ethical principles

### Character-based ethics

>Socrates – Take that action that reflects a life of striving for human excellence and wisdom.
>Plato – Take that action that reflects a virtuous life in accordance with the dictates of reason.
>Aristotle – Take that action that is thoughtful, reasonable and honest, and reflects the life you want to live.
>Jesus – Take that action that reflects unconditional love (empathy and compassion) and is the way you would like to be treated out of love.

### Deontology rule-based ethics

>Divine Command theory – Recognize your obligation to God and perform that action that adheres to God's commands.
>Kant – Do your duty which requires that you always treat people with dignity, and that your action can be universalized as the moral law for all people in similar circumstances.

### Utilitarianism

>Bentham-Mill – Take that action that results in the greatest happiness for the greatest number of people or minimizes the most harm.

### Power-based ethics

>Machiavelli – Take that action that ensures that you come out on top.

### Legal approach

Hobbes – Take that action that complies with the law or the prevailing contract.

### Rights approach

Locke – Take any action you wish as long as you do not impinge on the agreed upon and accepted rights of others.

### Moral relativism

Take that action that appeals to your personal preferences and biases since there are no overriding rules.

### Personalist ethics

*Situational ethics*

Fletcher – The situation called for a loving approach.

*Responsibility ethics*

Niebuhr – I did what I believed was the most fitting and responsible thing to do.

*Existentialist ethics*

Sartre – Because of who I am and my inner freedom, I know the right thing to do.

*Self-interest argument*

Take that action that ensures my own safety, welfare and interests.

*Feminist ethics*

Take that action that demonstrates care and that will best honor, preserve and enhance existing relationships.

## Executive summary

This chapter lays out some of the best-known ethical principles that have evolved throughout the history of Western civilization. Many of these principles are invoked daily without us being consciously aware that we are doing so.

It might be helpful to look at these principles in conjunction with our discussion on moral development in Chapter 4 and as I have summarized next. Bear in mind these are only ideas and guides to prompt reflection and questioning.

I would argue that what is essential is that every leader, manager or educated citizen should be aware of at least these ethical principles, how they were derived and how they might be applied. Based on my own personal experience and as someone who has worked as a corporate consultant for many decades, knowledge of ethical principles heightens people's cognitive and emotional intelligence.

*Table 6.1* Kohlberg stages and ethical principles

| *Kohlberg Stage* | *Ethical Principle* |
| --- | --- |
| 1 – Obey – fear | Machiavelli – power principle<br>Divine Command theory<br>Self-interest argument |
| 2 – What's in it for me? | Golden Rule; self-interest argument |
| 3 – Approval, loyalty | Golden Rule; feminist ethics; Self-<br>interest argument |
| 4 – Law and order | Law; contracts; rights; utilitarianism<br>Duty/Deontology |
| 5 and 6<br>Social contract<br>Decisions of conscience<br>Principled living | Virtue ethics; deontology; utilitarianism<br>Existentialism |
| Feminist ethics | Personalist ethics, Responsibility ethics |

## Questions for reflection

- Which ethical principle/s appeal to you the most? What energizes you around this or these principles?
- Think of your partner or best friend. What ethical principles do they typically use?
- What ethical principle does your boss seem to defer to?
- What ethical principles manifest themselves in your work culture?
- Do you care about your character and what it says about you?

## Key terms

Categorical imperative   192
Character   183
Deontology   188
Ethical quest   181
Existentialism   213
Golden mean   185
Humility   183
Imperative   185
Love   180

Majority   196
Moderation   185
Moral reasoning   182
Natural law   185
Power   181
Rights   202
Teleology   185
Utilitarianism   195
Virtue ethics   183

## Notes

1  I do not provide exhaustive coverage of all available principles. Also, my focus is on Western thought, and I have thus excluded the many principles provided by other traditions.
2  Leviathan is a mythological sea monster in the Jewish tradition. It is referred to in the Hebrew Bible in the Book of Job, the Psalms, The Book of Isaiah, and the Book of Amos.
3  Written during the turmoil of the English Civil War, *Leviathan* is a work of political philosophy. Claiming that man's essential nature is competitive and selfish, Hobbes formulates the case for a powerful sovereign – or "Leviathan" – to enforce peace and the law, substituting security for the anarchic freedom he believed human beings would otherwise experience. The original edition was written in 1651.
4  Three Enlightenment thinkers are usually credited with establishing a standard view of social contract theory: Thomas Hobbes, John Locke and Jean-Jacques Rousseau. They each had different interpretations of social contracts, but the underlying idea was similar.
    The definition of a social contract is – the voluntary agreement among individuals by which an organized society is brought into being and invested with the right to secure mutual protection and welfare or to regulate the relations among its members.
5  Sartre and his *Existentialism is a Humanism*. New Haven, CT: Yale University Press, 2007.
6  Chapter 9 which describes a moral reasoning framework also spells out the implications of professional codes of conduct.

## References

Anderson, Thomas C. *Sartre's Two Ethics: From Authenticity to Integral Humanity*. Chicago: Open Court, 1993.

Aristotle. *Nicomachean Ethics*. Cambridge, Massachusetts: Hackett Publishing Company, Inc, 1999.

Coppleston, Frederick, S. J. *A History of Philosophy*, Volume 8. New York: Doubleday, 1984.

Garvey, James and Jeremy Stangroom. *The Story of Philosophy*. London, Great Britain: Querus Editions, Ltd, 2013.

Gilligan, Carol. *In a Different Voice*. Cambridge, MA: Harvard University Press, 1993.

Hobbes, Thomas. *Leviathan*. New York: Penguin Classic, 1982 (based on 1651 text).

Machiavelli, Niccolo. *The Prince*. Translated and Edited by Angelo M. Codevilla. New Haven, CT: Yale University Press, 1997.

Mill, John Stuart and George Sher. *Utilitarianism*, Second Edition. New York: Hackett Publishing Co. Inc., 2002.

Noddings, Nel. *Caring: A Feminine Approach to Ethics and Moral Education*. Berkeley, CA: University of California Press, 1984.

Sullivan, Rojer J. *Immanuel Kant's Moral Theory*. New York: Cambridge University Press, 1991.

Tong, Rosemarie. *Feminine and Feminist Ethics*. Belmont, CA: Wadsworth Publishing Company Inc., 1982.

Wood, Allen W. editor. *Basic Writings of Kant*. New York: The Modern Library, 2001.

# 7 Justice

## Contents

## That is not fair!

You are the manager of the automotive spare parts group in a large, privately held company based in Florida. Although the company is profitable and growing, expenses are very tightly controlled. Headcount is a particularly carefully scrutinized item. It is difficult to get approval to hire new staff and, when staff members resign, senior management is reluctant to replace them.

You have worked for the organization for eight years and you have been instrumental in helping manage both its growth and the control of expenses. You believe your department is lean and very efficient. There is one problem that you and your staff are struggling with. An old friend of the CEO, who was also an employee with the firm for thirty-eight years, is a member of your department. The man's name is Harold. Harold, a widower, is now eighty-three years old. After Harold retired, the CEO offered him a part-time position in the organization. People infer that this is probably due to loyalty and a desire to help Harold from being lonely and feeling worthless. Harold is a nice guy but is getting more and more unreliable and ineffective each month. He is slow, forgetful and makes many errors. Your staff spends a fair amount of time fixing Harold's mistakes. More recently he has become almost deaf yet persists in answering the phone when customers call. Although Harold supposedly reports to you, in reality he does not report to anyone. He has no standards of performance to meet and is not evaluated in any way. The CEO has told you to take it easy on "poor old Harold."

Your staff works long hours and are expected to meet rigorous performance standards. They have been asking for more people in the division to help deal with growth. You have approached the CEO who keeps reminding you that times are tight, and that survival depends on running a tight ship. Resentment regarding Harold is beginning to take hold. Morale is deteriorating. Your staff has begun complaining that a position or a half-a-position is being squandered by giving it to Harold. You want to take this up with the CEO because it is not fair! This is not organizational justice, something the CEO pontificates on frequently. Taking this up with the CEO is a very delicate issue and may affect your relationship with him. Is it worth it?

Ever been stuck with the boss's friend or favorite nonperformer?

## Questions

What is the issue here? Do you think justice is at stake? What principle or argument would you use to challenge your boss about Harold's position?

## Creating a just society

In January 1996, I enrolled into the Social Ethics doctoral program at Boston University (BU). I had just completed a master's degree in Theology, with a specialty in ethics, at a Jesuit College. After graduation, I thought I knew quite a bit about ethics. I was in for a humbling surprise. The rigors of Jesuit education had stretched me further than I ever imagined possible, however, my doctorate was a whole new mind shaping experience.

Social ethics is concerned with the question of what makes a good society, where "good" means "just."

The intensive three-year social ethics curriculum included a study of comparative religions and ethics, anthropology, sociology, theology, philosophy, political science and developmental psychology. The idea was to explore social ethics, i.e., justice, as understood through the lens of different traditions, cultures, religions and ethnicities. As you can imagine, this is a vast terrain.

One thing I learned from my studies, is that justice is greatly influenced by a society's physical necessities (i.e., its geography and ecology), belief systems, and social values. While in most societies, justice is administered through laws of various kinds, there are also subtle agreements and bonds of reciprocation that exist. Justice is therefore both formal and informal, explicit and implicit, weaving a complex psychological thread that holds a society together. Once that thread begins to unravel, a society's demise is usually imminent. (See Chapter 10.)

In this text, until now, I have focused on ethics as it pertains to individuals engaging with one another or within the organization as the vessel of action. The subject of justice – a cardinal virtue for both Plato and Aristotle as we have discussed – takes ethics beyond personal and organizational relations, to society as a whole and extends to the environment.

As we look at society and the environment, we must bear in mind the systems perspective we discussed in Chapter 2. Chapter 8 is devoted to justice as a social and environmental responsibility. In this chapter we focus more narrowly on justice between people and organizations.

A critical thing we can never lose sight of is that a just society is made up of just institutions. Society does not function apart from its institutions. It **is** its institutions, in concert, evincing either cacophony or harmony. And as with other ethical principles, our perspective of justice is dependent on where we stand. With justice, however, perhaps more than any other ethical principle or moral norm, we are obliged to consider multiple perspectives or different stakeholder viewpoints. This alone makes the attainment of justice all the more challenging.

Leaders, politicians and ministers lavishly lace their rhetoric with all manner of appeals to issues of justice. Yet, despite ubiquitous usage, the practical interpretation and exercise of justice remains cloudy and is frequently contested. A major contributing factor to this discord lies in the fact that justice is a highly value-laden and deeply personal concept. Each one of us believes we know what is just, and we insist that we most certainly know what is unjust!

Wearing our business ethics hats, we now set out to see what justice means and how one might create a just institution/organization that supports and reflects a just society. In pursuing this question, the first matter we must attend to is what is justice and how does it manifest itself? And then, what are the elements of a just institution or society?

Justice is often depicted as a young blindfolded woman holding the human scales in one hand and a sword in the other. The young woman represents a virgin, not in the sexual sense, but rather as someone who has not yet been tainted, spoiled or embittered. A person of this disposition is most likely to have a free and open mind.

The female element is intended to depict mercy or human tenderness which contrasts with the severity of the sharp sword she is holding. The blindfold stands for impartiality; the scales for the competing claims, and the sword for the power of the law to dispense justice, i.e., to make a clear, decisive and fair determination by cutting through competing interests.

Aristotle, the Greek philosopher who we discussed in Chapters 3 and 6, said the just person is a very special person in that he or she is not solely concerned with him or herself, but is concerned with seeing that the right thing is done by others. This takes a noble mind; a mind that can rise above individual circumstance or need and can see the larger picture; a mind that seeks harmony rather than partisanship. Aristotle's taxonomy of justice as laid out in his *Nicomachean Ethics* (1999), still plays a significant role in our understanding and practice of justice to this day.

## Defining justice

### Claims and obligations

Broadly speaking, justice can be defined as "giving and getting one's due," materially, emotionally, psychologically, and spiritually (Solomon, 1990). This means justice has something to do with honoring rightful claims. It also implies that an agent (a person or organization), has an obligation to dispense justice by recognizing those claims. So justice is about claims and obligations. Some claims are enforceable under a law or a social convention. Some are unenforceable as in the case of gifts or a will where neither the beneficiaries nor anyone else can force the giver to show justice or fairness.

Claims that are non-material, for example regarding one's reputation, are often far more difficult to concretize than those that are.

Although justice is centrally a matter of how individuals are treated, we are frequently concerned with the justice of groups, for example when the government is allocating resources between different categories of citizens. Here each group is treated as though it were a separate individual for the purposes of a just allocation.

### Scope of justice

Justice refers to both actions taken and those not taken. How is this possible? Well, what we must bear in mind is that all our encounters and actions in life are relational. Whatever we experience or do is in relation to either ourselves, another or others, the community, the nation or the planet. Nothing exists in a void. In this sense, justice is inherent in everything. How we treat ourselves, one another, our community and the planet. From the fidelity between lovers, stealing at work, loafing at home, or polluting the planet, the scales of justice are always being tested. So when we raise questions about the scope of justice, it is ubiquitous; omnipresent. The justice question is always before us.

### Enforceable claims

We have already encountered the idea that there are situations in which claims of justice may not be enforceable even if the idea of justice is relevant. So who can make enforceable claims of justice, and who might have the corresponding obligation/s to meet them? Does this depend on the kind of thing that is being claimed? If comparative principles are being applied, who should be counted as part of the comparison group? Do some principles of justice have universal scope – they apply whenever agent A acts towards recipient B, regardless of the relationship between them – while others are contextual in character, applying only within social or political relationships of a certain kind? As we discuss below, and with a little help from our friend Aristotle, there are some broad guidelines to which we can turn.

### Impartiality

A principle implied as part and parcel of the concept of justice is that of impartiality. The term justice conveys the opposite of arbitrariness. This means that where two cases are relevantly alike, they should be treated in the same way. Therefore, if there is a rule or law that specifies what is due to a person who has features X, Y, Z, whenever such a person is encountered, that rule or law will apply. Although the rule or law need not be unchangeable, it must be relatively stable. This explains why justice is exemplified in the rules of law, where laws are understood as general rules impartially applied over time. Outside of the law itself, individuals and institutions that want to behave justly are obliged to mimic the law in as many ways as possible to demonstrate relevance and impartiality.

### Justice and agency

The issue of justice is prompted when an agent has in some manner contributed to bringing about an unjust state. The agent might be a person, a group, an organization or the state. Agents can also create injustice by an act of omission. For example, it is not unjust – though it is undoubtedly regrettable – that some children are born with a cleft lip. It may be unjust to deny remedial surgery to children whose lives would be blighted by the condition. The problems lie in defining the agent who has committed the injustice, and which agent has the obligation and ability to dispense justice as a result.

## Justice summary

- Goodness refers to demonstrating/manifesting justice.
- Justice is inherent in all our actions because all our actions are relational.
- Justice can be defined as "giving and getting one's due," materially, emotionally, psychologically, and spiritually.
- Justice is concerned with claims, obligations, and balancing competing stakeholder interests.
- Justice is concerned with individuals, organizations and societal harmony.
- Some agent is the cause of the state of injustice.
- The dispensation of justice requires consistency and impartiality.

## Questions of justice

The issue of justice raises at least the following questions:

- Which claims and obligations are enforceable, and which are not?
- How far does justice extend? Are there any limits?
- Does there have to be some relationship or reciprocal obligation between the parties for justice to apply?
- Does justice always imply objectivity or does emotion have a part to play?
- What if there is no agent? Is there such a thing as cosmic justice or cosmic injustice such as act of God?
- Are there objective principles by which to measure whether justice has been administered?
- Is the dispensation of justice purely context dependent?
- Are there goals for justice? For example, does justice mean establishing equality? For some? For everyone?
- Is justice concerned with ensuring that everyone has what they need?
- Is justice the same as liberty where everyone is free to be who they are and do what they like as long as they do not harm others?
- Does justice imply a commitment to the social good?
- Is justice purely determined by culture?

Let us look at some practical examples that elucidate some of these questions.

## I want justice!

### *A personal divorce*

Let us take a divorce settlement. Imagine the conflicting claims for justice from the various parties (him, her, the in-laws, the kids). Each party is sure to claim their position is fair.

Here are some perspectives from the various stakeholders:

- I want revenge.
- I want her to get her fair share.
- I think he should not pay her a penny as she was so unfaithful.
- I want her to be compensated for what she has been through.
- I want them both to get their fair share.
- I want to see that he gets nothing – he has destroyed her life.
- I want to see the nuptial contract fulfilled to the letter.
- I want to see her in the same place she was before she married the cad.
- I want to see him compensated for her spendthrift behavior.
- He gave her everything while they lived together, and now she still wants half the estate – that is unfair!
- I want my inheritance now that they have split up.

How does one establish justice in this situation? Which claims should be honored? How can all stakeholders feel that justice has been executed? Is that even possible?

We said that justice means giving and getting one's due or what one deserves. Where there are multiple, competing claims, as in this example, it is not always easy to ascertain what different people deserve. The benchmark for what someone deserves might be highly subjective or dependent on qualitative rather than quantitative parameters. Clearly establishing justice in these types of cases is no easy task. Even if in this example, the nuptial contract spelled out in detail the terms in case of a divorce, and say the contract was drawn up thirty-five years ago, should current mitigating circumstances not be considered?

As we know, in complex cases, lawyers look to precedent to help them find their way. Even with precedent, the context and the times are never the same. Establishing justice requires great insight and discernment, and as Aristotle pointed out, a noble mind.

### *A business divorce*

In a business organization the question of justice is equally challenging. Let us take divorce of another kind, for example lay-offs or downsizing. In deciding the layoff policy let us consider the competing claims of justice here.

- Senior managers cost the company the most. They should be laid off first.
- It is senior managers' fault the company is in trouble, they should bear the brunt and be laid off first.
- Senior employees who are no longer fit and creative should be laid off first.
- People with disabilities should be laid off first. They can still get their disability benefits.
- Only men should be laid off as they earn more than women.
- Only women should be laid off because they have husbands or men to support them.
- People under thirty should be laid off first because they will find a job more easily than others.
- The most productive people should be laid off as they will find a job more easily than others.
- Only the most productive people should be kept. The less productive should go first.
- The most recently hired people should be laid off first as the company owes them less loyalty.
- Old timers should be laid off first. New energetic blood is needed to save the firm.
- Old timers should not be laid off as the company owes them something for their loyalty.
- Lay off an equal percentage of each of these groups so as to spread the pain across the board.
- Decide by drawing names out of a hat.

What is justice here? In my experience, I have yet to meet a person who has been laid off, no matter what the circumstances, who feels they have been treated justly.

This example raises a further question as to whether in the case of competing claims, all parties can experience justice. Or whether justice is a zero-sum game. If I get justice, you do not. What are your thoughts?

### The state moves in

When Brazil hosted the 2014 World Cup Soccer, the government forced more than 250,000 people to leave their homes. The government managed to find $14 billion to host the games. Many argued that this money should rather have been spent to benefit the poor.

More violence followed in advance of the 2016 Olympic Games in Rio de Janeiro. About 70,000 people were displaced, and almost a thousand poor people – mostly black men – were killed during "pacification" efforts to clean up the city's image. Similar, less violent, displacements occurred in anticipation of Olympic preparations in Vancouver, London and Beijing.

In all cases, the cities argued that their countries benefitted hugely by hosting the Olympic Games which brought in new revenue streams, increased tourism, enhanced their countries' image, and sparked new investments in technology and infrastructure projects. Supposedly the benefits far exceeded the costs (the utilitarian argument we discussed in Chapter 6). Cleaning up unsanitary areas was essential to make this possible and the revenues that resulted from the games provided the needed funds and the social impetus. Some of the poor were recompensed. The homeless of course "lost whatever precinct they knew as home."

The media is already speculating in anticipation of the 2028 Olympic Games what the cost will be to Los Angeles' myriad homeless who live next door to some of the richest suburbs in the world.

Let us consider some of the competing claims of justice here:

- Cities have a social and moral duty to clean up their act so that they can compete fairly with other cities around the world. It is right and fair that they take the opportunity.
- The Olympic Games provides a valid reason to gentrify neighborhoods and reduce crime which is only fair to law abiding citizens.
- Wealthy neighborhoods add value and prestige to cities, contrary to the derelict areas and the slums. It is just to use opportunities to clean these up.
- Recompensing the poor for being displaced provides just compensation as they probably would not have been able to sell whatever possessions they had on the open market.
- It is unjust to force people to leave their homes even if compensation is offered.
- It is only fair to businesses to give them an opportunity to benefit from the huge marketing benefits that result from a city hosting the Olympic Games.
- It is unjust to make the poor pay for the benefits that will go to businesses and the rich.

- If business prospers the poor will benefit too. It is fair to all parties.
- Is it fair to socialize the costs of the Olympic Games across society and saddle them with a debt that may take thirty years to repay?

How does one settle these countervailing claims and provide an acceptable level of justice? Who should decide?

## Justice and the law

In most countries, the "law" is referred to as the justice system. The questions that arises frequently is whether all laws are just?

The justice system is divided into criminal justice which deals with the rules of law and order, and its counterpart, civil justice, which deals with the rights and obligations between citizens. It is the civil justice system that gives us the opportunity to debate our contractual obligations and our rights (remember Hobbes and Locke in Chapter 6).

Justice, as we have just discussed, means giving people what they deserve. Societies determine which behaviors are worthy of honor and reward and which are not (Sandal, 2007). The justice system, through the medium of laws, determines who deserves what based on these recognized behaviors. The justice system thus upholds the societal values-based paradigm. What is rewarded in many of the so-called developed countries is status, power and wealth. The justice system in these countries reinforces these social biases. Recall that the law is the codification of certain ethical principles. What gets codified is decided mostly by those in power. Once again – those in power make the rules.

### Executing justice

The practice of executing justice poses (at least) three essential problems. The first concerns what justice means in a specific context. The second relates to which perspective or stakeholder issue gets favored treatment. And the third problem is that executing justice entails not only assessing the outcome of a particular action or actions, but also the process that led to the action. For example, an outcome might seem unjust (the laying off of thousands of employees), yet the process might be justly formulated and executed (for example, personal circumstances were taken into consideration in deciding who should be laid off). How does one talk about justice in this example? Did the process matter or did the outcome? The process element refers to procedural justice, and many people place great store on procedural justice.

### Procedural justice

Procedural justice relates to the fairness and transparency of the processes used in order to arrive at just actions. This is often referred to as "due process." Clear communication of the issues at stake and the tensions involved at arriving at a just decision greatly improves the perception that the procedures for decision-making are just. Giving parties affected by a decision an opportunity to voice their views is an important part of making a process procedurally fair. In business organizations, if employees are given the opportunity and the right to give voice to their opinions, they usually feel respected and valued. This gives them a sense that organizational justice does exist. Research shows that evidence of procedural justice improves employee morale and consequently job performance. It also improves employees' perception of the outcome of a decision even if it is not in their favor.

## Help from the past

Until now, I have provided some definitions and broad principles that define justice and we have looked at three examples of typical claims related to justice. What is missing are some practical guidelines or rules that might help us nail down the definition and provide a justice implementation framework. Do these exist?

Let us turn to the past, namely to Plato and Aristotle, who set the initial curriculum for the study of justice, to see what they have to say.

### Plato

It was Plato, in his mighty work, the *Republic*, who canonized the question "What is justice?" For him, there were only three things worthwhile in this world: Truth, Beauty and Justice (the Good). In one of Plato's dialogues, Socrates (alias Plato), states that "a just man is a man in just the right place, doing his best, and giving the full equivalent of what he receives" (*The Republic, Chapter II, Book IV,*) This means that justice implies a form of appropriate reciprocity dispensed by a person who is a noble and thoughtful. Justice also takes the situation into account.

For Plato, a society of just men (women did not count in those days), would create a highly harmonious and efficient group due to their appropriate reciprocal interactions. I use the term appropriate to indicate that the reciprocity fits the relationship and the situation. Harmony results from everyone giving everyone else their due in harmonious balance.

In Plato's schema, justice means "effective coordination." This means the harmonious functioning of the elements in "man." Justice means not mere strength, but harmonious strength. Justice means not only the right of the stronger, but also the effective harmony of the whole. For Plato, all moral conceptions revolve around the good of the whole. Morality begins with the association and the interdependence and organization of society. Life in society requires the concession of some part of the individual's sovereignty to the common order, and ultimately the norms of conduct are dictated by concern for the welfare of the group. A prudent compromise is an important feature of justice. You could call this Plato's version of the social contract which we discussed under Hobbes in the previous chapter.

In sum, for Plato justice means promoting harmony of the group through thoughtful give and take.

### Aristotle

Aristotle, you may recall, named justice one of the cardinal virtues, and like all of Aristotle's virtues, justice describes the mean between extremes. Injustice, he refers to as an excess or defect in relation to the mean.

Aristotle believed justice concerned good judgment and a sense of fairness (giving people what they deserve), as well as a state of character. He viewed justice as a virtue of the highest degree in that, of all the virtues, justice is one that exists for another's good. All other virtues – courage, temperance and prudence – focus on concern for oneself. Aristotle believed that one finds it easier to exercise virtue in relation to oneself than to others. Therefore, for Aristotle, the just person exemplifies the virtuous person. The just person is a person of character par excellence.

Aristotle classified justice into various categories. This categorization facilitates the framing of justice claims so as to make them enforceable. Aristotle's categories are still used in the formulations of our justice system today. These can be summarized as:

> **Universal justice:** This places emphasis on consideration of the rights of others. This is the high-level concept of justice. An example is the issue of human rights.
> **Particular justice:** This relates to specific acts of justice which are further divided into distributive justice and rectificatory justice.
> **Distributive justice**: This raises the question of the distribution of wealth in society and whether the public should assist the needy. Should the state intervene when it comes to how wealth and opportunity is distributed?

According to Aristotle, if any assistance is provided it should be in accordance with the "proportion." By proportion Aristotle meant that equals deserve equal assistance and unequals deserve unequal assistance. The "unjust," is where the proportion is violated. What Aristotle means is that there is some benchmark relationship that defines a just proportion. For example, ten equal people should get ten equal shares of the cake. In the case of "unequal" people, their share may be more or less than one tenth, depending on the circumstances. Aristotle claims that where this "proportion" is not appropriately meted out, injustice exists. He does not give us any details on how to define quality or how to calculate or measure the proportion, or how to make adjustments to the proportion. The notion of fairness thus becomes a contentious debate.

> **Rectificatory justice**: This applies to restitution in the event of a theft or a loss. Justice in this instance ensures the person a return to their state prior to the theft or loss.

**Reciprocity:** This refers to justice-in-exchange or commercial justice. According to Aristotle, to ensure justice, everything should be related to the same measure of exchange. We know this principle only too well in that everything, it seems, is made in some way to be measurable in monetary terms, even happiness!

**Equity:** Aristotle distinguished between justice and equity. He claimed that the law cannot provide for everything, therefore one also needs equity. Equity exists as a corrective to legal justice in that it takes unusual circumstances into account and decides accordingly. By applying equity, the common law is moderated by ethics, fairness and an intuitive intelligence. Good judges know how to incorporate equity into their decisions. Equity is the highest form of justice.

The snapshot of Aristotle's thinking provided here sets out some of his major categories of justice. Despite his detailed writings on the topic, Aristotle fails to provide any simple, practical steps one can take to mete out justice. He relies on prudence and practical wisdom or judgment (*phronesis*). A capacity, he claims, comes with developing one's character.

From an organizational perspective, managers are expected to have the wisdom to exercise equity. This is by no means easy. It requires balancing many opposing needs, wants, rights and expectations. It also demands carrying out a thoughtful analysis of the problem and establishing appropriate criteria for evaluation. There is also the tyranny of precedence that often shuts down opportunities for new and creative solutions.

### Religious perspectives on justice

#### Judaism

The Jewish approach to justice is influenced by the Ten Commandments, the *Torah* and the *Halakhah* (Jewish Law). The Jewish people have a strong sensitivity to equal justice for all. Besides having myriad laws on personal behavior towards God, there are some very specific rules regarding behavior towards others. These include not taking advantage of the weak and needy even if someone might be viewed as an enemy. Jews are not to bear false testimony; not to take bribes, and to avoid all kinds of violence, even towards slaves.

Influenced by the *Code of Hammurabi*, there was in earlier Hebrew times a strong sense of justice that was tied to retribution. This is expressed in the well-known phrase "an eye for an eye and a tooth for a tooth."

#### Christianity

In Christian ethics, God is the ultimate in righteousness or justice. He remains faithful to His divinely established relationship with human beings. His behavior sets the tone and provides the benchmark for human behavior, not only toward

God, but between one another. Justice is considered a virtue that reflects a state of character where the just person acts in ways that promotes human flourishing. Justice is carried out by acting with impartiality towards others and ensuring they get their due or just dessert. Justice is influenced and shaped by love of God and neighbor.

Christian ethics also places great emphasis on justice as a matter of mercy. Christians consider justice and mercy to be two sides of the same coin. Justice or righteousness means being merciful to both the victim and the accused. Mercy means showing compassion and understanding for the parties concerned. Justice and mercy are not in opposition. Rather for Christians, true justice always includes an element of compassion and mercy.

### Islam

Muslims are expected to live and act according to the Quran. The Quran emphasizes the importance of justice as being close to Godliness. Justice is deemed a supreme moral virtue. It is interpreted as placing things in their rightful place, and in giving others equal treatment except when that does not result in fairness.

Justice is expected to be exercised to all. There is to be no discrimination. According to the Quran, everyone, regardless of race, color, creed or social class is to be given fair dealings. Equity is considered an important aspect of justice, especially in the case of distributive justice.

Where no clear injunctions or guidance is provided, Muslims are advised to use the intelligence God has given humans and to rely on the innate sense of justice written by God on the tablet of their souls.

Muslims are expected to do good, be fair, see the view from the other side and place truth over expediency. Muslims are encouraged to battle any injustice imposed on them.

### Hinduism

Hindus refer to the term *dharma* to describe their sense of religious, moral and social duty. Dharma refers to the laws that govern the natural world as well as the world of human activity. The dharma prescribes duty, obligations, law and ethics. When people ignore their duties, not just the social order but the cosmic order is threatened. Proper behavior literally keeps the world from falling apart, and proper behavior means everyone doing his or her universally assigned duty.

Hindus do not refer to having a personal moral of justice but rather to a cosmic one. This form of justice they refer to as *karma*, where each act has its consequences from which no-one can escape. People who complete their *dharmic* duties build up good karma and are thus likely to be reborn into more auspicious circumstances in the next life. Those who fail to do so generate bad karma and may find themselves reborn into a lower social caste or even a lower form of life. For many Hindus, concern for a better rebirth and ultimately liberation from the wheel of reincarnation serves as a great motivator to take their dharmic responsibilities seriously. One guiding rule is the Golden Rule where in several of their holy writings there is an injunction "to not behave toward others in a way which is disagreeable to oneself" (*Mahabharata*, (5:1517)).

*Confucianism*

Confucius, the Chinese philosopher, taught a doctrine of reciprocity and neighborliness. He taught: "To regard everyone as an important guest, to manage the people as one would assist at a sacrifice, not to do to others what you would not have them do to you" (Analects 15:23).

Confucius' main legacy is the teaching of *jen/ren*. *Jen* refers to the virtue of the "superior man," the gentleman. It refers to loyalty to one's own heart and conscience; to reciprocity and respect and consideration for others. *Jen* can be translated also as goodness, benevolence and human heartedness.

*Jen* is related to the concept *li*, which means propriety or ritual. The Confucian view is that life has inherent ritual, pattern and order. This should not be violated but always respected. This pattern and order are reflected in the manner in which people behave to one another. Familial relations provide a model for perfect social behavior.

---

### Your turn – facing Mecca

You are the CEO of a small publishing company. You have a staff of thirty people and you have been in business for twenty-five years. The business has done well because you understand your market and you have built a robust team who work hard and enjoy their work. Most of them have been with you for ten years or more.

You recently hired Mushid Abdal as one of your copyeditors. Mushid comes from Tunisia and is a devout Muslim. On taking the job, Mushid informed you that he needed to honor his prayer commitments of five times a day and would like a small, private space to do so. Eager to show your cross-cultural competence and empathy, you gave him a small room that used to be used for stocking old materials. Mushid has now turned this private prayer room into his own space where he has a prayer mat laid out facing Mecca, a pile of books including the Quran, along with some of his personal items.

Mushid disappears for prayers at midday and during the afternoon. While the prayers need only last five minutes, he is often in his room for thirty minutes or more. Several of your staff are annoyed. They feel that he is getting special treatment – which he is. His prayer time is not counted as part of his official lunch break. Mushid also leaves in the middle of meetings in the afternoon when he says he must pray. Discontent among the other staff is growing. They feel Mushid is taking advantage and they say they also want a private room for themselves as they all sit in an open plan office which is noisy and disruptive.

## Questions

- How are you going to handle this?
- What are the justice issues here?
- Will insisting the Mushid only pray for five minutes each time resolve the issue?
- Should you make him use this time as his lunch time?

This brief review of some of the religious perspectives of justice reveals the broad moral terrain justice covers. Based on our review of Plato and Aristotle, we can also conclude that regarding specific guidelines, help from the past is limited. To continue our search for some practical guidelines or insights as to how to execute justice, let us now look at whether some contemporary theories may provide any clearer answers.

## Perspectives of justice

Our review of justice shows that the concept embraces the following perspectives:

- Reciprocity
- Achieving harmony and promoting inter-relatedness
- Sacrifice for the common good
- Impartiality in giving people their due
- Fairness
- Carrying out the law
- Some form of equality
- Some form of distribution according to proportion
- Rectification of loss to a prior state
- Retribution in the case of harm
- Taking care of the weak and needy
- Promoting human flourishing
- Acting with love
- Showing mercy and compassion
- Eliminating discrimination
- Fair dealings
- Benevolence, human heartedness
- Demonstrating equity

It is important to note that justice is highly personal and culturally determined. Different societies interpret what is "due" to someone differently. For some it is retribution, for others mercy. For some it is based on the law or God's word, for others it is about creating harmony. The more pluralist the society or group, the wider the range of perspectives.

As you can see from the many perspectives I have provided, justice is a complicated matter. Place ten people in a room with a justice dilemma and you will get at least eight different answers. These different perspectives of justice are a source of a great deal of disharmony between people and within and between societies.

# A tragic case

Brian Scott was a senior engineer for a large contracts engineering company. He had a team of ten people working for him and was held in very high regard in the industry. He worked hard and earned well. His team respected his skills, but in general did not appreciate his off-hand, often rude manner. They saw him as self-centered and disinterested in them, both as colleagues and people.

Brian frequently met with customers to negotiate new contracts. Due to his expertise he was the lead negotiator with most of the company's important clients. One Wednesday, Brian met a team of engineers, who worked for an important client, for lunch in a friendly, rural restaurant about fifteen miles from the office. After a rather long lunch in which some alcohol was consumed, Brian drove back to the office.

No-one knows what really happened. A horrific accident took place. Brian's large Ford sedan had a head on collision with an oncoming Volkswagen filled with four children and the driver, being the mother of one of them. All the children were under the age of ten years. Only one child survived with severe brain injuries leaving him damaged for the rest of his life. The mother driving the Volkswagen had just collected the children from school and was taking them to their homes as part of a lift scheme. While Brian had alcohol in his system, he was found to be under the legal limit. He sustained head injuries. He was able to return to work after three months. Brian claimed he did not remember a thing and could therefore not explain how the accident occurred.

The four families affected were devastated. The community in the area where the company had its offices expressed outrage. The parents of the deceased children phoned the CFO (me), asking that the company pay all claims related to the deaths. People sent angry letters to the CEO and several articles damning the company appeared in the local newspapers.

# The issues

- The families wanted the company to pay all damages plus some form of restitution.
- The father who lost his wife and who was left with the brain-damaged child desperately needed financial help with medical bills.
- The newspaper articles included claims that Brian should lose his job.
- Several clients of the company placed their contract negotiations for new contracts with the company on hold.
- Morale at the company plummeted.
- Brian was given the best hospital care paid fully by the company.
- The lawyers said there was no legal case against the company or Brian as there were no witnesses. They advised that no money exchange hands.

# Questions

- What do you make of this case? What are your assumptions, biases and prejudices?

- What are the issues of justice here? How would you articulate them referring to the justice discussion above?
- If you were the CEO of the contracts engineering company, what would you do? What actions would you take with justice in mind?
- Why would you do what you would do? How would you explain your motivation? (Chapters 4 and 6.)

## Justice today

As we have seen, basic notions of justice are concerned with fairness, deservedness, benevolence, love and compassion, and concern for the common good. A person has been treated justly when he or she has been given his or her due.

Since Plato and Aristotle, many philosophers, theologians and social advocates have weighed in with their ideas of justice, yet the challenge of creating a just society remains. Many would argue that the challenges have mounted as societies have become larger, and less homogenous.

We might also remind ourselves that Adam Smith (Chapter 1), believed that humans are inherently just and that this innate sentiment tempers their otherwise self-interested intentions. Not too many other philosophers or social activists have been that confident in this aspect of human nature.

What is the role of justice in society today? Is it as Hobbes insisted, all about creating security and safety? Is it John Locke's view that justice is concerned with protecting our property and liberty? Or is it more about harmony and the common good?

While these aspects always play some part, a significant emphasis of contemporary justice theories center on the huge and growing disparities between the wealthy and the less wealthy. In the US for instance, how can one reconcile the inalienable right of individuals to life, liberty and the pursuit of happiness with the existence of extreme poverty and misery within the same society? Questions this raises include: Do the standards of justice in society in fact favor the stronger or more powerful citizens? Does the free market contribute to creating a just society? How should one interpret the meaning of "equality" in consideration of justice? And should people be expected to make sacrifices for the common good or should human freedom to be and do as they please prevail?

Rival theories of justice tackle these thorny questions differently. Common to most theories, however, stands the principle that like cases should be treated alike: i.e., equals ought to be treated equally, and un-equals unequally – remember Aristotle. This principle of justice does not, however, provide guidance on how to determine equality or proportion, and therefore lacks substance as a specific guide to just conduct. If we take any group of persons, many ways exist in which they have similarities and differences. Therefore, one must understand this account of equality as equality in relevant matters. Defining these "relevant" matters is a complicated exercise in justice itself.

# Justice in society

## *Distributive justice*

Since one of the consequences of globalization seems to be the growing disparity between rich and poor, distributive justice has become a highly charged matter of societal concern. In attempts to redress this reality, several political philosophers have proposed different versions of distributive justice (sometimes called social justice) with a view to re-allocating certain types of societal burdens and benefits. Here are some examples of the different principles put forward.

Give –

> To each person an equal share
> To each person according to individual need
> To each person according to that person's rights
> To each person according to individual effort
> To each person according to societal contribution
> To each person according to merit.

In the face of these conflicting ideas, how does one decide what is a "just" entitlement? Egalitarian principles of justice emphasize equal access to primary goods; Marxist theories emphasize distribution according to need; libertarian theories emphasize rights to social and economic liberty; utilitarian theories emphasize a mixed use of criteria aimed at maximizing both public and private utility (remember utility is a measure of happiness).

> **What do you think? What views do you have on distributive justice?**
>
> **What about at work? Should all people earn equally; according to need; according to seniority; according to merit; according to effort?**
>
> **How much should the senior management earn as a proportion relative to the average worker – 10 times as much; 100 times as much; 500 times as much? What is fair, just? Based on which principles?**

## *Justice debates*

Two Harvard professors, John Rawls and Robert Nozick, set the twentieth-century agenda in the US for the ongoing debate on issues of social justice. Much has been written by and about these authors' theories. My synopsis of their thoughts is by design brief, intended to give the you, the reader, the main gist of their different approaches to justice as their arguments remain part of the political debate to this day not only in the US but in other countries cognizant of the challenges of creating a just society.

*John Rawls*

John Rawls, in *A Theory of Justice* (1971), adopted a contractarian approach to the justice issue. A contractarian approach places emphasis on the social contract of a society where members compromise their own needs in the interests of the overall welfare of society (remember Plato). Rawls contended that we should distribute all economic goods and services equally except in those cases where unequal distribution would work to everyone's advantage or would at least benefit the worst off in society. Governments should intervene to implement these principles through one or more social programs.

Rawls is famous for his use of a device he called the *Original Position*. Here the social contract is based on principles of justice created from behind a veil of ignorance. This "veil" is one that a person assumes as blinding them to any facts about themselves so that they cannot tailor any principles to their advantage. For example, if one were not to know one's place in society, one's class, one's social status, the level of one's wealth, the extent of one's intelligence, one's physical capabilities or lack thereof, one is likely to develop principles of justice that take care of the weakest person, as the weakest person may turn out to be ourselves. If an individual does not know where he or she might end up, or where her fortunes may or may not lie, Rawls' theorized that he or she would develop a scheme of justice that treats everyone fairly.

Rawls claimed that parties in the original position would focus on granting equality as the basic principle of justice. They would, however, defer to a *difference principle* which would permit the inequality of distribution if those inequalities benefitted the worst-off members of society.

For all the hype, Rawls' argument was a hypothetical one. It is not possible to create a real-life situation where the veil of ignorance truly exists. The proposed outcomes of his argument have thus never been tried out. Therefore, we don't know that a veil of ignorance would indeed arrive at the approach to justice that he hypothesized. It is interesting however, that his thought experiment has captured the imagination of many as to how one might establish a just society. Some social theorists strongly support this egalitarian approach.

> **Distributive justice injunction**: *Take that action that protects the weakest and most vulnerable in society.*

*Robert Nozick*

Robert Nozick challenged Rawls' ideas. He explained his approach to justice in his "entitlement theory" as explicated in *Anarchy, State, and Utopia* (1974). He stated that government action is only justified when it protects the fundamental rights of citizens. Therefore, unless illegality has occurred, the government should not try to redistribute the economic benefits and burdens of society. As long as procedural justice has been carried out, Nozick argues to let the chips fall where they may. Government should stay out of any redistribution efforts.

Nozick emphasized that a distribution of goods is just when it is brought about by a free exchange among consenting adults from a just starting position. This means that the focus should be on everyone having equal opportunity from early in life. After that, it is up to effort, opportunity and even fortune, but no external interference can or should try to level the playing field.

> **Contributive liberty injunction**: *Take that action that does not interfere with anyone's rights to self-development and self-fulfillment.*

### Cosmic Justice

Thomas Sowell, in his book, *The Quest for Cosmic Justice*, (2002), attempts to address the reactions against the great inequalities of income and wealth that dominate the times. Sowell argues quite vehemently that while there are undeserved inequalities that arise for all kinds of reasons, politicizing them by insisting on all kinds of redistribution strategies is not the answer. Many of the inequalities that have arisen, for example race, gender and social circumstances at birth, have resulted from the cosmic throw of the dice. He questions how one can redress these disparities as there is no way to unscramble the egg.

Justice, he writes, is a process, not an enforced correction. Justice must deal with the here and now and not attempt to correct the past, as how far back does one go? What would corrective justice even look like, he asks?

Sowell suggests that the government cannot create social justice and should not even try. At best it can try to focus on economic policies going forward rather than, through redistributions, fix the distortions and alleged discriminations of the past. In a nutshell, Sowell claims that the government should exercise minimum interference other than to ensure that economic policies are sound . . . whatever that means.

### Ongoing challenge

The difficulties in defining and assuring distributive justice are likely to grow in complexity. As multicultural, pluralistic cultures develop and claim more and more individual and group rights, they no longer have the desire or the goal to establish "equality." They want to be both equal and different! For, as Aristotle at one point articulated, "the equal wish to be unequal, and the unequal equal." Further, as the gap between the rich and the poor continues to grow in more countries, this tension is at some point likely to stimulate (or revolutionize) new theories of distributive justice.

## Environmental justice

According to the US Environmental Protection Agency (EPA) the definition of environmental justice is as follows:

> Environmental justice is the fair treatment and meaningful involvement of all people regardless of race, color, national origin, or income with respect

to the development, implementation, and enforcement of environmental laws, regulations, and policies. The EPA has this goal for all communities and persons across this nation. It will be achieved when everyone enjoys the same degree of protection from environmental and health hazards and equal access to the decision-making process to have a healthy environment in which to live, learn, and work.

(EPA website)

Environmental justice seeks to redress environmental discrimination largely against non-dominant minorities and low-income groups. Typically, waste management and high pollution sites are located in proximity to these disadvantaged groups. They are frequently vulnerable to landfill sites, incinerators, and other potentially toxic facilities and harmful factories. This is deemed environmental discrimination because it is placing a harmful entity in a place where the people often don't have the means to fight back against big corporations.

Environmental discrimination has historically been evident in the process of selecting and building environmentally hazardous sites, including waste disposal, manufacturing, and energy production facilities. The location of transportation infrastructures, including highways, ports and airports, has also been viewed as a source of environmental injustice. The environmental justice movement has initiated laws and legal redress for circumstances where this occurs. Regrettably there is still a long way to go.

We discuss this issue in detail in the next chapter on corporate social responsibility.

## Justice reflection

What have we learned from this brief reflection on the very important matter of justice?

- First, there are several types of justice, for example criminal justice or social justice. These various types of justice attempt to set the context in which the claim for justice exists. There are some universal principles of justice, such as human rights, which we have not yet discussed but investigate in the next chapter.
- Second, I have provided a few of the better-known principles of justice many of which are anchored in the law.
- Third, different people have different ideas about what justice means. This makes creating a just society or a just organization challenging.
- Fourth, applying the motto that equal people should be treated equally, and unequal people unequally sounds simple, but defining what equal and unequal means in what respects is almost impossible. We are all equal in some ways and unequal in others.
- Fifth, applying the principle of equity is what takes justice to the next level. Here the dryness of the laws, rules or policies is watered with mercy and intuitive intelligence. But that takes great maturity and wisdom!

The best we can say is that justice is an ongoing work in progress. As our social consciousness changes, so does our idea of justice. Our interpretations change and our applications of justice alter. Think of how same sex marriage has influenced the interpretation of justice. Not until recently did we think, talk and argue about the essentiality of environmental justice and justice towards the planet. The Australian ethicist, Peter Singer, awoke us to our obligations to animals (Singer, 2009). Now we understand that justice applies not only to all animals but to the planet itself. All in all, it is our sensitivity and appreciation of the notion of justice that brings out the best of our humanness. So frustrating as it maybe, we must persevere in seeking and striving to keep on reinterpreting justice so that its lovingkindness can touch all that exists.

## A little discrimination

Joanne Corcoran was appointed as Vice President of HI-TECH Systems Inc., at the beginning of 2013. She has worked for the organization for seven years and is a very effective executive. She spent four months looking for someone to fill her previous position as director of marketing.

Allison Snow, who has worked at HI-TECH for twelve years, who was eager to get the vice president position, also applied. Allison has all the technical skills and knows the company inside out. She is intelligent, adaptable to change and a problem solver. Unfortunately, she is inclined to be controlling, confrontational and convinced that no-one's standards meet her own. While she achieves excellent results, she is not popular with some people, while others think her strengths more than compensate for her flaws.

Joanne, along with the hiring committee, decided that Allison would be too challenging if she were recruited into the director of marketing job. Instead they hired Sean Grady, a young MBA graduate who has had several years marketing experience in technology-related organizations. Sean came with good references that reflected his inexperience. He has an appealing personality and is inclined to put people at ease. The hiring committee was convinced that he would be a good fit.

It is now December of 2013. During the last six months, Allison was made to report to Sean in July 2013. Over the past four months she has increasingly bypassed Sean as her boss and reported or appealed directly to Joanne. Initially Joanne did nothing, but the frequency with which Allison undermined Sean grew. Joanne decided to have a serious meeting with Allison to get her back into line. At the meeting Allison explains that while Sean is charming, his execution is abysmal. According to her, he is slow, ineffective and does not get critical things done. Joanne has noticed that Sean does not take the initiative and is substantially behind in the achievement of his goals. She has been too busy to take him to task. She has also hoped that the "problem" would go away.

Irritated, Joanne tells Allison that she cannot keep making an end run to her office. She needs to find a way to work with Sean and to get things done through him. If he is ineffective, she, Allison must help him become more effective. Her job is to help him be a success.

Allison is furious. For one she knows that Sean earns a tidy salary, much greater than her own. Also, she feels while she can support a competent boss, she is not there to shore up an incompetent one. Why was she not given a chance? No-one is perfect but at least she works very hard and delivers the results. Would they have treated her like this if she were a guy?

## Questions

- Is this an issue of justice? Has Allison been fairly treated?
- What would justice look like in this situation?
- If you were Joanne, what next steps would you take?
- What is your rationale? What is your motivation?

My Comment: I regret to say that in my many decades of corporate consulting, I could write this case over just with different details many, many times!

## Justice and mercy

> *And earthly power doth act like God's*
> *When mercy seasons justice*
>
> (Shakespeare, *The Merchant of Venice*, ACT iv, scene 1)

As a teacher of ethics to both young students and mature professionals, I have concluded that we have a long way to go when it comes to practicing empathy. From my observations, few of us can look at a situation from multiple perspectives and genuinely set aside our own viewpoints and show concern or genuine empathy for the position of a person with whom we disagree. Many of us fail to understand that empathy is not what we would do or how we would feel in another person's shoes. Empathy is walking in the other person's shoes as them! This of course requires an understanding of the other person, his or her self-image, fears, hopes, dreams, sorrows, goals . . . and so on. It means trying to imagine what the world is like from that other person's perspective, while also suspending judgment.

To be truly empathetic is a great gift. Unfortunately, many of us are rarely able to put true empathy into practice. Therefore, fair judgment, or justice tempered by mercy, is a rare commodity and a ray of sunshine when it occurs.

The second struggle that many of us have is getting past our conviction that we know what is right. We find it difficult to hold the intellectual tension of another perspective without reverting to our own point of view.

The third struggle is finding compassion for the person who may have engaged in some wrong-doing. People are quick to point out the stupidity or evil intent of the guilty parties. We forget that all of us struggle with the ethics-morality gap where we actually do that thing we want and not the thing we hate. (Remember Chapter 3.)

The picture of Lady Justice as a woman is a reminder that true justice is tempered by mercy. And mercy results from empathy and compassion.

## Justice at work

Justice as we have seen, is a complex subject. Even so, our concern is how business leaders can incorporate justice into their organizations. Furthermore, when an organization trades across the globe, how can it act justly in the eyes of the many different stakeholders who have their own interpretations of justice? Yet, no matter how challenging the notion of justice might be, it is one of the most important elements of ethical deliberation as it is inherent in all actions. For without a sense of justice, we would live in an anarchic, pathological and diabolical world.

### *Some justice considerations at work*

- Nepotism
- Discrimination
- Sexual harassment
- Equal pay for equal work
- Equal opportunity for advancement
- Basis of remuneration policies
- Leave policy – e.g., maternity or childcare
- Healthcare and benefit policies
- Recruitment policies
- Procedures for disciplinary actions
- Methodology for layoffs
- Safety matters
- Customer care and service
- Supplier care
- Attention to the environment

Different organizations approach the justice issue differently. In my experience, justice is most explicitly addressed through human resource issues, many of which are included in the list above. Training for managers in the concept of justice and its practical implications, rarely occurs. Mostly matters of justice are viewed from a legal standpoint. That certainly helps to keep the organization out of the courts but does not necessarily promote the true spirit of justice in the organization. Recall, Chapter 6, where I stated that the law is a minimalist approach to ethics.

It would take many chapters to address a few, never mind all the areas to which the organization must pay attention. A good starting point is to include the matter of justice in the organization's conversations as part of its practicing ethics. It also means reviewing all organizational policies and procedures along with an attention to procedural justice. The exercise of procedural justice, while not assuring a just outcome, provides at least a thoughtful process in which multiple stakeholders can participate.

## Managing with equity

One of the biggest challenges facing managers is how to manage justly and thereby create a culture of justice. Managers need to be perceived as people who understand the subtleties of fairness and fair play. They also need to emphasize clear and consistent criteria for evaluating ethical dilemmas along with opportunities for employees to openly engage in the discussions leading up to resolutions.

Decision-making that reflects justice takes great skill and usually requires the collaboration of several parties. It is extremely challenging for a manager on his or her own to act justly without the benefit of discussion and consultation with others who can help him or her see multiple viewpoints. It also challenging for the manager to cope with the following tensions without dialogue and collaboration:

- What is good for an individual or individuals versus what is good for the group?
- What are the tensions between a short- term solution and the longer term? Where or when might more justice be achieved?
- Is objectivity and impartiality better than partisanship and caring?
- How and to what extent does precedent play a role?
- Where does one draw the line between strict fairness and mercy and compassion?
- To what extent and how should equal people be treated equally and unequal people unequally? In other words, how and where should one make allowances?
- To what extent should the "weaker" party be taken care of?
- When should the rules be changed or broken?
- Can the principles or rules be interpreted differently?

An ethical manager who practices just behavior is a huge asset to the organization. Sensitivity and compassion do not absolve people from their misdeeds but ensures that the justice dispensed is appropriate. Research shows that where people experience a sense of justice in the organization there usually is a greater culture of trust.

And as we discussed, the highest form of justice is the exercise of equity. Ethically competent managers exercise equity in their decisions. Equity requires practical wisdom; wisdom that is evidenced in the understanding of what is just and fair moderated by timing and circumstance. Practicing ethics enhances the ability to exercise equity and wisdom. Leaders who consciously engage in practicing ethics do far better than those who do not.

## He ain't heavy, he is my brother

### *The* Parable of the Sadhu

I often use the *Parable of the Sadhu* (McCoy, 2007), as an opening case in my ethics bootcamps and seminars. It is a true story that has been presented to a gathering of ethicists at Harvard University for their reactions. What is yours?

### *Story*

Buzz McCoy, who works for Morgan Stanley, takes a six-month sabbatical. He chooses to go mountain climbing in Nepal. He is accompanied by his friend, Stephen, an anthropologist. They hire a sherpa guide named *Pasang*.

They were halfway through the sixty-day Himalayan part of the trip when they reached a high point that they would have to traverse to reach the ancient holy place for pilgrims called *Muklinath*. They needed to get over the steep part of the climb before the sun melted the steppes and they could not get through the pass. This would have destroyed a once-in-a-life trip for McCoy.

Just after daybreak, as they were resting in anticipation of the last part of their journey, a New Zealander, part of a group ahead of them, came staggering towards them with a body slung across his shoulders. He dumped an almost naked, barefoot body of an Indian holy man – a sadhu – at Buzz McCoy's feet. The New Zealander felt he had done what he could and was eager to leave so that he could join his group and get over the pass.

Buzz McCoy was concerned about his growing altitude sickness and wanted to get over the pass. Buzz decided to keep going up over the pass leaving the fate of the sadhu to others. Stephen was concerned about the sadhu and did not want to abandon him. He and Pasang walked down the pass until they encountered the next group of climbers, a party of Japanese. The Japanese were not eager to take responsibility for the sadhu, and after giving him food, pointed out to him that he could walk further down to a hut for some cover from the elements. Stephen and Pasang resumed their climb toward the pass to join McCoy.

On meeting McCoy, who was elated at having reached the summit, Stephen challenged their behavior. "How do you feel like contributing to the death of a fellow man?" he asked. "What would you have done if the sadhu had been a well-dressed Western woman? No one person was willing to assume ultimate responsibility. Each was willing to do his bit just as long as it was not too inconvenient." Buzz McCoy responded "We had our own well-being to worry about. What right does an almost naked pilgrim have to disrupt our lives?" (McCoy, 1987 p. 108)

### Questions

- What are the justice issues here? How would you articulate them?
- What would you have done if you were Buzz McCoy?
- What is your motivation for your actions?

### Ethical theories and justice

Let us briefly examine how the ethical theories set out in the previous chapter address the issue of justice.

#### Character-based ethics

Socrates – *Take that action that reflects a life of striving for human excellence and wisdom.*

**Justice results due to the person's character, humility and striving to live a good life filled with wisdom.**

Plato – *Take that action that reflects a virtuous life in accordance with the dictates of reason.*

**A life guided by reason will result in reasonable behavior in all things**.

Aristotle – *Take that action that is thoughtful, reasonable and honest, and reflects the life you want to live.*

**A virtuous life includes practicing the cardinal virtue of justice which would translate to moderation in behavior, responses, and finding the dynamic and creative middle ground in all things**.

Jesus – *Take that action that reflects unconditional love (empathy and compassion) and is the way you would like to be treated out of love.*

**Acting with pure, unconditional, sacrificial love in all things reflects a divine form of justice**.

*Deontology rule-based ethics*

Divine Command theory – *Recognize your obligation to God and perform that action that adheres to God's commands.*

**By following God's commands, one acts justly as God is the measure of justice**.

Kant – *Do your duty which requires that you always treat people with dignity and that your action can be universalized as the moral law for all people in similar circumstances.*

**By doing one's moral duty as revealed to one through reason, and by not using people as means to an end, one acts justly**.

*Utilitarianism*

Bentham-Mill – *Take that action that results in the greatest happiness for the greatest number of people or minimizes the most harm.*

**Do that action that benefits the majority is the optimal method of assuring justice is dispensed**.

*Power-Bbased ethics*

Machiavelli – *Take that action that ensures that you come out on top.*

**There is no such thing as justice. Staying in power is what is best for everyone**.

### Legal approach

> Hobbes − *Take that action that complies with the law or the prevailing contract.*

**Follow the law as that is the formal system of justice for everyone's benefit.**

### Rights approach

> Locke − *Take any action you wish as long as you do not impinge on the agreed upon and accepted rights of others.*

**Acting justly means not interfering with the rights of others**.

> Rawls − *Distributive justice injunction: Take that action that protects the weakest and most vulnerable in society.*

> Nozick − *Contributive liberty injunction: Take that action that does not interfere with anyone's rights to self-development and self-fulfillment.*

### Moral relativism

> *Take that action that appeals to your personal preferences and biases since there are no overriding rules.*

**Justice results from the liberty to act as I wish.**

### Personalist ethics

> Situational ethics
> Fletcher − *The situation called for a loving approach.*

**Actions out of love are just**.

### Responsibility ethics

> Niebuhr − *I did what I believed was the most fitting and responsible thing to do.*

**By being a responsible person, I act justly**.

### Existentialist ethics

> Sartre − *Because of who I am and my inner freedom, I know the right thing to do.*

**Acting from a place of freedom, I act justly**.

### Self-interest argument

> *Take that action that ensures my own safety, welfare and interests.*

**The only just thing is that I survive**.

*Feminist ethics*

> *Take that action that demonstrates care and that will best honor, preserve and enhance existing relationships.*

**Justice results when we take care of relationships first and foremost.**

---

### Your turn – justice in action

1   Three men are shipwrecked with no help in sight. After a week, two of the men kill the third, who is a teenager and who is unconscious with fatigue and lack of food, so that they have food to eat. Their argument is that he was the weakest and by killing him at least two of them survived. Was this just? Which principle/s did you apply?

2   In India, very poor people sell their bones and their organs in advance of their death simply to get a bit of money. Are the people who buy these "body parts" acting justly? What principle/s would you apply?

3   Is surrogate motherhood just? For which parties? And the child? Which principle/s would you apply?

4   Is affirmative action just? What principle/s would you apply?

5   Should people who are seriously ill have a right to the drugs that might save them regardless of cost? What principle/s would you apply?

---

### Executive summary

Justice, for many people, refers to fairness. But while justice is important to almost everyone, it means different things to different groups. Justice is also inherent in everything we do hence ethics is largely concerned with justice.

In this chapter we cover the different kinds of justice, for instance:

- Social justice is the notion that everyone deserves equal economic, political, and social opportunities irrespective of race, gender, or religion.
- Distributive justice refers to the equitable allocation of assets in society.
- Environmental justice is the fair treatment of all people with regard to environmental burdens and benefits.
- Restorative or corrective justice seeks to make whole those who have suffered unfairly.
- Retributive justice seeks to punish wrongdoers objectively and proportionately.
- Procedural justice refers to implementing legal decisions in accordance with fair and unbiased processes.

We discuss the various perspectives that certain religious traditions bring to the topic along with the many challenges that arise in implementing justice. While there are many guidelines, no hard and fast framework exists that can be readily implemented.

Justice, like the rest of ethics, is about principles, reflection and discernment and most certainly about love – love of self, love of other and love of the world.

## Questions for reflection

- What do you think is the most important element of justice?
- Do you think justice demands always being impartial?
- Is the culture at your work a just one? What support can you provide?
- When did you last have an ethical challenge that was clearly a matter of justice? Which principle/s did you apply?
- What kind of justice training do you think managers should receive?

## Key terms

Agency   219
Civil law   223
Compassion   227
Contractarian   233
Distributive justice   225
Due process   223
Equity   226

Impartiality   217
Intuitive intelligence   226
Mercy   217
Procedural justice   223
Reciprocity   224
Rectificatory justice   225

## References

Aristotle. *Nicomachean Ethics*, Second Edition. Translated by Terence Irwin. Cambridge, MA: Hackett Publishing Company Inc., 1999.
McCoy, Buzz. *The Parable of the Sadhu. Harvard Business Review*, page 108, 1987.
McCoy, Buzz. *Living into Leadership*. Stanford, Connecticut: Stanford Business Books, 2007.
Nozick, Robert. *Anarchy, State 7 Utopia*. New York: Basic Books, 1974.
Plato. *The Collected Dialogues*. Edited by Edith Hamilton and Huntington Cairns. Bollingen Series LXXI. NJ: Princeton University Press, 1989.
Rawls, John. *A Theory of Justice*. New York: The belknap Press, 1971.
Sandal, Michael, editor. *Justice: A Reader*. New York: Oxford University Press, 2007.
Shakespeare, William. *The Oxford Shakespeare: The Complete Works*. 2nd edition. Oxford, UK: Oxford University Press, 2005.
Singer, Peter. *Animal Liberation*. Cambridge, United Kingdom: Harper Perennial Modern Classics, 2009.
Solomon, Robert C. and Mark Murphy, editors. *What Is Justice? Classic and Contemporary Readings*. New York: Oxford University press, 1990.
Sowell, Thomas. *The Quest for Cosmic Justice*. New York: Free Press, 2002.

# 8 The path to global corporate citizenship

## Contents

## Am I my brother's keeper? revisited

The very first case, in the first chapter of this book, is titled, "Am I My Brother's Keeper?" The choice of this title was intentional. In my opinion, the "brother's keeper" question, is one of the most important questions of our time. All other ethical challenges stem from this one question presented to us eons ago.

In the first book of the Hebrew Bible, Genesis, there is the story of Cain who kills his brother Abel. God comes looking for Abel. He asks Cain where he might find him. Cain feigns ignorance, and even disinterest, retorting defiantly with: I have no idea where Abel is and why should I; am I my brother's keeper? (Genesis 4:9)

This bedeviling question has faced us since the beginning of time. Its eternal persistence challenges us every day, be it the beggar on the street, refugees fleeing into our towns from a war-torn country, or taking care of the natural environment. Who indeed is my brother (sister), and what does it mean to be his (her) keeper? Right off the bat, the first story after humankind leaves the Garden of Eden concerns fratricide followed by that haunting question: Am I my brother's keeper?

The Hebrew Bible presents us with an in-your-face challenge. Do we murder our brothers and sisters, or do we have to care about them? Even more, do we have to put ourselves out to know whether the other is ok? Do we perhaps even have to participate in ensuring the other's welfare? Or, does it suffice that we do our thing, stay within the law, and do no harm? What about the John Locke argument? You take care of yours, and I take care of mine. Alternatively, should I go out of my way to make sure that I contribute to your well-being and not just avoid harming you? What if someone else is causing harm to you, should I intervene? And then, what about nature? Is that my brother or sister too? The animals, insects, flowers, trees, seas? Where does justice begin or end?

Maybe this is what justice really means. Maybe this is what giving and getting one's due is truly about. Maybe this is the eternal drama of love of neighbor. Maybe justice means love.

## A system's view of the world

Currently we face many new global realities. We could sum these up as collectively challenging us to create healthy, sustainable organizations, communities and societies that do not interfere with or harm nature's inherent ability to maintain and sustain life.

As we look at these challenges, a most important point, that we seem to keep forgetting is that everything on our planet is intrinsically interconnected, and directly impacts our well-being.

The first obstacle we must overcome, is our stubborn resistance to changing our minds and the way we do things. We all know the saying about not solving problems at the same level at which they are created, yet we persist in doing so. We remain caught up in a view that we are independent and in charge. We remain caught up in the fallacy that we can dominate, manipulate and extract to no end from the bounty of resources available – be it from people or the Earth.

We remain caught up in a mechanistic view of the world that supposedly behaves in a tidy cause and effect fashion. And we remain averse to complex problems, so we minimize them and leap into quick-fix solutions. Time to change.

### The essentiality of systems thinking

In Chapter 2, I devoted several pages to laying out the significance and essential elements of systems thinking. I reminded us that everything that exists, is a system, and that every system is embedded in other systems. I highlighted that due to the nature of systems, everything is interdependent and in reciprocal relationship with everything else. The fate of one part of a system impacts the rest.

I now add two further attributes of living systems. The first is that all living systems are autopoietic. This means they have an innate ability to reproduce and maintain themselves. The second is the idea of resilience.

Resilience comes from flexibility and diversity.

System behavior is dynamic in that it moves back and forth in cycles guided by non-linear feedback loops. These fluctuations, along with diversity within the system, build resilience. As long as fluctuations do not exceed certain tolerance levels, systems are remarkably resilient and robust. Once tolerance limits are exceeded for extended periods of time, systems invariably break down and can no longer maintain, and worse still, reproduce themselves. This is how we get sick, our communities become unhealthy and parts of the Earth that sustain us begin to die. It is a breakdown in the system.

In previous chapters, I pointed out that a key ethical principle is the principle of limits. That is moderation in all things. Excess or deficiency is in principle, unethical. Excess and deficiency violate tolerance limits and are unsustainable.

In Chapter 1, we discussed that the illusion of perpetual growth in every sphere, namely business, the economy, the population, without any appreciation of limits, is totally unrealistic and unethical. No system can sustain unlimited growth. It is unnatural and unhealthy. Basically – it is a killer! We even have a name for it. It is called cancer.

As a leadership and change executive, I strongly agree with Fritjof Capra's comment in his powerful book, *The Systems View of Life*, (2014), that the track record for implementing change in organizations is "very poor" (Ibid, p. 315). People do not want to change, least of all their minds. They find systems thinking too complex or too taxing. They readily nod when one mentions systems thinking, yet most people choose not to practice it. Organizational change initiatives lack systems thinking approaches and hence are mostly unsuccessful and are often highly detrimental to the company. Yet, all the world's current problems are systemic and require systemic solutions. What we need now are leaders that can take a systemic view.

### Think ecology

Capra claims that for us to develop sustainable businesses, communities and societies, we need greater ecological literacy. He points out that ecology comes from the Greek *oikos*, which means household. Ecology is therefore the study of the

Earth's household where everyone and everything is in relationship, connected and interdependent. As I like to emphasize, ecology teaches us that **everyone and everything is my brother or sister**.

The well-known and respected systems analyst and professor of Environmental Studies at Dartmouth College in New Hampshire, Donella H. Meadows, wrote in her book, *Beyond the Limits* (1992), that the present way of doing things is unsustainable (this was over twenty-seven years ago). Trying to solve societies' problems through constant expansion is a self-defeating illusion. She claims that the answer lies in human beings collaboratively working together from a basis of love. The sustainability revolution requires a societal transformation that encourages the best of human nature to be expressed and nurtured. And that is love of one another and the world in which we live.

## Leaders need competence in systems thinking

The largest gap in the intellectual ability needed for effective leadership in the knowledge age is systems thinking. Without it, leaders can't understand the relation of global forces to local pressures, macro policy to micro implementation, and social character to individual personality. Without it, their organizational vision will lack coherence. When linear thinkers connect the dots, they draw straight lines rather than the dynamic interactive force-field that represents the knowledge-age organization (Maccoby, 2007, p. 186).

## A just society depends on just institutions

Corporate social responsibility (CSR) is about justice. It concerns the giving and getting one's due where the sphere of influence extends beyond the individual or organizational, to include society and the entire environment, every bit of it, right down to last speck of dust. Why? Because we are at last recognizing that the environment – all of it – has systemic significance for the well-being of our planet and therefore us. Many native people around the world have always lived with this mentality and have been trying to tell us this for hundreds of years.

Business organizations can no longer deny reality and pretend to operate in an isolated bubble called the economy by conveniently ignoring that they depend entirely on the well-being of people, the harmony of society, and the health of the environment in order to function.

As I emphasized in Chapter 6, a just society depends on just institutions, and just institutions are socially and environmentally responsible, not only reactively, but proactively.

In Chapter 3 we discussed the question of who is the corporation? We noted that while certain laws exist that make the corporation a legal persona, it's a little like funny money. The corporation is a separate entity, and it isn't. Corporate social responsibility, yes, rests on the accountability of the corporation as an entity, but clearly decisions are made by people, mostly senior management, who shape the organization's culture, decide on principles and priorities and control the purse strings. Therefore, we need leaders and business managers who understand that they are the stewards of the environment and not just nomads passing through. (Discussed in the Introduction.)

If we desire a good society, we must create good institutions. If we want to see justice dispensed, we must have just institutions. If we want people to be able to exercise their rights, to be safe, to have an opportunity to prosper and flourish, we must have institutions that include these goals as part of their mission and their actions. If we do not directly link individual and institutional responsibility, we will continue to wonder why the happiness and well-being we desire continuously eludes us.

Business organizations have huge reach and huge power. If the leadership of these institutions fails to recognize the tie between individual responsibility and that of the organization, we will continue to see the dehumanization of organizational life and the lack of commitment to global corporate citizenship. The idea of global corporate citizenship means that there is no place to hide. Every organizational action, in every corner of the globe, is subject to scrutiny and self-accountability. Global citizenship also means, self-interested or not, for better or for worse, "I **am** my brother's keeper!"

## Flashpoint 8.1 – a planet in crisis

1   The message from a monumental study of the Intergovernmental Panel on Climate Change (IPCC) is that to avoid drastic repercussions, the world must slash carbon emissions by 45% by 2030, and completely decarbonize by 2050. Currently emissions continue to rise.

2   Antarctica is melting three times faster than a decade ago, and Greenland is losing ice quickly as well. If both ice sheets disappear, sea level rise could reach 200-plus feet, resulting in utter devastation, including the loss of the entire Atlantic seaboard on both the European and American continents and land now inhabited by more than 1 billion Asians.

3   Coral is dying, insects are disappearing, and the population of all mammals and bees are in decline. Coral, a critical part of an ocean system that provides protein to hundreds of millions of people, helps blunt coastal storm surges, and supports the livelihoods of people working in fishing and tourism.

4   The journal *Biological Conservation* predicts that 40% of insect species face extinction within the next few decades. Insects are essential link in the food chain and their loss would starve the birds and mammals that feed on them plus reduce pollination needed for agriculture.

5   Humans have destroyed more than 90% of the planet's grassland, most of it to produce food.

6   The US environmental protection system continues being dismantled. The EPA and Department of Interior are reversing years of protections for air, water, and land. In 2018, the Trump administration has opened up offshore waters and rolled back safety rules for drilling and has made it easier to build dirty coal plants.

7   In pointed contrast to the US, other countries are taking the environment seriously. France has committed to shut coal plants by 2021, India cancelled plans for coal plants, and China banned 500 inefficient models of cars.
8   North America is losing 1.5 million acres of open prairie to agriculture each year.
9   Air pollution is a major problem in most of the world's large cities, in some to such an extent it is now a major health risk.

## Supply chain blues

You are the Vice President of Operations of Belle Chain Inc., a robotic toy company. Manufacturing takes place in China and Vietnam. Eighty percent is carried out in China where you have three contract manufacturers (cms) responsible for eight different products. Your two main products are single sourced through your most efficient and only Tier one cm. The other cms are not nearly as efficient or as organized and only qualify for a Tier 3 rating. The two main products are responsible for 60% of the organization's revenue. The other six products are dual sourced through all three cms and the smallest cm based in an industrial zone outside Hanoi.

You have just arrived in China for your regular bi-monthly visit. You are concerned because business is booming and the cms are under pressure to produce products on time. The head office, based in Atlanta, Georgia, USA, has been emphasizing the need for business units to keep up with demand and meet revenue goals. The share price has been shaky, so meeting revenue growth targets is critical.

Based on previous volumes, Belle Chain has only contracted to fill 50% of the Tier 1 cm's product line. Your Tier 1 cm cannot commit more capacity to your goods and is now threatening to reduce the contracted capacity as it can command a much higher price from other organizations.

Another blow is that you learn that one of your key component suppliers has been using paint that has lead in it. The situation gets worse when you find that your second most important cm has not paid its suppliers for over five months and is $20 million in arears. Now, to top it up, your newly appointed supplier in Hanoi is using child labor in some of its factories. You had hoped to move some of your volume from the Tier I cm in China to the one in Hanoi. This would reduce your exposure in China and give you strong cost negotiating opportunities in Vietnam. Now, what will you do? And what about the supplier with the lead paint? To switch suppliers now, halfway through the year, will be expensive and margins are tight.

If you refuse to work with the cm in Vietnam until it tidies up its act regarding child labor, you will not meet production deadlines. If you cannot move some of your volume from the Tier 1 cm in China, the general manager is asking for a "production bonus" payment of $500,000 to keep meeting your current volume. Neither of your other two Chinese cms can absorb any more volume or take on new products for at least another eighteen months.

Should you pay the production bonus of $500,000 and then start looking for new cms? Should you ignore the child labor in Hanoi just for six months until you can figure this out? You have already calculated that any penalty you might have to pay is miniscule compared with not meeting production goals. And what about the cm who is behind in paying suppliers? What if the suppliers stop providing component parts? Should you pay them? Should you prop up the cm who is clearly in trouble? But what if corruption is involved? And what about the Foreign Corrupt Practices Act that prohibits bribes? Or Human Rights Watch? So far, your supply chain has stayed within the law. Could a small slip really matter, just for a short time?

What should you do? If you miss your production numbers, you lose an enormous bonus as does your very hard-working staff. You will also lose tremendous credibility at Belle Chain. So far, you have never not been able to figure things out. But this is more than you have ever encountered.

## Questions

- What went wrong here? How did all of these things "suddenly" occur?
- What are the ethical issues in this case?
- What risks is Belle Chain facing?
- Which ethical principle/s will guide you best here?

## Corporate colonialism

David Korten, who we met in Chapter 1, does not think we live in just societies, nor that we have just institutions.

Korten, a Vietnam veteran and a Stanford University MBA graduate, has lived around the world, first as a development worker in Africa, Latin America and Asia, and then with the Ford Foundation, followed by a stint with the US Agency for International Development (USAID). Thereafter, he started a global citizen's network known as the Living Economies Forum. More recently he, along with fifty NGO leaders, convened the International Forum on Globalization (IFG). He claims his personal aim is not only to promote local empowerment, but to curb the relentless and unchecked power of global corporations.

In his highly regarded, best-selling book, *When Corporations Rule the World* (2015), Korten delivers a devastating critique of global capitalism and the mega corporations that prop it up. He claims that the emerging Fourth Industrial Revolution (explained later) has become the new form of colonialism where corporate empires, as opposed to nations, now dominate the world. He is particularly critical of the pursuit of growth at all costs and the belief that a growing GDP (gross domestic product) solves everyone's problems. He writes with great intensity about the collateral damage resulting from the consolidation of corporate power. He also discusses in detail how global capitalism drives wages to the bottom, leads to intense competition for land and natural resources, and results in social disintegration and environmental destruction.

Korten insists that real wealth lies in human and environmental health which includes fertile soil, clean air and water, well paid and cared for labor, the free flow of ideas and the constructive use of technology. He argues that people want a secure livelihood, a decent place to live, healthy and uncontaminated food, a good education, accessible healthcare, and a clean and vital natural environment. Instead, globalization, he says, denies many, and a growing number of people, these basic rights.

On the people and society front, Korten blames corporations for the creation of sweatshops, substandard wages, and the negative impact on traditional societies and the fabric of relationships on which they depend. He criticizes mega-corporations for the pressure they place on labor costs, the practice of modern slavery, poor working conditions, and the death of unions.

He claims that large corporations are responsible for shifting their environmental problems to the other side of the globe. They readily export their waste and polluting factories to countries who are sold a bill of goods called greater employment. There is a general abuse of nature's bounty as corporations take control of land and forests that used to be the homes of local people. They ignore the limits of the Earth's renewable resources generating huge amounts of toxic waste the environment is unable to absorb. Local water is contaminated; over-fishing is rife; severe land degradation is creating vast new tracts of deserts, and poor countries, particularly in Africa, are the dumping grounds for surplus goods.

Korten decries the oppressive policies of the World Bank and the International Monetary Fund. He claims they have lost their independence and are now subservient to the transnational corporate system. They lend to governments based on contracts with large firms that dictate the terms. Poor countries, desperate to attract investment capital, are forced to accept coercive terms and are treated severely when they fall behind in debt repayments.

He asserts that organizations need to take society and the environment into account in everything they do. They must honor and promote societal relations even if these are not regulated or legislated and they need to be philanthropic and proactive in furthering the welfare of society. They must contribute to social progress, address problems in society and help correct social injustices. All in all, they must act like globally engaged citizens.

---

### Business and the environment

- Japan shifted its aluminum smelting capacity to the Philippines where it now produces all its high-grade copper cathodes. To create room for these factories, thousands of acres of land were land expropriated from citizens and the gas and waste emissions in the Philippines have soared contaminating, among things, fresh water supplies.
- "Thailand is among the world's most dangerous countries in which to oppose powerful interests that profit from coal plants, toxic waste dumping, land grabs or illegal logging." Many environmentalists are killed with little or no recourse through the courts. (*New York Times*, May 2016.)

- The US Census Bureau 2018 report on export data for shipments of plastic waste generated in the US and sent to other countries showed that 78% (0.83 million metric tons) of 2018 US plastic waste was sent to countries with waste "mismanagement rates" of greater than 5%. That means about 157,000 large 20-ft shipping containers (429 per day) of US plastic waste were sent to countries known to be overwhelmed with plastic waste. A major portion of this waste is now dumped in the ocean.

Finally, Korten argues that CSR, as a self-regulatory endeavor, does not work. Strict legislation is needed to ensure corporations clean up their messes, take responsibility for their externalities, and are limited in their ready access to environmental resources. The principle of environmental justice, he says, is a healthy society and a healthy life. Corporations have civic and social responsibilities to contribute to both.

While much of Korten's criticisms remain valid, as environmental problems escalate, and the plight of the planet's health is now evident to all except those who are stubborn or indifferent, times are a changing. The pressure to address some of the issues Korten so eloquently describes, is on the increase.

However, before we review some positive measures now being taken, let us take a brief look at the state of the world as it exists now in 2019, five years since Korten completed his book and how bad it had to get to shake us out of our ethical lethargy.

**Walmart corporate rap sheet**

Walmart, the largest company on the world by far according to revenue as one financial measure, has a very poor employee practices rap sheet. It has been or is being sued for –

- Gender and racial discrimination
- Forcing pregnant workers to take unpaid leave
- Exploitative low wages
- Poor working conditions

In 2016, an investigative group used a hidden camera to detect children as young as nine working in a factory in Cambridge, New York. The children were packaging high-end lotions and skin cream for brands like Acure and Savannah Bee, suppliers to well-known chain retailers including Whole Foods, Amazon, Target and Walmart.

Workers in Bangladesh, Cambodia, India and Indonesia who make clothes for Walmart (WMT) face "intensive labor exploitation and abuse," according to a report released by the Asia Floor Wage Alliance, an international coalition of trade unions and human rights organizations (*New York Times*, June 2016).

## Our current challenges

Our number one challenge has to be the rapid degeneration of the environment. Human beings are using natural assets faster than nature is regenerating them. This ecological strain is exacerbated by continued population growth mainly on the African and Asian continents. The global population, currently at 7.5 billion, could, according to the UN, reach 9.3 billion by 2045. Consequently, the pressure on natural assets will increase.

Another significant reality is climate change. In the past few years the world has experienced some extreme weather conditions that are posing new risks not to mention a huge cost in lives and trillions of dollars.

On the technology front, ubiquitous social media platforms are creating a world reflected in a surreal mix of radical transparency as well as often deceptive, malicious and fake news. Communication and technological advances are leading to the creation of huge data banks that are vulnerable, among other things, to privacy violations. And technology's advances in robotics, artificial intelligence, 3D printing, nanotechnology and biotechnology are impacting all walks of life.

If we consider the impact of these new realities plus the emerging Fourth Industrial Revolution and the Global Risks report generated at World Economic Forum (2019) outlined below, we must surely acknowledge there is a lot on our plate.

### *The Fourth Industrial Revolution*

Klaus Schwab, founder and executive chairman of the World Economic Forum, wrote a compelling review of the emerging Fourth Industrial Revolution in anticipation of the 2019 World Economic Forum.

Schwab describes the emerging revolution as characterized by a fusion of technologies that are blurring the lines between the physical, digital, and biological spheres. The speed and scope of these technological developments are breathtaking and are disrupting almost every industry in every country.

### *Challenges and opportunities*

Like the revolutions that preceded it, Schwab points out the Fourth Industrial Revolution has the potential to raise global income levels and improve the quality of life for populations around the world. To date, he says, those who have gained the most have been those able to afford and access the digital world.

On the flip side, he posits that the revolution could result in greater inequality, particularly with its potential to disrupt labor markets. As automation substitutes for labor across entire economies, the net displacement of workers by machines is likely to exacerbate the gap between returns to capital and returns to labor (Something we discussed in Chapter 1). Besides being a key economic concern, he sees inequality as representing the greatest societal concern associated with the Fourth Industrial Revolution.

*Innovation remains key*

The shift from simple digitization (the Third Industrial Revolution) to innovation based on combinations of technologies (the Fourth Industrial Revolution) is having a huge impact on organizations who are forced to reexamine the way they do business. To stay ahead of the game, business leaders and senior executives need to understand their changing environment, challenge the assumptions of their operating teams, and relentlessly and continuously innovate. This will of course accelerate the disruption of industries in a never-ending cycle of creative destruction (Recall Schumpeter – Chapter 1).

*Impact on government*

Schwab predicts that as the physical, digital and biological worlds continue to converge, new technologies and platforms will increasingly enable citizens to engage with governments, voice their opinions, coordinate their efforts, and circumvent the supervision of public authorities. In turn, governments will gain new technological powers to increase their control over populations. They will have the ability to use pervasive surveillance systems and will strive to control digital infrastructure.

*Impact on people*

Schwab is most concerned that the Fourth Industrial Revolution will change not only what we do but also who we are. It will affect our identity and all the issues associated with it along with our health and how we prioritize our time. Being in constant digital connection may deprive us of one of life's most important assets, he writes, namely "the time to pause, reflect, and engage in meaningful conversation."

*Shaping the future*

Schwab insists that neither technology nor the disruption that comes with it is an external force over which humans have no control. He asserts that everyone should take responsibility in guiding its evolution towards a future that reflects common objectives and values. People need to be put first, he insists.

According to him, in its most pessimistic, dehumanized form, the Fourth Industrial Revolution has the potential to "robotize" humanity thereby depriving us of "our heart and soul." On the other hand, it also has the potential to "lift humanity into a new collective and moral consciousness based on a shared sense of destiny." What is important is that we all recognize our responsibility to make sure the latter prevails.

## World Economic Forum Global Risks report 2019

*Extract from the executive report*

- A primary concern is the weakening of collective responses to emerging global challenges. Global co-operation has deteriorated radically making the finding of systemic solutions more difficult.

- Financial market volatility has increased and the headwinds facing the global economy have intensified. The global debt burden is significantly higher than before the global financial crisis of 2008, at around 225% of GDP.
- Geopolitical and geo-economic tensions are rising among the world's major powers. These tensions represent the most urgent global risks at present. Against this backdrop, it is likely to become more difficult to make collective progress on other global challenges – from protecting the environment to responding to the ethical challenges of the Fourth Industrial Revolution.
- Environmental risks continue to dominate. Extreme weather is of greatest concern along with environmental policy failure. The accelerating pace of biodiversity loss is a great concern. Species abundance is down by 60% since 1970.
- Technology continues to play a profound role in shaping the global risks landscape. Concerns about data fraud and cyber-attacks are prominent. There were further massive data breaches in 2018.
- Worldwide, mental health problems now affect an estimated 700 million people. Complex transformations – societal, technological and work-related – are having a profound impact on people's lives. A common theme is psychological stress due to a sense of lack of control in the face of uncertainty.
- Rapidly growing cities and ongoing effects of climate change are making more people vulnerable to rising sea levels. Two-thirds of the global population is expected to live in cities by 2050 and already an estimated 800 million people live in more than 570 coastal cities vulnerable to a sea-level rise of 0.5 meters by 2050.

### A glimpse at environmental issues around the world

**Asia:** Population growth and economic development create huge pressures on land, habitat destruction, loss of biodiversity, water scarcity and water pollution, air pollution, leading to global warming and climate change.

**Australia:** Marine conservation and protection of the Great Barrier Reef. The Great Barrier Reef's environmental pressures include water quality from runoff, climate change and mass coral bleaching, and overfishing.

**Canada:** Air pollution is a major concern as it affects wildlife, vegetation, soil and water. Air pollution causes acid rain and contributes to climate change.

**China:** Air pollution, water shortages, desertification and soil pollution.

**Europe:** Air quality problems are the most serious.

**India:** Severe pollution (air, water, soil, noise) is of primary concern. This is affecting climate change, shortage of clean water, health and biodiversity

**Latin America**: Air pollution; rivers flowing through industrial centers are tremendously contaminated by industrial wastes; rapid deforestation and soil erosion.

**New Zealand:** Wildlife is threatened by habitat loss, pollution, deforestation, air pollution and soil erosion.

**Russia:** Deforestation, energy inefficiencies, pollution and nuclear waste.

**United States:** Climate change, air pollution, energy efficiencies, species conservation, invasive species, deforestation, mining, pesticides, waste and over-population.

**Sub-Saharan Africa:** Serious environmental problems, climate change, water pollution, population growth, coal mining, nuclear waste, deforestation, overfishing and deteriorating yields in agriculture.

*Note*: Summary of a variety of reports and environmental articles published during 2018/2019.

## Population explosion

In 1798, an English clergyman named Thomas Malthus published an essay on *The Principle of Population*. Therein he concluded that "the power of population is infinitely greater than the power of the Earth to produce subsistence for man." If people kept procreating, Malthus argued, we would run out of planet. However, with illness and wars and new territories being discovered, people very soon laughed off Malthus' predictions.

Then in 1968, in his book, *The Population Bomb*, American biologist Paul Erhlich predicted that by 1980, 4.4 billion humans would begin to starve en masse. And here we are, all 7.5 billion of us, gobbling up our food, drinking bottled water by the gallons, swishing down our wine, enjoying our heat or air-conditioned homes and driving our cars.

Now the prediction is that there will be 9.3 billion people by 2045. How will we survive? Where will we all live? Will the world become one massive suburban wallpaper, burping up burgers, receiving packages from Amazon, and clicking away at technological gadgets? According to scientists, right now we use 86% of the Earth's fresh water for food alone and uncontaminated water supplies are dwindling fast. And what about pollution? This is a huge problem right now. What will it be like with 9.3 billion people gasping for fresh oxygen? And even if we survive, what quality of life will we have as we have stripped our environment of its regenerating vitality?

Many scientists are predicting a tipping point – but what will it be, and can responsible global citizenship halt this inexorable trend toward some huge calamity? It sounds as if it is just a matter of when!

## Global social contract

In modern times, most democratic countries have some form of social contract implicit among its members. These social contracts regulate the rights and responsibilities between citizens and communicate an understanding among members about a shared sense of purpose and vision for the community. (We discuss social contracts in Chapter 6.)

The social contract concerns the community's safety, quality of life and well-being, especially for its descendants. In order to bring this vision to reality, the members have some arrangement regarding powers of government, law and order, and member rights and responsibilities. Responsibilities refer to the obligations toward the government and towards individual others or the collective.

In response to globalization and the multiple significant challenges the world's people are facing on a global level, there is an increasing clamor in some quarters for some form of social contract at the global level. The prevailing argument by human rights organizations, NGOs (non-governmental organizations), international non-profits and social activists supported by some progressive organizations, is that the "flattening" of the world has rendered us all citizens of the world. According to their way of thinking, just as we have duties and obligations to our nation states, we now have duties and obligations to "the world." By the same token, just as we have rights and entitlements in our nation states, we now have some of these at the global level. What these are of course varies depending on who one asks or what perspective one brings.

Despite the efforts of social activists, NGOs, and progressive organizations, that global social contract is slow in coming. For one, there is no global government that has the power to exact certain behaviors or responsibilities from either individuals or institutions across national boundaries. There are several international bodies and courts of law that have some ability to operate at the global level, but even in that capacity they are often hampered by local government activities or disagreements. As mentioned earlier, many multinational corporations have far more power and resources than many nation state governments. As they sweep the world with their goods and services there is little to curb their powers. Local governments try to defend their territories from what they consider to be aggressive invasions by using tariffs, duties and import restrictions. Often these are not effective.

Global governance is a collective effort by sovereign states, international organizations and other non-state actors who try to address common challenges and endeavor to seize opportunities that transcend national frontiers. Until now, this has been a hit-or-miss affair. Given the current geopolitical climate, governance standards could even deteriorate. Perhaps the only way left to curb the global stampede of corporations is to appeal to their honor as caring global citizens concerned with their brothers' and sisters' welfare. The other option is to rely on concerned global citizens who use communications technology to highlight corporate ethical lapses and abusive behaviors. The former option is doubtless preferable.

## Global corporate citizenship

In 1927, the then Dean of the Harvard Business School wrote an article entitled, "The Social Significance of Business." There he stressed that the development, strengthening, and multiplication of socially minded businessmen is the central problem of business. Well, here we are ninety plus years later and what has changed? Can we say that we have progressed at all?

Despite the growing emphasis on CSR since the 1950s when Howard Bowen, who supposedly was the first to use the term corporate social responsibility, published his book, *Social Responsibilities of the Businessman* (1953), it seems we still have a long way to go. Admittedly, the world has changed faster than ever, and the problems are more complex. However, our growing technical prowess has inflated our egos and distracted us from our systemic responsibilities and any respect for limits.

### Global citizenship versus corporate social responsibility

Global corporate citizenship (GCC) and CSR are sometimes used inter-change-ably. The term "corporate citizenship" however, is broader in scope and responsibility than that of CSR. With CSR, the focus is on an organization behaving in a socially responsible manner. This means that it will minimize any harm that might result from its operations, it will pay attention to stake-holder needs, it will care for the environment and it will be an ethical and responsible employer.

Corporate citizenship type behavior demands more than this. Here the emphasis has shifted from simply minimizing harm, obeying the law, and ensuring that an organization's operations do not create negative impacts on society, to one where management's mindset is now directed toward becoming a positive contributor to society. Under the corporate citizenship banner, organizations are expected to care about significant societal issues, such as health, safety, the environment and women and children's welfare. They are no longer viewed as economic institutions with narrowly delineated boundaries of rights and responsibilities.

---

### Definition of a global business citizen

A global business citizen is a business enterprise and its managers that respon-sibly exercises its rights and implements its duties to individuals, stakehold-ers and societies within and across national and cultural boundaries.

(Wood et al., 2006, p. 4)

---

As global citizens, organizations, especially those who participate on the global landscape, are expected to be concerned with their social, cultural, environ-mental, economic and technological impact in the societies within which they participate. They must take note of their "organizational footprint" on the world as it is under scrutiny by many watchdog bodies and, of course, many civilians who are either existing or potential customers.

The pressure to act in the manner of a global citizen has arisen in response to the relentless and unstoppable progress of globalization. Globalization, as we discussed at length in Chapter 1 and now in this chapter, has brought with it both positive and negative effects. On the one hand, many argue it has raised the standard of living of millions of people across the world. It has brought industries and healthcare to many who reside in "rural backwaters." It has brought education and job opportunities to those who would have previously had access to neither. It has improved healthcare, reduced the impact of major diseases, and improved infant mortality rates.

On the other hand, globalization has increased the pressure on organizations to demonstrate financial performance and success. This has increased the tendency toward short-term thinking in order to boost financial results. Korten (as mentioned in chapter) and many others have accused large multinationals of taking advantage of local conditions by tolerating shabby and even highly unsafe work conditions, intolerably long work hours and very low wages. Supply chains now crisscross the world where they take advantage of lower wages and lower costs and most often far lower standards of safety, quality and environmental oversight.

Land grabbing for industrial use has been on the rise. Corruption and bribes, especially regarding access to natural resources, has been rife between large corporations and corrupt local government officials. Millions of people continue to be displaced to make way for factories, plantations and huge infrastructure projects.

The number of stakeholders now affected by organizations has radically increased as has the number of conflicting interests they might have. The current GINI index reflects the rapidly growing divide between the rich and the poor. (The GINI index is a measure of statistical dispersion that represents the income distribution of a nation's residents and is the most commonly used measure of inequality.)

Despite Korten and many others who have been chafing at globalization and the lack of CSR since the turn of this century, local, national and supranational governance has not been able to keep up with the tide of rapid investment and growth across the globe. Bad behaviors by corporations continue. Short-term thinking by management is rewarded. Rapid financial returns on the back of human rights abuses, destruction of the environment and ethical misdemeanors abound. Governments have little or no power to inhibit the unchecked growth plans of determined multinationals. Penalties these organizations are sometimes required to pay for unethical or illegal behavior frequently pales in contrast with the fortunes they make as they discover hitherto untapped economic opportunities.

### *The question for this century has become how to create a global capitalism that is sustainable*

Corporate citizenship recognizes the moral duty to ensure that corporations engage in development that is sustainable. This means that the needs of the present are met without compromising the ability of future generations.

As almost all countries are moving toward a free market system, fighting capitalism and its globalizing trend, is both a waste of time and not really the goal. In recognition that globalization is destined to continue and that capitalism will remain the dominant market system, several key international initiatives are underway that underscore and reinforce the idea of global corporate citizenship.

**Discourse, regulation, compliance and investment**

All kinds of acronyms are currently employed to refer to CSR. We have discussed the Triple Bottom Line – People, Planet and Profits. Some organizations refer to People, Principles and Profits or variations on that theme. Most organizations feel impelled to include some form of CSR principle within their mission statement that incorporates themes of environmental sensitivity as these are important to employees, customers, and other stakeholders. Many organizations include a page on their websites explaining their commitment to corporate citizenship.

*Discourse*

The worldwide concern regarding climate change and the threat to the environment has raised the level of public discourse on CSR and environmentalism. A growing number of consumers, environmentalists and investors are demanding accountability for costs and environmental degradation that has hitherto been ignored, avoided or shoved aside as a problem for NGOs to mop up.

Further, as communities grapple with the cultural and social impact of business institutions, they frequently look to organizations to provide vital services and support charitable causes. There is thus growing pressure for companies to take on social and moral responsibilities.

*Regulation and compliance*

Even though regulation has been somewhat selective and sporadic, this too is on the increase. Greater enforcement procedures are in place and penalties are also more severe. New EU directives have been mandated since the VW emissions scandal (Chapter 3) and these will impact organizations worldwide. Even China is paying attention to pollution and to workers' employment standards.

Then there are new initiatives, such as the GRI (global reporting initiative) and integrated reporting (see following), calling for both greater quantity and quality of CSR disclosures. There is also a movement toward standardization of reports so as to improve comparability between reporting companies. Corporate social responsibility litigation and investigations have increased, and human rights abuses are receiving heightened scrutiny.

*Investment*

Corporate social responsibility used to be the focus of niche investors and large pension funds. Now it has become more mainstream and part of most investor considerations.

Environmental, social and governance (ESG) reporting standards, which are largely stock exchange driven, are mandatory requirements in many countries.

The importance of ESG reports is that they refer to central factors in measuring the sustainability and ethical impact of an investment in a company or business from a risk/return perspective. This helps investors evaluate the likely future performance of the organization, taking ESG risk factors into account. In practical terms, this means that organizations are obliged to spell out what they see as potential risks, for example, how climate change might impact their business. corporate social responsibility and ESG benchmarking are on the rise.

Investors are also eager to see that organizations have a board that is concerned with being good citizens, and that an internal steering committee exists charged with oversight and governance in this area.

While there are many investment funds and investment advertisements or articles that report that investing in organizations that are socially responsible pays off handsomely with increased returns, I will not elaborate on that here. I am averse to the consequentialist or "the means justifies the ends" approach to ethical thinking. I hold that global corporate citizenship should stand on its own and be done for its own sake; not because it generates more money. You may recall the Ring of Gyges (Chapter 3), and the argument that being ethical has intrinsic value.

---

### BlackRock's 2018 letter to CEOs

BlackRock is the world's largest asset manager with more than $6 trillion under management. Larry Fink, the President and CEO, included the following in his 2018 letter to CEOs:

> Every company must deliver financial performance and show how it is making a positive contribution to society. Companies must benefit all their stakeholders, including shareholders, employees, customers, and communities in which they operate. Without a social purpose, a company cannot achieve its full potential, will succumb to short-term pressures and ultimately provide subpar returns to long term investors.

Fink has committed to increasing the size of his investment stewardship team as he expands BlackRock's investment process. He commented:

> A company's ability to manage environmental, social and governance matters demonstrates the leadership and good governance that is so essential to sustainable growth, which is why we are increasingly integrating these issues into our investment process.
>
> Larry Fink, President and CEO

---

### An ego flying high

In October 2017, it surfaced that former General Electric CEO, Jeff Immelt, for many years had an empty business jet follow his corporate plane on several trips around the world. The second plane was used as a backup, in case the one Immelt was flying in had "mechanical problems."

General Electric knew that this practice would be perceived as unethical and wasteful, so flight crews for both planes were forbidden to reveal the existence of the unfilled jet. The story of the empty jet surfaced a few months after new General Electric CEO, John Flannery, slashed thousands of jobs to cut costs.

## A stakeholder management approach

By contrast to global corporate citizenship and CSR, another approach to managing business ethical obligations is that of stakeholder management.

While the term "stakeholder," was introduced into strategic management in the 1960s, the stakeholder concept swept into the business ethics arena through the efforts of several people, notably Darden University Professor of Business Administration R. Edward Freeman. The stakeholder approach provides a conceptual framework to assist organizations in dealing with the increase and complexity of changes in the environment, and the multiplicity of stakeholders that are impacted by its actions.

The underlying philosophy of this approach is that the organization should provide value for all stakeholders and not just the stockholders.

The definition of stakeholder is taken to be "any group or individual who is affected by or can affect the achievement of an organization's objectives" (Freeman, 2007).

The stakeholder approach takes a form of systems perspective of the many environments in which a business is embedded. Here the organization identifies its primary and secondary stakeholders while also distinguishing those that are internal stakeholders to the firm, e.g., employees, and external customers and the environment. The idea is to identify the different stakes that these constituencies have in the organization's activities and where their interests lie. By mapping the various stakeholders, their coalitions, their interests, claims and strategies, the organization is made more aware of its broader responsibilities than to just its stockholders, and it can better formulate its ethical responses. In this manner, ethical behavior is subsumed into the organization's strategic behavior.

Freeman provides a detailed framework for evaluating the interests of stakeholders and their corresponding ethical claims on the organization. While this framework is most helpful, I have yet to see it practiced in a coherent way in any organization. This is no reflection on Freeman or others who work with him. It may simply be that like with systems thinking, people find this cognitively too taxing or complex.

## Sustainability

There is no doubt that for organizations to survive in the longer term, they must focus on sustainable practices. As we can see, this is vitally important for everyone – all stakeholders, including individuals like you and me and the entire planet.

Young and Dhanda, in their comprehensive tome, *Sustainability: Essentials for Business* (2013), argue that sustainability is far more than just going green. They insist that sustainability needs to be inherent in every part of the business and needs to factor into all strategy development.

In their book, they identify four sets of drivers related to sustainability. These are –

Set 1 – pollution, waste, and material consumption
Set 2 – NGOs and their impact on society
Set 3 – emerging disruptive technologies
Set 4 – increase in population, poverty and inequity arising for globalization.

Young and Dhanda break these drivers down into sustainable strategies for today and tomorrow, and they illustrate how appropriate strategies provide a variety of bottom line payoffs including long term sustainable value creation. They recommend that the organization work its way up the 'ladder of sustainability" – there are many such models and organizations can create their own – in order to ensure that progressive steps are taken and remain part of the business's ongoing strategy.

What we are seeing here is that sustainability become like the Total Quality Management (TQM) movement. It needs to pervade all thinking and all doing within and throughout the corporation. It is not an add on, but intrinsic to all activities and should become a measure of organizational excellence. Regrettably, it appears that it is the smaller- or medium-sized businesses or non-profits that have truly taken sustainability to heart.

## Northeast Delta Dental a corporate citizen par excellence

Northeast Delta Dental is the preeminent dental insurance company in northern New England. In its mission statement it states its commitment to acting as a corporate citizen that balances profitability and community involvement, with colleagues working together to create a corporate environment built upon high trust and mutual respect.

It has won numerous awards for its social responsibility and community engagement along with being one of the best companies to work for in New Hampshire at least eight times. Two outstanding awards include that of being the most psychologically healthy place to work and the other is the State Quality award supported by the Malcolm Baldrige principles.

Tom Raffio, President and CEO of Northeast Delta Dental since 1995, has worked with his senior leadership team to create a remarkable organization with highly engaged employees while following best practices in all aspects of the business. Tom himself has collected multiple awards for his leadership and his social and environmental commitment.

I have known Tom for many years and have observed his leadership style throughout several economic ups and downs. In a recent discussion with him, he shared some of his philosophy. First of all, he takes a long-term view. He believes in building bonds for their own sake, i.e., because it is good to do so and not because he is waiting for any payoff. He is very aware that the health of the organization and that of the community are intertwined. To this end he encourages great generosity toward the community. He serves on many boards and participates in several different fundraising events. He encourages his employees to do the same and Northeast Delta Dental pays for time off (up to 7.5 hours per year) for them to engage in volunteer efforts.

Two examples of community support include sponsoring a soccer field and an athletics stadium to encourage healthy outdoor activities. Tom advocates to secure dental insurance for the poor and underserved and works with his dental network to maintain reasonable insurance rates.

Tom also believes in moderation. For example, he mentioned that he could probably raise insurance rates and make more money, however the organization is sufficiently profitable and has reserves, so why put pressure on others. There is such a thing as fairness. Excess is unnecessary, and in the long run nobody gains.

Northeast Delta Dental invests a great deal in staff development. Training is provided in both technical and personal development areas. An example of some of the wide-ranging training, development and wellness opportunities they offer include mindfulness, meditation, team building, financial planning, meeting management and specific training related to core job functions.

The great payoff for Tom, Northeast Delta Dental and the community is that the culture that he has created has fostered a tremendous corporate citizen spirit in employees. Talking with them one finds they are almost zealous when it comes to caring for the community and the environment. More organizations with this philosophy are sorely needed.

## Corporate governance

I discussed corporate governance, its role and scope, in Chapter 2. Here I expand on the board's responsibilities in the current climate.

Boards of directors are responsible for corporate governance. Governance includes providing strategic direction, ensuring the company stays within the law, oversight of internal checks and balances, and consideration of stakeholders. Stakeholders include society and the environment.

The board must also ensure that the company cultivates an ethical climate and that it upholds values of dignity, responsibility, accountability, fairness and transparency.

At this time, boards are under increasing pressure to ensure that the company acts as a corporate citizen, and for global companies as global citizens. As I mentioned, simple CSR behavior no longer suffices. Proactive care and concern for people, society and the environment are important matters on most boards' agendas.

Human rights (HR) issues are also significant. This is a difficult area, as local regulations and conditions vary. The main HR objective is that the dignity and respect for humans is recognized as well as concern for creating sustaining conditions where human potential can develop and flourish. Unfair discrimination is, in theory, no longer tolerated.

### Conflicts of interest

Although there are many other board responsibilities, I will only mention two others here, as they surface regularly and are ethical in nature.

The first is the matter of conflict of interests. This, too, is a complicated topic.

A definition of a conflict of interest is: "A conflict of interest is a set of circumstances that creates a risk that professional judgement or impartial actions regarding a primary interest will be unduly influenced by a secondary interest."

A primary interest refers to the principal goals of the profession or activity, such as the protection of clients, the health of patients, the integrity of research, and the duties of a public officer.

A secondary interest includes personal benefit and is not limited to only financial gain but also such motives as the desire for professional advancement, or the wish to do favors for family and friends. These secondary interests are not treated as wrong in and of themselves, but become objectionable when they are believed to have greater weight than the primary interests.

Alas, a great deal of the corruption that exists in the corporate world is as a result of, often significant and blatant, conflicts of interest. In my personal experience, having sat on several boards, conflicts of interest are always present. Being transparent about them by completing a Conflicts of Interest form does not eliminate the conflict. This so-called transparency, if anything, provides a bizarre form of endorsement.

### Risk management

The second area of board responsibility is that of risk management. This includes not only basic business risks, but risks related to ethical issues, and sustainability and environmental matters.

Here, I defer again to my personal experience as an accountant, corporate financier and leadership and ethics consultant. In general, most people are not good at risk assessment or risk management. One can speculate why this is so. It may be due to lack of appropriate training and education. It may be due to the emphasis on short-term thinking. It may be because most business managers are harried and hurried and rarely take sufficient time to engage in proper scenario planning or calculating risk alternatives.

I have found that those who have been trained in finance or economics are usually more adept at understanding and quantifying risks. In the corporate world, while many have their MBAs, this too is no guarantee that they are good at thinking systems, seeing the bigger picture, or evaluating short, and long-term risks. Even though risk and return are hammered into them – or at least I do to my MBA students – few know how to really identify and quantify risks.

In sum, the chances are that most boards are not competent, never mind sophisticated, in risk assessment. This is an important point to bear in mind when reading the implementation struggles of the global reporting initiative mentioned next.

### Value creation

A final and important comment regarding corporate governance is that of value creation. Along with global citizenship, boards are now expected to focus on how the organization adds value in the three spheres of the economy, society and environment. In the economy, creativity and innovation add value. In society, positively contributing to society's well-being (mental and physical), adds value. With respect to the environment, the board should take an active role in the reduction of emissions, improving energy efficiencies, recycling, reduction of waste and other creative methods for reducing the organization's footprint so as to add value.

All in all, board responsibility and fields of activity are destined to grow in scope, and accountability for performance is also likely to increase (Huse, 2007).

## Global reporting initiative and the International Integrated Reporting Council

Until recently, minimal reporting standards have not helped encourage global corporate citizenship and sustainability management. Over the past decade however, there has been a growing interest in developing more formal and comprehensive reports that reflect the true economics of organizations and the longer-term impact of their activities on society and the environment.

A strong argument that supports a sound reporting framework is that it will influence the way organizational leaders and managers think about sustainable management, and that this will improve their ability to manage and communicate the impact on the environment. It will enable companies to measure, track and improve their performance on issues such as, for example, energy consumption and waste or water usage. Regular reporting also facilitates comparing a company's performance to those of its competitors. Despite these obvious benefits, CSR and sustainability reporting, other than the ESG reports required by various stock exchanges, remains largely voluntary.

### Global reporting initiative

In 1997, a partnership of CERES (coalition for environmentally responsible economies) and the United Nations Environment Program established the Global Reporting Initiative (GRI). The GRI standards were created in line with international labor practices, and any environmental impact was assessed by conducting independent audits according to various International Organization for Standardization (ISO) standards.

By the early 2000s, there was a growing recognition that social impact and sustainability reporting remained ineffective. Organizations persisted in providing separate reports; one the usual set of financial statements, and the second, a sustainability report based on the then GRI guidelines.

At the end of 2009, during a meeting at St James' Palace called by His Royal Highness Prince Charles and attended by many significant organizations, discussions were held on how organizations might discharge their social and environmental duties of accountability based on more integrated financial and sustainability reports. The outcome of this meeting led to the formation of the International Integrated Reporting Council (IIRC) chaired by former South African Supreme Court judge, Mervyn King.

### The International Integrated Reporting Council

The mission of the IIRC is to establish integrated thinking and reporting within mainstream business practice as the norm. Its vision is to align capital allocation and corporate behavior to wider goals of financial stability and sustainable development. Its hope is to change the corporate reporting system so that integrated reporting becomes a global norm.

The IIRC was given the remit to develop a globally accepted integrated reporting (IR) framework that elicits from organizations material information about their strategy, governance, performance and prospects in a clear, concise and comparable format. The idea here was also to intertwine both financial and nonfinancial information.

### Integrated Reporting

The IR framework stresses that company value creation consists of major inputs that can be listed under six capitals, namely: financial, manufactured, human, intellectual, natural and social. The key idea is that a company should consider these six capitals when developing its business strategy instead of merely focusing on financial capital. By taking this systemic approach, a company's board is directed to pay attention and care for the broader outcomes (or impacts) of a company's business model rather than leaving these to regulators and NGO's to clean up.

The outcomes-based approach of integrated reporting is to look at the value creation chain from inputs into the company's business model, to its outputs, being its product or service, and the effects these have on society based on the three critical dimensions of sustainable development – the economy, society and the environment. This outcomes-based approach has now been integrated into the Sustainable Development Goals of the UN in April 2015, in which the UN states that in order to achieve sustainable development by 2030, account must be taken of the integrated dimensions of the economy, society and the environment. The UN has set the goal of 2030 to highlight the urgency of attending to the Earth's sustainability.

The whole idea of integrated reporting is to get at the real story behind the financials and to see how well the organization is positioned for the future. The

IR framework is intended to encourage disciplined business practices that take an integral approach to understanding the organization and its interface with the environment.

What the IR framework must consider is that an integrated report requires a whole new way of understanding and representing financials. Financial accounting principles are based on historical activity. Sustainability reporting takes one into the world of finance which is about the future based on projections and risks. Not only does this require a different mindset (as I mentioned under Corporate Governance earlier), it requires many different reporting principles which will need a certain competence for their interpretation. As an accountant turned financier, I am aware of the wide differences between an accounting mentality and a finance/economics one. Making the report integral is key and certainly a laudable goal.

The IR framework directs companies to report annually the positive and negative impacts of how the company made its money through engagement with the economy, society and the environment. And as discussed under corporate governance, good corporate citizenry demands that the Board develops a strategy that takes these spheres of engagement into account.

### One report

Harvard professor, Robert Eccles and Grant Thornton LLP partner, Michael Krzus, document in their book, *One Report* (2010), the need for an integrated report that provides a "single version of the truth" to all organizational stakeholders. They agree with Mervyn King and the IR framework that both financial and non-financial information should be woven together in relating the organization's position and should not be set apart as currently most often practiced, in separate statements.

Eccles and Krzus also support the idea that a company's strategy cannot be divorced from what is happening in society and the environment and that they need to take this into account proactively. While they discuss some of the details that can be incorporated in "one report," they do not provide a distinct framework as such. They claim to be working with many organizations in promoting the one report approach.

### Outlook

Whether it be through stakeholder pressure or enlightenment on behalf of corporate executives, attention to CSR and sustainability is growing. Future corporate reporting is heading in the direction of greater transparency, ease or comparability, and greater integration of the critical relationships between financial and other performance metrics. The pressure from many stakeholders to become a responsible global citizen is also likely to accelerate the integrated reporting approach.

I predict that a mandatory reporting framework is on the horizon. One caution I would make is that the new integrated reporting framework, however it is structured, does not add to the complexity and already voluminous tomes of the current financial reports. Most people cannot decipher or absorb the multitude of notes to current reports nor do they have, or want, to make the time to wade through fifty to one hundred pages. If sustainability reporting becomes another dreaded compliance exercise, it will defeat the purpose of conveying an important story that needs to be communicated.

## The United Nations Global Compact

The UN Global Compact is the world's largest corporate citizenship and sustainability initiative. Since its official launch on July 26, 2000, the initiative has grown to more than 12,000 participants, including over 8,000 businesses in approximately 145 countries around the world (https://www.unglobalcompact.org/what-is-gc).

Participation in Global Compact is voluntary. It is open to any company that is serious about its commitment to work towards implementation of Global Compact principles throughout its operations and sphere of influence, and to communicate on its progress.

The UN Global Compact's ten principles in the areas of human rights, labor, the environment and anti-corruption enjoy universal consensus and are derived from:

*   The Universal Declaration of Human Rights
*   The International Labor Organization's Declaration on Fundamental Principles and Rights at Work
*   The Rio Declaration on Environment and Development
*   The United Nations Convention Against Corruption

The UN Global Compact asks companies to embrace, support and enact, within their sphere of influence, a set of core values in the areas of human rights, labor standards, the environment and anti-corruption:

### Human Rights

Principle 1: Businesses should support and respect the protection of internationally proclaimed human rights; and
Principle 2: make sure that they are not complicit in human rights abuses.

### Labor

Principle 3: Businesses should uphold the freedom of association and the effective recognition of the right to collective bargaining;
Principle 4: the elimination of all forms of forced and compulsory labor;
Principle 5: the effective abolition of child labor; and
Principle 6: the elimination of discrimination in respect of employment and occupation.

## Environment

> Principle 7: Businesses should support a precautionary approach to environmental challenges;
>
> Principle 8: undertake initiatives to promote greater environmental responsibility; and
>
> Principle 9: encourage the development and diffusion of environmentally friendly technologies.

## Anti-Corruption

> Principle 10: Businesses should work against corruption in all its forms, including extortion and bribery.

## Cultural relativism

You may recall the discussion of moral relativism in Chapter 2 and in Chapter 6. Cultural relativism is moral relativism according to culture or ethnicity. It raises the question as to whether when in Rome to do as the Romans do?

From the global citizen perspective, this question is particularly challenging. Should a company that operates in other countries use its own moral standards and ethical guidelines or should it defer to the moral standards of the local country?

The UN's Global Compact is one place where the organization may get some guidelines. As outlines, this compact seeks to project certain universal values and asks businesses operating globally to act on certain universal principles.

In my opinion, while the Global Compact's guidelines are helpful, the decisions made as a result of referring to these principles will depend on the wisdom of how their principles are interpreted and implemented. Forums and discussions such as those hosted by the Global Compact are helpful in that they give executives and managers an opportunity to confer and consult with one another.

As to cultural relativism questions in real life situations, I recommend that managers engage in as much collaborative engagement and discussions as possible. Experience that people have had on the ground in different countries is invaluable. The opportunity to learn from one another and to understand the opportunities, pitfalls and trade-offs when making policy decisions on a global basis can be enormous.

One thing to note is that the UN Guiding Principles on Business and Human Rights and other international norms for companies are not legally binding. Companies can, and sometimes do, ignore them or take them up half-heartedly and ineffectively. Many companies have inadequate or no human rights due diligence measures in place, and their actions cause or contribute to human rights abuses. For more than two decades in every region of the world Human Rights Watch has documented human rights abuses in the context of global supply chains in agriculture, the garment and footwear industry, mining, construction and other sectors.

## Equity in Saudi Arabia

You are the newly appointed general manager of the manufacturing division of EXTEX. You have been sent to establish a plant in Saudi Arabia. You are going to need all kinds of manual workers, engineers and administrative staff. Although some organizations are now hiring women into management positions in Saudi Arabia, this is in no manner the normal trend.

The area in which you will establish the plant is known to be a rather traditional one where most people are Sunni Muslims. You learn that both Shias and women are discriminated against in Saudi Arabia especially among the more traditional Sunni Muslims. You must establish a hiring policy with the new plant manager, who happens to be a Sunni Muslim. How are you going to handle the employment of women and Shias? Will they even be hired? If so, will they be entitled to the same remuneration and promotion opportunities as others? Will you implement the same reward system as used by the head office in San Francisco? How will you arrive at an equitable approach given that employment policies may negatively impact your ability to employ certain people and may even inhibit the growth of sales within Saudi Arabia if people object to your policies?

## Facebook – a plague?

Mark Zuckerberg's journey to moguldom began ignobly with Facemash.com, a meanspirited site that encouraged his fellow male students at Harvard College to rate women on campus by their looks.

Zuckerberg created the Facebook precursor by hacking into Harvard web pages to gain access to the women's identification photos. Harvard called his behavior a "violation of individual privacy," and hauled Mr. Zuckerberg before its administrative board. Mark deactivated his site and apologized.

The Zuckerberg style continues like this. Something bad happens of increasingly severe consequence on Facebook (say, Russian election meddling in the United States, or the incitement of ethnic cleansing in Myanmar). After it is called out, Mr. Zuckerberg or another company official vows to do better. And when the heat is off, the cycle begins anew.

The pattern repeated last week when a meticulously reported *New York Times* investigation revealed Facebook's bare-knuckled efforts to deflect blame and undermine critics as it came under scrutiny for enabling the spread of misinformation in the run-up to the 2016 election.

It was a baffling explanation for anyone who took Zuckerberg and his deputy, Sheryl Sandberg, at face value when they swore, not long ago, that they would work openly to assert more control over the platform to stop misinformation campaigns, privacy breaches and incitements to violence.

Nothing was more at variance with their promises of transparency than the *New York Times's* revelation that the company had hired Definers Public Affairs, whose founders are known in Republican circles as lords of the so-called "dark arts" of political opposition research. Sandberg first said she knew nothing about it. Later she claimed she did not realize the implications . . . Extract from the *NY Times* November 2018.

---

### Your turn – Are You a Global Citizen?

* Do you think corporations have a responsibility to provide jobs locally or nationally? Should they refrain from outsourcing in foreign countries or using automation?
* Should corporations actively lobby to reduce regulation or environmental standards?
* Do you think the corporation should apply equal pay policies across the board regardless of country?
* Do you support affirmative action in hiring procedures?
* Should a one child policy be instituted worldwide?
* Who should pay for the recycling of electronic equipment – the corporation who makes them or the customer?
* Should corporations contribute toward helping the one million plus Rohingya in Bangladesh who are now being used as undocumented, very lowly paid laborers in garment factories?

---

## Creating a culture of global corporate citizenship

Surely, the greatest legacy organizations can leave is a planet healthy and prosperous for generations to come. Organizations can do this by instilling a global citizen ethos among their employees. The hallmark of a "good," i.e., just, organization is one where the culture encourages and supports personal and organizational excellence reflected in good global citizenship behavior. And good global citizenship behavior is ethical and just.

Well-known organizational psychologist Edgar Schein said that multi-stakeholder consciousness is integral to the moral development of executives (Schein, 1996). And the ability to take a systemic, integral view of stakeholder conflicting concerns and interests enables executives to demonstrate real leadership. This means that leaders and managers need to talk about what it means to be a global citizen and to educate employees on global issues. Leaders also need to role model systems thinking and encourage their employees to see the world as an inter-dependent system right down to the last speck of dust!

While most businesses boast ethics codes, most of them written in carefully crafted, politically correct language, few of them have teeth in the daily life of the organization. Making these codes a lived reality requires real commitment and love of the company and the world.

### *Give up instrumentality*

A personal issue that I have is with much of the instrumentality of global corporate citizenship and sustainability behavior.

Research carried out by a group of ethics scholars and written up in the *Business Ethics Quarterly* (April 2017), the official journal of the Society of Business Ethics in the US, confirms that that most organizations take an instrumental perspective on sustainable business practices. This means they see it as a means to an end, and not an end in itself. It is done either to enhance the organization's image or branding, and of course mostly to improve the bottom line.

Besides vitiating the integrity of the endeavor (recall ethical motivation is more important than the action itself), it makes CSR and sustainability conditional and subject to the vagaries of the budget and financial goals. Every employee knows the true reason why a corporation behaves responsibly, whether it is fear of being caught, pressure from activists, boosting sales, or for the sheer dignity and love of life and the world. So – which is it to be?

### Some suggestions

- Ensure that your employees are aware of all the countries in where your organization operates.
- Provide information, videos, webinars or seminars that explain the history, geography, culture, religion and environment of those countries.
- Arrange reciprocal visits between members of your company and those of your overseas partners.
- Sponsor the learning of another language particularly that of the countries in which the organization does its business.
- Distribute international newspapers to your employees on a regular basis.
- Regularly show films or videos on the beauty of nature and the planet and the challenges the planet is facing due to the human footprint.

## Executive summary

In this chapter we explored justice as it pertains to corporate global citizenship, CSR and sustainable business practices. Key points covered include:

- The essentiality of seeing the world from systems perspective and the ethical obligation to care for one's brother or sister.
- The notion that a just society is founded on just institutions. Just institutions are socially and environmentally responsible.
- The emergence of the Fourth Industrial Revolution and how that is challenging everything we do. It is also creating new social and environmental challenges.
- The current dire state of the environment and the desperate need for corporations to step up and help redress the many environmental hazards that are creating climate change and destroying the planet.
- The real challenge of population explosion.
- The heightened demand for corporations to see themselves as global corporate citizens and to become proactive in helping society and the environment.

- New legislation and new reporting measures are afoot, and organizations need take heed and begin aligning themselves to these realities.
- Cultural relativism is a challenge for organizations who operate globally and navigating these waters requires ethical prudence.
- Organizational leaders and managers need to actively shape and influence their culture to act locally and think globally.
- One way of looking at global corporate citizenship and sustainability is from a perspective of love of self, others and the world.

## Key questions

- What do you think prevents organizations from being more socially responsible?
- Would you say your organization practices CSR or global citizenship?
- How would you influence the culture of a business to become more environmentally aware?
- Do you support CSR by only buying from organizations who are socially and environmentally sensitive?
- Do you support more intensive legislation?

## Key terms

Autopoietic   247
Conflict of interest   266
Corporate citizenship   249
Corporate colonialism   251
Cultural relativism   271
Digitization   255
Fourth Industrial Revolution   251
Ecology   247

Human rights   251
Integrated reporting   261
Risk   250
Social contract   257
Stakeholders   259
Sustainability   248
Value creation   264

## References

Benn, Suzanne and Dianne Bolton. *Key Concepts in Corporate Social Responsibility*. London, UK: Sage, 2011.
Capra, Fritjof and Pier Luigi Luisi. *The Systems View of Life: A Unifying Vision*. Cambridge, UK: Cambridge University Press, 2014.
Eccles, Robert G. and Michael P. Krzus. *One Report: Integrated Reporting for a Sustainable Strategy*. Hoboken, NJ: John Wiley & Sons Inc., 2010.
Freeman, R. Edward, R. Edward Freeman, Jeffrey S. Harrison, and Andrew C. Wicks. *Managing for Stakeholders: Survival, Reputation and Success*. New Haven, CT: Yale University Press, 2007.
Habisch, Andre, Andre Habisch, Jan Jonker, Martina Wegner, and Rene Schmindpeter, editors. *Corporate Social Responsibility Across Europe*. Berlin, Germany: Springer, 2005.
Huse, Morten. *Boards, Governance and Value Creation*. Cambridge, UK: Cambridge University Press, 2007.
Korten, David C. *When Corporations Rule the World*, 20th Anniversary Edition. Oakland, CA: Berrett-Koehler Publishers Inc., 2015.

Maccoby, Michael. *The Leaders We Need: And What Makes Us Follow*. Boston, MA: Harvard Business School Press, 2007.

Meadows, Donella H. *Beyond the Limits*. Post Mills, Vermont: Chelsea Green Publishing Company, 1992.

Schein, Edgar H. *Organizational Culture and Leadership*. San Francisco, California: 1996.

Schuler, Douglas, Andreas Rasche, Drod Etzion, and Lisa Newton. Corporate Sustainability Management and Environmental Ethics. *Business Ethics Quarterly*, Vol. 27, No. 2, April 2017, Cambridge University Press.

Spinello, Richard A. *Business Ethics: Contemporary Issues and Cases*. London, UK: Sage Publications, 2020.

Weiss, Joseph, W. *Business Ethics 4th Edition. A Stakeholder and Issues Management Approach*. Mason, OH: Thomson South-Western, 2006.

Wood, Donna, Jeanne M. Logsdon, Patsy Lewellyn, Kim Davenport. *Global Business Citizenship: A Transformative Framework for Ethics and Sustainable Capitalism*. Abingdon, United Kingdom: Routledge, 2006.

Young, Scott T. and K. Kathy Dhanda. *Sustainability: Essentials for Business*. London, UK: Sage, 2013.

# 9 The moral reasoning framework

## Contents

## A Moral Reasoning Framework

In the pages that follow, I have set out a comprehensive moral reasoning framework (MRF) which provides a structured process for evaluating ethical dilemmas and formulating moral strategies for action.

This framework can be used either as presented here, or reduced to a simpler version, and/or customized to meet the needs of the organization. You can also use the "short-hand" version by using the five fingers on your hand as prompts.

Now that you have this framework available, there is no excuse for ignoring the ethical dimension in the daily choices of life!

## Practicing Ethics

One of the major aims of this book is to enhance our ethical competency so that we become wiser decision makers and are better able to navigate our way through this turbulent and complex world that places many demands on our decision-making capacities.

Being ethically competent provides us with a multitude of advantages. To mention a few:

- We enhance our cognitive and moral maturity.
- We advance our moral development.
- We become wiser decision makers.
- We are better able to explain our decisions and communicate our moral reasoning process.
- We convey with greater clarity our perspective on a moral dilemma, the issues at stake, the factors that require consideration, and the trade-offs involved.
- We feel better about ourselves and how we live in the world.

As we know, one develops ethical competency by practicing ethics. Practicing ethics means intentionally and diligently practicing one's moral reasoning processes as one engages in the moral dilemmas of everyday life. Being ethical, something we have discussed at length in the previous chapters, means asking: How do I live my life? According to which principles do I live my life? Do I make choices with the intention of advancing goodness? Do I weigh different options and look at decisions from multiple perspectives, including those that don't suit me? Can I set aside my personal feelings and emotions and wrestle with what it is I ought to do? Can I go beyond my egoic fears and needs and choose wisely guided by my highest self? Do I have the courage to follow through on my ethical intentions? The MRF guides us through some of these questions.

## Ethical Competency

Teaching people codes or rules does not make them ethical. Teaching them how to practice ethics, and how to develop their ethical competency, however, besides the benefits I have just pointed out, greatly advances their wisdom in applying codes and rules more effectively.

### Ethical competence spelled out

#### 1   Defining the issue

Ethical competence begins with defining the ethical issues at stake. This does not mean defining the business issue, the legal issue or the compliance default, although they are important too. It means specifically defining the ethical issue(s) in the language of ethics. Once one begins the defining process, frequently one finds that more than one ethical issue requires consideration.

#### 2   Establishing significance

Ethical competence means being able to assess the significance of the problem and its risk to oneself and/or the organization. Due to hasty analysis the significance is frequently misunderstood or underestimated.

#### 3   Clarifying the dilemma

Ethical competence means being able to deliberate and truly grasp what makes the ethical dilemma a dilemma. What is it about the dilemma that makes the various options in solving the dilemma so complex or unpalatable?

Ethical dilemmas invariably challenge our own values, emotions and judgments. These challenges are what make for a dilemma in the first place and what makes our being objective difficult.

It is important to recognize the difference between a problem and a dilemma. Problems we can typically solve – there is a clear solution even if there is a price to pay. Dilemmas are difficult problems in that there are no solutions as such. With dilemmas, at best, we can optimize among certain alternatives, many of which hold some uncomfortable compromises. (Discussed in Chapter 4.)

A dilemma often requires transcending the current situation and being creative by finding new ground or a new perspective. We discuss this possibility under moral imagination later in the chapter.

*4   Using the language of ethics and morals*

Ethical competence means knowing the language of ethics and morals, and being able to objectify the problem so that difficult conversations can be held around ethical principles rather than around personal feelings and biases.

*5   Framing*

Ethical competence means carefully framing the issue and strategizing the best way to identify the trade-offs associated with different courses of action. Different framing usually implies different courses of action.

*6   Risks and harms*

Ethical competence means being able to anticipate the ethical harms and risks associated with various decision options.

*7   Reviewing ethical principles and personal values*

Ethical competence requires using wisdom and grounded judgement where one mindfully interweaves thought and action.

*8   Integrated thinking*

Ethical competence is based on an integration of motivation, intention, the use of ethical principles, and the wise display of moral courage.

## Ethical competency

- Defining the issue
- Establishing significance
- Clarifying the dilemma
- Using the language of ethics and morals
- Framing
- Risks and harms
- Reviewing ethical principles and personal values
- Integrated thinking

## Importance of language

Every discipline incorporates its own lexicon of concepts. Learning these concepts and being able to apply them appropriately is one of the hurdles and hallmarks of competence in that discipline.

In accounting one talks of debits, credits, the bottom line, profits, losses, equity and shareholders. In finance one talks about free cash flows, discount or hurdle rates, net present value, risk and return, and opportunity costs. In biology one talks about metabolism, organisms, cells, adaptation and homeostasis. In ethics one talks about self-examination, virtue, deontology, utilitarianism, justice, moral relativism, moderation, consequences and conscience.

All concepts convey depths of meaning. They are abstract terms that synthesize a collection of ideas, thoughts, feelings and processes. A concept replaces a paragraph of words, pictures or sounds. They provide a shorthand method of communicating effectively and efficiently.

In ethics, concepts are particularly important as they refer to the principles of thought, feeling and experience in the choices that pave the journey of our lives. Let us take the example of justice. I could enter into a long, personal ramble about how someone had broken an agreement we had and that I felt he was wrong. That he had let me down, hurt my feelings, got away with something that was not his by right, left me the worse off, betrayed my loyalty etc., or I could mention that an injustice had been committed.

The ethical issue to be dealt with is a violation of the principle of justice. Having now diligently studied Chapters 6 and 7 on justice, we know that it refers to the principle of giving and getting one's due. We know that I have not received my due and that requires some form of rectification.

My hurt feelings, sense of being wronged, and anger may be justified as a result of the injustice I have suffered. Only I can resolve those feelings. If I am recompensed, that might be easy to do although I might still feel embittered. If I am not recompensed, then I have likely even greater psychological and emotional work to do. Fair or not – that is my work to do. The ethical issue, in the ethical domain, is justice.

Being able to articulate ethical issues using the language of ethics is extremely important when it comes to challenging others – something we discuss later in this chapter. If we make our ethics personal and relative to our feelings, then discussions typically devolve into whose feelings are more worthwhile. However, once we refer to principles, we can discuss their value and appropriateness more objectively, and we can refer to comparatives, benchmarks, standards or precedence. I am not saying applying ethical principles is easy. On the contrary, the two examples next provide some of the challenges we currently experience.

### The erosion of moral discourse

Prior to the twentieth century, moral discourse took place publicly – on the commons – and privately as people wrestled with how to live according to the times.[1] The twentieth century changed that. Whether it was the two devastating world wars and the great depression that left people morally speechless, or the rapid scientific and technological advances that literally propelled us into the stratosphere, or a combination of all three, morality is no longer the bread and butter of daily discourse and public life.

Jeffrey Stout, in *Ethics After Babel*, (1988), questions our ability to relate current Western morality to the philosophical and religious traditions of the past. He suggests that we have become individually adept at developing a moral bricolage in our attempts to attune traditional ethical theory to modern day moral problems.

Stout claims that we speak not one moral language, but several and that they serve us poorly. According to him, the primary language in which we understand ourselves has individualism shot through it and that it is ill-suited for public discourse for the common good or for shaping meaningful lives.

In the research I completed for my PhD dissertation and have continued since, I would concur with Stout. In my investigation with hundreds of senior managers, few take an active interest in ethics education or personal moral development. They attend courses mandated by their professions or their companies, however it is a rare exception to find a person who takes things further and makes a point to develop some level of ethical competence and facility in discussing ethical issues.

### All My Life is Feelings!

Jacob Needleman in his book,[2] *Why Can't We Be Good?* (2008), writes about his challenges of discussing ethics with his students. He describes how no-one seems to have an idea of what ethics really means. Not that the students do not experience decision-making dilemmas, but they have no idea of referring to principles, he claims. Everything redounds to what makes them *feel* good, bad or guilty. Not whether by any objective measure it was good or bad or morally blameworthy.

Needleman describes the universal moral relativism of modern young people. The fashion seems to be to deny moral absolutes in the ethical sphere. The argument goes as, to who or what is to say what is good or bad, or right or wrong? It is simply accepted that all morality is relative to time, place, ethnicity, religion, social class, nationality and so on. The interesting point is that the question of moral relativism is not even considered or possibly even known to exist. It is simply how it is. Obviously, people who live this paradigm have no ability to speak the language of ethics and morals. Everything is simply a matter of personal feeling or preference. (In Chapters 1 and 3, I explained this personalist trend.)

My own teaching experience mirrors that of Needleman's. I would add that it is not just young students who think this way. Many adults who have years of work experience, some of whom are in managerial and even senior leadership positions, reflect these same personalist perspectives. Regrettably, these people have never had the experience of "doing ethics." Ethics, as we have covered from various vantage points, is about self-examination, reflection, deliberation and questioning. Needless to say, it is difficult to build an ethical culture if one does not understand what ethics is about, just as it would be very difficult to coach baseball or soccer if one has never been on the field, played the game or read up the rules. Baseball and soccer have their own language too!

## The five pillars of the moral reasoning framework

The moral reasoning framework provides a disciplined approach to working through moral dilemmas. It encourages critical thinking and helps one to objectify the moral dilemma by using a methodical process as a basis for discussion and deliberation. Using this framework eliminates the typical personal and self-referential approach in which many moral dilemmas are resolved. Most importantly it provides a methodology that can be included as part of an organization's decision-making processes.

*Pillar one: frame the ethical problem*

The first step is to frame the dilemma in ethical rather than legal or economic terms. This does not mean that the latter aspects are eliminated. What it does means is that the focus of the problem definition lies in determining what makes the dilemma an ethical one. Other aspects of the problem are also considered but do not drive the main line of questioning. For example: The dilemma concerns theft, fidelity, stewardship, transparency and so on.

*Pillar two: deliberate*

The second step is to work through all the angles that make this challenge a moral dilemma for you. Here is where you look at what is at stake for you personally. You roll up our sleeves and get into the messy particulars of your insecurities and your defenses. Here is where you carry out honest self-examination and look at what imprisons you and what frees you. You raise questions such as how this dilemma impacts your moral freedom; your economic and psychological safety; your family, your ego, identity and self-esteem. Where do your personal value conflicts lie? What role does fear play? What about your sense of competence and power? What is at risk and what might you lose or gain?

Next you consider the internal systemic pressures that inhibit you from speaking openly and freely. There may be physical pressures, culture and community pressures, professional duties, and authority issues that serve to inhibit your moral freedom. Then there might be external pressures such as religious commitments, community values, political positions, and economic circumstances that all play a role in making this a dilemma for you.

*Pillar three: test against ethical principles*

The third step requires working through the dilemma by taking the various perspectives presented by different ethical principles. Here you can include the organization's set of acclaimed ethical values. As you work through this section you will note that, by applying different principles to the dilemma you will be presented with alternative courses of action for consideration.

*Pillar four: draw up a moral balance sheet*

The fourth step requires drawing up an ethical "balance sheet" or "a pros and cons" analysis that summarizes the ethical "assets" and "liabilities" (the trade-offs) associated with following through on anyone of the ethical principles or values considered.

*Pillar five: moral plan of action*

The fifth step results in formulating a moral plan of action with specific steps for follow through. This step also recognizes the implications of alternative actions that will not be followed, i.e., the risks associated with both the actions to be taken and not taken.

*Figure 9.1* Short Hand Version

**Thumb:** What is the ethical issue here and how significant is it? Can I lose my hand?

**Forefinger:** What makes this a dilemma? What forces are pushing me in which different directions? What value conflicts am I experiencing?

**Middle finger:** What are the different perspectives I can take? Which ethical principles guide me in which direction? For example, my character versus the law, or my duty versus the consequences.

**Ring finger:** How can I sum up the different perspectives and their advantages and disadvantages?

**Little Finger:** What plan of action will I make? Will I have the courage to follow through with it? What might it take?

Now we will work through the Cuba case using the detailed version of the MRF.

## Dilemma from Cuba

You work for an organization that develops special steel-cutting equipment. You are the vice president of sales who has a sturdy record of achieving sales targets. As the year end is approaching, you are anxious to achieve your forecasts. This seems highly likely given the last quarter's sales performance. Your organization's profits depend upon your sales team meeting their goals. Your pride depends upon it too and your bonus will be a healthy one if you do.

Two days before the end of the organization's financial year, wandering around the warehouse you find several large containers marked "goods returned." On closer inspection, you notice the goods have been returned from Cuba. You are astonished. You know the organization does not sell to Cuba as it adheres strictly to US embargo laws that forbid the sale of any goods to Cuba. How did this happen? What is going on? You do some investigation and you establish that one of your major Canadian customers has redirected your organization's goods to Cuba.

You are left with several major considerations:

1   Should you recognize the returns within the current financial year since this will have a significant impact on achieving sales targets?
2   Will you challenge your Canadian customer and insist that in future your goods may not be redirected to Cuba since it is against US trade policies?
3   Will you be transparent with senior management about this event and will you also bring up the likelihood that other customers might be reselling or redirecting the organization's products into embargoed territories?

These questions will of course challenge your competence not only regarding meeting sales targets just when it is really needed but concerning your ability to set customer policy. How many customers might the organization lose if you check where they redirect their sales?

## Questions

- What are you going to do?
- What is your rationale and motivation for your choice of action?
- Which ethical principle/s is/are guiding you most?
- What are the greatest trade-offs you need to consider?
- What is the worst thing that might happen?
- Who are the stakeholders affected?

## Dilemma from Cuba

### Section 1: framing the moral problem

This section is the most important. It is here that we get to understand the nature of the dilemma and its impact. It is also here that we get the first signs of what responses or actions might be possible. How we frame the dilemma will radically impact our further analysis. We begin with establishing the scope of the dilemma, and its significance. The framing of will also influence the ethical principles that might guide our actions. It also informs what we will choose to do and how we will do it.

### *Defining the ethical issue*

In my experience, many people use ineffective problem-solving strategies. What stands out is that few people spend sufficient time to thoughtfully define the nature

# Moral Reasoning Framework

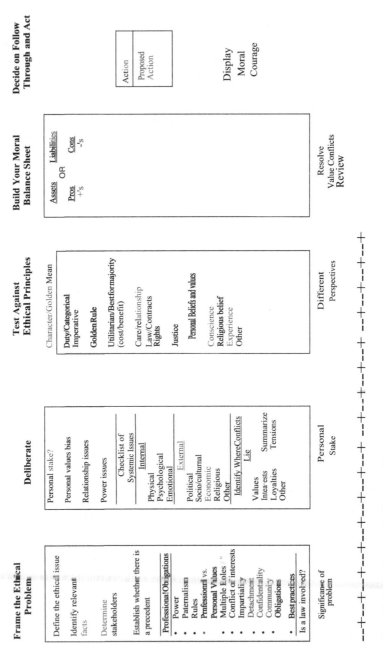

| Frame the Ethical Problem | Deliberate | Test Against Ethical Principles | Build Your Moral Balance Sheet | Decide on Follow Through and Act |
|---|---|---|---|---|

**Frame the Ethical Problem**

Define the ethical issue

Identify relevant facts

Determine stakeholders

Establish whether there is a precedent

Professional Obligations
- Power
  - Paternalism
  - Rules
  - Professional vs. Personal Values
  - Multiple Roles
  - Conflict of interests
  - Impartiality
  - Detachment
  - Confidentiality
  - Community
  - Obligations
- Best practices
- Is a law involved?

Significance of problem

**Deliberate**

Personal stake?

Personal values bias

Relationship issues

Power issues

Checklist of Systemic Issues

Internal
Physical
Psychological
Emotional

External
Political
Socio/cultural
Economic
Religious
Other

Identify Where Conflicts Lie
Values        Summarize
Interests     Tensions
Loyalties
Other

Personal Stake

**Test Against Ethical Principles**

Character/Golden Mean

Duty/Categorical Imperative

Golden Rule

Utilitarian/Best for majority (cost/benefit)

Care/relationship
Law/Contracts
Rights

Justice

Personal Beliefs and values

Conscience
Religious belief
Experience
Other

Different Perspectives

**Build Your Moral Balance Sheet**

Assets     Liabilities

OR

Pros       Cons
+'s        -'s

Resolve Value Conflicts
Review

**Decide on Follow Through and Act**

| Action |
|---|
| Proposed Action |

Display Moral Courage

*Figure 9.2* Moral reasoning framework

of the problem in an organized or coherent manner. Even fewer people try to get below the surface symptoms to explore where the root cause of the problem might lie, i.e., identifying the real problem under consideration. And then there are those who propose courses of action before they have even defined the problem at all. This latter tendency is particularly prevalent when it comes to moral dilemmas. As discussed earlier, feelings and biases leap to the fore and solutions are vehemently proposed before anyone has even grappled with what it is they are trying to solve.

The tendency to rush to conclusions and perform habitual ways of responding is alarming. Many people find great difficulty in setting aside their personal viewpoints and considering others. They seem to have made up their minds whether they understand the true nature of the problem or not. I have found, however, that practice does improve decision-making strategies. By practice, I mean repeatedly using an explicit framework that provides a rigorous approach to defining the problem. Good problem solvers know that a thoughtful problem definition shines light on the most effective solution or response. If a problem is well defined, half the battle of discerning the best course of action has been won.

### Cuba case

Let us look at the ethical issues that come to light in the Cuba case. It is important to identify them and spell them out. For starters we could name honesty, adhering to generally accepted accounting principles, complying with the law, customer accountability, loyalty and protecting relationships.

It is important to shake out as many of the ethical issues that one can. This helps us look at the problem from multiple perspectives which also begins to guide us as to where the trade-offs and the ultimate choice of action might lie.

What can you add to the list I have provided?

### Identifying relevant facts

Here we want to establish the facts we know and identify the gaps, i.e., the facts we do not know. We also want to ask ourselves whether there might be some relevant questions or facts that are outside of our awareness. Invariably there will be gaps in our knowledge. This is where our assumptions and inferences play an important role. What kind of assumptions are we going to make to fill our gaps in knowledge? Are we even aware of the assumptions we are making? Are they good ones and do they reflect critical thinking? (Recall our discussion on the relevance of critical thinking to understanding assumptions in Chapter 5.)

### Cuba case

We do not have that many facts, but what we do know is:

- You are anxious to make sales forecasts
- Your organization's profits depend on you and your team achieving the sales forecasts

- You will get a healthy bonus if the organization has a profit
- You feel proud if you make sales forecasts – assumption you feel you have failed if you do not
- Two days are left to the end of the year – so you are nearly there
- You (unexpectedly – assumption) find containers with goods returned from Cuba
- US embargo laws do not allow US companies to sell to Cuba
- One of your major customers is redirecting your organization's good to Cuba.

### Determining stakeholders affected

A great deal has been written on stakeholder analysis and the various methods by which one can determine the direct and indirect stakeholders of the organization (Explained in Chapter 8).

In this section of the problem definition what we are seeking to determine is the ripple effect of the ethical dilemma. Who, directly or indirectly will be affected and how? Stakeholders include both personal relationships and/or people and groups involved with the organization.

The number of people affected by a moral dilemma is often far greater than one first imagines. For example, if you lose your job as a result of how you handle this dilemma, your entire family will be affected, not to mention the organization, your peers and your sub-ordinates. Thoughtful stakeholder analysis is advised at this early stage of the problem definition as it informs the scope of the problem and the risks that may be entailed.

### Cuba case

Consider the wide number of people impacted in the Cuba case.

- Yourself
- Your family who is affected by your successes and failures
- Your sales team and their families
- Senior management and their families
- The organization as a whole – the viability of the organization as a system
- The stockholders and their families
- Your customers – existing and new

Can you name any others?

### Consider the extent of harm and risks

Here we want to imagine the greatest harm that might occur as a result of our moral dilemma. The harm might be a personal one and/or one that impacts certain specific stakeholders or the entire well-being of the organization. We also want to consider what types of risks are associated with our taking an action or doing nothing.

*Cuba case*

In the Cuba case, would you consider this a serious case based on a reasonable assessment of the number of stakeholders affected and the potential harms and risks?

*Possible harms and risks*

- You could lose your job.
- Your sales team might be downsized.
- You may lose several customers.
- The organization might make a loss having to lay off people or curb operations.
- The organization may have to pay legal fines.
- The image of the organization might be negatively impacted.
- The share price might plummet.
- Liquidity might be affected and put the company at financial risk.

Can you add to this list?

*Is there a precedent?*

A former boss of mine once said: "If we are not thoughtful, precedents can make us consistent fools!"

Precedents can provide helpful guidelines. They can also act as obstacles and blinders to new possibilities. We need to consider precedents wisely. On the one hand, precedents establish a course of action and following this consistently has its advantages. On the other hand, there might be some nuance in our situation that challenges the precedent and invites a new course of action. Breaking precedents or creating new ones requires careful thinking, tenacity and persuasion, and often, courage!

*Cuba case*

We are not made aware of any precedent here.

(Since the Cuba dilemma relates to a corporation and not a professional business, we will omit the Professional Obligations section and return to this later.)

*Is a law involved?*

Frequently in decision-making the first question posed is whether there is a law to which one can defer to resolve an issue. I suggest that this should not be the first question asked, as looking to the law often closes the door to more ethical and creative options. It also makes us approach the problem from a moral rather than an ethical perspective. Clearly the existence of laws is significant and must be taken into consideration. However, laws are made by humans and depend on time, context and interpretation. Even legal guidelines may not be that clear cut and require further deliberation, interpretation and discernment.

### Cuba case

In the Cuba case a law exists that places an embargo on goods being shipped to Cuba. Breaking that law could lead to fines and even to being placed under further scrutiny by the US federal government. Clearly this cannot be taken lightly.

### Conclusion – significance of the problem

Here at the end of Section 1, we consider the profile and scope of the moral dilemma under investigation and its significance. If we deem it significant, i.e., it affects many people or it has a huge financial or negative image impact on the organization, we need to incorporate thoughtful discernment as we proceed through the next steps of the MRF. If we conclude that our dilemma is a relatively insignificant one, then we may decide not to carry out the next steps in any detail, although still asking ourselves the important questions.

### Cuba case

I think we might consider the Cuba case to be a morally significant one. An initial review tells us that the organization might be indirectly breaking the law. We also realize that many people's welfare is at stake and the organization is facing some clear risks. The future policies needed to ensure that customers do not place the organization at risk, is a sensitive one. Customers in other countries may object to having to comply with US embargo rules. The incident of returns also raises the question of complying with generally accepted accounting principles that require recognition of a returned sale in the year in which it occurs. This is an important compliance issue that also has legal consequences if there is failure to comply.

Morally significant cases obviously demand in-depth analysis.

## Section 2: deliberate

This section of the Moral Reasoning Framework questions why the issue is a moral dilemma for you and/or the firm. Most often decision-making processes do not allow for personal issues or so called "baggage" of the people involved to be openly and candidly taken into account. Invariably it is because there is something personal at stake that makes the dilemma a dilemma. It is much easier for us to make decisions and to take action where we have no personal investment or where the range of outcomes do not impact our own personal well-being. If an organization is facing an ethical issue, for example dealing with sexual harassment claims, it always redounds back to individuals. Recall – there is no such thing as "the corporation!"

To do this section justice, requires complete candor and personal honesty about how certain courses of action stimulate fear, aversion, anger, envy or power plays. We are human and these are very real emotions that we must deal with. Acknowledging these emotions does not make us bad people. On the contrary, admitting our struggles is what gives us authenticity and character. It also helps us have compassion for others as we understand the path they might also be trying to walk.

### Personal stake

Here we consider what personal stake we have in the outcome of any decision we might make.

### Cuba case

In the dilemma from Cuba, there are several personal aspects at stake.
  For example:

- You want to make our sales forecasts because you wish to be seen as competent; as an effective performer; as someone who can deliver.
- You have a vested interest in the company making a profit.
- You do not want to lose your bonus or be the cause of other people losing theirs.
- You do not want to acknowledge that maybe you have a problem with some of your existing customer base and that you may have to develop a new one.
- Bringing the Cuba sales situation to senior management's attention would make you extremely unpopular and personally vulnerable.
- If you do nothing, however, and the returns are discovered by someone else, you might be deemed incompetent.

Can you think of other relevant perspectives?

### Personal value bias

Here we deliberate about what our personal values would encourage us to do. This does not mean we will follow through on them; however, it does help us see where the value tensions lie.

### Cuba case

- You may not support the idea of embargoes to any country.
- Maybe one of your relatives is Cuban.
- Alternatively, you may be a staunch believer in the embargo to Cuba and thus wish to see the embargo strictly adhered to.

- You may feel that you deserve a bonus whether the company makes a profit or not, as you have contributed your share to its earnings.
- You may feel that customers outside of the US should not be bound by US embargo laws. If you were to change sales policies to insist that they do, you may not be able to build a strong customer base.

### Relationship issues

Part of our deliberation concerns the impact our actions might have on our relationships. These relationships may be either personal or professional or both.

### Cuba case

- Here you would consider the impact on our family if you do not bring home that bonus. Maybe the family was depending upon it. This was to be for the special holiday; or new car; or student education fund. How would they feel if this did not materialize? How can you let them down?
- Then there is the question of fellow employees? What will happen to your relationship with them if they do not get their bonuses because you choose to be so ethical? Is it worth it?
- You may be concerned that your relationship with your boss might be impaired. Until now, you have always delivered the results, and he trusts you implicitly. Could this trust now be broken?

### Power issues

Here we consider how the dilemma may or may not impact your own personal power. It may impact your relational power with others, or it may impact your power as someone who is competent or professional.

### Cuba case

In the Cuba example you would certainly lose both relational power and competency power if you did not achieve your targets whatever the reason. This does not mean that your power cannot be recouped, but you will be rendered vulnerable for a period, at least. Being vulnerable is a dangerous place to be! Can you perhaps avoid this?

### Internal systemic issues

Internal systemic issues relate especially to your sense of moral freedom within the organization. Do you feel physically, psychologically, economically and emotionally free to make good ethical decisions? If you have an open and transparent discussion about the Cuba issue with your peers and senior management will there be any adverse repercussions?

You may recall, in Chapters 2 and 4 we discussed some of the systemic barriers to ethical behavior in organizations. Here is where we might consider whether any of those barriers apply in how we respond to our problem. Are there any inherent dynamics in the organization that are either helping you or holding you back?

## *Cuba case*

We have insufficient information to make any inferences here. You may not economically need that bonus, but psychologically perhaps you do! You may fear authority and find it difficult to tell those in positions of authority the truth.

## *External systemic issues*

External systemic issues refer to any major constraints in the external environment that have an impact on the dilemma. These might be political, cultural, economic, religious and so on.

## *Cuba case*

In the Cuba case there are political issues related to dealing with Cuba. There are possibly economic issues regarding the Canadian economy and the financial health of your customers.

## *Identification of conflicts*

Here you want to identify all the tensions you are personally experiencing as a result of this dilemma, whether these tensions are rationally valid or not. The most important thing is looking at where personal value conflicts lie. These might be, for example, personal values versus organizational values. Or they could be loyalty to your family versus telling the truth.

## *Cuba case*

We mentioned that on the one hand you may not believe in embargoes. On the other, you may wish to uphold the embargo, but you are torn by your concern for the impact on the relationships, personal and other, that you have. There is the loyalty to your employees to get their bonuses versus your loyalty to senior management to see that the organization is not doing something against the law or complying with acceptable accounting policies. Then there is your concern that you need to develop a new customer base and your fear of being able to achieve that within an acceptable period. A major tension is likely to be when to tell what to whom and how that will impact the way people see you.

### Conclusion – personal stake

At the end of Section 2, you want to have a good, conscious understanding of why this is a dilemma for you and which major factors inhibit certain courses of action. If possible, by now you would like to have established the major stumbling blocks to making this a simple case of immediately telling the truth to all concerned.

## Section 3: test against ethical principles

Psychologists say that a measure of maturity is a person's ability to entertain multiple different and competing concepts or ideas at the same time, without losing his or her ability to take a stand on their own (Kegan, 1982). Section 3 of our Moral Reasoning Framework asks us to do just this – take many different perspectives, some of which will be opposing ones – and view what each perspective contributes to the problem solution. I have personally witnessed the enormous strides in cognitive maturity that results from this exercise.

In this section we are going to use a variety of ethical principles to guide us in our choice of action regarding the moral dilemma we have profiled. We are going to combine all that we have established and deliberated on so far and see how taking different ethical perspectives shape our response.

We can select any variety of ethical principles plus we can add the organization's own avowed values or principles as part of our list. Chapters 6 and 7 laid out some ethical principles we could use. We might also wish to add some personal guidelines of our own such as religious beliefs, or values learned from personal experience.

Ethical injunctions we could use:

*   Character/ Virtue Ethics: Take that action that is honest, open, truthful and reflects the life I want to live.
*   Golden Rule: Do unto others as you would have them do to you.
*   Duty/Categorical Imperative: Do your duty. Ask what action could be taken that could be made a universal rule regardless of the consequences. Don't use people as means. Treat them as ends.
*   Utilitarian approach: Take that action that results in the greatest good for the majority or minimizes harm.
*   Care/Relationship Approach: Take that action that reflects caring for the most important relationships involved.
*   Justice: Take that action that is fair to all parties involved and that promotes the greatest overall harmony.
*   Law/Contracts Approach: Take that action that adheres to the law or honors the contractual relations between parties.
*   Rights Approach: Take any action you wish as long as you do not impinge on the rights of others.
*   Am I My Brother's Keeper?: Take that action that reflects concern and compassion for those in a weaker position than you.

- Corporate Citizenship: Consider the role modeling a responsible corporate citizen would demonstrate in this case.
- Sleep Test: Take that action that squares with your conscience and allows you to sleep at night.

(Refer to Chapters 6 and 7 for full list.)

### Cuba case

In the Cuba case, what would each of these ethical principles invite you to do? Some of them may not appear relevant to the case – which is fine. Some of the principles might seem contradictory – so how will you mediate that conflict? Recall from our discussions that ethics is about questioning, interpretation, reflection and judgment. Ethics is NOT rules. Ethics invites us to think and adapt with one goal in mind: How will this principle help me to advance goodness, flourishing, potential, authenticity and the truth?

## Section 4: build your moral balance sheet

In this Section you summarize the pros and cons of taking each action according to the ethical guideline used. I use the term "moral balance sheet" as many people in business can relate to that as an analogy for reviewing positive and negative resource commitments. You can of course use another name, for example guiding moral actions analysis. One organization I worked with called it their "Ethical Review Analysis" (ERA). The main idea is simply to juxtapose those ethical guidelines that you consider help you arrive at a positive course of action and those that detract from that. Some ethical principles may do both. In those cases, list both the pros and the cons.

### Cuba case

For example, using our Cuba case and the injunction to do our duty:
 Our duty would be to act as a responsible employee concerned for the assets and welfare of the company.
 The assets or pros could be summarized as –

- Saving the company from a potential lawsuit (law),
- Being a dutiful employee who can be trusted (duty),
- Adhering to accounting standards and thus promoting financial integrity (duty),
- Supporting the political goals of the government (duty), and
- Doing what is best for the majority (utilitarianism).

The liabilities or cons could be summarized as –

- Not giving the Canadian company the opportunity of a warning (character/justice- mercy),
- Being too ethical as many companies close their eyes to the redirection of sales (duty),
- Having no concern for the impact on shareholders when sales fall short (promote short term thinking) (utilitarianism),
- Having no concern for the needs of the employees (care/relationship),
- Ignoring the impact on one's own financial welfare (self-interest),
- Putting one's family at risk (relationship), and
- Being viewed as a sanctimonious bureaucrat obsessed with the letter of the law (duty).

The MRF asks that one complete this analysis in detail taking the various stakeholders impacted by the dilemma into account. It is important to be as frank as possible. The efficacy of this analysis will be greatly enhanced if it is carried out by several people working together rather than just the individual problem-solver working alone. Discussion will unpack many of the issues and highlight some of the tensions along with some aspects that call for a variety of responses.

At the end of this deliberation, the trade-offs need to be summarized, the value conflicts considered, and then the "wisest" option chosen. There is no rule or answer as to which is the wisest option. Wisdom only has a chance to display her presence where there is genuine open discussion and discernment.

## Section 5: decide and act

While the MRF is presented as a linear process, that is misleading. The best way to use the framework is to ensure that it remains a dynamic list of questions that are dealt with iteratively. This means that each section remains open to further questioning as one works through the process. Each section maybe revisited repeatedly as one gains a finer understanding of the problem at hand. Discussions should thus go back and forth as new questions fine tune the dilemma and the issues at stake.

Ultimately, thoughtful definition of the moral dilemma and careful follow through of the questions as outlined in the MRF usually brings the optimal problem solution to the surface. This does not mean that the choice is easy or simple. The idea here is to understand all the elements that came into play in making the decision and to learn from them. It is the process itself that strengthens decision-making skills and enhances wisdom.

Most choices imply trade-offs. As I say often: There is no such a thing as a free lunch. One of the biggest challenges in deciding on a path of action is deciding how to settle value conflicts without feeling that one has sold one's soul. Discussion with others and recognition of the cost of making certain decisions is critical. And then there is moral imagination.

### Moral imagination

> *Let him who is without sin among you be the first to throw a stone at her.*
>
> John 8:7

If there is one person who demonstrated moral imagination, it was Jesus. Time and again, he would reframe, turn things around, take a different perspective, and with dignity and poise disarm his adversaries who were blinded by a tunnel-like moral vision that could only see the literal letter of the Hebrew moral law.

In one instance, Jesus was presented with a moral dilemma when the scribes and the Pharisees brought a woman before him who had been caught in adultery. According to the law of Moses, adultery called for death by stoning of the woman. The guy got off scot free! So Jesus had a dilemma. Would he refute the sacred law of Moses by not supporting her stoning (rule-based ethics), or would he go against his own character ethics (remember Chapter 6), by supporting her stoning? Of course, the crowd was delighted at the spot he was in, and were no doubt anticipating the gory spectacle of a stoning. Instead, Jesus turned the tables on everyone. He reframed the issue saying, "Let him who is without sin among you be the first to throw a stone at her." He placed the dilemma back in everyone else's laps by pointing out: Who are we to judge? We who are sinners too, dare we throw stones?

Moral imagination is like that. It generates new and creative alternatives or solutions to our moral dilemmas. It requires a sensitivity and awareness of the depths of emotions, feelings and experiences that affect and influence people. It searches out what is meaningful and where core values lie.

Moral imagination is inspired by reframing issues, engaging conflicting viewpoints, encouraging dialogue, using metaphors and allegories to draw out possibilities that are unusual. Turning things around or upside down or back-to-front generates creativity and new viewing points. Most of all, moral imagination requires empathy – empathy for all parties to the situation and for the situation itself.

### Moral courage

Taking the high road takes courage. The high road can be steep, and one can find oneself alone. The high road requires commitment and determination and that, too, does not attract the crowds.

We have discussed the ethics-morality gap several times, largely because it is such a prevalent issue. Most of us mean well, but sometimes we get tripped up in the delivery. One can do an impressive job working through the MRF and even deciding on the wisest course of action, and then when we are actually called to do it – to follow through, to speak up or out, to confront, clean-up or challenge, we can get cold feet.

Developing moral courage is part of practicing ethics. The more you practice ethics, the more you practice moral courage. And the more you practice anything the better at it you become. (I discuss courage in greater detail in Chapter 10.)

### Execution and action

Now you must take a stance and decide. What will you do? How will you do it? With whom will you engage first? And what is the appropriate timing?

As I explained in the Introduction, the key components of ethics include reflection, deliberation, choice and action.

Reflection and deliberation refer to identifying the issues and wrestling with alternative choices. As we know, moral dilemmas present us with difficult choices. Once we have made a choice, the way in which it is enacted has a direct impact on the appropriateness and the effectiveness of the choice we made.

Deciding **what** to do is one major part of solving our dilemma. Deciding **how to execute** our decision is another. Let us work through some of the considerations regarding what we are going to do and how, and then we can turn to having the ethical conversation.

### Action strategies

> *Timing* – Responding to an ethical dilemma sooner is always better than later. It is important, however, that you have established the necessary facts and carried out any relevant research or data analysis. Shooting from the hip with unsupported evidence, suppositions, and untested assumptions is never a good idea.

Selecting the right moment of the day or week and the right place is an important matter. Try to be sensitive and selective in when you are going to make your first move. Monday morning 8 a.m. in the hallway as people are arriving at work may not be the optimal choice.

Your taking action may also require several conversations. Maybe you confer first with thoughtful colleagues or an understanding boss and then in collaboration with them, take the next steps.

> *Engagement* – With whom will you engage first? I suggest that before one does anything else, one confers with one or two other people, preferably those not directly engaged in the problem or issue you are addressing. Discuss your deliberations with them and get their perspective or feedback. After you have had the benefit of a sounding board, then you can decide to whom you wish to take on or report your dilemma.

In certain instances, maybe because the matter is a confidential one, your choices of whom you might talk with are limited. Here again be strategic about who you approach first. Once you have revealed your hand there is no going back. Where there is a legal issue at stake, you may have to get expert opinion before you take in other actions. In some cases, due to the legality or illegality of the situation, the matter might be taken right out of your hands.

*Challenging or confronting someone* – One lesson I was taught as a very young professional is never to confront or accuse anyone without first posing an inquiring or non-judgmental question. The idea here is that there may be some significant information of which one is unaware. It is only fair and ethical to give people an opportunity to explain themselves before they are publicly challenged or condemned.

In the case where you wish to challenge someone's actions or behaviors because you consider them to be unethical, I highly recommend speaking with them in private and alone first. Public challenging matches rarely get a constructive response, and you can be seen to be as much of the problem as the person or persons you are challenging.

*Personal involvement* – If the dilemma involves you, as in the Cuba case, where you have to decide as sales manager what the ethical course of action would look like, then a very important step in your deliberations is the consideration of who is affected by the dilemma and how. The largest or most important stakeholder should in most cases be told of the ethical circumstances and should be invited to participate in the problem solving. An invitation to participate is always more appealing to people than confrontation or didactic demands. Once he, she or they have had an opportunity to think and talk things through, other stakeholders should be brought into the conversation. Transparency wherever possible is preferred to clandestine meetings, memos and actions. Each case requires its own appropriateness.

## Having the difficult conversation

### Framing the issue

Having honest discussions about ethical issues is not easy. If it were easy more people would be doing it! One reason that moral discussions do not take place is that people do not know how to have them. They do not have a moral language or framework with which to share the moral decision-making process.

Another challenge to having ethical discussions is that people think that their values are the right ones or the only ones, and do not factor in that other people do not see the world as they do. This is the value confusion we discussed in Chapter 2. Without due caution, ethical discussions can devolve quite quickly into a contest or conflict of whose values or world views are better or "right." These discussions typically go nowhere. All that is achieved is misunderstandings, defensiveness and resentment.

In deciding whether to discuss your ethical dilemma with others or whether you intend to pursue a certain action, frame the problem that you are addressing as an important part of the solution.

First and foremost, you want to try to depersonalize the issue. The problem or challenge should not smack of a personal judgment as to someone's ethical competence or integrity. Those kinds of discussions are far too value laden. The "I think," "I feel," "We should," discussions should be omitted. The rallying cry should be around principles: principles regarding truth, honesty, stewardship, justice, loyalty, fidelity, duty and courage. One of the goals of this book is to help business managers find the moral language with which they can frame ethical issues and have productive discussions. This moral language should be embedded in the language of the situation in which you are working. If it is a business dilemma then relate the moral language to business, for example, the use of a moral balance sheet which is in no way intended to reflect utilitarian thinking, but to relate moral evaluation to business language. If the situation is a family or church situation, then the moral language should be adjusted to relate to that context.

The importance of a carefully crafted message cannot be over-estimated. To whom to address your message, timing, setting out your purpose or goal of the discussion and being sensitive to the way people react is all part of the practical wisdom that is needed and comes with the practice of doing ethics.

### Stick to principles

Once discussions begin, it is important to hold steady around addressing the principles at stake rather than personal values or preferences. "I do not think that is fair! That is not the right way to treat people. I think she should put her family first. The customers have some rights you know!" These kinds of claims assert what I think and leave no room for what you think. The tendency is also to make moral claims in a moralistic tone of voice that imply that I know better than you do, or I am more ethical than you. I think about moral things and you don't seem to. You don't know what is important. I do.

Conversations of this nature go nowhere especially if you wish to make a point to someone in power. Business people are trained in rational discussions. That is how they evaluate investment decisions, allocate money and measure performance. They appreciate assessment, consideration and rational processes. This does not mean emotion should be avoided. It means that emotion needs to be aligned with whatever has been rationally thought about. Remaining rational and clear about the business issues at stake, not your personal issues, will gain you far greater ground than arguing your personal case. Depersonalizing the issue is essential in order to make progress.

### Speaking truth to power

Most of us fear "speaking truth to power" especially when the truth might challenge the world view or moral behaviors of those in positions of authority. Many people in power are afraid their power will be taken away from them. Any conflict is seen as a challenge to their power, and rightly so, because often it is. Those in power are continually on their guard against this occurrence. This makes them wary, sometimes on the defensive, and less open to ideas other than their own. Their fear might be communicated through anger, aggression, bullying tactics and conceited behavior. The disrespect some people in power show is intended to intimidate others so that they dare not challenge them. Where this is the case it is difficult for those with less power to speak up. (Recall fear defenses in Chapter 3.)

If you have been asked by the CEO (someone in power) to, for example, cook the books (remember Richard Evans in Chapter 4), exclaiming in anger "that is wrong" will not gain you much credence, even if the CEO agrees with you. You are likely to lose any negotiating opportunity there and then. You are far better off taking a step back and doing your moral homework around the issue.

Here are some suggestions about how you might "speak truth to power" without losing his or her respect, or ear, and your own moral ground:

- Maintain your role as a problem solver. You (the organization has) have a moral problem and you are working on finding the best and most appropriate solution. You are not a wimp. You are someone who has thought through the problem as you would in any business situation. As with other business situations, you present your findings and possible options to your boss. You are doing the same here.
- Using appropriate language explain what you have to share is not a challenge or a negotiation but a combined learning opportunity.
- You are in business and you make business decisions using the language of business – return on investment, cost-benefit analysis, competitive strategies and so on. Use moral language to discuss the moral issue.
- Share your moral reasoning process. Be sure to use the language of moral motivation, obligation, intention and consequences. Take him or her through the process step by step. Invite discussion and listen to other points of view. Incorporate them into your "workings."
- You may select to withhold a discussion about your own personal dilemma in the early stages of the discussion. See how the other person responds first. It is better to leave one's personal value system out of the initial discussion. Let the principles and the perspectives they bring speak for themselves.
- Beware of making yourself the issue. Depersonalize your language. Avoid comments such as "That is wrong," or "I think that is unethical," or "That is dishonest." Rather talk about the principles of truth and honesty that are at stake.
- Avoid getting into a power tussle. You have looked at the problem from a number of perspectives. You are more comfortable with some of these perspectives than others. You are open to hearing your boss's views. You may agree to disagree but at least some principled thought has gone into the decision process.

The conversation could proceed something like this.

"I have given your proposal to 'rework the numbers' very careful consideration. Maybe we could discuss this proposal from an ethical perspective as our moral choices might have significant consequences for all involved. In my position as CFO, it is my responsibility to look at possible alternative actions and their consequences and risks, and to present these to you for your due consideration. Using different ethical guidelines here are the moral trade-offs I have come up with. Maybe we could explore these possible outcomes together."

Once again, being ethical asks us to be courageous and to stand our ground even in the face of anger, accusation or deflection. How we raise and discuss the issues is critical to how they will be received. Of course, if the issue is outright dishonesty and corruption, we don't need to tread so softly provided we have the evidence and have covered our bases.

I now shift to focus on the ethical nuances that apply to professionals.

## Professional ethical obligations

This section on professional obligations applies to people and firms that identify as professionals or professions and who usually have a code of professional ethics or conduct to which they must adhere.

## Etymology of the word "profession"

The word "profession" derives from the Latin *professus*, which means "to affirm openly." To profess, means to assert or claim something. In common parlance it refers to standing for something. The act of professing refers to open declaration, public avowal or acknowledgment. A professional is therefore someone who openly declares or stands for something. The assumption is that this "something" in some manner is for the common good.

The earliest professions were related to theology, law and medicine and were only open to men. Over time the number of professionals has proliferated and now also includes women.

## Definition of "profession"

- A profession is an occupation that requires extensive training and the study and mastery of specialized knowledge and/or skills. Examples include accounting, medical, legal, nursing, educational and financial professions.
- A profession is usually regulated by a professional association that sets standards of performance, a process of certification or licensing and an ethical code.
- Professions claim to be self-regulating by enforcing standards and disciplines on themselves.
- Professions are generally exclusive which means that lay people are either legally prohibited from or lack the wherewithal to practice the profession. For example, people are generally prohibited by law from practicing medicine without a license.

A member of a profession is termed a professional. The term "professional" is also used for the acceptance of payments of an activity in that capacity in contrast to payments made to an amateur. A professional boxer, for example, is one who receives payment for participating in a sport, but boxing is not generally considered a profession.

## Definition of a "professional"

Professionals are individuals who claim to be engaged in an occupation or business they "profess" to understand. This means they claim to have mastered the discipline of their occupation or business and they are able to exhibit special competence in that field. The professions in which professionals engage require considerable training and specialized study.

In order to stay up to date in their field, professionals undertake ongoing training and study referred to as "professional development."

The following conditions are implicit in the concept of a "professional":

- They are prepared to exercise their knowledge and/or skills in the interest of others.
- They exhibit mastery and competence in their field.
- They have an ability to exercise judgment related to their field.
- They define their sphere of practice and communicate clearly the limits of the field in which they have competence.
- They adhere to high ethical standards and conform to a professional code.
- Their engagement with clients or customers is most often subject to professional rules of confidentiality.
- They are appropriately qualified or licensed to carry out the responsibility of their profession.
- They honor a responsibility to the public for its welfare, health and safety.

Nowadays almost any occupational group can proclaim that they perform as professionals with the cachet it entails. This is not necessarily negative or misrepresentative, as long as the group organizes itself and comports itself in accordance with the expectations of a professional body.

Professionalism is commonly understood as honesty, competence and responsibility to other parties. In general, therefore, acting in a "professional" manner is deemed a good thing, whether one is the butcher, baker or candlestick maker!

## Professional ethical codes

Professional ethics is not one body of knowledge but rather an amalgam of professional codes applicable to different professions. Professional ethics, as such, also includes certain unique characteristics. These unique characteristics relate to certain prescriptive norms that regulate the conduct of professionals in different ways to the norms associated with other areas of social behavior. An example is the professional's obligation to uphold confidentiality where otherwise transparency would be called for. The tensions between professional ethics and personal morality is something we explored in Chapter 2.

A professional code describes specific professional ethical responsibilities associated with a specific profession. The professional association that regulates the profession usually compiles its profession's ethical code.

In Chapter 3, I laid out the Values-Ethics-Morality-Law-Professional Codes framework. I pointed out that professional codes are an eclectic mix of ethical principles and moral rules. Each profession has its own collection of ethical obligations, however most of the codes include some of the professional ethical obligations I have included in the MRF, and which I discuss next.

Many professional associations have disciplinary procedures to deal with people who violate the code.

### Organizational codes of ethics

In the context of an organization, a Code of Ethics is usually a formal statement that sets out the organization's values pertaining to certain ethical and social issues. Most codes set out general principles about the organization's values regarding quality, stakeholder relationships, or the environment. Words such as dignity, respect, care and honesty are frequently included. Whether people walk that talk, is another matter!

## The profession as a social role

Professionals take on social roles to fulfill the needs of society. The first social roles were that of the priest, the lawyer and the doctor. In contemporary society, we now have dozens of professions that take up a host of different social roles.

In early Greek society, a person who fulfilled a socially allotted role or function well was considered a good or virtuous person. In other words, a good soldier who was strong, loyal and courageous was deemed a good person by virtue of the excellence with which he performed his role. In this way, Greek society was held together by everyone performing his or her socially assigned role, and so "harmony" was established. Everyone knew their place. This social-role structure exists in several societies today but is rapidly disintegrating as a societal framework. Capitalism has contributed to this disintegration as people step out of their assigned roles and claim their individual right to choose who they want to be. Some say this trend is detrimental to society and contributes to our increasing social ills and perhaps the 700 million people facing mental health difficulties (Chapter 8).

Nowadays, in our twenty-first-century world, we do not confound the perfection of the social role with the moral virtue of the person. In other words, a good doctor, someone who is skilled at taking care of patients is not necessarily a good or virtuous person. We might find that contrary to professional behavior, a good doctor may have highly questionable personal values and motives.

The question this raises is where does true morality lie? Is it in the performance of the professional *qua* professional or as a person in his or her own moral capacity?

We can ask the question the other way around. Should a professional violate a professional ethical obligation if it clashes with their own ethical principles? I raised this question in Chapter 3. Well, what do you think? And, what it everyone did it?

## Moral reasoning framework and professional ethical obligations

Here I include a generic list of ethical issues that are frequently part and parcel of a professional Code of Ethics. Each organization can adapt this list to suit its type of business and professional obligations.

### Power differential

The issue of power differentials always prompts ethical issues. Rarely are two or more people power equals. In the case of the professional, he or she has a power advantage over the person who is dependent on his or her knowledge and skills. Usually the professional is privy to information and insights that the customer or client does not have. A major challenge facing the professional is how not to abuse that power advantage and how to hold appropriate boundaries with customers and clients.

### Paternalism

Power differentials also raise the issue of paternalism (maternalism). Paternalism refers to treating people in a "fatherly" (motherly) way. While this can be viewed as thoughtful and caring, it can also infantilize the other person thus denying him or her individual rights. It might also lead to a failure to educate or empower the other in a responsible fashion.

Paternalism raises the dilemma of how much to "look after" the other, and what is best for them. To act appropriately in this regard requires true caring (not ego-driven self-importance), and good judgment.

### Following the rules

Professional codes provide both principled guidelines and specific rules. A challenge that professionals face is whether simply following the rules always assures behaving responsibly. Is literal or blind following of the rules acceptable or should there be a discretionary or intelligent interpretation of the rules? The professional must consider when the circumstances and the context ask for something more than simple compliance. The ethical challenge lies in determining the spirit rather than the letter of the rules.

One famous example is that of the doctor appointed by an insurance company to examine an injured party demanding reparation. During the doctor's examination he accidentally discovered that the injured person had a life-threatening brain tumor. In his contract with the insurance company the doctor was only bound to report on the injuries sustained by the accident. Following the rules of his professional contract the doctor failed to report to both the insurance company and the injured party his other findings. Was this acceptable professional behavior?

## Professional versus personal values

From time to time professionals are faced with a conflict between the ethics dictated by their profession and their own personal values. One example is where they are expected to make a judgment that benefits the majority. This might be closing a subsidiary company that is making losses (the professional decision) knowing that many of the employees to be laid off will be unable to find new jobs (the personal values dilemma). The professional must consider how to handle this conflict and whether to make it public. Not an easy call.

## Organizational versus personal values

Conflicts between organizational and personal values are not ethical issues peculiar to professionals. They arise for all types of employees in organizations and need to be mediated in an open and honest manner.

Examples include:

- Rewarding merit as opposed to length of service,
- Emphasizing profitability as the organization's primary concern versus the well-being of its employees,
- Emphasizing attention to the environment rather than increasing people's pay, and
- The non-promotion of women to senior positions.

I am sure there are many more you can think of or you might have experienced. Being aware of the tension and then discussing it with others is always a healthy way to go. Remember the value confusion we discussed in Chapter 2 and the importance of focusing on principles rather than personal preferences.

## Conflicts of interest

To act "professionally" usually denotes being objective. This means to demonstrate a lack of personal interest in the outcome of any event, transaction or engagement with the person or organization the professional is dealing with. Conflicts of interest occur where the professional cannot be truly independent as he or she has a personal relationship or has a personal stake in the outcome of the activity in which he or she is engaged.

As we know, true independence is hard to find as the professional is paid by the organization or client and thus has a vested interest in keeping the organization or client satisfied. (Discussed in Chapter 8.)

### Impartiality

Professionals are expected to be impartial when executing their work. This means they should not show any partisan feelings toward a person or a group with whom they are working. An example is a manager mediating a conflict between employees. This may not be easy in that professionals are human and naturally favor some people over others. A question for us is whether impartiality is always a good thing? What if the life or livelihood of someone close is at stake? Surely our feelings or passions are an important part of our considerations and actions.

### Professional detachment

Just as with impartiality, professionals are expected to be detached in performing their work. This means their own emotions and feelings about the work or their client should not affect or influence their performance. Again, one might question whether this is realistic or a good thing. Many argue that we cannot really be ethical if our emotions are disengaged as it is our feelings that motivate us to be invested and act. Being emotionally shutdown does not enhance ethicality.

### Confidentiality versus transparency

Many professional roles such as that of the priest, doctor or therapist insist on confidentiality of client information. While confidentiality can protect the client, this is directly counter to the call for transparency that supposedly enhances moral conduct between people in society.

A dramatic example is what does the therapist do when her client tells her that his compulsive urges lead him to stalk women at night? Should she report him to the police? To you and me this might sound like a no brainer! In the eyes of the law and judicial process this is by no means a clear-cut case.

### Community obligations

Implicit in the definition "professional" is recognition that he or she has a responsibility to the community. This means that sometimes the professional might have to choose between what is best for the individual client versus what might serve the greater community. An example might be the professional accountant who is approached by a client to assist in raising funds for an organization whose pollutants will negatively impact the local environment. The professional has a judgment call to make on whether he uses his professional skills to assist his client or whether he foregoes this opportunity in favor of the welfare of the community.

*Best practices*

Here the professional must consider what best practices the profession would advise or dictate and being ethical implies being competent in those best practices.

## Executive summary

This chapter lays out what it means to practice ethics. It also explains the Moral Reasoning Framework and shows how this can be used by working through a detailed case study.

Guidance is provided on how to proceed once a decision has been made. Action strategies are set out along with suggestions on how one might hold a difficult conversation that revolves around ethical issues.

What it means to be a professional is outlined along with the ethical expectations of professionals.

## Key terms

| | |
|---|---|
| Confidentiality   303 | Moral bricolage   281 |
| Detachment   307 | Paternalism   305 |
| Etymology   302 | Precedent   289 |
| Framing   280 | Profession   281 |
| Integrated thinking   280 | Professional   283 |
| Impartiality   307 | Systemic issues   292 |

## Notes

1  In their book, *Common Fire*, Daloz et al. (1996), discuss how our modern way of living, with its emphasis on individualism and a coarsening of society, has destroyed the spirit of the commons. The commons used to be the central place in the town where people would come together to practice dialogue, discussion and democracy. Here people would discuss ethical issues and moral actions. The meaning of a moral life was openly explored.
2  This is part of the lyrics of the song "Feelings," written by Brazilian singer Morris Albert in 1957.

## References

Daloz, et al. *Common Fire: Lives of Commitment in a Complex World.* Boston, MA: Beacon Press, 1996.
Kegan, Robert. *The Evolving Self.* Cambridge, Massachusetts: Harvard University Press, 1982.
Needleman, Jacob. *Why Can't We Be Good?* New York, USA: Penguin Group Inc., 2008.
Stout, Jeffrey. *Ethics after Babel.* Boston, MA: Beacon Press, 1988.

# 10 Ethical leadership and good practice

## Contents

## The leadership challenge

It is a little blunt, but let's call a spade a spade. The world is in severe turmoil right now. On many dimensions, things are spiraling out of control. We are paying dearly for our material achievements. Life maybe richer, broader in focus and more stimulating but it is also more complicated, more exhausting, more uncertain, and more self-alienating. As someone recently summed it up, we are experiencing a "suffocating planet gasping for air and suffocating people gasping for meaning."

As we know from our discussions on systems theory (Chapter 2), the macrocosm mirrors the microcosm and vice versa. Global collaboration is in disarray. We have messed up capitalism. Here was a system that did indeed deliver on many promises and then we got greedy, and now it has gone awry. And we can't blame the system – because we are the system. We are it! There is no such a thing as good or bad capitalism, just as there is no such a thing as a greedy, power hungry corporation. This sort of talk keeps us from being accountable for our own moral culpability because everything redounds on us – you and me. And how we love to lay the blame somewhere for our failings even if we must resort to personification to give us the foil we need. (Recall Chapter 4.) The truth is, we have given up on constraints, on limits, on self-discipline, on moderation. We just want more for less: less effort, less self-discipline, less moral accountability.

Then there is the environment. How bad does it have to get before we respond with urgency? In my book, *Leadership and Change Management*, (2009), I explain our tendency to put off new realities for as long as possible until they hit us like a tsunami and then we are forced to react. Once we are in reactive mode, our options are radically diminished and we become hasty and rush for the quick fix. We fail to think systemically, so we do not address the problem holistically, and ultimately it is rarely really resolved. Added to this, we are so busy dealing with the old reality that we are treating as a new one, that we miss the arrival of the true new realities and so we are caught in the reactive cycle once again.

Can you believe Rachel Carson wrote her powerful book, *Silent Spring*, in 1962? That is nearly sixty years ago! Therein, she warned us of our impact on the environment. We talked a lot about her book at the time, as we usually do, and were slow to do anything substantial about it. To this day, toxic chemicals and waste are still to be found in the livers of birds and animals on every oceanic island of the planet. However, Carson's work did make some difference in that it led to the creation of the US Environmental Protection Agency in 1970, which now as agencies around the world that are engaged in promoting policies to protect the environment. Even so, here we are sixty odd years later treating the whole environment 'thing' as if it were a new reality.

Other features of the times are that the new religion is technology. With this comes the age of manufactured identities dependent on superficial approval ratings, compliments of the social media. We also live in a post truth era. Ethics has gone out of the window. Moral relativism has taken hold, and nobody stands for anything for long or with any depth. And we have such a poor experience of meaning-making that we think it can be done by machines ironically named AI. All in all, we are failing where it matters most because we have lost touch with our own core selves.

Testament to the above is the devastating statistics of the Davos Risk report (Chapter 8), where worldwide there are now 700 million people suffering from mental illness. That is slightly less than 10% of the entire world population. If we were to add to this number the people experiencing everyday stress, anxiety and a sense of purposelessness, we would possibly be talking about half the population of the world! The statistics on suicide are also disheartening as annual numbers mount, and the age of those in such despair keeps dropping. For all our gadgets, so called opportunities, and advances in medicine and the sciences, hundreds of thousands of young people feel hopeless. Has all this materialism really brought us to a better place? We may be less poor in "things," but what has happened to our souls? Was Max Weber correct – are we trapped in an iron cage? (Chapter 1.)

### The stage of decadence

Margaret Wheatley writes in her recent book, *Who Do We Choose to Be?* (2017), that the world does not need more entrepreneurs or techies or technological breakthroughs. It needs leaders. Leaders, she says, who can create islands of sanity amidst chaotic conditions, lack of support, isolation and loneliness. It needs leaders who can lead beyond the ego, put service over self, stay present and hold steadfast during these careening times.

Wheatley cites the works of Joseph Painter in *The Collapse of Complex Societies* (1988) and Sir John Glubb in *The Fate of Empires and the Search for Survival* (1976). Independently Painter and Glubb studied many different societies. Both noted that a recurrent feature of every society is collapse, and that the patterns that precede this collapse are almost identical no matter the geography, ethnicity or spiritual tradition.

According to Glubb, the stage of decadence always precedes collapse and can always be identified by the following traits:

- Politics are increasingly corrupt, and life increasingly unjust.
- A cabal of insiders accrues wealth and power at the expense of the citizenry fostering an opposition between haves and have nots.
- There is increased narcissism, materialism and consumerism.
- The masses are distracted by entertainment, sporting events and a celebrity culture.
- There is a general abandonment of moral restraint and leaders are in charge who believe they will govern forever.

### The warrior leader

Wheatley claims we need warrior leaders who can help steward the world through times of disintegration, fear and loss. Our system has become too complex to be humanely manageable. It has become a beast that can no longer be fed.

During these times, Wheatley writes, leaders typically create wars, make promises they do not keep, and create a distorted sense of reality by inflating the economy and fabricating a false sense of prosperity. Their real purpose is to preserve their own power.

Wheatley argues for an old school warrior type of leader. This is someone with strong ethics and a strong sense of honor. They have compassion and insight and confidence in themselves. They are humble and self-aware, full of hope and able to move beyond their fears. They are also systemic thinkers who combine their hearts and their heads. And Wheatley is looking to business leaders to be some of those warriors.

## Corporations must take up the leadership baton

Undoubtedly, the new stewards of the planet are corporations and their leaders. The baton has long since passed from the Church, whose steeples used to dwarf and dominate every town, to the philosophers and politicians, who sought to create rational forms of government and governance, to businesses. Businesses now comprise the predominant form of all organizations, and businesses lead most new trends across the world.

Businesses have the savvy, the reach, the entrepreneurial spirit, the global view and the resources to make a difference. Businesses employ billions of people, they reach across cultures and their impact is ubiquitous.

Business leaders are globally inter-connected. They have the information and the technology to make things happen with a rapidity and efficiency that exceeds any government or nation state. They have power, as they can influence one another, governments and regimes, for better or for worse. People in business are trained in managing, politicians are not.

Businesses form the thick web that holds together nearly every society. They provide safety, identity and meaning. Even the younger generation, that claim disinterest in materialism (except they all want to be tech millionaires), and that job hop at the drop of a hat, are empty of meaning and look vainly to businesses to fill the hollowness within themselves.

Business leaders now have the responsibility to take the helm; to grab the leadership baton; to look realities in the face and deal with them; and to correct the current pendulum swing away from indulgence, greed and immoderation. Business leaders need to step up and role model good leadership – where good means ethical. They must create just institutions so that there can be just societies (Chapter 7). They can no longer hide behind economics or the bottom line. They need to cease advocating for their own interest and recognize that as citizens of the world, they have multiple responsibilities to multiple stakeholders.

One cannot have one's cake and eat it. We cannot luxuriate in warm tubs of excess and simultaneously enjoy a paradigm of moderation and modesty. If only we had stuck to the original blueprint that Adam Smith and others laid out; if only we had curbed our greed and our attachment to a good thing, always wanting more. If only we had remained butchers and bakers and candlestick makers, maybe life would not be so complex. Things would not have spiraled out of control. If only . . .

If onlys are for dreamers. We didn't, and now we must face the music and dance appropriately. Business leaders must lead the dance.

## Conscious capitalism

Here we have it again – that anthropomorphism that we cannot get away from. By now we know that capitalism cannot be conscious. As people, we might be able to practice capitalistic behavior consciously. And that is what John Mackey and Raj Sisodia are advocating in their book, *Conscious Capitalism*, (2014).

Mackey and Sisoda, write about conscious leaders who are thoughtful and authentic. These conscious leaders integrate their hearts and their heads by developing self-awareness, and emotional intelligence, and empowering others to do the same. Conscious leaders operate with a higher sense of purpose, integrate the interests of stakeholders, and build a culture of trust, accountability and caring.

Mackey and Sisoda extol the benefits of capitalism and its extraordinary ability to generate wealth. They also argue that capitalism is a heroic force that can be used for the good. They agree that, at this time, capitalism has gone off the rails and has now earned a bad name which it deserves.

Their book catalogs all the positive and constructive things that a business should do to take care of its stakeholders. It reads like a manifesto for the best companies' award. It barely takes a breath to consider the trade-offs and difficulties that prevent organizations from taking the moral road they may consciously wish to take. They ignore the fact that to be conscious is difficult, and doesn't result from training courses or seminars, no matter how enthusiastic they might be – see my discussion on ethics and mindfulness later in this chapter.

Being conscious means being fully attentive, fully present, fully aware, in mind, body and soul. Being conscious takes real, heartfelt commitment and training, and it takes time to inculcate conscious behavior in both individuals and organizations because currently it is so greatly lacking.

Mackey's company, Whole Foods, a high-end grocery chain, often referred to by shoppers as Whole-Pay-Packet as its prices are so high, is held up as the model of excellence. Throughout the book, Mackey cites example after example of everything he and his management team did to create, what reads like, a company made in heaven. Alas, the trade-offs cashed in and heaven came to an end it seems, when Wholefoods began losing market share, closing stores, laying off people and generating lower profits. (These details are not described in the book.)

Responding to frustrated shareholders, Whole Foods sold out to, of all the organizations in the world, the voracious, behemoth Amazon! Amazon would not at this time rate as a conscious capitalist organization. It does not have a good reputation for job pay, working conditions and care for the environment. I wonder whether it is part of the conscious capitalist movement Mackey and Sisoda have spawned?

Since the merger took place in 2017, it is reported that the culture at Whole Foods is changing. People are disgruntled and comfortable work practices are being dismantled. Was selling his beloved company to Amazon a conscious decision by Mackey? I guess so!

The important part of the Whole Foods story is that the capitalist spirit is unbridled; the system encourages growth at all costs, and there is no effective oversight as to the size and the power of organizations. (Discussed in Chapter 1.) It seems that only the large and the powerful survive in the long run. Business leaders are thus challenged to continuously make trade-offs, some of them difficult, and some of them that would not classify as part of an ideal world. But then, who is talking about an ideal world?

## Being ethical in a non-ideal world

### Living the question

Given a review of the global capitalist macrocosm and the inner dynamics of organizations, it is clear we do not live in an ideal world. But has there ever been a time one could call an "ideal world" to which everyone would agree?

So given the world in which we currently live, how does one live an ethical life, and as a manager or CEO, how does one create or foster an ethical organization? What must one do, or more importantly, how should one **be** so that one can constructively influence people to be ethical even if the environment (macro or micro), is inimical to ethical behavior? (The question was raised in Chapter 2.)

Before we try to answer these questions, let us remind ourselves of the questions that lie at the heart of ethics. These are: How should we live? What does it mean to live a good life? What does "good" mean? What is the meaning of justice? How does one create a just institution? And I am adding the question: Am I my brother or sister's keeper?

These are by no means easy questions as we know. And, throughout this book, I have not provided any hard and fast answers. There is a reason for this – there are none! I have instead provided guidelines, questions and ideas – but no absolute, once and for all, answers.

I am sure you are not surprised because ethics, as I have belabored, is a cognitive process where one wrestles with thoughtful questions and does not look to trotting out answers. Ethics is about living the question and knowing that no sooner that one has arrived at an answer, new questions arise. One is always seeking to refine any answer with ever new questions.

If we wish to cross the Delphic threshold, and claim that we know ourselves, we would have to admit that there is almost nothing we know irrefutably, absolutely, unquestionably and for sure. We may have some answers, even seemingly good ones, and some theories, rules or codes, but they are just crutches to help us get by. Yet we need those crutches. They have a role to play as we cannot remain in our heads but must make choices and act. And what we choose or do not choose, and how we act, falls under the rubric of ethics, too.

Ethics, which means character (Chapter 2), or character development, is about reflection, deliberation, choice and action. It is about how we shape our character with every decision we make. With character development, every moment is a defining moment, as every moment is filled with choices that weave the tapestry of our lives.

Being an ethical person, someone who does not live life blindly conforming to norms or conventions (Kohlberg stages 5 and 6 – Chapter 4), means one is someone who tests alternative guiding principles for their appropriateness and selects the wisest (most virtuous) option possible and follows through with courage.

An ethical person asks that most difficult of questions: Is it better to survive, be liked, save face, stay with the crowd, defer to authority . . . or be ethical? What will it be? Or, who will I be?

### Moral development, ethical leadership and practicing ethics

As we discussed in Chapter 4, we all have a responsibility to engage in moral development. Especially if we are senior leaders or managers, it behooves us to develop an independence of mind where we are prepared to question and challenge on ethical grounds, the validity and appropriateness of the norms, customs and laws of a group, organization or society. We also need to be able to set aside our egos – discussed later in the chapter – so that we are less dependent on others for approval and acceptance and, instead, care that we live out of a developed conscience that makes us self-defining.

One way to improve our ethical capacity is to practice ethics. In Chapter 9, I spelled out what practicing ethics entails. I also stressed that it is helpful to use some formalized moral reasoning framework that interjects rigor and discipline into often rancorous, personalist, unstructured arguments and debates.

Organizations urgently need leaders and managers who will role model ethical behavior and who will not succumb to the material excesses that capitalism may offer (crazy salaries and stock options), or the cockroach-like behavior possible in the unswept corners of the corporate culture (cheating, bullying and deflecting blame). As I mentioned in the Introduction and point out in my article – see article why Ethics Training Does not Work on page 326 – the organization itself must help with the moral development process. This means that senior management needs to make moral development a distinctive strategy as part of the development of the corporate culture. Managers also must coach and mentor their employees in communicating ethically and knowing some of the language of ethics so they can articulate their moral positions effectively.

Those who have earned positions of authority, either formal or informal ones, have an ethical responsibility to understand the emotionally regressive forces of authority on individual behavior and to avoid using those forces to their advantage. (Remember Milgram and fear of authority – Chapter 4.)

As always, everything redounds to "good" leadership. Good leaders realize that the quality of people's motivation and behavior and their mature attachment to the vision and goals of the organization determines the success of everything.[1]

### Transactional versus transformational approach

In shaping the moral culture of the organization, leaders can choose whether to take a transactional or a transformational approach.

Transactional methods consist of control strategies, while transformational approaches consist of empowerment strategies. In transactional strategies, employees are like robots that require programming. While empowerment strategies attempt to coach and transform employees into greater self-awareness and self-accountability. Control strategies lead towards compliance, while transformational strategies lead to personal growth and people functioning as creative, autonomous persons.

The transactional leader typically favors an abundance of rules and prescribed procedures as a method of keeping people on the straight and narrow. The transformational leader is likely to prefer the virtue or character-based approach. Either way, to attain corporate moral excellence, businesses need a supportive corporate culture and a clear articulation of the ethical expectations. They should explicitly encourage the practicing of ethics. And employees should be given an opportunity to engage in moral discourse and moral reasoning and should be encouraged and guided in their reflections and deliberations.

In my experience, the transformational approach is the far more sustainable and effective one.

## Ethics and mindfulness

There is nothing as new as the old! For thousands of years, every cultural tradition known to humankind has insisted that the most important and beneficial thing a human being can do is to get to know themselves. The paths to this knowing are many. It may be contemplation, prayer, meditation or other forms of altered states of consciousness, yet the goal is always the same, deeper self-knowledge and a life of contentment (Recall Chapter 3.)

Solitude, silence and reflection were upheld as essential features of a healthy life being good for one physically, mentally and emotionally, as well as providing essential balm for the soul. With self-examination, self-awareness and solitude, the ancients argued, came wisdom.

And here we are in the twenty-first century, celebrating this supposed new find called mindfulness! Endorsed by many neuroscience studies that allegedly prove what the ancients knew without any scientific instruments or laboratories, Mindfulness, a form of Buddhist meditation packaged as psychology for those with an aversion to religion, yet carrying hints of ochre garbs and sayings of the great Buddha, is slowly pervading many corridors of life including those of many corporations.

### *What is mindfulness?*

Simply put, mindfulness is paying attention to our attention moment by moment. In each conscious (aware) moment of our lives, we **are** our attention. In other words, we are consciously living (experiencing) whatever we are attending to, namely thoughts, emotions, feelings and sensations.

By paying attention to our attention, we have a direct, immediate experience of what it is we are giving our attention to and how we are experiencing it. In a sense, we are experiencing our experience.

Our attention could be absorbed with happy or sad thoughts. It could be thoughts of regret, guilt or envy. It could be emotions of excitement, anxiety, confusion or despair. It could be feelings of hurt, pride, fear or joy. It could be sensations of attraction, pain or irritation.

Paying attention to our attention also means being aware of the experiencing within our bodies. With mindful attention we recognize the continuous changes in our body: its comfort level, its aches and pains, its feeling of relaxation and ease, and the fluctuations of our heartbeat as it responds to the rhythms of the day. We are consciously **in** our bodies. In fact, we realize we **are** our bodies – an integrated being of mind, body and soul.

With mindfulness we are fully present. We are all there – every part of us – aligned in conscious-awake-awareness. There are no distracting thoughts or feelings. We are completely attuned to whatever it is we are engaged in and experiencing.

Mindfulness is akin to self-examination, something we explored at some length in Chapter 3. There we discussed how the early Greeks, advocated that self-examination is good for the soul, leads to a good life and contributes to our experience of happiness. Mindfulness, too, delivers on these promises.

### Mindful lessons

With mindfulness, our first deep lesson is that something or someone is paying attention to our attention. We come to realize that there is a witnessing "I" who is not the same as the contents of our attention. For example, when I say, "I am sad," I am really saying, "I am experiencing sadness." The experiencing "I" and the experience are separate. I am not my sadness. This process, known as disidentification, has huge implications for how we experience our lives.

The next thing we learn is how transient, erratic, repetitive, often irrational and contradictory the contents of our attention can be. One minute we are contented and the next minute, when someone has cut us off on the highway, we are furious! We soon learn how reactive we are to external stimuli.

We notice, too, how moment by moment our attention flits between one thing and another. It is scattered, all over the place, until we sit down and do something mindfully.

With mindfulness, we become more aware of the deep judgments, expectations, hopes, fears and aversions we have about almost everything! From the moment we wake up, we are passing judgments. "What a dreary day it is today!" "Thank heavens it is Friday!" "Oh God, another day of boring meetings!" Everything is value laden, personal, and about me and my comfort. We begin to notice that our ego gets out of bed before we do. We also notice the assumptions behind our judgments. We observe ourselves swiftly turning away from the beggar in the gutter; averting our eyes; lifting our noses. And it comes home to us that we may have got it wrong. If circumstances changed, that person in the gutter could be you or me and we are not simply drunken bums! (Recall Chapter 5.)

As we become more and more mindful, we learn how conditioned our responses are to external events or encounters so that we respond like programmed machines. We learn how unaware and inattentive we are to the mechanical existence we are living, where we are seldom at "home," always distracted in some way, and rarely paying true attention. Our mechanical conditioned mind is in the driver's seat most of the time (Deezel and Raffio, 2018).

## *The power of mindfulness*

The power of mindfulness lies in its direct experience. By paying attention to our attention in the moment, as things are taking place, the true mirror of our existence is held before us. This mirror is uncompromising. We are confronted with who we really are, how we really think, what triggers us, what makes us afraid, what gives us hope and meaning, our rapid impulses and how we sell ourselves out moment by moment.

With mindfulness we observe in real time our own betrayals, lies, greed, insecurities, perversions, deflections and the cowardice behind many of our words and actions. We also note that without paying due attention we cannot be ethical. We miss cues, skip over details, succumb to our fears, react out of patterned behaviors and dismiss the need for reflection and deliberation.

One of the greatest benefits of mindfulness is that we get to slow down. We create space between stimulus and response, allowing us time to breathe and stall our usual rapid-fire reactions.

Mindfulness is also the mirror that reveals our shadow selves; those parts of us we tossed into the basement as not being part of the persona that we have so artfully crafted for public consumption. (Chapter 4.) We also find in this basement some gifts and possibilities that we have not embraced or lived into for some reason or another.

Lastly, for our brief discussion here, mindfulness is about compassion. As we observe ourselves and learn about who we truly are, we are called to be compassionate. Mindfulness is not another opportunity to beat ourselves up or to cringe at our limitations or to embrace self-loathing. On the contrary, by being compassionate we heal the inner wounds that led to some of our insecurities and fears, and we acknowledge that we are not perfect and yet we are still ok. We are in fact way better than ok! We are courageous because we take the risk of choosing time and again. We make decisions and sometimes we fail and fall, but we get up and keep trying. With mindfulness we realize we have a lot of goodness within us, and as we move closer to the source (our core selves), and find our inner freedom, we find we have an almost infinite potential for more.

*Developing ethical capacity*

In what we would call ancient times, ethics and mindfulness were part of "yoga." Yoga means the uniting or yoking to the Divine or the core that lies deep within us. Yoga was a way of living; a spiritual path or what we would call, the way to a good life. But as we are wont to do, we have once again created our specializations: Yoga as physical exercises on Saturday mornings; mindfulness for one hour on Tuesday evenings; and ethics when we are in a fix. We now have separate teachers, books, linguistic terms and dogma for each of these new specializations that were once part of a seamless, cohesive philosophy of being.

As the ancients knew, mindfulness, or self-awareness, builds our ethical capacity. The deeper our self-examination, the deeper we drop into ourselves. The more we drop into ourselves, the more we see our inner contradictions, our capacity for good and evil, our capacity for love and hate and our capacity for immense kindness and incalculable cruelty. Any moral self-concealment is blown apart in moments of lucid awakening to our darker selves.

As we grow in self-awareness, we also witness the ethical principles that do or do not guide our lives. We live the ethics-morality gap (Chapter 3) with greater consciousness, and we strive to make more of our decisions from a place of freedom: freedom from fear, freedom from peer pressure, freedom from wanting to be liked, freedom from wanting to not stand out, freedom to risk the loss of material safety in favor of our personal integrity. Self-awareness and ethics go hand in hand.

Self-awareness also gets us to explore our own conscience. As we self-examine what we stand for, "we see through a mirror darkly, but in time we shall see face to face" (1 Cor. 13:12). In other words, over time, with deeper self-awareness we come to see reality as it truly is. Our commitment to the journey of inquiry grows our conscience into a deeper truth.

Deep self-awareness gets us to confront the reality of who we are now and who we have the potential to be. We come to realize that we can indeed consciously engage in the journey from our current being to our becoming (our potential), and that we can answer Wheatley's question in the title of her book and consciously choose who it is we want to be.

Our growth in self-awareness builds our inner confidence as we recognize we have far more agency over our lives than we often think. It also helps us to set aside our ego, those structures of the mind that give us self-understanding and identity, but that, from time to time, as Danielle Grant of LeaderShape Global says, needs to be put aside and take the passenger seat.

With self-awareness we come to realize that it is the quality of our attention that can free us from our egoic reactions. It is when we set aside the ego, that we can make incredible acts of generosity and sacrifice, and that we can see new and creative perspectives that raises everyone and everything to a new level.

It is through our struggles presented by our growing self-awareness that our capacity for humility, compassion, justice and love grows. It is this capacity out of which we can become ethical beings and act morally. It is out of this capacity that we can love our neighbors, our brothers and our sisters, as we love ourselves. It is out of this capacity that we can grow in wisdom.

Each one of us has an ethical and moral responsibility to develop this capacity, most especially those who wish to take on the role of leaders.

### Stress and anxiety

A very high proportion of people claim that they are continuously stressed and anxious – something we noted above. Our frenzied, materialistic lives, with a high emphasis on doing, clearly has not helped our states of mind whatever our bank balance.

Discussions during my ethics bootcamps often center around stress and exhaustion and how these factors inhibit people from making good decisions. In describing the MRF (Chapter 9), many people respond by saying that no-one has the time to do that kind of analysis. Even when I show them the "short-hand" version, they seem too overwhelmed to want to think things through. Decisions are to be made quickly, got off the desk and the box ticked.

Mindfulness, and its partner meditation, is renowned for its positive impact on people's stress levels. Simply slowing down, not multitasking, but mindfully tackling one task diligently at a time, makes all the difference to both the person and the quality of the task performed.

It is so easy to forget that the quality of what we do is always a quality of the function of our conscious attention. We may fool ourselves that we are getting things off the desk or off the list, however, frequently due to a rushed, not thought through, shoddy job, the same issue arrives back on our desk or list in no time again. No wonder we are stressed. By being in a continuous hurry, with often self-imposed deadlines and limitations, we are over-burdened, over-anxious and underperforming. Mindfulness reduces stress. The less stressed we are the better decision makers we become.

## Transpersonal leadership

A new type of leadership is emerging in response to the challenges the times. This leadership incorporates some of the oldest tools of wisdom known to humankind. These tools include self-awareness that arises from disciplined self-examination; systemic thinking based on an understanding of the inter-relatedness of everything; high relational integrity founded on a sense of universal unity and harmony, and last but by no means least, recognition and engagement of the spiritual dimension vested in all humanity. This new leadership is called transpersonal leadership.

### The emergence of transpersonal leadership

Many people consider Abraham Maslow (1908–1970) outdated. They say they want something new. What they forget is that there is nothing new in this world! All new theories stand on the shoulders of great people who went before. And few know that Maslow is one of those great people who too stood on the shoulders of others, in his case, notably Aristotle.

It is Maslow who talked about "being" values as opposed to "doing" values. It is Maslow who identified deficiency motivations – Feed me! Love me! Respect me! – versus growth motivations that focus on inner self-sufficiency, autonomy, transcendence and striving to live one's potential (Maslow, 1999).

Among many other things, it is Maslow who coined the term "transpersonal psychology" from which the notion of transpersonal leadership has emerged (Maslow, 1993).

It is Maslow who tried to teach the corporate world that in each person there is a deeper self that is experienced in transcendent states of consciousness. These transcendent states of consciousness are achieved when we rise above our own limited and limiting egos. In these states of being, our human potential extends to infinite possibilities. Interestingly, Maslow also encouraged meditation for personal growth – and that was the 1960s!

It is Maslow who tried fervently, and at the time in vain, to educate business organizations to understand people's innate need for transcendence and personal growth beyond the ego. Due to the fragility of this inner call against the tumult of the outer world, he tried to get businesses to pay attention and nourish this inner potential which he insisted would be to everyone's benefit.

### Maslow revisited

While Maslow's Hierarchy of Needs remains a popular framework that lays out his theory of motivation, there has not been much development of his ideas on self-actualization (the top part of his pyramid) and his theories on transpersonal psychology until recently. People pay great lip service towards the need to have self-actualizing employees, but many are not really sure what that means or entails. (I run seminars on self-actualization and can speak well to the confusions.)

Self-actualization refers to the movement of a person from "being to becoming," where becoming means moving toward one's full potential (This is what Aristotle referred to as *entelechy* – see Chapter 3). This movement is the inner motivation to attain one's potential or wholeness, and thereby become more fully human. Maslow, among many, many other psychologists, claimed that if this movement is frustrated it leads to neurosis, poor health and torpor, and detracts from the person's ethical sensitivities. (Remember that Aristotle claimed we had a moral obligation to strive to attain our potential – Chapter 3.)

Maslow wrote a great deal about peak experiences and about the true self (the whole self) that is experienced in transcendent states of consciousness. The significance of these peak experiences lies in their transporting the person from their usual day-to-day consciousness to a heightened consciousness where the usual boundaries between people and the environment are eradicated. (Remember Tolstoy and the transcendent purpose in life – Chapter 3.)

During a peak experience, the person experiences a sense of deep well-being and a feeling of being totally at one with the universe. This feeling is usually accompanied by feelings of love, compassion, care and acceptance. With this intense awareness of unity, everything is part of one harmonious whole. In these states, nothing but this awareness exists. These states, Maslow argued, as would chorus all the ancients across time, accesses our deepest, inner awareness that is a source of wisdom, health and harmony. It taps into our full humanness or "best self."

Maslow coined the term *eupsychia* to refer to human-oriented organizations, societies and communities where self-actualizing people would evolve and thrive by moving more closely into the transpersonal realm. In practical terms this would mean people being able to work with a sense of "flow" or being "in the zone." To create this type of culture requires enlightened management practices that encourage people's creativity and need for self-transcendence. The benefit to organizations would be a leadership that would role model the greatly needed attributes of vulnerability, authenticity, humility and openness to learning.

Despite Maslow's huge popularity with business organizations, he could never get any traction with these ideas. Maybe Maslow's time has come. If self-transcendence could become a new corporate (and societal) motto, we may just embrace some aspect of the glorious ages of the past where virtue and humility were the foundations of a just society.

### Leading beyond the ego

LeaderShape Global, a UK based organization headed by John Knights and his colleagues, Danielle Grant and Greg Young, have published a comprehensive book entitled, *Leading Beyond the Ego* (2018), that provides a detailed curriculum on how to become a transpersonal leader.

Knights, who has extensive international corporate experience both as a CEO and entrepreneur, along with co-founder Young was inspired to promote the transpersonal leadership approach based on his repeated findings that senior managers do not care or know how to show they care for their employees. Many of them are also woefully lacking in emotional intelligence (EI), and empathy. (See Chapter 7). Not only that, many decisions are ego driven, and the senior management team are frequently busy cleaning up their own mistakes rather than running the company and embracing the future.

In 2003, LeaderShape Global was launched. Since then, based on research involving several thousand executives, Knights et al., found that across the board, key leadership elements that are largely missing include empathy, developing others, conflict management, the ability to be a change catalyst and inspirational leadership. Knights and his team seek to counter these leadership deficiencies by developing the transpersonal leadership approach.

The *Leading Beyond the Ego* book provides a comprehensive plan that charts the transition from being a rational, ego-based, as usual leader (starting point), to the intermediate stage, where one becomes a robust, emotionally aware leader. The advanced journey is one that integrates all three intelligences – rational, emotional and spiritual – and leads to one becoming a radical, ethical and authentic leader, namely a transpersonal leader.

Spiritual intelligence is incorporated in the *Leading Beyond the Ego* model as conscience and self-determination. These culminate in two critical questions: Who am I? and What do I do with who I am? These are similar questions posed by our Greek friends, Socrates, Plato and Aristotle, and Margaret Wheatley discussed earlier.

Transpersonal leadership ala Knights et al., also places a great deal of emphasis on inner development where they mention mindfulness, ethics, understanding one's own motivation and what they identify as transpersonal values.[2] They also provide some interesting practices that reinforce the transpersonal leadership approach.

Judging by the growing interest in transpersonal leadership, Knights and team are creating a transpersonal leadership movement and working at providing the bridge that Maslow was unable to create.

## Courage – the heart of ethics

> *The secret of happiness is freedom, and the secret of freedom is a brave heart.*
>
> Pericles' Funeral Oration

Few if any business ethics (or leadership) books discuss the topic of courage. How is this possible? Why does no-one want to discuss the essentiality of courage? One cannot be ethical without courage and one certainly cannot lead well without ethical courage.

Ethics, by virtue of its claim on us, demands courage. Ethics asks us to make wise decisions, not self-interested ones or ones motivated by our need to be liked. This means setting aside our egos and making a just choice that may leave us vulnerable. It requires us to work through the systemic barriers that serve as force-fields pulling and pushing us in various directions, many of which are scary as they render us out of control.

In Chapter 3 we explored the ethics-morality gap that presents itself frequently in most of our lives. We discussed how we so often end up doing the very thing that we do not really want to do or refraining from doing the thing we know we ought to do. We can readily supply reasons for these deviations, some of which fall into the categories I outlined in Chapters 2 to 4.

For example, there are the pressures of organizational culture and the implicit pact of what it means to belong. There is the power of the group and the understandable fear of becoming an outsider. Bureaucracy adds to feelings of alienation and loss of autonomy. Then there is the power of authority and our own personal baggage and projections associated with authority. Added to all this is our anthropomorphizing tendencies where we distance ourselves from our own moral agency and hand it over to "the company." And then of course, there is our own self-interest, our ego that gets in the way.

As I have discussed several times, to be ethical requires self-examination, and self-examination assuredly requires courage. With self-examination we have to be brutally honest and face the reality of our fears, some of which are misplaced and some of which make us feel ashamed. In my experience, shame is one of the most difficult things to face and to work through.

To be ethical requires courage. It takes courage to advocate taking a path that others do not want to take. It takes courage to break with precedent. It takes courage to challenge the law and lawyers. It takes courage to set aside one's ego and be vulnerable. It takes courage to be prepared to pay the price for striving for rightness. It takes courage to work at living fully out of oneself.

### Understanding courage

Courage is the ability to act despite our fears. It does not mean an absence of fear. Aristotle named courage a great virtue. He had much to say about fear and courage. He was clear that being afraid when confronted with fearful things is appropriate. He insisted that fearlessness is not courage and the fearless person is more dangerous to have around than the coward. What he did stress however, is that there are some things we fear that we should not and there are ways we act out our fears that are not constructive.

It takes courage to look at what lies behind our fears and to understand what causes them. And it is by facing both the fear itself and what creates that fear, something that is often painful, that motivates people to act courageously and be brave. Courage involves "pushing" through the fear, and bravery is acting in the face of that fear. It means working with one's fear; not denying it, avoiding it, or suppressing it. Courage means facing one's fears head on. Ethical leadership requires great courage.

Aristotle observed that we become brave by doing brave acts. It is back to his insistence on practice.

Brave acts are far more mundane and less spectacular than we normally imagine. Brave acts are the small, mindful decisions we make each day as we weigh our choices and strive to make good ones.

Brave acts, according to Aristotle, are fearing the right things, for the right motives, in the right way, at the right time and according to the merits of each case. A brave person is someone who holds fear in the right perspective and acts accordingly. A brave person takes his or her fear into account when pursuing any action.

Courage, derived from the word *coeur* meaning "heart" in French, is that vital activity of the heart that makes us brave enough to press on even though we fear. And sometimes, we fear for our lives.

Practicing ethics invites us to practice courage. It calls us to speak up, to give voice to our principles, to honestly seek out creative solutions and to take actions that sometimes place us in positions of vulnerability.

Ethical decision makers are usually people who demonstrate courage. It takes courage to take risks; it takes courage to take the high road in the face of opposition; it takes courage to stand apart from the group and break the pact of collusion; it takes courage to create new precedents, new norms and new conventions. It takes courage to have difficult conversations around ethical and moral matters.

It takes courage to risk one's own safety, psychological, economic or physical, in the service of a principle or a life-giving action. It takes courage to speak truth to power. It takes courage to act justly and to show equity as opposed to appeasing one's friends or alliances. It takes courage to be an ethical manager and to be able to be part of the group and yet stand apart when decisions and actions call for self-determination and self-trust. However, the more we practice courage, the more we realize the truth in Pericles' words: Courage is the secret to freedom and thus happiness.

## Creating the ethical organization

Creating an ethical organization is no small matter. Unfortunately, many organizations for whatever reason have resorted to short-cuts, played minimally to the law's requirements, and have succumbed to the slippery slope.

One of the responsibilities of the management team and each manager is to create an ethical organization. That is an organization that promotes the moral development of its employees. How does it do this? Firstly, there needs to be an organizational and cultural commitment to make ethics apart and parcel of all decision-making. Ethics needs to be understood as the fabric of organizational life as opposed to it being a watch dog or compliance function. The culture of the organization needs to be one attuned to good citizenship as discussed in Chapter 8 and management needs to be clear that ethical behavior is a priority.

Since ethical considerations are part of decision-making and taking effective action, managers and employees should be encouraged to practice ethics. They need to operate in an environment that seeks to promote trust and honesty, where questioning is encouraged and where the slavish following of rules or behaviors that demonstrate lack of personal responsibility or accountability are discouraged. Everyone in the organization should be impressed with the reality that they are the organization, and that every one of their actions or decisions has an organizational impact. They need to understand that silence is not golden and that their ability to take personal ownership of their actions is vital to advancing the ethical culture of the organization.

In this environment managers should be expected to demonstrate ethical competency (Chapter 9). They need to demonstrate moral imagination and the ability to discern, deliberate and exercise good judgment. Good judgment comes with collaborative and open discussions and practice. Good judgment is enhanced by reflection on previous decisions and review of what might be learned with the benefit of hindsight. Good judgment develops by reviewing one's decisions and actions and reflecting on their efficacy.

The ethical manager should be rewarded and affirmed. He or she should help eliminate fear from the organization and should be ready to tackle the resistances and "stuckness" that sometimes occurs with the group mind. The ethical manager should understand the importance of creating an environment of moral freedom so that employees feel empowered and free to act with self-determination and personal accountability. Subservience to the institution or the go with the flow mentality should be discouraged.

Most of all, the ethical manager will need to have courage and be encouraged to take risks, to ask difficult questions, to pursue creative and different options and to combine his or her heart's instincts with intellectual rigor and critical thinking.

How does one achieve this culture and tutor these managers? By having the ethical intention to live the ethical quest and by affording the opportunity to practice, practice, practice! Practice what? Open reflection, rigorous deliberation and thoughtful choice followed by courageous action.

## Why ethics training doesn't work

### *New Hampshire Business Review – January 24, 2014*

I heartily support the call by Mark Connolly and Mark DiSalvo to stop the ethical merry-go-round so evident across all our sectors ("Stop the unethical merry-go-round," Dec. 27–Jan. 9, 2014 – *New Hampshire Business Review* -NHBR). The unrelenting scandals are a sad testimony to the most important and powerful institutions in our country, notably business and government.

As a former ethics professor who has taught many MBAs and developed a course, Ethics Across the Professions, I can attest to the fact that ethics training as currently delivered does not have much impact on participants. In the interests of brevity, I cite a few observations:

- Most ethics training is heavily based on the stories, dilemmas or actions of other people, and minimal emphasis is placed on the moral dilemmas the students or the professionals are personally facing. As a result, discussions are an abstraction. People seem more interested in how and why people are caught than in the real-life emotional wrestling that results in misconduct.
- Online ethics tools are a travesty. How can one take these seriously? Selecting the supposed correct answer from a list of multiple alternatives hardly teaches anyone about ethical deliberation, judgment and moral reasoning. The heart of ethics is deliberation and judgment, not ticking boxes. Yet online tools are how we train many of our professionals!
- Most MBAs have their sights on gargantuan salaries and huge share options. Any discussion regarding excess CEO pay, for example, even when the company has clearly lost significant market value over a sustained period, is typically shrugged off with, "Well whatever is legal is OK."
- Some of the case studies I have presented regarding the financial fallout and the granting of inappropriate mortgages to irresponsible or naive citizens invariably ends with a clear injunction from both MBAs and professionals that the "buyer beware" and the professional have no responsibility other than disclosure of risks. The notion of "I am my brother's keeper" is not something most MBAs or business professionals subscribe to.

- Most organizations have reward systems that emphasize financial performance. There are few checks and balances regarding their impact. Ethics research shows that reward systems have a major impact on ethical behavior.

A good society has good institutions. Our unethical institutions and the rampant corruption that appears everywhere is thus a reflection on us. Connolly and DiSalvo mention instilling a sense of citizenship and personal responsibility across society. I could not agree more. As such, I would like to propose a somewhat different approach to business ethics education:

- Ethics education should be carried out at the workplace. Forget the classroom.
- Employees should be encouraged to practice ethics and use a formal moral reasoning framework for significant business decisions.
- The ethics program would include an ethics audit of some of the organization's most significant decisions made throughout the year for their ethical impact.
- The audit would be carried out once or twice annually. It would be overseen by a random group of people chosen from across the organization, several representatives from key stakeholder groups and one or two members from the community at large. Lawyers and accountants should be excluded, as they have a tendency to focus on rationalizing the rules or the law.
- The audit should be written up and presented in a transparency report attached to the annual financial statements and posted on the organization's website.
- The conclusion of the report should include a discussion of lessons learned and the impact on being a good corporate citizen. This should be followed by remedial action if any is required.
- A synopsis of the report should be presented at an organization town meeting and, for a public company at a selected shareholder meeting.

All in all, the entire spirit of ethics education needs to be one of advancing learning, transformation and wisdom, not catching "bad" people. Creating this atmosphere will be important.

## Mandate for the ethical leader

> *If you are not afraid of dying there is nothing you cannot achieve.*
>
> Tao Te Ching

Our world depends on leaders. Leaders are there to guide us into the future as it arrives, i.e., guide us through the paths of change. This is a huge responsibility and a difficult task (Beerel, 2009).

The responsibility is huge as how we embrace the future shapes the future. It is a difficult task as most people do not like change. Change challenges egos, brings up fear and deconstructs norms. Under these circumstances, unethical behavior readily rears its head.

To answer the primary ethical question: How should I live? And, What does it mean to live a good life? I propose the following leadership mandate.

This mandate is applicable to anyone interested in living an ethical life, and most especially, it is relevant to leaders and managers and those who guide and influence others. I hope you will make it your own.

## Leadership mandate

1  Self-examination and self-awareness
2  Mindfulness practices
3  Ethical principles and moral actions
4  Do it for its own sake
5  Systems thinking
6  Power
7  Courage
8  Limits and moderation
9  Justice
10  Promoting the practice of ethics
11  Professional development
12  Looking in the mirror

### 1    *Self-examination and self-awareness*

Clearly, self-examination and self-awareness are primary factors needing attention. I have gone so far as to say that we are ethically responsible to develop our ethical capacities, and that the most powerful way to do this is through self-examination or mindfulness strategies. I have Socrates to back me up!

We need to commit to growing in self-awareness with respect to our own strengths and weaknesses; self-awareness regarding our emotions and how they impact our behavior; self-awareness regarding our shadow side; our issues with authority; our desire to be respected and admired, and our fears and how we handle them.

Self-awareness is a sign of maturity. It provides an indicator that one is self-reflective, and that one can look at oneself critically. Self-awareness shows an interest in and a concern for the kind of person one is and how one engages in the world. Self-awareness is a critical component of cognitive and emotional intelligence. Without it one is less adept in dealing with complex and stressful situations. Unreflective people are less thoughtful and aware of other's states of mind or feelings. Dealing with the stresses of change and developing one's adaptive capacity requires unremitting focus on self-reflection and self-awareness.

> Suggested exercise: Write down the greatest insight you have had about yourself during the past week (or in reading this book). Analyze the ethical implications of this insight and what you have learned as a result.

## 2   *Mindfulness practice*

Being mindful and present with quality attention is essential for any form of leadership. Demonstrating presence and giving quality attention to everything one encounters enhances relationships and provides clarity to decisions. It also makes one observant.

New realities are revealed in the present moment. Only by seeing the present with curious and attentive eyes can one recognize many of the new realities that seem hidden in plain sight. Mindfulness brings curiosity, openness, patience and thoughtfulness to the unfolding of new phenomena. Being in tune with these new realities as they arise is the hallmark of effective leadership.

> Suggested exercise: Write down what you observed today as new realities in your organizational system. This could be what you saw, heard, felt, smelled, read, intuited. What did you learn?

## 3   *Ethical principles and moral actions*

Seek to get in touch with the ethical principles that typically guide your choices, and name them when you can. The point is not to quibble with whether they are the right ones or not, but simply to raise awareness. How do I lead my life? Am I a consequentialist where I care mostly about results? Or am I more character driven where I care what I say and do says about me as a person? It is helpful to know one's ethical leanings.

It is also important to know whether there are any ethical principles that drive your life and that you are willing to "die" for.

Now to the matter of moral relativism. Observe your own moral relativism. In what circumstances do you find yourself making decisions based on personal bias or a sense of "I know what is right!" and how and when does conscience act as your guide?

> Suggested exercise: Take your most recent moral decision of any significance and analyze it as explained above. What did you learn?

## 4   *Do it for its own sake*

Make ethical choices for their own sake. Choose the wise, prudent, just and loving thing simply because it has value in and for itself.

It is a travesty when we feel we need to justify honorable, decent, ethical behavior with a business case. It simply vitiates the quality of our ethics. It turns our actions into a moral equation supported by some ridiculous accounting calculation or some ostensible stock market trends.

"Have diversity on your board – it is good for business! Be environmentally sensitive – it is good for business! Empower women – it is good for business!" Surely this is a prostitution of ethical principles. Recall that doing the right thing for the wrong reason is the most heinous of all moral acts!

Role modelling ethical and honorable behavior has its own rewards (Chapter 2).

> Suggested exercise: Review your own and the organization's rhetoric for justifying ethical behavior.

### 5    Systems thinking

The ability to see the big picture and to detect patterns and relationships is essential for both effective and ethical leadership. Bad behavior does not occur in a vacuum, is rarely isolated and is invariably attributable to a systemic issue. Likewise, creating an ethical organization requires taking a systems perspective (Chapter 2).

> Suggested exercise: By referring to systems thinking as laid out in Chapter 2, and any other material you might have, using an ethical lens analyze the systemic impact of your organization's reward system on the various systems that constitute your organizational system.

### 6    Power

At various junctures in the previous chapters, I have emphasized that those in power make the rules. Ethics is invariably entangled with power issues. I also pointed out in Chapter 4, how important it is that those who have authority use it wisely and benevolently. Power is an energy to get things done. Ethical leadership is about getting good things done.

Looking at power from a different aspect all together, an important element of ethical leadership is personal willpower. I am not advocating a stubbornness or intransigence but rather the willpower to see things through, to strive for what is right, and to persevere in trying to make the wisest choice. No-one can ever ask for more than that.

> Suggested exercise: Ask yourself the following questions:
>
> - Do I use my power to make the rules serve me and my interests or do I use my power benevolently, namely, to serve the good of others or the common good?
> - Is mine a top down power or a shared power?
> - Do I realize that rules are not immutable and that rules provide needed safety and boundaries, but do not enhance people's development or growth?

### 7    Courage

As discussed above, courage is essential for the ethical leader. Courage is required to stand up to the challenges of others, to be able to hold steady when one fails their projections and expectations, and when one is blamed for the discomfort of having to change and adapt to new realities.

Courage is needed to resist the personal temptations and seductions of power and glory and gargantuan pay packets. Courage is required to be able to face one's own fears and not project them onto others. To be able to be vulnerable and to say, "I don't know, I am confused, I need help," takes courage.

It takes courage not to have all the answers and to tell others what to do. It takes courage to give people the work back and to help them do their own learning even when they prefer someone else giving them instructions.

Only courageous people can face the truth when it is unpleasant and try to make others do the same regardless of the personal cost. Only courageous people challenge unfair norms, biased precedents and the coercive power of groups or systems.

As I mentioned in Chapter 3, moral courage lies at the heart of character, moral competence, effective leadership and good citizenship.

> Suggested exercise: List the courageous actions you have taken over the last week. What can you learn from reviewing this list?

## 8   Limits and moderation

As we have discussed in several chapters, ethics is foremost about moderation and limits. It is about Aristotle's golden mean and Jesus' Golden Rule. Moderation is that precious middle ground between excess and deficiency where there is not too much and not too little. Prudence, defined as practical wisdom, is needed to determine this delicate place that reflects balance and harmony. Being an ethical person implies that we recognize this fundamental principle and try to live it throughout our lives. This of course calls for being attentive and open. As leaders and managers, we need to role model moderation and we need to set limits. The most effective way to do this is by example.

> Suggested exercise: Review the way you live moderation and limits in your life. Ask yourself: As a role model, do you show respect for limits in your organization? Does the organizational culture reflect a respect for moderation and limits? (Consider its payment policies, reward systems and expense accounts.)

## 9   Justice

Chapter 7 was devoted to the mighty topic of justice. Naturally, I could only provide the essentials of this intricate subject in this text.

It is important for the mature adult, and certainly the manager and leader to understand the basic rubrics of justice and how it plays out in various systemic settings.

You may wish to consider you own views on the topic and how it influences your overall view of life. For example, what comes up for you regarding politics, the stock market, taxes, healthcare matters, immigration, the environment and so on? These are all matters that are entangled in the wide web of justice.

> Suggested exercise: Reflect on what is the most important justice issue for you in your life? Then consider: Does your organization have a just culture? When did you last have to adjudicate or advise on a matter of justice? What did you learn?

## 10   Promoting the practice of ethics

The more one practices ethics the better one becomes at being more ethical and more ethically sensitive.

Throughout this book I have stressed the need to practice ethics. Let me add that in reading this book you have practiced ethics.

Chapter 9 is devoted to bringing the ideas of practicing ethics together. I hope you can use the examples provided to bring ethics into an explicit practice in both your personal and organizational life.

> Suggested exercise: Review your own approach and that of your organization to practicing ethics? How might you make this a more explicit process?

## 11   Personal development

Our development as a human being has a direct bearing on our ethical capacity and ethical sensitivities.

I have provided the Kohlberg Moral Development model as one of many human development models. Another useful model is that provided by Harvard Professor Robert Kegan which he names "The Five Stages of the Evolving Self" (Kegan, 1982). Both Kohlberg and Kegan used the pioneering work of Jean Piaget as the basis for developing their theories.

There is another useful framework provided by Ken Wilber, known for his Integral Theory and his AQUAL model (Wilber, 1998).

The key point of all these models is that they track our shifts in consciousness as we mature and develop. The sign of maturity or personal development is a "vertical" movement in our consciousness, where we "transcend and include." What this means is that at one level of maturity or consciousness, whatever was a subjective experience, such as I hate him or I feel insecure, is transcended in that it is no longer subject but becomes object. For example, it now becomes: He triggers my disdain, or the situation challenges my competency. This shift from subject to object enables me to transcend the situation and look at it rather than experiencing it as overwhelming me. This also applies to what is no longer me, as in our discussions on the shadow, to realizing an ever-wider ambit of what is part of me.

As we transcend to new perspectives or viewing points, we do not discard the previous experience. We simply hold them differently. This transcending and including, is a move to greater maturity, acceptance, compassion and wisdom. Some of this shift in consciousness occurs simply by virtue of our "growing up," yet not all people grow to the same maturity level. After a certain stage, typically young adulthood, we need to positively engage in consciousness shifting experiences and developmental opportunities to continue the development process.

Whichever developmental model you find most useful, all of them provide indicators that personal development leads to shifts in consciousness and that shift make us more ethical.

> Suggested exercise: Write down examples of shifts in consciousness you have experienced, i.e., you understand something from a whole new deeper perspective. What have you learned?

### 12 *Looking in the mirror*

Engage in the tough questions set out here. Ask yourself these questions from time to time.

## Personal reflection – the tough questions

1 Do you see yourself as a reflective and self-aware person? If you asked three other people you know, would they agree with your answer?
2 Are you someone who is mindful and observant? Do you have presence? If you asked three other people you know, would they agree with your answer?
3 Are you able to see the big picture? Are you able to hold both the big picture and details at the same time? List two circumstances where you have demonstrated this capacity.
4 Do you see yourself as a courageous person? If you asked three other people you know, would they agree with your answer?
5 Are you a pleaser? Do you avoid conflict? Do you find it hard to have difficult conversations and so you bypass them?
6 Are you self-accountable? Can you own your mistakes without blaming others? Can you always find a learning opportunity in errors? Do you promote a blaming culture at work?
7 Are you a critical thinker? Do you test your assumptions?
8 Do you use principles to guide your actions or do you defer to what you know is best based on experience, hunch or what someone else suggested?
9 Do you engage in continuous personal development?
10 Can you be humble and vulnerable? If you asked three other people you know, would they agree with your answer?
11 Do you have a good sense of humor? Not a sarcastic one, but a warm, funny one?
12 Do you have a transcendent purpose in life? Is it part and parcel of your life at work?

What have you learned from this reflection?

## A last word – staying inside yourself

What does it mean to "stay inside yourself?" I am sure if you had pressed me at five years of age, I would not have been able to articulate clearly what that meant. All I knew at the time is that it was a feeling, a sense of being in touch with something that was "myself."

Since then I have had many, many experiences, and done a lot of soul searching. Every ethical question I have posed in this book, I have wrestled with at a deep personal level. All the shadows, fears, ego driven reactions, blind spots and slippery slopes I have visited myself. Or they have visited me. As I have learned, none of us escape.

What I do know is that whenever I lose touch with my grounded self, I am in trouble. I have also learned how easy it is to lose, and how readily one can give this grounded self away by one's neediness for love and safety, and by projecting one's fears, expectations and hopes onto others.

When I entered the Jesuit College twenty-six years ago, the first course I signed up for was ethics. And right there, slap bang, without any ceremony, I was confronted with all these questions and deliberations I have shared with you. It was a humbling experience to say the least.

So back to this question of staying inside yourself. Staying inside yourself is a connection that is beyond articulation or intellectualizing. It is a knowing that emanates from the silence within.

Staying inside yourself means being grounded on the inside. It is an alignment with the center of gravity that is found at the core of one's being. It was this alignment that unwittingly kept me balanced, and not reeling all over the place in response to the energy currents of the factory as they swished around me on those chaotic Saturday mornings.

Staying inside yourself means trusting who you are even if parts of you are elusive or a mystery. It is a deep resonance with something inside that is impervious to the volatile, frivolous, vacillating, temporal ups and downs of everyday life.

Staying inside yourself is an ability to look at yourself and hold yourself accountable for your reactions and responses to the external forces in all their various guises, and to in some way latch onto the anchor of the inner self, so that you can step above or aside from the negative forces that trigger your shadow energies.

In this business ethics text, I have referred to the importance of "love" several times. Some of you may have thought: How can a business ethics text refer to love? Business ethics is about rational, unemotional, down-to-earth behavior. What is this love business?

Well, I disagree! And then, why, can or should business ethics not include love? Love is the greatest motivator of all. It is love that brings out the best in us and inspires our call to transcendence. Love can withstand most things and follow through on all things.

We rarely intentionally hurt who or what we love. As I said in the Preface, business ethics is about loving what we do and who we do it with – employee, supplier, customer, the environment, you name it, no matter who or what they are. And business ethics – in fact ethics – is about staying inside yourself. Because when you stay inside yourself you realize that everything is about love.

At last! You want an answer, a rule, an injunction for ethics. Something that holds in all circumstances. That has no "depends" attached to it. That is context free. Here it is! Ethics is all about love. It is as simple as that.

## Reflection across all chapters

- Do you think money is a measure of moral worth?
- In your experience, has global capitalism contributed to flourishing of all life on Earth? Some life? Your life?
- Do you think it is better to survive than be ethical? Always? Sometimes? Which times?
- Are you mindful of your communication and how what and how you say things conveys something about your ethical sensitivities?
- When did you last exhibit moral courage?
- Do you consider yourself to be an ethical person?
- How personally empowered do you feel in the face of authority? What if the "authority" is represented by a group, for example, a committee or the board?
- Have you ever made a list of some of the contents of your shadow?
- Can you identify one action that has no ethical or moral implication whatsoever?
- Which ethical principle is most prevalent in your organization?
- Is justice something you have thought about in a serious manner? Is it important to you?
- Are you your brother or sister's keeper? Why yes or why no? Or is it some-times? Then when?
- Who do you choose to be?

## Key terms

| | |
|---|---|
| Attention 316 | Personal development 332 |
| Courage 314 | Power 310 |
| Ego 311 | Stage of decadence 311 |
| Ethical capacity 315 | Staying inside yourself 334 |
| Eupsychia 322 | Stress 310 |
| Hierarchy of needs 321 | Transactional leadership 316 |
| Love 310 | Transformational leadership 316 |
| Mindfulness 313 | Transpersonal leadership 320 |

## Interesting ethics research results

Factors that negatively impact ethical behavior:

- Stress, alienation, loss of purpose or meaning
- Exhaustion
- Frustration, sense of powerlessness
- Job insecurity

- Toxic power dynamics
- Fear driven the culture
- Employees trained to be smilers and overly friendly and accommodating to customers
- High paying reward systems
- Lack of accountability
- Size of organization – the larger the greater the tendency towards bureaucracy and unethical behavior.

**Interesting note:** Research shows that in general, women are not more ethical than men.

*Source:* Annabel Beerel Doctoral Dissertation 2013 and multiple research studies.

## Notes

1 I deliberately use the word mature here as leaders need to be cognizant of the dynamic explained in Chapter 4 with respect to projection and creating the organizational ideal.
2 John Knights has written an excellent paper on Ethical leadership – this can be found at J. Knights. *Ethical Leadership: Becoming an Ethical Leader.* Abingdon, UK: Routledge, 2016. http://bit.ly/1Uh6vHL.

## References

Beerel, Annabel. *Leadership and Change Management.* London, UK: Sage Publications, 2009.

Beerel, Annabel and Tom Raffio. *Mindfulness: A Better Me, Better You, Better World.* Boston, MA: Self-Published, 2018.

Ericka R. Lawrence and K. Michele Kacma. Exploring the Impact of Job Insecurity on Employees' Unethical Behavior. *Business Ethics Quarterly*, Vol. 27, No. 1, January 2017, published by Cambridge Journals.

Kegan, Robert. *The Evolving Self.* Cambridge, MA: Harvard Business School Press, 1982.

Knights, John, Danielle Grant and Greg Young, editors. *Leading Beyond the Ego: How to Become a Transpersonal Leader.* New York: Routledge, 2018.

Mackey, John and Rajendra Sisodia. *Conscious Capitalism.* Cambridge, Massachusetts: Harvard Business Review, 2014.

Maslow, Abraham. *The Farthest Reaches of Human Nature.* New York: Penguin Books, 1993.

Maslow, Abraham. *Toward a Psychology of Being*, Third Edition. New York: John Wiley & Sons Inc., 1999.

Wheatley, Margaret J. *Who Do We Choose to Be?* San Francisco, CA: Berrett-Koehler Publishers Inc., 2017.

Wilber, Ken. *The Essential Ken Wilber.* Boston, MA: Shambhala, 1998.

# Glossary

## The vocabulary of ethics

**Absolutism**   Holds that a moral principle or claim holds everywhere, in every circumstance and can never be overridden.

**Alienation**   A sense of emotional isolation or disassociation.

**Altruism**   A disinterested benevolence and unselfish concern for the welfare of others. Amoral   Operating completely outside the realm of moral value.

**Assumption**   A principle or proposition that is taken for granted.

**Autonomous (person)**   Independent in mind or judgment; self-directed.

**Business ethics**   An academic discipline that seeks to apply ethical principles to the moral challenges experienced in the business context.

**Capitalism**   A socio-economic system based on the right to private property and the competition existent in a free market.

**Casuistry**   A method of evaluating ethical problems situationally by analyzing the circumstances of a case.

**Categorical imperative**   Refers to universalizing an ethical maxim so that it can be considered a universal law.

**Cognitive dissonance**   A disconnect between a person's inner and outer worlds.

**Compassion**   Deep awareness of the suffering of another.

**Concept of limits**   Notion that everything has a natural limit or boundary that defines excess or deficiency.

**Confidential**   Acting or communicating in confidence or secret – not to be shared or divulged with others.

**Consequentialism**   Ethical theory that focuses solely on the consequences of actions.

**Corporate governance**   That system of checks and balances within a corporation that aids the organization in achieving its primary business purpose, both lawfully and ethically.

**Corporate social responsibility (CSR)**   The term used to refer to corporate attention to legal, moral and social effects of running a business.

**Culpability (moral)**   Deserving of blame or censure.

**Deontology**   Greek word for necessary or imperative. Commonly referred to as rule-based ethics.

**Determinism**   The philosophical view that maintains that all events in the universe, including human events, are absolutely determined or conditioned by necessary and sufficient antecedent causes. The determinist rejects the idea of human free will claiming that every action is the result of a necessary chain of causes.

**Egoism**   An ethical theory claiming that the pursuit of self-interest is morally correct and rational.

**Emotivism**   The doctrine that all moral judgments are nothing but expressions of preference, attitude or feeling.

**Ethical relativism**   The ethical theory that denies the existence of universal moral truths and proposes that right and wrong must be based on differences in cultural norms and mores.

**Ethics**   The discipline that studies analyzes and reflects on moral behavior, values and virtues.

**Eudaimonia**   Ancient Greek for happiness or well-being usually associated with the views of Aristotle as being the main goal in life.

**Existentialism**   Existentialists believe that the source of moral authority rests in humans and not in abstract principles.

**Feminist ethics**   Supports a relationship ethic that focuses on care for the relationship. Fiduciary duty – A duty to be trustworthy and act in the best interests of those one represents.

**Freedom (moral)**   The unrestricted and independent ability to make choices.

**Free market**   In a free market system buyers and sellers can freely enter and leave the market and prices are set by voluntary agreements to buy and sell.

**Golden mean**   Aristotle's ethical principle that refers to moderation or balance.

**Golden Rule**   Attributed to Jesus as the moral injunction to "do unto others as you would have them do unto you."

**Goodness**   A description of a person's general inner orientation or disposition of the heart.

**Hedonism**   The ethical theory that claims that the pursuit of pleasure should be the aim of all action.

**Human rights ethics**   This principle holds that anyone can do as they please as long as they do not impinge on the rights of others.

**Impartiality**   A disposition that lacks bias or prejudice.

**Intrinsic value**   The worth a thing has in and of itself independent of its relationship to anything else.

**Justice**   The concept that people are equal and that everyone should receive his or her fair due.

**Laissez faire**   The French for "hands off." A doctrine that champions non-government intervention.

**Machiavellianism**   An ethical theory proposed by Niccolo Machiavelli that posits that the only actions morally worthwhile are those that keep one in power.

**Means and ends**   Refers to the manner or strategies (means) by which we achieve our desired goals or outcomes (ends).

**Moral competence**   The ability to recognize moral issues and to apply critical moral thinking and reasoning to a moral dilemma.

**Moral courage**   The ability to follow through on one's moral obligations and intentions and convert them into definitive moral action.

**Moral intention**   Refers to the moral purpose or desire that lies behind our actions.

**Morality**   What people believe to be right or wrong based on the customs of their community/society.

**Moral motivation**   That cause, e.g., loyalty or fear, that induces one to act in a particular manner.

**Moral obligation**   Where knowing how one should act places an actual claim on one's selection of moral choices.

**Moral reasoning**   The process by which we work through a moral dilemma from identification of the moral issue through to the choice of moral action to pursue.

**Moral relativism**   Describes the belief that no absolute, universal or objective ethical principles exist. Moral standards are considered subject to context, circumstance or personal preference.

**Morals**   Norms and standards of behavior established within a community or society.

**Moral vision**   The ability to recognize that a moral issue exists now or potentially in the future.

**Personalist ethics**   Ethical theories (several exist) that view morality as an expression of conscience, feeling or love. There are no universal objective principles. The source of ethics stems from the person.

**Pluralism**   A condition in society where numerous ethnic, religious or cultural groups co-exist.

**Prudence**   Includes wisdom, perception, appropriate caution, the demonstration of moral pragmatism.

**Rational**   Using reason, being logical

**Reason**   Capacity for logical, rational and analytic thought.

**Relativism**   The rules governing any situation are to be determined by their relation to something else, e.g., customs or culture of a country.

**Right(s)**   A sense of entitlement.

**Sarbanes–Oxley Act**   Legislation passed in 2002 to address the financial scandals. The Act emphasizes management responsibility for financial statements and tightened board oversight.

**Self-interest**   An ethical principle that upholds the importance of placing emphasis on one's own interests or needs.

**Situation ethics**   This ethical principle holds that context and situation influences one's moral choice. The guiding rule is that love should always be served.

**Skepticism**   Denies there are objective moral values and denies there are true or false moral judgments. There are no objective bases for any norms or principles.

**Stakeholder**   Someone who has an interest in or is affected by a decision of the organization or institution.

**Stakeholder concept**   Holds that management resolves ethical quandaries by giving equal consideration to the legitimate interests of all stakeholders.

**Stockholder theory**   Holds that management resolve ethical problems by taking those actions that increase the long-term profits to stockholders.

**Subjectivism**   Insists that the sole source of knowledge or authority is in the perception of the individual.

**Survival ethic**   This ethic insists that, where one's survival is at stake, all actions that promote self-care are justified.

**Telos**   Greek word meaning goal, end, or purpose.

**Transparency**   an ethical principle that promotes openness, honesty, lack of guile, deceit or secrecy.

**Utilitarianism**   An ethical theory that focuses the net utility (or benefit) of actions. Ethical behavior according to this theory means taking that action which consequences will benefit the majority of people.

**Utility**   Measures the happiness or unhappiness that results from a particular action.

**Values**   states of affairs desired by and for people, e.g., enhance people's freedom.

**Virtue**   A desirable human condition that promotes a full human life and a good society.

**Virtues**   Refers to excellences of character that include courage, wisdom, self-control and justice as some of the cardinal virtues.

# Index

Note: Page numbers in *italic* indicate a figure and page numbers in **bold** indicate a table.